TOKYO

Judith CONNOR, Mayumi YOSHIDA

CITY

GUIDE

INTRODUCTION
HOW TO USE THIS BOOK
CONTENTS
TOKYO
ACCOMMODATION
EATING OUT
SHOPPING
ENTERTAINMENT
NIGHT LIFE
ARTS
SIGHTSEEING
HEALTH AND BEAUTY
THE BASICS
LANGUAGE
APPENDIX
MAP
INDEX

TOKYO CITY GUIDE

Judith CONNOR, Mayumi YOSHIDA

Published by Ryuko Tsushin Co., Ltd., in cooperation with Kodansha International Ltd.

Design Director: Shuhei TSUJI
Illustrator: Isamu UEMOTO
Photographer: Tobias PFEIL
Editors: Yoichi MATSUI, Chieko NOSE
Distributed in the United States by Kodansha International/USA, Ltd., through Harper & Row, Publishers, Inc., 10 East 53rd Street, New York, New York 10022. Published by Ryuko Tsushin Co., Ltd., 2-35, Honmura-cho, Ichigaya, Shinjuku-ku, Tokyo 162, in cooperation with Kodansha International Ltd., 12-21, Otowa 2-chome, Bunkyo-ku, Tokyo 112, and Kodansha International/USA, Ltd., with offices at 10 East 53rd Street, New York, New York 10022 and The Hearst Building, 5 Third Street, Suite 430, San Francisco, California 94103. Copyright in Japan 1984 by Judith CONNOR, Mayumi YOSHIDA, and Ryuko Tsushin Co., Ltd.
All rights reserved. Printed in Japan by Nissha Printing Co., Ltd.
ISBN-0-87011-725-4
LCC 85-40064
First edition, 1984
3rd printing, 1985

INTRODUCTION

Four years ago when I first came to Japan from America, I didn't buy a guidebook to the city. The books available directed the tourist to bus tours, expensive imported designer boutiques in Ginza, to ancient nightclubs and cabarets. It was just intuition at the time, but I knew there must be more than that going on in Tokyo, and decided to find out what it was.

Over the years Mayumi and I have guided hundreds of friends through the city. We became experts at drawing maps and running off xerox handouts of information on where to go, what to do, and where to find what. It was always fun, always great to see people get as excited about the city as we were. Still, we often wished that there was a single volume, collecting all the information, which we could give to visitors. The book should have been published long ago, and when no one else did it, we decided we'd better do it ourselves.

In the past few years Tokyo has received more good PR overseas than any other city in the world. More and more people are coming to the city, most of them with different reasons and expectations from those people came with ten or even five years ago. For some the city is disappointingly westernized, for others it's a super technopolis of the future. For yet others it's simply frustrating. But few people fail to be intrigued, if not captivated, by the curious combination of new technology, internationalism, traditional behavior and aesthetics, and the cross-cultural kitsch that make up Tokyo's special brand of urban life.

The city casts its spell over even the most adamantly unhappy of its foreign residents. Conversations here turn with an almost predictable frequency to Japan and the Japanese. Much of the talk consists of complaints, accusations, stories about silly Mr. Suzuki, or games of one-upmanship as to who has read the most hysterical, the most bizarre, or the most obscene misprinted English phrase of the day. But love or hate, the fascination never dies.

The repertoire of complaints is fairly standardized: the ugliness of the city, people rudely pushing and shoving their way through crowds, the noise pollution, the difficulty of getting around with no consistent system of addresses or street names, the constant pointing and staring at foreigners and the audible "*gaijin da!*" ("it's a foreigner!"), the pervasive belief that foreigners can't learn the impossible Japanese language. But most vehemently criticized is the general sense of regimentation and the overall lack of individuality in the people—the inability to do anything that doesn't go by the rules or isn't decided after lengthy discussion with the "group".

The criticisms are at least partially justified, the frustrations undeniable. You can go into a coffee shop and order a ham and cheese sandwich, hold the ham (or even just the mustard), and it provokes a major crisis. If you're feeling assertive, you'll get angry, wondering why something so simple can't be done. But that's how things work here and the best way to deal with it is to eat your sandwich ham and all, quietly take it off yourself, or simply leave Japan.

The aggressive individuality most foreigners were raised to believe in doesn't figure in the Japanese scheme of things. The Japanese do not believe in individuality, but in the concept of a group where every single person has his place, duties, and responsibilities. This one basic difference leads to more misunderstanding and frustration than any of the multitude of other cultural differences. Individualism is great and makes for a vibrant and actively creative society. But it's not the only way to organize life, and certainly not the Japanese way. To their credit, the Japanese have managed to work out a system that keeps most of the population healthy, happy, and prosperous—if lacking in individuals. For skeptics it's worth noting that the state of Japan is analogous to a hypothetical situation where half the population of the U.S. would be squeezed into Southern California. All those American individuals would probably end up killing each other off within the week. You pay one way or the other.

The bad parts of the city are the most blatantly obvious, while in a typically discreet Japanese fashion, the good parts are often found in the easily overlooked small things—the careful wrapping of the most humble purchase, the hot *oshibori* towel before a meal, the safety, the backstreets swept spotlessly clean by the local residents—all of which are just day to day manifestations of the general Japanese attitude towards life.

It may sound simplistic, but for us, the good parts of the city are a more than equal trade-off for the bad.

We both came to the city as temporary residents. Mayumi arrived as a college student 10 years ago from Sapporo, a city in northern Japan. Her reactions were at first similar to those of any tourist and she often thought of leaving. But after spending a year in London, she returned with a new interest in things Japanese and an objective appreciation for Tokyo.

I came from Seattle, a provincial city on the west coast of America. Tokyo was to be the first stop on a trip around the world. I stayed and learned the language. Curiosity kept me here as three months turned into four years, and I'm still curious.

We both have a great time in Tokyo. We like the technopolitan city that's built on an unshakably Japanese foundation. Tokyo lacks the glamour and sophistication of New York and Paris, but the combination of new and old, the ceaseless input of new cultural variables from around the world, the friction between what gets accepted and what doesn't, give the city an energy—the excitement of a contemporary urban culture constantly in the process of creation.

When we started this book over six months ago, we naively thought it would take much less time and trouble than it has. In the process we have reexplored the city, remembering things we had forgotten, learning things we had never known. There's still much more to learn. This book is a good introduction to getting the best out of the city. It's the book we both wished we had had when we came to Tokyo. It's about how we enjoy it now, and how, with a bit of imagination, you can too.

HOW TO USE THIS BOOK

Cross Referencing

The book is divided into three main sections. The beginning covers the history of the city, its districts and neighborhoods. The middle section is divided into guide chapters covering specific topics: accommodations, restaurants, shopping, arts, etc. The book ends with the map sections. There are 50 maps charting most of the listings found in the guide sections, and covering the districts described in the first chapter. Next to each map is a list of its contents with the text page reference number for each entry.

The idea is to provide a complete cross referencing system. Ideally, you should browse through the entire book. But if you're in a hurry and are looking for something specific, e.g. a *sushi* restaurant, then you can look one up in the restaurant chapter under *sushi*. Then, if you want to spend a day in a particular district, read the first chapter history and description of the district, then turn to the map to see what the area has to offer in terms of shops and restaurants.

How We Selected

Even with a book this size, only a fraction of what the city has to offer can be included. But then, we didn't intend to compile a phone directory. We have selected what we feel is the best of Tokyo. Our selections cover a broad range of prices, and a huge range of possibilities. Convenience figured to some extent. Some places we couldn't include because the Japanese owners didn't want to be made public.

While the decisions were basically our own, we consulted various local "experts" to discover new places, and to reconfirm that our decisions were not made purely on the basis of sentimental association. Our "experts" included born and bred Tokyoites aged 60 plus, resident foreigners, journalists, artists, shop owners, etc. Many of the older shops

and restaurants are famous Japanese institutions, the newer places are often known by only a limited group of Japanese "in the know".
How You Can Select
There is a lot of information in the book. For a future resident or long term visitor it can be great, but for a short term tourist possibly confusing. Our suggestion is to pick one new and one historical district to explore—for example Harajuku or Shinjuku for the contemporary side and Asakusa for old Tokyo. Spend the evening in Roppongi. From our listings for restaurants (or accommodations), you can choose according to price range. All offer excellent quality for the price.
Listings
The shops, restaurants, hotels, etc., listed in this book, with few exceptions, correspond to a number on one of the maps in the map section. The map reference number is marked after each entry as, for example, [M-3], meaning "Map #3". The exceptions are not located on any of our maps and are marked [off Map]. Sometimes we have included instructions for how to get there, or sometimes just the nearest station.

The prices and addresses are valid as of July 1984, but Tokyo changes very quickly. Some of our favorite places closed down while we were writing the book, and more will doubtless close within the next year. In most cases it won't be necessary, but if you're planning to go out of your way to visit a particular shop or restaurant, we suggest you call ahead just to make sure it's still in business.

Most addresses have been written in English, but for some of the more difficult places we have included the names and addresses written in Japanese so you can show them to someone if and when you get lost.

When a place appears more than once in the text, the address, hours, etc., have been noted with the main entry.
Proper Names
Japanese proper names have been written in the Japanese way with family name first.
Place Names
They have been written in the Japanese form. For example Yoyogi Kōen means Yoyogi Park, but if you ask a Japanese person where Yoyogi Park is, few people will understand you. The same goes for museums, gardens, temples, etc. Sometimes we have listed an entry as, for example, Sensō-ji Temple. The "ji" means temple, so the entry literally translates as Sensō Temple Temple. There is no practical way around this.
Italics
In all but a few isolated cases, all words in italics are Japanese terms that are not personal or place names.

Pronunciation

We recommend that you consult the pronunciation guide in the language section before attempting to use any Japanese. In most places throughout the book long vowels have been indicated, with the notable exception of the word Tokyo.

Romanizations of Japanese words in the text are slightly different from those normally used for teaching Japanese, but we have attempted to make them as easy to read as possible for those not acquainted with the Japanese language.

Language Section

The chapter on the Japanese language was written by Peter Barakan, a ten year Tokyo resident with flawless Japanese and a university degree in the language. He is British, which is important for non-British speakers of the English language to remember when following the instructions for pronunciation.

In addition to endless research and telephoning, we have walked the streets of Tokyo trying to make this book as error free as possible. But in spite of our efforts, we know there will be some mistakes—hours and prices will change, shops open and close, the maps may have a few minor omissions. For this we would like to apologize.

Each chapter in this book begins with a title plate. The front page designs are taken from kimono stencil patterns popular in the Edo period. These patterns, called "Edo Komon", are still used on formal kimono. For the inner pages we have selected award-winning examples of Japanese commercial design. All were posters or magazine advertisements originally produced for commercial purposes.

CONTENTS

INTRODUCTION——5

HOW TO USE THIS BOOK——8

TOKYO——17
THE CITY——19
THE DISTRICTS——22
ROPPONGI——22　NISHI-AZABU–HIRŌ——23　SHIBUYA——23
DAIKAN-YAMA——24　HARAJUKU——24　AOYAMA——25
SHINJUKU——26　IKEBUKURO——27
AKASAKA–NAGATACHŌ——28　GINZA——29
HIBIYA–KASUMIGASEKI–YŪRAKUCHŌ——31　MARUNOUCHI——32
SHIMBASHI–SHIBA–HAMAMATSUCHŌ——33
NIHOMBASHI–KYŌBASHI——34　TSUKIJI——35
KANDA–JIMBŌCHŌ——35
OCHANOMIZU–HONGŌ–YUSHIMA——36　AKIHABARA——36
KŌRAKUEN——36　SHINAGAWA——37　NINGYŌCHŌ——37
ASAKUSA——38　UENO——39
ASAKUSABASHI–KURAMAE–RYŌGOKU——41
FUKAGAWA–KIBA–TSUKUDAJIMA——41

ACCOMMODATIONS——43
HOTELS——45
RYOKAN——52
CHEAP ACCOMMODATIONS——53
CAPSULE HOTELS——55

EATING OUT——57
EATING OUT IN TOKYO——60
　DISTRICTS——63
　ETIQUETTE——63
JAPANESE FOOD——64
　ORDERING——64
JAPANESE RESTAURANTS——67
　KAISEKI-RYŌRI——67　SHŌJIN-RYŌRI——68　SUSHI——69
　TEMPURA——72　YAKITORI——73　ROBATA-YAKI——75
　KUSHI-AGE——76　TONKATSU——77
　SUKIYAKI AND SHABU-SHABU——78　SOBA——80　UDON——81
　UNAGI——82　FUGU-RYŌRI——83　ODEN——83
　TŌFU-RYŌRI——84　OKONOMIYAKI——84　RĀMEN——85
　KATEI-RYŌRI——86　YŌSHOKU——87
HEALTH FOOD RESTAURANTS——88
OTHER ASIAN FOOD——89
　KOREAN——89　CHINESE——90　TAIWANESE——91
　CAMBODIAN——91　VIETNAMESE——91　INDIAN——91
WESTERN FOOD——91
　FRENCH——91　ITALIAN——92　AMERICAN——93
　MEXICAN——93　RUSSIAN——93
DESSERT AND COFFEE SHOPS——94

SHOPPING——97
- SHOPPING DISTRICTS——99　DEPARTMENT STORES——100
- FASHION BUILDINGS——103　SPECIAL BUILDINGS——104
- ARCADES——105　TAX-FREE STORES——105
- WHOLESALE MARKETS——106

FASHION——107
- DESIGNER BOUTIQUES——107　CHEAP FASHION——110

ELECTRONICS AND CAMERAS——112
- SHOWROOMS——112　ELECTRONICS AND COMPUTERS——113
- CAMERAS——114

TRADITIONAL ARTS AND CRAFTS——115
- GENERAL SHOPS——116　MINGEI—FOLKCRAFTS——116
- EDO GANGU—TOYS——116　TAKO—KITES——117
- KOINOBORI—CARP BANNERS——117　NINGYŌ—DOLLS——117
- WASHI—PAPER——118　FUDE—BRUSHES——119
- TSUZURA—LACQUERED BAMBOO TRUNKS——119
- SUDARE—BAMBOO BLINDS——119
- CHŌCHIN—PAPER LANTERNS——120　INTERIOR LAMPS——120
- KASA—UMBRELLAS——120　KŌ—INCENSE——121
- CHA-DŌGU—TEA CEREMONY UTENSILS——121
- KATANA—SWORDS——121
- HŌCHŌ AND HASAMI—KNIVES AND SCISSORS——122
- SASHIMONO—FURNITURE——122　OKE—WOODEN BUCKETS——123
- YŌJI—TOOTHPICKS——123　SHIKKI—LACQUER WARE——123
- TŌJIKI—CERAMICS——124　UKIYOE—WOODBLOCK PRINTS——125

TRADITIONAL INSTRUMENTS——126
- SHAMISEN——126　KOTO——126　BIWA——126
- SHAKUHACHI——126　DRUMS——127

TRADITIONAL CLOTHING AND ACCESSORIES——127
- KIMONO——127　OBI——128　KIMONO ACCESSORIES——129
- GETA AND ZŌRI——129　TABI—SOCKS——129
- SENSU—FANS——130
- KUSHI AND KANZASHI—COMBS AND HAIR ORNAMENTS——130
- KESHŌHIN—COSMETICS——131　FESTIVAL CLOTHING——131
- WORKMEN'S CLOTHING——132
- TRADITIONAL DANCE ACCESSORIES——132
- TENUGUI—TOWELS——132　MEN—MASKS——132
- MARTIAL ARTS CLOTHING AND EQUIPMENT——133

ANTIQUES——133
- ANTIQUE STORES——133　FLEA MARKETS——133
- ANTIQUE KIMONO——134　OTHER SECONDHAND CLOTHES——135

FOOD AND DRINKS——135
- TRADITIONAL SWEETS——135　SEMBEI—CRACKERS——137
- SAKE——138　OCHA—TEA——138
- OSHINKO (TSUKEMONO)—PICKLES——139　TSUKUDANI——139
- GROCERY STORES——139

RECORDS——140
- CLASSICAL JAPANESE MUSIC——141　RECORD SHOPS——141

BOOKS——142
- GENERAL BOOKSTORES——142　SPECIALIZED BOOKSTORES——143
- JIMBŌCHŌ BOOK DISTRICT——143

OTHER SHOPS——144
    ART AND OFFICE SUPPLIES——144   COSMETICS——144
    DISCOUNT SHOPS——144   FABRICS——144   INTERIORS——145
    LUGGAGE——145   PEARLS——145   SHOES——146   TOYS——146
    MISCELLANEOUS SHOPS——146

ENTERTAINMENT——149
TRADITIONAL THEATER——151
    GAGAKU AND BUGAKU——151   NŌ——152   KYŌGEN——153
    BUNRAKU——153   KABUKI——154   SHIMPA——156
    RAKUGO——157   GEISHA——157
    TICKETS, THEATERS, AND INFORMATION——158
CONTEMPORARY THEATER——159
    CONCERT HALLS AND THEATERS——161   TICKET OUTLETS——162
SPORTS——162
    SUMŌ——162   MARTIAL ARTS——165   BASEBALL——166
MOVIES——167

NIGHTLIFE——169
DISTRICTS——171
BARS——172
    GENERAL BARS——173   EXPATRIATES' HANG-OUTS——174
    GAY BARS——175
BEER HALLS AND BEER GARDENS——175
DISCOS——176
LIVE MUSIC——177
    ROCK AND MODERN MUSIC——177
    JAZZ——178   COUNTRY AND WESTERN——178   KARAOKE——178
CABARET AND HOSTESS BARS——179
X-RATED——180
    X-RATED TOKYO——180   LOVE HOTELS——181

ARTS——183
MUSEUMS——185
    JAPANESE TRADITIONAL ARTS——186
    MODERN JAPANESE AND WESTERN ARTS——187
    SPECIALIST MUSEUMS——188   OUTSIDE TOKYO——192
CONTEMPORARY ARTS GALLERIES——192
    GALLERIES——194   CERAMICS AND CRAFTS——196
    CONTEMPORARY PRINTS——196   PHOTOGRAPHY——197
    VIDEO——197
TRADITIONAL ARTS——198
    IKEBANA——199   TEA CEREMONY——199   CALLIGRAPHY——199

SIGHTSEEING——201
TEMPLES AND SHRINES——203
PARKS AND GARDENS——209
ZOOS——212
PLEASURE GROUNDS——212
HISTORICAL SITES AND BUILDINGS——213

CEMETERIES——214
CONTEMPORARY ARCHITECTURE——215
GUIDED TOURS——216
WALKING COURSES——216

HEALTH AND BEAUTY——227
ASIAN MEDICINE——229
   HARI–ACUPUNCTURE——229   SEITAI–CHIROPRACTIC——230
WESTERN MEDICINE——230
   CLINICS——230   HOSPITALS——230   DENTAL CARE——231
   OPTICAL CARE——231   PHARMACIES——231
SENTŌ—PUBLIC BATHS——231
SAUNAS, STEAM BATHS, AND MASSAGE——232
SPORTS FACILITIES——233
   HEALTH CLUBS——233   SWIMMING POOLS——234
   JOGGING COURSES——235   CYCLING COURSES——235
BEAUTY CARE——236

THE BASICS——237
PLANNING——239
   CLIMATE——239   WHEN TO TRAVEL——239
   SPECIAL DEALS–BEFORE YOU GO——240
   PACKING AND SUPPLIES——241   VISAS——242
ARRIVAL——243
   FORMALITIES——245   CUSTOMS——245
   PASSENGER SERVICE FACILITY CHARGE——246
   AIRPORT SERVICES——246   TRANSPORTATION TO TOKYO——246
   HANEDA AIRPORT——247
DETAILS——248
   MONEY——248   TIPPING-SERVICE, CHARGES-TAXES——248
   BUSINESS HOURS——248   METRIC——249   ELECTRICITY——249
   FOOD AND DRINK——249   JAPANESE TOILETS——250
   SAFETY——250
COMMUNICATIONS——251
   MAIL——251   TELEGRAMS AND CABLES——251
   TELEPHONES——252
GETTING AROUND——253
   TRAINS AND SUBWAYS——253   TAXIS——255   BUSES——255
   GETTING THERE——256   GETTING LOST——257
   LOST AND FOUND——257
TOURIST SERVICES——257

LANGUAGE——259

APPENDIX——273

MAPS——299

ACKNOWLEDGEMENTS——352
INDEX——353

東京
TOKYO

"The Ginza Story". One of the first districts in Tokyo to "modernize", since the Meiji period Ginza has stood for all that was new, innovative, and elegant. This poster celebrates Matsuya Department Store's 60th anniversary in Ginza.

TOKYO

THE CITY

It's often said, by Japanese and foreigners alike, that Tokyo is not the "real" Japan. What they mean is that it's not the "ideal" Japan, the Japan of a people unspoiled by the west, where the descendants of the Sun Goddess live in spiritual harmony with nature in the land of the rising sun.

The nostalgia is understandable. With a population of nearly 12 million, Tokyo reads at times like a lexicon of the problems confronting Japan today. But the "ideal" Japan, like all objects of nostalgic devotion, is part of an irretrievable past. With barely 100 years of modern history, the Japanese still suffer from growing pains. The events of those 100 years, the greatest successes and the greatest defeats, were first felt in Tokyo.

Kyōto was the center of the country during the golden days of Japan. There, in the rarefied air of the emperor's presence, a court aristocracy pursued a life of aesthetic sensitivity and refinement. What was most important was the turn of a phrase in a cryptic poem, the perfect harmony in 12 layers of subtly shaded *kimono*, the just-so sweep of a brush across a sheet of immaculate paper. The present site of Tokyo was then called Musashi no Kuni, a land of fields and thickly forested hills.

Tokyo came of age with Tokugawa Ieyasu's rise to power in 1600. The *daimyō*, feudal lords, were brought to submission and the country was ruled for 250 years of domestic peace and isolation from the world under the Tokugawa shogunate based in *Edo*.

Edo had prospered since the mid-15th century as a castle town built by the minor *daimyō* Ōta Dōkan. Throughout Japan, the *daimyō* consolidated their power in castle towns that grew into provincial capitals of cultural and economic activity centered on the needs of the lord and the *samurai* aristocracy. Primarily constructed for defense, the castles were surrounded by concentric circles of moats and ramparts, the streets laid out in irregular zigzag patterns to surprise and confuse an attacking enemy. The seemingly random pattern of Tokyo streets today is a survival of this early urban planning.

Edo became the greatest castle in the land. The city grew rapidly as the *daimyō* built homes within the castle walls, alternating residence between their provincial domains and mandatory service on the *shōgun* in *Edo*. With the influx of *daimyō* and *samurai* troops, the need for a service class increased. Tokugawa Ieyasu invited merchants and artisans to the city, assigning them quarters in the eastern marshes by the sea, now the lands stretching west and southwest from Hibiya. Dirt from the top of Surugadai, one of Tokyo's larger hills, was provided to start the process of reclamation from the sea that continues today. By the 1700's, the population of *Edo* was close to a million, making it possibly the largest city in the world at the time.

The conservative *Edo* period government legally enforced a strict division of classes, placing the *samurai* at the top and the theoretically unproductive merchant at the bottom. But the urban *samurai* had become utterly dependant, and increasingly indebted to, the merchant class. Despite government efforts to enforce the status quo, the merchants continued to prosper. Restricted to *"shitamachi"*, the crowded downtown districts, from the merchant and artisan classes emerged a culture that was as vibrantly creative as it was unabashedly vulgar. In the amusement quarters of the city, the merchants escaped from the pressures of the rigid social system and the demands of business. Under their patronage, the arts flourished—the *bunraku* and *kabuki* theaters, *geisha*, and *ukiyoe* were all products of the time.

Tokugawa rule ended shortly after the arrival in Tokyo Bay of Commodore Perry and the U.S. Navy in 1853. Unable to protect the country from the "Southern Barbarians", the government had lost its claim to legitimacy. A coalition of powerful families from the southern and western provinces seized power from the shogunate, and in the 1868 *Meiji* Restoration reestablished Imperial rule. The Emperor was moved to *Edo* castle and the city renamed Tokyo—the "eastern capital".

The new government quickly realized that national security could best be achieved by meeting the west on its own terms, and a program was undertaken to promote rapid modernization. Things western were adopted and praised as far superior to Japanese. Foreign experts were sought and extravagantly paid. Tokyo took on a new air as brick buildings, trains, and tailored suits came into vogue.

Patterns of urban use also changed. The *daimyō* packed up and moved back to the provinces leaving vast stretches of vacant land in the castle area. No longer confined to *shitamachi*, the wealthy merchants moved to the western, hilly parts of town. Without their patronage, the arts and entertainment forms of *Edo* popular culture lost their major source of support. The old pleasure quarters and theaters fell on hard times and *shitamachi* was left to the poor.

Tokyo continued to grow, and by the 1920's had a population of over 2 million. Then, in 1923, the Great Kantō Earthquake struck. The earthquake, and the fires and tidal waves that followed, left nearly 140 thousand people dead and half of the city destroyed. Tokyo was rebuilt and in less than ten years the population was again at pre-earthquake levels. In 1932, the city limits were expanded to the current 23 wards, boosting the population another 2 million.

The city has suffered over the years from a variety of natural and unnatural disasters—in the *Edo* period from over 500 major fires, from floods, typhoons, earthquakes, and in 1945 from the fire bombing of World War II. Each time the people reconstructed the city and resumed their lives with a stoic resilience. Tokyo has no tradition of permanence.

Now, the second largest city in the world, Tokyo sprawls across more than 800 square miles of the Kantō plain. As an urban environment, the capital shows little concern for outward appearances, and evokes neither the alien exoticism of an Asian city, nor the sense of wonder and awe one expects from a city of its size and international importance. But while westerners build monuments to the future, the Japanese have built and rebuilt for the present. The chaos of the city today is the function of an attitude that puts the exigencies of survival above all other concerns. A major earthquake has been predicted in Tokyo. They happen every 60 years or so; the last one was in 1923, and the next is already overdue. The city keeps building its functional modern highrises and just waits.

Yet the "technopolitan" Tokyo of first impressions is really just a thin veneer that hides what remains in essence a city of villages. Within walking distance of almost any of the city's major districts are back street neighborhoods where life operates pretty much the same as in any small suburban community. Shops and homes line the narrow wandering streets where children play and grandmothers chat at the corner fruit stand. The man next door waters his street side garden in his pajamas each morning and the *tōfu* seller tours the neighborhood in the evening by bicycle, calling out to the local housewives with his distinctive horn.

The districts and neighborhoods that divide Tokyo make it a city of varied pleasures and endless discovery. Each has a history, each growing up at a different stage in the life of the city. Some, aging, are museum of the past; others are still in the first neon flush of youth.

THE DISTRICTS
Roppongi

The most international district in Tokyo, Roppongi is famous as one of the city's major nightlife districts. Less expensive and established than Ginza and Akasaka, more sophisticated than Shinjuku and Shibuya, Roppongi claims some of the best restaurants, bars and nightclubs, and a crowd with more blond hair and blue eyes than any other part of town.

It is also one of the city's high-rent residential areas, a reputation the area has had since the *Edo* period. One theory on the origin of the district's "six trees" name claims that six *Edo* period *samurai*, whose names included the character for tree, lived in the neighborhood. In the *Meiji* period the area was inhabited by wealthy Japanese and foreigners connected with the newly established embassies. Later the military set up camp towards Nogizaka where the Self-Defense Force headquarters are located today. After the war more foreigners moved in as embassies relocated to the area, and the U.S. military established a base on part of the former Japanese Army lands. It was still a quiet district, with a street car running along the main thoroughfare and a few western style bars and restaurants serving burgers and pizza.

During the late 50's and early 60's, as the post war prosperity took hold, the Japanese began to look beyond the need for survival, and the traditional values propagated by the nationalistic wartime government. Roppongi, with its international air, attracted the new cosmopolitan Japanese. In a few cafés and bars—Nicola's, Gino's, and the still famous Chianti—gathered the liberal elite of intellectuals, entertainers, fashion designers and other notables. The district's popularity grew, more bars and restaurants opened, and the young Japanese who frequented the area were dubbed the "*Roppongi-zoku*"—the Roppongi people.

Life in Roppongi starts at the Roppongi crossing and its tribute to the Japanese love of coffee shops and kitsch architecture—the famous Almond (pronounced "*amando*")—a multi-story pink coffee shop with some of the worst coffee and cakes in town. This is, however, a major landmark and the corner in front a favorite rendezvous spot. Another famous landmark is the Square Building, a potential entrant in the Guinness Book of World Records for housing seven discos in its ten stories.

By day, Roppongi is relatively quiet. Two fairly recent buildings make it worth a daytime trip: the Axis Building full of shops specializing in contemporary interior goods, and Wave, the most advanced record store in the world.

A short walk down the hill from the main crossing is Azabu-Jūban, a neighborhood shopping area that grew up as a textile center producing linen cloth, *asa*, from which the area gets its name. The area has two community festivals each year around the 20th of August and on the second Saturday and Sunday in September.

Nishi-Azabu—Hirō

As Roppongi slowly reaches a nightclub saturation point, the fallout from the district's burgeoning prosperity has drifted towards the west and southwest into two formerly quiet residential areas—Nishi-Azabu and Hirō (pronounced Hiro-o).

Nishi-Azabu is centered around Kasumichō crossing at the bottom of the hill to the west of Roppongi, along the main road to Shibuya. Now the back streets are the refuge of a growing number of small interesting clubs following in a tradition set by a fellow named Tommy a few years back. Tommy opened a basement bar, predictably called "Tommy's House". Tiny, with loud music and backgammon boards, the place was invariably packed. The sign still remains, but Tommy closed his bar in 1983 and his mother opened a restaurant on the site. In 1982, the nearby Red Shoes was the Bar of the Year and drew a steady crowd of Tokyo's more creative community to its tiny red interior. The new clubs that have opened in the area are heirs to the scene.

More residential than the Kasumichō area, Hirō has a rather dubious reputation as the "*gaijin* ghetto" (*gaijin* means "foreigner"). Expensive company subsidized apartment complexes are full of foreign executives and their families, while two large western style supermarkets help comfort the homesick. One street near the station is a more traditional Japanese style shopping area, and Arisugawa Park is a short walk away.

Shibuya

One of the first things anyone should know about Shibuya is the heart-warming story of Hachikō, a dog of the native Japanese Akita breed. Hachi would escort his master, a professor at Tokyo University, to Shibuya station each morning and return in the evening to meet him on his way home from work. One day the professor suffered a stroke and never came home, but the faithful Hachi returned to the station each evening to wait. This went on for seven years. When Hachi finally died in 1935, he got the front page of all the major newspapers. Gifts and letters poured in from around the country, and a bronze statue of Hachikō was erected in the plaza in front of the station. Hachikō Square (North Exit) is probably the most famous meeting place in the city. The real Hachi was stuffed and is part of the collection of the Tokyo Museum of Art.

As a district, Shibuya fits somewhere between the wildness of Shinjuku, the kids of Harajuku and the sophistication of Roppongi. A moderately fashionable area, its main attractions are the Seibu Department Store and the three part Parco, offering one-stop shopping for the best Japanese designers. There is an abundance of record stores and theaters, and at night the area draws crowds of students and young office workers to its cheap discotheques and *nomiya* (Japanese style bars).

Until recently, Shibuya was a quiet residential area. Named after the Shibuya family whose castle was located here, during the *Edo* period the district was just one step up from the provinces. After the *Meiji* Restoration, the *samurai* residents vacated the area, which was then used as tea fields and ranch lands. When the earthquake destroyed much of Tokyo in 1923, people moved from the center of town and undeveloped districts like Shibuya, Meguro, and Setagaya became heavily residential. After the war, Shibuya had one of the city's largest black markets. Nearby was the office of a famous ghost writer of love letters to U.S. soldiers on behalf of lovelorn Japanese women. He still operates a translation office in the same place.

Daikan-yama

A short distance from Shibuya, Daikan-yama is a rising star among the city's peripheral residential districts. Since the 70's when the Hillside Terrance apartments and shops were built (designed by architect Tange Kenzō), the area has grown slowly and more gracefully than any other neighborhood in Tokyo. The general feeling is curiously reminiscent of Los Angeles, and there is even a Mexican restaurant (though the food is unmistakably not from Southern California). Public transportation to the area is unusually bad for Tokyo, the one station being Daikan-yama on the suburban Tōyoko Line from Shibuya. But then that helps the Los Angeles illusion—you need a car to get around. The area has a growing number of chic boutiques, restaurants, and residents.

Harajuku

Dedicated to youth, fashion trendiness, and the belief that all consumers under 25 are created equal, Harajuku thrives as the kid's capital of Tokyo. The district swarms with the well-dressed pampered youth of Japan, raised in an era of post war prosperity and carefree consumerism. But the rigorous school system and the pressures for conformity to the salaryman and satisfied housewife pattern of life have their young victims. Many of the dancers who fill Harajuku's Yoyogi Park on Sundays are the ones who can't make it in the system or simply don't care to try. In an ironic display of rebellious behavior, the kids dance in well choreographed, polite groups—boys with boys, girls with girls. The original dancers in the late 70's were named the *Takenoko-zoku*, or "bamboo-shoot people", after the bright Asian style costumes made by a boutique called Takenoko, now the James Dean look and 50's nostalgia reign.

The spirit of Harajuku is as infectious as it is insipid. For fashion the district beats any other part of Tokyo. Most of the big designers' shops are in nearby Aoyama and Shibuya, but cheap knock-offs and play clothes overflow from the hundreds of shops near the central crossing and lining the back streets. The main landmark is the La Foret fashion building, and down the street towards Tōgō Jinja Shrine is Takeshita-dōri, famous as one of the city's cheapest shopping areas.

North of the district is Yoyogi Park, the Meiji Jingū Shrine and its outer gardens. The park attracts some of the more exhibitionist Tokyo inhabitants—dancers and street performers of all kinds, and towards the north end of the park are always a few saxophonists or trumpeters practicing their instruments into the bushes.

Aoyama
The post Harajuku generation finds more of interest in the neighbor-

The signs on this old house announce that it is absolutely not for sale. Behind towers a new apartment complex.

ing Aoyama district, where life moves at a more sophisticated, expensive pace. The main street, Aoyama-dōri, stretches from Shibuya to Akasaka, meeting along the way a number of side streets spawning ever growing numbers of boutiques, specialty shops and restaurants. Kottō-dōri, on the Shibuya end, is famous as one of Tokyo's antique shop streets. The Nezu Museum is nearby. Along Killer-dōri (named by designer Koshino Junko who used to have a boutique along the street) is more of the same, boutiques, shops and restaurants all potentially dangerous for your budget.

The *Edo* period Aoyama *daimyō* family lived here, leaving for posterity their name and the family graveyard, now the Aoyama-bochi, a great place for a quiet stroll or for viewing the spring cherry blossoms.

On the Akasaka end of Aoyama-dōri is a huge walled-in green spot. Inside is the Akasaka Detached Palace, an official state guest house modeled after Buckingham Palace on the outside and Versailles on the inside. Across the street is the Sōgetsu Kaikan, center of the famous school of contemporary *ikebana*.

Shinjuku

A showcase for all the worst aspects of the city's chaos, Shinjuku has, at the same time, a stronger, more vibrant spirit than any other part of town. Much of the spirit borders on sleaze. Shinjuku is the latest of the late night districts, and one of the cheapest. It's here that night-time revelers come to escape the sophistication and civility of the city's chic southwest districts.

Shinjuku has always had a rather questionable reputation. In the *Edo* period it was a small lodging town, not even within the city limits. A fight between a local brothel owner and the younger brother of an influential *samurai* official led to the area's disappearance. But 50 years later it grew up again and became a major pleasure quarter frequented by the lower classes.

In 1889 Shinjuku station was built with a new train line servicing the western suburbs. The area immediately prospered. The residential population increased, as did the number of pleasure houses. When courtesans were liberated in 1872, the formalities of the *geisha* entertainments were abandoned, and most of the former *geisha* houses became simple houses of prostitution with rooms for rent. Shinjuku was notorious for having more rooms than any other part of town. Plans to clean up the neighborhood and relocate the pleasure quarter were drawn up but never put into effect.

The area continued to grow and in 1920 part of it was annexed into the city's Yotsuya ward. The rest of the district became a part of Tokyo in 1932 when the city limits were redrawn. The station became increasingly important as a commuter transfer point and is now the largest in the country, handling over 2 million passengers a day.

Shinjuku has prospered. Around the station are found the highest rents in Japan. Department stores, boutiques, fashion buildings and the huge Shinjuku station underground arcade serve commuters on their way home or suburbanites in for the weekends when the major thoroughfare becomes a pedestrian "paradise" (or "hell" depending on how much you like mobs). Students from the surrounding universities form another big part of the crowd.

But life in Shinjuku really begins after dark. Kabukichō is the center of the action. The *kabuki* theater originally planned as a cultural focus for the neighborhood never materialized, but gave the district its name. In its place a modern pleasure quarter grew up after the war. The area has numerous movie theaters, and the surrounding streets are famous for their x-rated shops: no-panty coffee shops, pick up shops, strip shows, "pink" cabaret (in Japan "pink" is the symbolic x-rated color). This is the area where you're most likely to spot *yakuza* types (the Japanese mafia—easily recognized by their typical gangster-style dress, their squared-off crew cuts, and the notable absence of fingers).

Gōruden-gai, another famous neighborhood, is a street full of tiny closet-sized bars, and is one of the few parts of town where a little caution is advised. Shomben-yokochō, near the train tracks on the west side of the station is yet another drinking area. Full of cheap *nomiya*, the name literally translates as "piss alley." Ni-chōme is the gay bar district.

The *nishi-guchi* (west side) of Shinjuku claims more skyscrapers than any other part of Tokyo. Built on land that was formerly a water and sewage treatment plant, the area is properly antiseptic. The oldest building dates from 1971.

Ikebukuro

Ikebukuro is basically a less interesting version of Shinjuku. A commuter's town, the district lacks any specific kind of character. The major attractions are the huge Seibu Department Store (the largest in the world) and the Sunshine City complex which at 60 stories is the tallest building in Asia.

Until the *Meiji* period the district was farm and forest lands, famous as a spot for viewing the summer fireflies. A small bag-shaped pond in the area gave the district its name—Ikebukuro means literally "pond bag". A train station was built in 1903 and served at the time about 30 passengers a day. Now it's second only to Shinjuku.

In the 30's Ikebukuro was a haunt of artists and writers, and the area was dubbed, in all seriousness, "Ikebukuro Montparnasse". The district later became the site of Tokyo prison. After World War II the prison was renamed Sugamo by the Occupation Authorities and was used to hold Japanese war criminals. Seven men, including Field Marshal Tōjō Hideki, were hung in the prison. In 1958 the name was changed back to Tokyo Prison, but the building was torn down in 1972 to build a new cultural center for the area. The Sunshine City Building stands on the site.

The west side of Ikebukuro station is similar in flavor to Shinjuku's Kabukichō. Here and the area behind the Bungeiza Theater to the east were, in the past, "dangerous" areas with the reputation for being the scene of an occasional gun battle between rival yakuza gangs.

Akasaka—Nagatachō

The side streets in Akasaka are lined with Japanese style buildings of a uniform sand color, with discreet signs telling the name of the restaurant. These are not places that the ordinary foreigner can enter, nor the ordinary Japanese for that matter. Most of these "*ryōtei*" restaurants require an introduction. In the evening *geisha* are called, and over bottles of *sake* (rice wine) and meals in the best Japanese tradition, politicians and big business types cement those bonds of friendship so important in the greater world of economics and governmental affairs. On a back street hill nearby is a row of empty rickshaws. In the mid *Meiji* period there were over 50,000 in the city, but the rickshaws are now used only by the *geisha* on their way to a party.

Yet the discreet *ryōtei* seem somehow anomalous in an area now dominated by the glitz and glamour of the entertainment scene centered around the hundreds of small hostess bars, cavernous cabarets like the Mikado and New Latin Quarter, and TBS Television, which since 1960 has ensured a steady flow of TV personalities and their fans into the neighborhood.

Hotels give the district an added international dimension. The major ones are the New Ōtani, the Akasaka Prince, the Akasaka Tōkyū (otherwise known as the "Pajama Hilton" for its pink and white striped exterior), the Capitol Tōkyū, and the remains of the ill-fated New Japan Hotel, which burned up along with a number of tourists in a fire that led to a wave of new safety regulations for hotels.

Top level *Edo* period *daimyō* had lived in the area during the Tokugawa reign. The neighboring Hie Jinja Shrine was one of the big three shrines of the time. In the early *Meiji* period, the *daimyō* moved out and the government confiscated the lands, turning them to agricultural uses. Akasaka became a hill of tea bushes and *akane*, plants that produced a red dye, giving the district its name meaning "red slope". The military moved in later, while the Nagatachō area north of Akasaka became the center of *Meiji* period state government. The reputation of the *"Akasaka ryōtei"*, and their tradition of serving power and politics, dates from this time. The *"Akasaka geisha"*, the lowest class of *geisha* during the *Edo* period, were upgraded to entertain the important clientele and are still considered some of the city's best.

Ginza

Ginza used to be synonymous with the glamour of big city life in Tokyo. Elegant, expensive, and at one time the most international part of the city, Ginza inspired a string of hit songs in the first half of the century. Best remembered are songs like "Ginza Rhapsody", "Ginza Can-Can Girl", and even the American surf-rock band the Ventures wrote a song called "Ginza for Two" (an interesting bit of trivia—the Ventures were a huge success here in the early 60's and still tour Japan every year). The name Ginza has now become another way of saying "shopping street"—there are some 450 "Ginza" streets throughout Japan, and the number is still growing.

Ginza started out as a swamp and was among the first areas reclaimed from the sea during Tokugawa Ieyasu's reign. Overshadowed by the

Taishō period Ginza.

more prosperous Nihombashi, Ginza grew up as a town of artisans and craftsmen. In 1612 the Tokugawa silver mint was moved to the area. "Gin" means silver and "za" means a licensed association of craftsmen; the district got its name from the numbers of artisans working in the metal. When the mint was moved in the *Meiji* period the name remained.

The Tokugawa (*Edo*) period ended with the challenge from the west, and Ginza was one of the first parts of town to feel the effects of the *Meiji* government's modernization program. When the area was destroyed by fire in 1872, the government hired the British architect Josiah Condor and planned a model western style urban center. Nearly 1,000 brick buildings were constructed, tiled pavements laid, and willow trees planted. The first horse trolley in Tokyo passed through Ginza to Nihombashi and Shimbashi. The first gas lights in the city were installed, turning Ginza into a night life area. Across the street from Matsuya Department Store a single lamp post remains.

While the brick buildings created quite a stir, most remained vacant long after completion. Though fireproof in theory, the buildings were badly ventilated and believed to be hazardous to health. Still, crowds of people turned out to see the novelty, and the commercial success of Ginza dates from this time. Shopping in Ginza by day, and evening strolling by gaslight, became a fad that led to the coining of a new term "ginbura" meaning wandering around in Ginza.

Another term coined in the *Meiji* era was *haikara*, or "high collar", a reference to western style shirts, and the *Meiji* era equivalent of the modern "trendy". At the time this meant "western" and Ginza more than any other part of Tokyo was the center for all that was western and new—men's suits, watches, meat eating, and coffee drinking.

The area was full of new ideas and entrepreneurs. The famous cosmetics company Shiseidō was started in a small Ginza pharmacy in 1872 by Fukuhara Akinobu, a former pharmacist for the navy. The Seikō watch company began as a retail and repair shop opened by Hattori Kintarō. By the *Taishō* period all the major department stores had opened branches in the area. The Ginza Matsuzakaya was the first department store in the country that didn't require its customers to take off their shoes.

After the war Ginza was the first place prosperity returned to. The department stores were crowded again, exclusive boutiques began to fill the back streets, and Ginza was called the "Fifth Avenue of Tokyo". The neighborhood became a treasury of expensive Japanese restaurants and clubs catering to the businessman of the future economic miracle. Even now Ginza claims the largest number of eating and drinking establishments in Tokyo.

But for the post war generation, Ginza has less to offer than the newer districts to the west. Too expensive, too conservative, yet not quite traditionally Japanese, Ginza is still crowded but somehow lacks spirit.

The trend may reverse—shops and restaurants that had drawn the younger population to the west have begun to move back downtown, and the largest concentration of contemporary art galleries is already here. The blend of old and new could be interesting, and is something that hasn't happened anywhere else in town.

Hibiya—Kasumigaseki—Yūrakuchō

Like Ginza, Hibiya was part of the marsh land reclaimed from the sea during the early *Edo* period. Close to the central part of the castle *daimyō* mansions occupied the grounds. With the early *Meiji* period exodus of *daimyō* families from the city, the lands were left an empty wasteland. Part of the land was used as the first parade ground for the new western style military. Nearby were built the Rokumeikan in 1883 and in 1890 the original Imperial Hotel.

The Rokumeikan was a state owned guest house designed by Josiah Condor. One of the more idealistic endeavors of the *Meiji* period establishment, it was believed that, by inviting foreign diplomats to parties given at the ornate western style building, Japan would be placed on the roster of civilized nations.

The Imperial Hotel was built on the site of the present hotel building. Originally designed by a Japanese, the second building was the work of American architect Frank Lloyd Wright. The Wright building was torn down in 1968 and the third and present hotel constructed.

The military gave its parade ground to the city in 1893. The initial plan was to build a concentration of government office buildings on the site, but when the land proved unable to support the weight of the proposed constructions, the area was made into the city's first western style park and opened in 1903. If you happen to take a bus tour that passes through the area, the tour guide is likely to make some slightly risqué joke about Hibiya Park's reputation as a favorite spot for lovers. As early as 1908, the police were raiding the park and fining indiscreet couples.

Hibiya is now the home of numerous theaters and movie houses, and the famous Takarazuka Theater.

The neighboring Yūrakuchō area is famous for its cheap *yakitoriya* beneath the elevated train tracks. During the first five years after the war General McArthur's headquarters were located in the Yūrakuchō Daiichi Seimei Building (the room remains, though you can't enter). The area had a large black market and was full of U.S. soldiers, prostitutes, orphans, and shoe shine boys.

Kasumigaseki is a short walk through the Hibiya Park. The government office district, there are ministries of just about everything—MITI (Ministry of International Trade and Industry), the National Diet building, and the Prime Minister's Official Residence. The 36 story Kasumigaseki Building, constructed in 1968, was known as the first Japanese skyscraper.

Marunouchi

Marunouchi is as prestigious as business addresses come in Japan, and most major corporations are located here. Little of the corporate income, however, is spent on image and the area is architecturally one of the least interesting in the city.

Marunouchi's reputation was set in the early part of the century. Like many of the city's central areas, the land had been vacated by the *samurai* at the start of the *Meiji* period and taken over by the new government. Owned by the military, the lands were left unused by all but rickshaw pullers and other *Meiji* period low life characters and became known as "Gambler's Field". The land was put up for sale and first offered to the Imperial Family, who were unable to raise sufficient funds. In 1889 it was bought by the already powerful Mitsubishi Company.

The Mitsubishi purchase was planned as a new business district and Josiah Condor was commissioned to build a brick office center modeled on London's Lombard Street. The first building was completed in 1894, and about 25 years and 27 brick buildings later the development was completed and became known as Tokyo's "Little London". The buildings were torn down after the war and the area took on its current middle of the road modern air.

The strategic location of Tokyo station was largely responsible for the success of the new development. Built as the main terminal for trains from the south, the main entrance faced towards the palace and the Mitsubishi buildings, rather than the more established Nihombashi and Kyōbashi districts. The Mitsubishi gamble paid off (whether someone else was paid off to ensure the pay-off is another story), and by 1922 over half of Japan's major corporations had already relocated there.

Tokyo station, home base of the famous *Shinkansen* "Bullet Train" was built in 1914, and is the oldest remaining station in the city. The Japanese had just beaten the Russians in war and, full of pride and patriotism, decided to build a station to shock the world. Amsterdam station was chosen as the unlikely model and a vaguely post-Victorian red brick station was erected. The old building can still be seen from the west side of the station. Uninspiring though the building may be, it was the site of two famous political assassinations: that of Prime Minister Hara

Takashi by a 19 year old youth in 1877, and in 1930 that of Prime Minster Hamaguchi Osachi by a right wing terrorist.

Shimbashi—Shiba—Hamamatsuchō

Situated at the southern end of Ginza, Shimbashi has always been the less illustrious neighborhood of the two. The station was one of the first in the city, and the original terminal for trains from the south. The surrounding area was known for its shopping arcades, bazaars and cheap drinking spots. The "*Shimbashi geisha*" quarter was one of the two great *geisha* districts in the *Meiji* period.

Ginza was centered closer towards Shimbashi during the early *Meiji* period. But with the opening of Tokyo station, Shimbashi lost its prominence and the center of Ginza moved north to the crossing where it remains today. The old station was closed and a new one built on the old drinking area. The shops moved to the side and the district is still known for its tiny restaurants, *nomiya* and salaryman clientele.

South from Shimbashi is Shiba, an important *Edo* period temple district protecting the castle from the south, a direction which, according to superstition, was a potentially dangerous one. Zōjōji, a Tokugawa family temple, was the area's greatest.

The sea reached as far as the Zōjōji *daimon* (main gate) at the beginning of the *Edo* period. A port served merchant vessels, and salt was made on the beaches. Hamarikyū, a villa of the Tokugawa *shōgun*, and its extravagant gardens stretched along the Shiba coast. Now only the gardens remain. Reclamation projects moved the sea far away, and by the *Meiji* period Shiba became one of the city's industrial districts.

Now Hamamatsuchō to the west of Shiba borders the sea, its coast lined with warehouses and piers. Takeshiba Sambashi pier serves ships to the islands lying off the Izu Peninsula. Hamamatsuchō is best known for its World Trade Center, built in 1970, which after the Kasumigaseki building became the tallest skyscraper in Japan. Connected to the Trade Center is the terminal for the monorail to Haneda Airport. In the Hamamatsuchō station is a copy of the Brussels Manniken-Pis. Since 1956 the statue of a small naked boy has collected an extensive wardrobe of clothing donated by concerned women passengers. The wardrobe now includes over 200 outfits, which may make the statue one of the best dressed works of public art in the world.

Another famous neighborhood copy is the Tokyo Tower. Built as a tourist attraction in 1958, the tower unfortunately fails to lend the area the hoped for European flair.

Nihombashi—Kyōbashi

Old money and conservatism usually go hand in hand, and Nihombashi is no exception. Nihombashi has been the center of big money in Japan since the *Edo* period, and most of the country's big mercantile families started off in this neighborhood.

Nihombashi was the first of the merchant neighborhoods designated by the *shōgun* to be reclaimed from the sea. With the construction of the Nihombashi Bridge in 1603, it became the official last stop on the famous Tōkaidō route from Kyōto and the point from which all roads in Japan were measured. Rebuilt in 1911, the Nihombashi and the nearby Tokiwa are the oldest bridges in the city.

The district grew up as the heart of commercial *Edo*, with the fish market, the shops of craftsmen and artisans, and the offices of money changers. One of the most densely populated districts of the city, wooden houses were cramped together along the narrow alleys and backstreets. The homes of wealthy merchants and a few of the *samurai* aristocracy lined the banks of the river.

Nearby was the Kyōbashi district, named for its "capital bridge" (the kyō in Kyōbashi is the same kyō as in Tōkyō and Kyōto). Next to the bridge was the first *kabuki* theater built in 1624 by Nakazawa Kanzaburō.

The Nihombashi and Kyōbashi areas had, in the early days, been full of theaters and temples, and neighboring Ningyōchō was famous for its pleasure quarters. But by the late *Edo* period all were moved to the northern outskirts of town by the conservative shogunate. The wealthy downtown merchants then traveled north for their pleasures, and the trip was usually by boat from the Kyōbashi bridge.

With the changes in the *Meiji* period, the wealthy merchants moved away from the area to the prestigious residential districts to the south and west. Not as receptive to change as Ginza and Marunouchi, Nihombashi was slow to catch up with the modernism of the new era. But by late *Meiji* the district had come into its own with a series of monumental buildings in an architectural style that blended European Classical elements with traditional Japanese. The Bank of Japan opened its new building in 1896, and more banks and government offices followed. The department stores—Mitsukoshi and Takashimaya—were expanding and adding floors.

Little remains from the early days—a few *Edo* period shops, and some bridges and buildings from the *Meiji* and *Taishō* periods. The commercial banks are still there as is the stock exchange. But of the major business districts in Tokyo, Nihombashi alone retains a sense of history and a quiet dignity.

Tsukiji

Tsukiji is one of Tokyo's more off beat tourist attractions. The main fish market for the city, buying and selling starts at about 5 a.m. and finishes shortly after noon. An early morning trip to the market for a fresh *sushi* breakfast is a great way to start off a day of sightseeing in Tokyo.

Until the 1923 earthquake, the fish market was located in the heart of Nihombashi, near the Bank of Japan and Mitsukoshi Department Store. When nearly 400 people died there during the post earthquake fires, the market was torn down and rebuilt on its present site.

Tsukiji, formerly the mouth of the Sumida River, was a major *Edo* period reclamation project, the name meaning "constructed land".

When the country was opened to the west in the *Meiji* period, Tsukiji was built as a foreign settlement to isolate and protect the citizens and foreigners from each other. The area was never much liked, except by the Christian missionaries who built St. Luke's Hospital and St. Paul University. Nearby was built the Hoterukan. An early attempt at western architecture, the hotel had over 200 rooms. In 1869 the Shibaura pleasure quarter was opened in Tsukiji by the government in an attempt to please the foreign population. The quarter had over 200 houses with nearly 2,000 *geisha* and courtesans, but the Shibaura was more than most of the prudish foreigners could take. The quarter never prospered and was shut down shortly afterwards.

At the end of the 19th century when the treaties with foreign powers were revised and autonomy returned to Japan, foreigners were permitted to live where they chose in the city. Most moved from the settlement and the remaining buildings burned down in the earthquake.

Kanda—Jimbōchō

It was with dirt from the top of Kanda's Surugadai hill that the marshlands of early *Edo* were reclaimed. Nearly half of the hill was carried off over the years and by the late Tokugawa (*Edo*) era the hill had a large flat plateau on the top.

Kanda means "god's field", the land having originally belonged to Ise Jingū Shrine, the oldest in Japan. The area developed as a town for workers and craftsmen; its fruit and vegetable market provision the castle. *Edo* period gangsters frequented the district and its bath houses, known for their rather tough breed of women.

The *Meiji* period "*haikara*" liberals and intellectuals found a home here; the Nikoraidō Russian Cathedral was an impressive foreign monument for the neighborhood, there were bookstores, and the highest concentration of universities in the city.

The district now has the feel of a classic university town. The nearby

Jimbōchō secondhand book district adds to the general intellectual atmosphere and over 60% of Japan's publishers are in the neighborhood. The district also has many sporting goods stores catering to the average student who, once through the "examination hell" of lower schools and into university, spends more time drinking, playing sports, or going to mah-jong parlors than studying.

Also in the Kanda district are a number of restaurants that date from the *Edo* period, including Tokyo's most famous noodle shop—Yabu Soba.

Ochanomizu—Hongō—Yushima

With Kanda, these areas make up the major students' districts of Tokyo. Always fond of foreign analogies, the Japanese like to call this the city's "Quartier Latin". The district's real name Ochanomizu means "tea water", a reference to the waters of a nearby spring that were used by Tokugawa Ieyasu for the tea ceremony.

The district's reputation for education dates from the *Edo* period with the construction of the official Confucian Academy for the shogunate. The Yushima Seidō Shrine, formerly part of school, still survives.

Hongō's Tokyo University, popularly known as "*Tōdai*", is the most prestigious university in the country. In January and February each year, hundreds of hopeful junior high and high school students make a pilgrimage to the area, walking from Yushima Seidō, to Yushima Shrine (dedicated to a famous *Heian* period scholar) and finally ending up at the gates of *Tōdai* heaven. Complementing the district's overall educational atmosphere is a concentration of love hotels nearby.

Akihabara

The electronics discount district of Tokyo, Akihabara is a good place to go to *experience* the productiveness of the country. Besides the electrical goods that interest most foreigners, the selection of home appliances built for the Japanese domestic market is also fun to browse through.

The district was formerly the grounds of an *Edo* period shrine called the Akiba, or autumn leaf. When the shrine was destroyed in one of Kanda's frequent fires, the lands were cleared as a fire break and became known as the fields of Akiba or Akibagahara. The land was later used as a freight depot by the *Meiji* government, and the name took on its current shortened, famous form.

Kōrakuen

Kōrakuen is best known among the Japanese for its baseball stadium, site of the yearly Japan Series. From 1871 until the end of World War I, the stadium grounds had been occupied by a government munitions factory which was then moved to Kyūshū. The stadium was built in 1934 and Babe Ruth was the honored guest of the opening.

The name Kōrakuen comes from the Koishikawa Kōrakuen Gardens that date from the early *Edo* period. One of the most famous and most beautiful in the city, the garden is a striking contrast to its namesake stadium and the surrounding pleasure grounds that now dominate the area.

Shinagawa

The original Shinagawa station, located nearer to the sea than the present one, served the first Japanese rail line that ran from here to Yokohama (Kanagawa prefecture). The line was later extended to Shimbashi. The railroads were one of the most striking of *Meiji* period modernization efforts, and the first were expensive and used only by the wealthy, government officials, and foreigners. A story is told of how when the Japanese first boarded the trains, they politely removed their shoes on the platform before entering the cars. Upon arrival, the Japanese passengers disembarked, astonished to find that their shoes were not waiting outside the door where they had left them.

Shinagawa had been a major stop on the *Edo* period Tōkaidō route to the south, growing up as a way station with inns and a pleasure quarter that was second only to the famous Yoshiwara. The pleasure quarter declined in the late *Meiji* period when the station was moved to its current site.

Meiji period Shinagawa was part of the city's industrial zone; though now little remains of the district's early flavor. The station is still an important transfer point, but the surrounding area is best known for its hotels and for being the location of the Sony headquarters.

Ningyōchō

Ningyōchō is a quiet neighborhood, known to most foreigners as the location of TCAT, the Tokyo City Air Terminal, with its bus service to Narita Airport. Close to the central *Edo* period business districts, Ningyōchō was a major amusement center with *kabuki* theaters, and the famous *Yoshiwara geisha* district. The area was named "doll town" for the number of shops selling dolls to the theater audiences.

Ningyōchō lost its *geisha*, and later its theaters, to Asakusa in the north. The city's doll shops are now in Asakusabashi. On the outer fringes of the *Meiji* period downtown development, Ningyōchō escaped the era's modernization madness and settled into the quiet *shitamachi* (downtown) neighborhood it remains today.

Along the main crossing is a shopping area. Some shops are historical, like Kotobuki selling the same traditional sweets they've been famous for since the late 1800's. Suitengū Shrine is still visited by expectant mothers and those with newborn babies.

Asakusa

Tokyo passed through various stages of growth, and the districts of the city followed along, or were left behind, as modernization and new modes of transportation changed the patterns of urban life. The original *shitamachi* areas—Nihombashi and Ginza—moved with the city into its *Meiji* period growth, and are, now, more memorable as districts from the early modern era. But the feeling of the *shitamachi* era remains in a district that was, in the early *Edo* period, a very distant neighborhood of marginal interest to the central downtown populace.

Asakusa flourished after the *Edo* period Tempō Reforms enacted by the financially unstable Tokugawa government. The theaters and pleasure quarters were moved here from the downtown districts in an attempt to encourage the merchants to lead more frugal lives, while the *samurai* class as a whole was slowly sinking into poverty. Asakusa thrived through the *Meiji* and *Taishō* periods, but when the railroads became important, Asakusa station remained a minor stop, and the modernization that changed the real downtown areas never affected it. Today Asakusa retains more of the old Tokyo *shitamachi* character than any other part of town.

The district is centered around Sensōji Temple, popularly known as the Asakusa Kannon-dera. Dating from the 8th century, the temple enshrines a small golden statue of *Kannon*, the Buddhist Goddess of Mercy, found by local fishermen in 628. At least that's how the legend goes. The statue is never on view and no one ever seems to have seen it, but its existence has never been questioned by the millions of pilgrims who flocked to the area and continue to come today.

This northern tip of the city was originally underwater, and later became a fishing village. As the temple attracted ever greater crowds of worshippers, the surrounding area filled up with shops, and the sometimes bawdy forms of entertainment typical of many *Edo* period temples. When the theaters and pleasure quarters entered the area its amusements increased and so did the crowds.

Moved from its original Ningyōchō home, Yoshiwara to the north was the most famous of *Edo* and *Meiji* period *geisha* districts. The downtown merchants traveled by boat from the southern parts of the city along the Sumida River, often finishing the trip on foot through the cherry tree lined park that stretches from the main Asakusa bridge north on both sides of the river.

At the start of the 20th century, Asakusa was still largely rural in character, and much of the city's rice land was found in the area. But by the end of the *Meiji* era, the district claimed the highest population density in the city. The Yoshiwara *geisha* quarter had declined with the advance of modernization, and was destroyed in the fire of 1911. When the district was rebuilt, its days of glory were clearly over.

Asakusa continued to prosper through the *Taishō* and early *Shōwa* periods. The *kabuki* theaters moved back to their original downtown home as the new day made the old popular culture respectable. Movie houses took their place and the first film showing in Japan was held in Asakusa in the early 30's.

The district was badly scarred by the war. Fire bombing destroyed most of its monuments. Asakusa and its temples were rebuilt, but the post war city looked more to the western districts and Asakusa was gradually left behind.

Asakusa is one of the last strongholds of the *Edokko*, the born and bred child of *Edo*. The *shitamachi* spirit and sensibilities remain here. Craftsmen work in their traditional shops, in the traditional way, maintaining the sense of pride the *Edokko* was famous for.

Ueno

When the fabled cherry blossoms burst out in spring, the favorite viewing spot for the average Tokyoite is Ueno Park. Since the *Edo* period Ueno Hill was famous for its blossoms, but surrounded by the Tokugawa family temple complex, the viewing was kept fairly sedate. Things have changed and, now, Ueno draws huge crowds to frolic beneath the blossoms.

It's quite a spectacle, though not nearly as poetic as might be imagined. On approximately 4 *tatami* mat-sized (about 8 m^2) sheets of plastic, cardboard or cloth the parties gather. A row of shoes fringe the sides of the mat, and each area is separated from its neighbor by ropes and strings tied between the trees. By day things remain quiet, with families making up the greater part of the crowd. But after dark, thousands of office workers make a mad rush for the little plot saved by a co-worker whose assignment for the day was to sit in the park and hold that space. Until 10 p.m. when the park closes, the crowds will eat, drink, and sing songs, getting for the most part absolutely plastered and feeling very Japanese. Stray foreigners are almost always invited to join a group—which can be amusing for a while. When the crowd disperses, the park is left quiet, filled with the pink blossoms and huge mountains of garbage deposited by the nature loving Japanese. This is one of the cultural experiences you shouldn't miss.

During the *Edo* period Ueno was one of the city's major temple districts. Being in the northeast quarter of town, the temples served to protect the castle from this traditionally dangerous direction (demons were believed to favor this route of attack). The temples were also planned to double as forts in the event of a military attack on the city. The main temple was Kan'eiji, where six of the 15 Tokugawa *shōgun* were buried.

At the time of the *Meiji* Restoration, the city of *Edo* was turned over to the new government without a fight. The few remaining Tokugawa loyalists retreated to the hills surrounding the temple and a final battle was fought. The loyalists were quickly defeated, but most of the temple complex was burned.

In early *Meiji*, plans were drawn up to build a medical school on the former temple grounds. When a German doctor was consulted about the project he suggested that the medical school be located elsewhere and the hill be turned into a park. His suggestion was followed and in 1873 Ueno became the first public park in the city. Officially named the Ueno Royal Park, the land was transferred to the royal family in 1890, and on the marriage of the present emperor in 1924, was returned to the city. The renaissance style building of the National Museum in the park was a gift from the citizens of Tokyo in commemoration of the emperor's wedding.

The park was the first place in Japan to have a museum and a zoo. It now has four major museums and the zoo that is famous for its pandas and the appalling condition the animals are kept in. Shinobazu Pond in the western portion of the park was originally part of the marshlands that covered most of the downtown districts. Annexed to the park in 1885, it was a favorite spot for viewing waterlilies.

Aside from its cultural attractions, Ueno is known for the large numbers of country people who stream into its station from the north. Less sophisticated than downtown Tokyo, old shops and restaurants remain from the *Edo* period when its main street was one of the busiest shopping areas in the city. After the war a large black market flourished beneath the railroad tracks. The market is still there and, though no longer a black market, Ameyoko retains much of the flavor of one.

Further north of Ueno is Yanaka, a continuation of the Ueno temple district. This area escaped the fires of the earthquake and World War II and numerous small temples, shrines and old shops remain. The Yanaka cemetery is another famous spot for cherry blossom viewing.

Asakusabashi—Kuramae—Ryōgoku

Asakusabashi is a wholesale district known for its shops selling dolls, toys, novelties, and seasonal decorations. The district is named for the Asakusa bridge that crosses the narrow Kanda River.

Yanagibashi, the "Willow Bridge", crosses the Kanda further down, close to the point where it meets the Sumida River. The bridge was famous for its *geisha* quarter and as a departure point for boat passage to the northern Yoshiwara. The Yanagibashi was the more conservative *geisha* district of the two. At its peak in the late *Edo* and early *Meiji* periods, it faithfully maintained the traditional ways. The boat houses later became *ryōtei*, the most exclusive type of Japanese restaurant. A few *ryōtei* remain in the neighborhood today, and boats can still be rented near the bridge.

Kuramae was a rice warehouse district in the *Edo* period. Since 1954, *sumō* tournaments have been held in the area's Kokugikan. But *sumō* really belongs to the other side of the Sumida River, to Ryōgoku. From January 1985 tournaments were again held here in the district's new Kokugikan.

Ryōgoku literally translates as "both countries", the Sumida River having long separated the districts on either side. In the *Edo* period, bridge building was restricted by the government in order to make an attack on the capital more difficult for potential invaders. But when hundreds of people were trapped and killed on the banks of the river during one of the many *Edo* fires, the shogunate permitted a bridge to be constructed in the area.

Ryōgoku remains the center of *sumō*. In the area are located many of the stables where *sumō* wrestlers live and train. During the Tokyo *sumō* tournaments the wrestlers wander around the streets in all their enormous glory.

Fukagawa—Kiba—Tsukudajima

Fukagawa lies on the east side of the Sumida River, south of Ryōgoku, bordering Tokyo Bay. The district and the neighboring Kiba were known through the *Edo* period for their lumberyards. The skills of the early lumberyard workers are now commemorated in a yearly festival in Kiba. Both areas often suffered damage from the frequent floods of the Sumida. Flood control banks have been built along the river's edge, protecting the lands but destroying much of the neighborhood's atmosphere.

Until the early *Meiji* period, Fukagawa was one of the less densely populated districts in the city. Convenient to cheap water transportation, it became one of the major industrial districts of *Meiji* period Tokyo.

Tsukudajima lies to the south west. The island has grown with post war reclamation projects, but the original part of the island escaped from the constant fires of the downtown district as well as those of World War II, and the back streets remain closer to those of the *Edo* period city than any other part of town.

ACCOMMODATION

Snow falls on a traditional Japanese home. *Ryokan* are typically of similar traditional architecture. Few, however, remain in Tokyo.

ACCOMMODATION

Your hotel in Tokyo is about the only place where you'll get away from the city's 11.50 million inhabitants. Obviously, this should be a subject for serious consideration. Unless you have a friend or relative in town, your choices will fall into four main categories: major hotels, business hotels, Japanese style lodgings, and hostels.

Which category you choose will most likely be a matter of budget. Your second criterion should be convenience to where you'll be doing most of your work or play. Equally important is accessibility to public transport. The train and subway systems are so efficient that even if you don't mind paying for a taxi, public transport can save you time (and time=money). If you're a "night person", consider staying in a hotel close to one of the nightlife districts. During the day you can travel by transit system, but after midnight the trains and subways go home to rest and you're left with your legs, or taxis with a 20% surcharge after 11 p.m.

HOTELS

We have selected what we consider the best of the major and business hotels, then divided them by districts. Best is defined here as good quality and service for the price, convenience, and accessibility to public transport. A list of "other" second choice hotels is supplied in the event that our recommended hotels are booked up. All hotels are safe and clean. Most provide cotton "*yukata*" robes. Distance on foot to the nearest station has been noted. Rates listed are basic room charges. In addition you'll pay a service charge of 10-15% and 10% tax. In mid-February when the university entrance exams are held in Tokyo it is almost impossible to find a room—book early.

Major Hotels—like everywhere in the world, these range from 1st class to not-particularly distinguished. Price is usually a good indication of quality. The number of rooms has not been noted, but most are large. The three best hotels in Tokyo are the **Ōkura**, the **Capitol Tōkyū** and the **Imperial**.

Business Hotels—theoretically for the "businessman", these are low priced hotels with minimal but efficient service. Most hotels with singles under ¥8,000 fall into this category. Rooms are generally quite small and rather Spartan. Bathrooms are strictly utilitarian molded-in-one-piece units. Televisions are usually provided, though sometimes they're coin operated with extra-charge "adult" video channels for lonely businessmen.

Ginza—Shimbashi—Hibiya

IMPERIAL HOTEL—in Japanese called the "Teikoku Hotel". Established in 1890, new tower completed in 1983.
帝国ホテル　千代田区内幸町1-1-1
1-1-1 Uchisaiwaichō, Chiyoda-ku.
Tel: 504-1111, TLX: 222-2346 IMPHO J. Cable: IMPHO TOKYO
Rates: Sgl. from ¥24,500, Dbl. from ¥28,500.
—Swimming pool, executive salon, good shopping arcade, excellent restaurants, 2 min. from Hibiya and Yūrakuchō stations [M-10].

GINZA TŌKYŪ HOTEL　銀座東急ホテル　中央区銀座5-15-9
5-15-9 Ginza, Chūō-ku. (close to the Kabukiza)
Tel: 541-2411. TLX: 252-2601/THCGIN J. Cable: GINZATOKYUTEL.
Rates: Sgl. from ¥11,000, Dbl. from ¥20,000, Japanese style: ¥33,000.
—1 min. from Higashi-Ginza station [M-8].

MITSUI URBAN HOTEL GINZA—Mitsui Urban chain hotel. Has a very good reputation.
三井アーバンホテル銀座　中央区銀座8-6-15
8-6-15 Ginza, Chūō-ku.
Tel: 572-4131. TLX: 252-2949.
Rates: Sgl. from ¥10,000, Dbl. from ¥13,800.
—1 min: from Shimbashi station [M-8].

HOTEL ATAMISŌ—formerly a *ryokan*, opened as a western style hotel in 1984.
ホテル熱海荘　中央区銀座4-14-3
4-14-3 Ginza, Chūō-ku.
Tel: 541-3621. TLX: 2524557.
Rates: Sgl. from ¥7,700, Dbl. from ¥15,000.
—2 min. from Higashi-Ginza station [M-8].

- **Other Hotels**

GINZA DAI-ICHI HOTEL　銀座第一ホテル　中央区銀座8-13-1
8-13-1 Ginza, Chūō-ku. Tel: 542-5311. TLX: 252-3714. Sgl. from ¥11,000, Dbl. from ¥16,000.
—5 min. from Shimbashi station [M-8].

SHIMBASHI DAI-ICHI HOTEL　新橋第一ホテル　港区新橋1-2-6
1-2-6 Shimbashi, Minato-ku. Tel: 501-4411. TLX: 222-2233. Sgl. from ¥9,000, Dbl. from ¥15,000.
—3 min. from Shimbashi station [M-11].

GINZA MARUNOUCHI HOTEL　銀座丸の内ホテル　中央区築地4-1-12
4-1-12 Tsukiji, Chūō-ku. Tel: 543-5431. TLX: 252-2214. Sgl. from ¥8,500, Dbl. from ¥16,000.
—2 min. from Higashi-Ginza station [M-22].

GINZA NIKKŌ HOTEL　銀座日航ホテル　中央区銀座8-4-21
8-4-21 Ginza, Chūō-ku. Tel: 571-4911. Sgl. from ¥9,400, Dbl. from ¥16,500.
—4 min. from Shimbashi station [M-8].

Tokyo—Marunouchi

PALACE HOTEL—a quiet and subdued atmosphere, the hotel overlooks the Imperial Palace moats and gardens.
パレスホテル　千代田区丸の内1-1-1
1-1-1 Marunouchi, Chiyoda-ku.
Tel: 211-5211. TLX: 222-2580. Cable: PALACEHOTEL TOKYO.
Rates: Sgl. from ¥14,500, Dbl. from ¥20,500.
—3 min. from Ōtemachi and 7 min. from Tokyo station [M-10].
HOTEL KOKUSAI KANKŌ　ホテル国際観光　千代田区丸の内1-8-3
1-8-3 Marunouchi, Chiyoda-ku.
Tel: 215-3281. Cable: KOKUSAIHOTEL TOKYO
Rates: Sgl. from ¥10,800, Dbl. from ¥18,000.
—1 min. from Tokyo station [M-9].
YAESU FUJIYA HOTEL　八重洲富士屋ホテル　中央区八重洲2-9-1
2-9-1 Yaesu, Chūō-ku.
Tel: 273-2111
Rates: Sgl. from ¥8,500, Dbl. from ¥14,000.
—2 min. from Tokyo station [M-9].
TOKYO CITY HOTEL　東京シティホテル　中央区日本橋本町1-9
1-9 Nihombashi Honchō, Chūō-ku.
Tel: 270-7671
Rates: Sgl. from ¥6,000, Dbl. from ¥8,200.
—2 min. from Mitsukoshi-mae station, 5 min. by taxi from Tokyo City Air Terminal [M-9].
• **Other Hotels**
TOKYO MARUNOUCHI HOTEL　東京丸の内ホテル　千代田区丸の内1-6-3
1-6-3 Marunouchi, Chiyoda-ku. Tel: 215-2151. TLX: 222-4655. Sgl. from ¥8,500, Dbl. from ¥18,000.
—5 min. from Tokyo station [M-10].
TOKYO STATION HOTEL　東京ステーションホテル　千代田区丸の内1-9-1
1-9-1 Marunouchi, Chiyoda-ku. Tel: 231-2511. Sgl. from ¥7,000 (w/o bath), Dbl. from ¥16,000 (w/o bath).
—at Tokyo station [M-10].

Akasaka—Nagatachō

CAPITOL TŌKYŪ HOTEL—formerly the Tokyo Hilton. Comfortable and relaxing atmosphere, the interiors are a blend of Japanese and western design.
キャピタル東急ホテル　千代田区永田町2-10-3
2-10-3 Nagatachō, Chiyoda-ku.
Tel: 581-4511. TLX: CAPTEL J24290. Cable: 222-3605 CAPTEL J.
Rates: Sgl. from ¥21,000, Dbl. from ¥27,500, Japanese style: ¥40,000.
—Swimming pool (summer only), excellent restaurants, 2 min. from Kokkai-gijidōmae station [M-6].
HOTEL NEW ŌTANI—the largest hotel in Asia. A new tower and old building combined in a sprawling and somewhat confusing fashion.
ホテルニューオータニ　千代田区紀尾井町4-1
4-1 Kioichō, Chiyoda-ku.
Tel: 265-1111. TLX: HTLOTANI J24719. Cable: HOTELNEWOTANI TOKYO.
Rates: Sgl. from ¥16,500, Dbl. from ¥24,500, Japanese style from ¥41,000.
—400 year old Japanese garden, health facilities.
—4 min. from Akasaka-mitsuke station [M-6].
AKASAKA PRINCE HOTEL—Prince chain hotel. New building opened in March 1983. Ultra-modern interiors. The lobby is austere white marble, the rooms are brightly white and efficiently furnished.
赤坂プリンスホテル　千代田区紀尾井町1-2
1-2 Kioichō, Chiyoda-ku.
Tel: 234-1111. TLX: 232-4028.

Rates: Sgl. from ¥19,500, Dbl. from ¥27,500, Japanese style from ¥70,000.
—All rooms have great views. Executive salon available.
—4 min. from Akasaka-mitsuke station [M-6].
HOTEL KAYŪ KAIKAN—Hotel Ōkura chain. Nice and quiet, smaller hotel.
ホテル霞友会館　千代田区三番町8-1
8-1 Sambanchō, Chiyoda-ku.
Tel: 230-1111. TLX: 232-3318.
Rates: Sgl. from ¥9,300, Dbl. from ¥15,500. Japanese style: ¥17,000.
—5 min. from Hanzōmon station [M-17].
DIAMOND HOTEL　ダイアモンドホテル　千代田区一番町25
25 Ichibanchō, Chiyoda-ku.
Tel: 263-2211. TLX: 232-2764. Cable: HOTELDIA TOKYO.
Rates: Sgl. from ¥6,500, Dbl. from ¥8,500.
—2 min. from Hanzōmon station [M-6].
- **Other Hotels**

AKASAKA TŌKYŪ HOTEL　赤坂東急ホテル　千代田区永田町2-14-3
2-14-3 Nagatachō, Chiyoda-ku. Tel: 580-2311. TLX: 222-4310. Sgl. from ¥14,000, Dbl. from ¥21,500.
—1 min. from Akasaka-mitsuke station [M-6].
HOTEL YŌKŌ AKASAKA　ホテル陽光赤坂　港区赤坂6-14-12
6-14-12 Akasaka, Minato-ku. Tel: 586-4050. Sgl. from ¥6,550, Dbl. from ¥10,800.
—4 min. from Akasaka station [M-6].

Roppongi—Toranomon—Shiba

HOTEL ŌKURA—officially rated the 2nd best hotel in the world. A favorite of Japanese and foreigners alike.
ホテルオークラ　港区虎の門2-10-4
2-10-4 Toranomon, Minato-ku.
Tel: 582-0111. TLX: J22790 HTLOKURA. Cable: HOTELOKURA TOKYO.
Rates: Sgl. from ¥22,000, Dbl. from ¥28,500, Japanese style from ¥53,000.
—Health facilities, executive salon, excellent restaurants.
—5-7 min. from Kamiyachō and Toranomon stations [M-11].
TOKYO PRINCE HOTEL—Prince chain hotel. Located next to Zōjōji temple. Large but comfortable quality hotel.
東京プリンスホテル　港区芝公園3-3-1
3-3-1 Shiba-kōen, Minato-ku.
Tel: 432-1111. TLX: 242-2488.
Rates: Sgl. from ¥17,500, Dbl. from ¥19,500.
—Swimming pool (summer only).
—3 min. from Onarimon and 6 min. from Kamiyachō stations [M-11].
SHIBA PARK HOTEL　芝パークホテル　港区芝公園1-5-10
1-5-10 Shiba-kōen, Minato-ku.
Tel: 433-4141. TLX: 242-2917 PARKHO J. Cable: HOTOSHIBA TOKYO.
Rates: Sgl. from ¥9,900, Dbl. from ¥16,000.
—3 min. from Onarimon station [M-11].
ROPPONGI PRINCE HOTEL六本木プリンスホテル　港区六本木3-2-7
3-2-7 Roppongi, Minato-ku.
Tel: 587-1111
Rates: Sgl. ¥16,000, Dbl. from ¥17,000.
—1 min. from Roppongi station [M-1].
- **Other Hotels**

TOKYO GRAND HOTEL　東京グランドホテル　港区芝2-5-3
2-5-3 Shiba, Minato-ku. Tel: 454-0311. TLX: 242-3147. Sgl. from ¥9,500, Dbl. from ¥14,000.
—2 min. from Shiba-kōen station [M-11].

Shibuya—Harajuku—Aoyama

THE PRESIDENT HOTEL AOYAMA—the best medium priced hotel in town.
プレジデントホテル青山　港区南青山2-2-3
2-2-3 Minami-Aoyama, Minato-ku.
Tel. 497-0111. TLX: J25575 HTLPRE.
Rates: Sgl. from ¥8,200, Dbl. from ¥10,500.
—1 min. from Aoyama Itchōme station [M-5].

HOTEL HARAJUKU TRIMM　ホテル原宿トリム　渋谷区神宮前6-28-6
6-28-6 Jingūmae, Shibuya-ku.
Tel: 498-2101
Rates: Sgl. from ¥6,000, Dbl. from ¥9,500. No credit cards/no foreign exchange.
—Sports facilities.
—3 min. from Harajuku or Meiji-Jingūmae stations [M-4].

SHIBUYA TŌBU HOTEL　渋谷東武ホテル　渋谷区宇田川町3-1
3-1 Udagawachō, Shibuya-ku.
Tel: 476-0111. TLX: 242-5585. Cable: SHIBUYATOBU HOTEL
Rates: Sgl. from ¥8,800, Dbl. from ¥15,100.
—6 min. from Shibuya station [M-3].

ASIA CENTER OF JAPAN—a cross between a business hotel and student lodgings, this is one of the best deals in town.
アジア会館　港区赤坂8-10-32
8-10-32 Akasaka, Minato-ku.
Tel: 402-6111. Cable: ASIACENTER TOKYO.
Rates: Sgl. w/o bath ¥3,960, w/bath ¥4,840. Dbl. w/o bath ¥5,280, w/bath ¥8,140.
—5 min. from Aoyama Itchōme, 8 min. from Roppongi stations [M-5].

• **Other Hotels**

HILLPORT HOTEL　ヒルポートホテル　渋谷区桜丘町23-19
23-19 Sakuragaokachō, Shibuya-ku. Tel: 462-5171. Sgl. from ¥7,000, Dbl. from ¥13,000.
—4 min. from Shibuya station [M-3].

SHIBUYA SUN ROUTE　渋谷サンルート　渋谷区南平台1-11
1-11 Nampeidaichō, Shibuya-ku. Tel: 464-6411. TLX: 242-4175. Sgl. from ¥5,000, Dbl. from ¥7,800.
—5 min. from Shibuya station [off Map].

TOKYO AOYAMA KAIKAN　東京青山会館　港区青山4-17-58
4-17-58 Aoyama, Minato-ku. Tel: 403-1541. Sgl. from ¥3,800, Dbl. from ¥6,800. This is a government sponsored facility for school teachers, so they're not used to foreigners.
—6 min. from Omotesandō station [M-5].

NIHON SEINENKAN　日本青年館　新宿区霞岳15
15 Kasumigaoka, Shinjuku-ku. Tel: 401-0101. Dbl. from ¥6,100 per person.
—10 min. from Sendagaya station [M-5].

Shinjuku

HILTON INTERNATIONAL—the new Hilton was completed in September 1984. The old hotel, now the Capitol Tōkyū, had an excellent reputation.
ヒルトンインターナショナル　新宿区西新宿6-6
6-6 Nishi-Shinjuku, Shinjuku-ku.
Tel: 344-5111. TLX: 232-4515.
Rates: Sgl. from ¥20,000, Dbl. from ¥19,000. Japanese style from ¥33,000.
—Executive salon, health facilities.
—8 min. from Shinjuku station [M-7].

KEIŌ PLAZA HOTEL—an International Hotel. A 45 story concrete and glass skyscraper of the most undistinguished kind. Interiors are more of the same.
京王プラザホテル　新宿区西新宿2-2-1
2-2-1 Nishi-Shinjuku, Shinjuku-ku.
Tel: 344-0111. TLX: J26874. Cable: KEIOPLATEL.
Rates: Sgl. from ¥16,500, Dbl. from ¥20,500, Japanese style: ¥50,000.

—Health facilities, executive salon
—6 min. from Shinjuku station [M-7].
HOTEL CENTURY HYATT—Another monolithic Shinjuku Hotel with Japanese style Hyatt Hotel service and interior.
ホテルセンチュリーハイアット　新宿区西新宿2-7-2
2-7-2 Nishi-Shinjuku, Shinjuku-ku.
Tel: 349-0111. TLX: J29411.
Rates: Sgl. from ¥16,000, Dbl. ¥20,000, Japanese style: ¥43,000.
—Health facilities, discotheque.
—9 min. from Shinjuku station [M-7].
HOTEL SUNROUTE TOKYO—Sunroute Chain Hotel.
ホテルサンルート東京　渋谷区代々木2-3-1
2-3-1 Yoyogi, Shibuya-ku.
Tel: 375-3211. TLX: Tokyo 232-2288.
Rates: Sgl. from ¥8,800, Dbl. from ¥16,000.
—2 min. from Shinjuku station [M-7].
WASHINGTON HOTEL—New hotel with computerized check in service. Human front desk clerks will show you how to use the system.
ワシントンホテル　新宿区西新宿3-2-9
3-2-9 Nishi-Shinjuku, Shinjuku-ku.
Tel: 343-3111. TLX: 232-2103.
Rates: Sgl. from ¥6,800, Dbl. from ¥11,000. No foreign exchange service, accepts Visa.
—8 min. from Shinjuku station [M-7].
- **Other Hotels**
SHINJUKU PRINCE HOTEL　新宿プリンスホテル　新宿区歌舞伎町1-30-1
1-30-1 Kabukichō, Shinjuku-ku. Tel: 205-1111. TLX: 232-4733. Sgl. from ¥10,000, Dbl. from ¥13,500.
—5 min. from Shinjuku station [M-7].

Ikebukuro

SUNSHINE CITY PRINCE HOTEL—Prince Hotel chain. Linked to the Sunshine City building, huge and rather impersonal.
サンシャインシティプリンスホテル　豊島区東池袋3-1-5
3-1-5 Higashi-Ikebukuro, Toshima-ku.
Tel: 988-1111. TLX: 272-3749.
Rates: Sgl. from ¥10,500, Dbl. from ¥19,000.
—10 min. from Ikebukuro station [M-18].
HOTEL METROPOLITAN—A new hotel trying to bring a touch of elegance to Ikebukuro.
ホテル メトロポリタン　豊島区西池袋1-6-1　1-6-1 Nishi-Ikebukuro, Toshima-ku.
Tel: 980-1111. TLX: 272-2787.
Rates: Sgl. from ¥10,500, Dbl. from ¥13,000.
—3 min. from Ikebukuro station [M-18].

Shinagawa

TAKANAWA PRINCE HOTEL—Prince Hotel chain.　高輪プリンスホテル　港区高輪3-13-1
3-13-1 Takanawa, Minato-ku.
Tel: 447-1111. TLX: 242-3232.
Rates: Sgl. from ¥16,000, Dbl. from ¥19,000, Japanese style from ¥30,000.
—Swimming pool (summer only).
—10 min. from Shinagawa station [M-37].
NEW TAKANAWA PRINCE HOTEL—New addition to the Takanawa Prince.
新高輪プリンスホテル　港区高輪3-13-1
3-13-1 Takanawa, Minato-ku.
Tel: 442-1111. TLX: 242-7418.
Rates: Sgl. from ¥18,000, Dbl. from ¥22,000.
—All rooms have a private balcony, swimming pool (summer only).

—10 min. from Shinagawa station [M-37].
SHINAGAWA PRINCE HOTEL—Prince Hotel chain. This hotel is adjoined to a huge sports center that includes skating rinks, tennis courts, swimming pool, and bowling facilities.
品川プリンスホテル　港区高輪4-10-30
4-10-30 Takanawa, Minato-ku.
Tel: 440-1111. TLX: 242-5178.
Rates: Sgl. from ¥7,000, no doubles but an extra bed can be added for ¥2,200.
—5 min. from Shinagawa station [M-37].
- **Other Hotels**
HOTEL PACIFIC　ホテルパシフィック　港区高輪3
3 Takanawa, Minato-ku. Tel: 445-6711. TLX: 242-3074. Sgl. from ¥16,000, Dbl. from ¥18,000.
—5 min. from Shinagawa station [M-37].

Meguro

MIYAKO HOTEL TOKYO—affiliated with the famous Miyako Hotel in Kyōto.
都ホテル東京　港区白金台1-1-50
1-1-50 Shiroganedai, Minato-ku.
Tel: 447-3111. TLX: 242-3111 MYKTKYJ. Cable: MIYAKO TKY.
Rates: Sgl. from ¥14,000, Dbl. from ¥19,000, Japanese style: ¥22,000.
—Health facilities, not particularly convenient but quiet.
—20 min. from Meguro station [M-19].
GAJOEN KANKŌ HOTEL—an eccentric older hotel with an interesting blend of western and Japanese interiors. Formerly associated with the Meguro Gajoen Ryokan next door.
雅叙園観光ホテル　目黒区下目黒1-8-1
1-8-1 Shimo-Meguro, Meguro-ku.
Tel: 491-0111. TLX: 246-6006. Cable: GAJOENHO TOKYO.
Rates: Sgl. w/shower ¥5,500, w/bath ¥9,350, Dbl. w/shower ¥8,800, w/bath ¥15,100.
—5 min. from Meguro station [M-19].

Ochanomizu—Kudan

HILLTOP HOTEL—a lovely older hotel. Erstwhile favorite of writers and artists.
山ノ上ホテル　千代田区神田駿河台1-1
1-1 Surugadai, Kanda, Chiyoda-ku.
Tel: 293-2311. TLX: 222-6712 HILTOP J. Cable: HILTOP TOKYO.
Rates: Sgl. from ¥9,500, Dbl. from ¥15,000.
—5 min. from Ochanomizu station [M-15].
KUDAN KAIKAN HOTEL—this *Meiji* period building houses a hotel and concert hall. Ask for a room facing the Imperial Palace.
九段会館ホテル　千代田区九段南1-6-5
1-6-5 Kudan-Minami, Chiyoda-ku.
Tel: 261-5521.
Rates: Sgl. from ¥9,500, Dbl. from ¥10,500, Japanese style: Dbl. use ¥15,100 (incl. tax & serv.).
—2 min. from Kudan-shita station [M-17].
- **Other Hotels**
HOTEL GRAND PALACE　ホテルグランドパレス　千代田区飯田橋1-1-1
1-1-1 Idabashi, Chiyoda-ku. Tel: 264-1111.TLX: 232-2981 GRAPA J. Sgl. from ¥11,500, Dbl. from ¥20,000.
—1 min. from Kudan-shita station [M-17].
FAIRMONT HOTEL　フェアモントホテル　千代田区九段南2-1-17
2-1-17 Kudan-Minami, Chiyoda-ku. Tel: 262-1151. TLX: 232-2883 FAIRHO J. Sgl. from ¥7,500, Dbl. from ¥14,000.
—6 min. from Kudan-shita station [M-17].

Tokyo City Air Terminal
HOLIDAY INN—just like in America. ホリディイン 中央区八丁堀1-13-7
1-13-7 Hatchōbori, Chūō-ku.
Tel: 553-6161. TLX: 252-3748.
Rates: Sgl. from ¥11,700, Dbl. from ¥18,500.
—Swimming pool (summer only).
—1 min. from Hatchōbori station, 3 min. by taxi to TCAT [M-25].
• **Other Hotels**
HOTEL KITCHŌ ホテル吉晁 中央区日本橋人形町2-32-8
2-32-8 Ningyōchō, Nihombashi, Chūō-ku. Tel: 666-6161. Sgl. from ¥7,550, Dbl. from ¥12,700.
—2 min. from Hamachō station [M-23].
KAYABACHŌ PEARL HOTEL 茅場町パールホテル 中央区新川1-2-5
1-2-5 Shinkawa, Chūō-ku. Tel: 553-2211. TLX: 252-3834. Sgl. from ¥6,200. Dbl. from ¥9,200.
—3 min. from Kayabachō station [off Map].
CITY PENSION ZEM シティペンションゼム 中央区日本橋蠣殻町2-16-9
2-16-9 Kakigarachō, Nihombashi, Chūō-ku. Tel: 661-0681. Sgl. from ¥7,000, Dbl. from ¥12,000.
—7 min. from Hamachō station [M-23].

Narita Airport
NARITA VIEW HOTEL 成田ビューホテル 千葉県成田市小菅700
700 Kosuge, Narita City, Chiba Prefecture.
Tel: (0476) 32-1111. Cable: NARIVIEWTEL NARITA.
Rates: Sgl. from ¥9,000, Dbl. from ¥13,000.
—Health facilities.
—next to Narita Airport and 10 min. by cab to Narita City train station [off Map].

RYOKAN

A Japanese inn "*ryokan*" may be the closest you'll get to staying in a traditional Japanese home. You'll sleep in a *tatami* straw matted room, in place of a bed, there will be a *futon*. Baths are Japanese style and often communal (sexes are segregated). Privacy and excellent service are another plus. Morning and evening meals will be served in your room and your *futon* laid out at night. Good *ryokan* are expensive. Prices range from ¥15,000 to ¥50,000, but two meals are included and the cuisine is often excellent.

Unfortunately, the best inns are not found in Tokyo. With land prices skyrocketing in the city, most innkeepers have opted for high-rise hotels. If you are planning to travel outside of Tokyo, you should perhaps save your *ryokan* experience until then.

Because the few exceptional *ryokan* in Tokyo will accept only "introduced" guests, we have listed one medium class *ryokan* and five inexpensive, somewhat tourist oriented inns that can give you a taste of this tradition. Major hotels often have Japanese style rooms. Most are expensive, but a few, like the **Kudan Kaikan** are very affordable.

MEGURO GAJOEN—a beautiful but rather unusual *ryokan*. The Gajoen has seen better days, but the incredible "Japanese baroque" interiors of the adjoining wedding hall and meeting rooms make it one of the most interesting places to stay in the city.
目黒雅叙園　目黒区下目黒1-8-1
1-8-1 Shimo-Meguro, Meguro-ku.
Tel: 491-0074.
Rates: from ¥14,000 per person (morning & evening meals, tax & service incl.), ¥9,000 per person (morning meal, tax & service incl.)
—3 min. walk from Meguro station [M-19].
YASHIMA—has both western and Japanese style rooms, communal bath, showers. Meals not included.
やしま　新宿区百人町1-15-5
1-15-5 Hyakuninchō, Shinjuku-ku.
Tel: 364-2534/368-7251.
Rates. Sgl. from ¥3,000, Dbl. from ¥4,600. Dbl. w/bath ¥7,000.
—1 min. from Okubo station [off Map].
SANSUISŌ—communal bath and showers, meals not included.
山水荘　品川区東五反田2-9-5
2-9-5 Higashi Gotanda, Shinagawa-ku.
Tel: 441-7475.
Rates: one person ¥3,600, two ¥6,600, for three ¥8,400.
—5 min. from Gotanda station [off Map].
SAWANOYA—close to Ueno Park. Meals not included.　澤の屋　台東区谷中2-3-11
2-3-11 Yanaka, Taitō-ku.
Tel: 822-2251.
Rates: one person ¥3,600 (w/o bath), ¥4,100 (w/bath), for two ¥6,600 (w/o bath), ¥7,000 (w/bath).
—7 min. from Nezu station [M-13].
INABASŌ—Japanese or western style rooms all with baths. Meals not included.
稲葉荘　新宿区新宿5-6-13
5-6-13 Shinjuku, Shinjuku-ku.
Tel: 341-9581.
Rates: one person ¥3,900-¥4,400, for two ¥7,000-¥8,000.
—3 min. from Shinjuku San-chōme station [M-7].
MIKAWAYA BEKKAN—located in the center of Asakusa. Communal baths, meals not included.
三河屋別館　台東区浅草1-31-11
1-31-11 Asakusa, Taitō-ku.
Tel: 843-2345.
Rates: one person ¥4,500, for two ¥8,600.
—5 min. from Asakusa station [M-12].

CHEAP ACCOMMODATIONS

If you're on a budget, there are a number of inexpensive alternatives to hotels. In addition to being cheap, most are inconveniently located, lacking in privacy, and offer only minimal service. They are, however, safe and maintain reasonable standards of cleanliness. Choices include YMCA and other youth hostels, peoples lodges "*kokumin shukusha*", "*minshuku*" family run lodging, and Buddhist Temples. We have listed a few, but for further information, contact one of the various organizations listed below.

Youth Hostels

Rates average ¥1,800, meals cost from ¥400-¥650. There is usually a central kitchen so you also cook for yourself. Rules are rather strict—including a 9 p.m. curfew. You must be a member of the "International Youth Hostel Federation". You can buy a membership at the Tokyo Y.H. office for ¥3,000 plus one passport photo.

JAPAN YOUTH HOSTELS ASSOCIATION 新宿区市ヶ谷砂土原町1-2保健会館3階
Hoken Kaikan, 3rd Fl., 1-2 Sadoharachō, Ichigaya, Shinjuku-ku. Tel: 269-5831/3.

Minshuku

The average rate is ¥5,000 a day. There are over 27,000 of these lodgings throughout the country. Make your reservations through one of the following organizations:

JAPAN MINSHUKU CENTER 日本民宿センター 千代田区有楽町2-10-1交通会館ビル
Kōtsū Kaikan Bldg., 2-10-1 Yūrakuchō, Chiyoda-ku. Tel: 216-6556.
JAPAN MINSHUKU ASSOCIATION 日本民宿協会 新宿区百人町2-10-8ニューパールビル
New Pearl Bldg., 2-10-8 Hyakuninchō, Shinjuku-ku. Tel: 371-8120.

Others

Japan Travel Bureau can reserve lodgings in Buddhist Temples and Peoples Lodges. TIC also has a pamphlet titled "Reasonable Accommodations in Japan". Listings of other inexpensive lodgings can be found in the "Tour Companion" and the "Tokyo Journal"

TOKYO YMCA 千代田区神田美土代町7
7 Mitoshirochō, Kanda, Chiyoda-ku. Tel: 293-1911. Rates: Sgl. from ¥4,900, Dbl. from ¥8,200.
—Communal bath, 1 min. from Shin-Ochanomizu station [M-14]
YMCA ASIA YOUTH CENTER 中央区猿楽町2-5-5
2-5-5 Sarugakuchō, Chiyoda-ku. Tel: 233-0611. Rates: Sgl. ¥5,500, Dbl. ¥9,000, Triple ¥12,000.
—Private bath, 5 min. from Suidobashi station [M-15].
JAPAN YWCA HOSTEL—Women only. 千代田区九段南4-8-8
4-8-8 Kudan-Minami, Chiyoda-ku. Tel: 264-0661. Rates: Western or Japanese style rooms at ¥4,300 per person.
—Communal bath, 4 min. from Ichigaya station [off Map].
TOKYO YWCA HOSTEL—Women only. 千代田区神田駿河台1-8
1-8 Surugadai, Kanda, Chiyoda-ku. Tel: 293-5421. Rates: Sgl. ¥4,300, Dbl. ¥8,000, Triple ¥10,500.
—Built in 1928, private bath, 4 min. from Ochanomizu station [M-15].
TOKYO YWCA SADOHARA HOSTEL 新宿区ヶ谷砂土原町3-1-1
3-1-1 Sadoharachō, Ichigaya, Shinjuku-ku. Tel: 268-7313. Rates: Sgl. from ¥4,000, Dbl. from ¥9,000. Married couples room with kitchenette ¥9,700.
—Communal bath, 7 min. from Ichigaya station [off Map].
TOKYO INTERNATIONAL HOUSE: Has various rooms around the center of Tokyo. Shared kitchen, living room and bath. Rates: from ¥1,000-¥2,000. Tel: 945-1699.
KOTANI HOUSE: Has two locations, both slightly outside of Ikebukuro. Tel: 962-4979. Rates: Sgl. from ¥1,900. Monthly rates: ¥33,000 for a shared room, ¥66,000 for a couple [off Map].
FOREIGNER'S HOUSE MATSUOKA: Three locations all within 15 min. from Shinjuku. Tel: 381-7026. Rooms are private or shared, communal kitchen, showers. Rates: on a weekly basis from ¥1,800-¥2,600 per day [off Map].

CAPSULE HOTELS

The capsule hotel phenomena provides an amusing insight into city life in Japan. Located in nightlife areas and near the major commuter train stations, these hotels have hundreds of tiny sleeping capsules stacked one on top of the other. Average capsule size is 1.1 m. wide, 1.2 m. high, and 2.2 m. long. Standard equipment includes: color T.V. with porn channel, radio, alarm clock, air conditioner, emergency button, and sprinkler system. The clientele is predominately intoxicated businessmen who missed the last train back to their suburban homes (women aren't allowed). The occupancy rate is very high, with the busiest check in hours being between 12 midnight and 3 a.m. The check out rush comes between 8—9 a.m. when the hundreds of very serious faced and blue-suited businessmen scurry off to work.

GREEN PLAZA SHINJUKU—the biggest capsule hotel in Japan, boasts 660 ''rooms''.
グリーンプラザ新宿　新宿区歌舞伎町1-29-3
1-29-3 Kabukichō, Shinjuku-ku.
Tel. 207-5411.
Rates: ¥3,800 per capsule, for an afternoon nap the rate is ¥1,000 for 2 hrs, 10 a.m.-5 p.m.
—Huge sauna, gym, and massage.
—2 min. from Shinjuku station [M-7].

HOTEL WHITE CITY　ホテルホワイトシティ　豊島区東池袋1-11-11
1-11-11 Higashi-Ikebukuro, Toshima-ku.
Tel: 987-3011.
Rates: same as above. Also have normal rooms from ¥6,350.
—Sauna.
—2 min. from Ikebukuro station [M-18].

EATING OUT

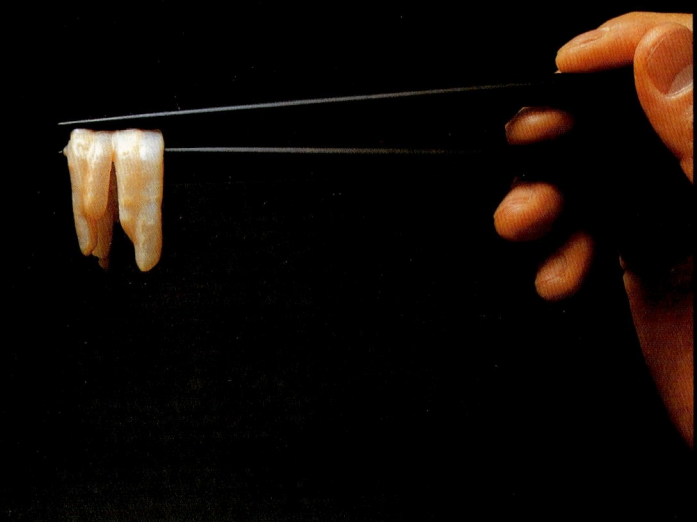

語呂は悪くてもゴロが大事です。|塩甘の塩辛|づくり。

紀文の「いか塩辛」は、材料の「いか」がちがいます。ほとんど北海道の身のしまった「するめいか」をつかいます。ゼイタクのようですが甘味があるのです。耳なれない言葉ですが、塩辛は「ゴロ」とともに醗酵させてつくります。「ゴロ」はいかの肝臓ですが、日本海の対馬から隠岐島の、秋口の「するめいか」が最高の味を引出すといわれています。紀文はいかを選び、ゴロを選び、塩まで選びます。塩にも差がずい分あります。長持ちより味本位、真のうまみのある甘口に仕上げます。最良の材料に肝臓を揃え、静かに時をかけて眠らせ、味を育てます。合成保存料などいっさい加えません。日本の味覚の文化を召しあがれ。

味の名門 紀文

EATING OUT

Japanese food is one of the truly great achievements of the Japanese. Its current popularity overseas is no surprise to the locals who even when traveling abroad will search out the neighborhood *sushi* bar (which is never quite as good as in Japan). But there is a lot more to Japanese cuisine than *sushi* and *tempura*. Most versions, however, do not appear outside of the country. For anyone interested in food, Tokyo can be a source of endless culinary experimentation.

For more than 2,000 years the Japanese diet has been based on rice, a fact often pointed to by the Japanese as a reason for the myriad of differences between "us" and "them", meaning western meat-eaters. For the common people, expensive white rice was never a main part of the meal. Rather a mixture of white and brown rice, millet and greens was consumed while the white rice crop was paid in land rents to the aristocracy. It wasn't until after WWII that perfectly white rice was democratized and became standard fare for all.

As meat consumers, the Japanese have a history of only just over 100 years. Considered unclean by the adopted Buddhist religion. Meat eating was outlawed in 675 by the emperor Temmu. Hunted animals such as deer and wild boar were allowed on occasion as a sort of medicinal food. In the *Edo* period, the practice of eating meat to increase strength became somewhat more common, though it was still disliked by the general public. In 1872, the emperor Meiji made headlines by declaring publicly "I shall eat meat". In the country's attempt to become as powerful as the invading westerners, meat eating seemed like a possible means of increasing Japanese strength. *Gyūnabeya*, beef restaurants, suddenly became popular especially among the *Meiji* period liberals. The beef was prepared "Japanese style", boiled in a broth with vegetables.

The basic diet of the people remained as before, the main part of every meal being the rice, *miso* soup and pickles served with side dishes of cooked vegetables and sometimes fish. Meals have always been seasonal in Japan. Today, one of the most difficult parts of ordering in restaurants is keeping up with the ever changing menu of what is particularly great at a particular time of the year.

Here are some statistics on general Japanese eating habits:
- Breakfast—more than 90% of the people eat at home. 74% eat a typical Japanese breakfast of: rice, *miso* soup, raw egg, fish and vegetables. 24% eat bread, coffee and milk. 13 years ago the percentages were 85% and 11% respectively.
- Lunch—for a typical "*sararīman*" (salary man). 1 out of 5 eats a "*bentō*"—a packed home-made lunch. The others spend an average of ¥500 a day to eat at the company cafeteria, or at a restaurant outside they will have a bowl of noodles or a cheap set menu called "*Teishoku*".
- Dinner—nearly 80% have it at home with their family, and 90% of them will eat rice with raw fish, grilled meat, or boiled fish and vegetables.
- The average Japanese family spends 27.5% of its income on food (a U.S. family spends 16.2%)
- The most popular foods are (in order of popularity): *Sashimi*, *yakiniku* (grilled meat), cooked vegetables, *sushi*, grilled fish, *tempura*, curry and rice.
- The most popular meals at home are: Curry and rice, cooked vegetables, hamburger steak, salad.

EATING OUT IN TOKYO

There are almost too many restaurants in Tokyo, over 45,000 at the last official counting. The majority tend to be small and moderately priced. The best, as anywhere in the world, are the most expensive.

Aside from sheer numbers, the variety of types of food is mind-boggling. Not only are there the numerous styles of Japanese cooking, but every imaginable kind of international cuisine is represented in some form (though not always a particularly recommendable one) somewhere in the city. We've concentrated on Japanese food, and tried to provide good explanations of the food, how to order and where to eat. Hopefully, after using this book at one of these recommended restaurants, you can venture off on your own. Restaurants included range in price from dirt cheap to the top of the line, but all offer good, if not excellent, quality for the price.

For international cuisine, we've selected primarily restaurants with a good reputation for quality. While excellent Japanese food can be had in a broad range of prices, international, particularly western food, doesn't come cheap. The less expensive places tend to serve a questionable mixture of Japanese and western cooking. It's edible, just a little disappointing, and certainly not what you'd expect the food to be.

The average seating capacity of Japanese restaurants is somewhere around 14 persons, which accounts in part for the astonishing numbers. Many of the less expensive restaurants do not take reservations or credit cards. The more expensive ones, Japanese and western, often require reservations, and most accept at least American Express and Diners Club. Travellers checks are only rarely accepted. Many restaurants close early, often by 9 or 10 p.m.

Following is a brief description of the general categories of eating places in Tokyo.

- **Very Expensive but High Quality**

Ryōtei—offering full course Tokyo or Kyōto style cooking, usually accompanied by traditional Japanese *geisha* entertainment, these are the most expensive places to dine, with prices easily ¥40,000 or more per person. Sand-colored Japanese style buildings, with discreet signs, shuttered windows and a pervasive air of secrecy, *ryōtei* are frequented by parties of politicians and businessmen. One wonders what goes on behind those walls—unfortunately an introduction is usually required.

Kaiseki-ryōri is a meal traditionally served at the tea ceremony. The most expensive restaurants, as with *ryōtei*, are patronized mainly by expense account businessmen. There are also several moderately priced *kaiseki* restaurants that attract a more average crowd.

- **Expensive to Medium Priced**

Tempura, sushi, sukiyaki, shabu-shabu, etc. can be quite expensive or reasonably priced depending on the restaurant, what part of town it's located in, the decor and service.

- **Cheap Food**

Katei-ryōri—Most restaurants in this category are called *shokudō* or *meshiya* (*meshi* means rice and by implication the meal itself). These places serve food just like mom used to make. Students, salarymen, workers are the main clientele. Many of the smaller home-cooking restaurants have an actual "mother" figure, who both cooks for and entertains the often regular customers.

Nomiya—*Yakitori, robatayaki, oden* usually fit in this category. These restaurants are usually small places located near train stations so the businessmen who stop off after work don't have to stumble too far to catch a train back to the suburbs. *Nomiya* literally means "drinking place". Theoretically what they serve are snacks to go along with drinks, but the "snacks" can be a full meal depending on how much you order.

Noodle Restaurants—Serving *soba, udon* and Chinese *rāmen* are another inexpensive type of food. Even the best noodle restaurants are still relatively cheap.

Yōshokuya—These are restaurants serving Japanese-style western food. Many of these places started in the *Meiji* period (1867-1911) when the country was reopened to western influences. Because English food was the first official import much of the food is typically British. Other favorites were food from Holland, Portugal, Spain and France. This kind of food is also popular for home-cooking. The food is very basic, but can be quite good. Typical items are hamburger steak and various kinds of croquettes.

Department Store and Arcade Restaurants—Perhaps the easiest and the cheapest way of eating in Tokyo is to go to one of the big underground arcades or the department store restaurant floors. The restaurants all have plastic food models which make ordering ever so simple. There is usually a wide variety of restaurants to choose from, all in one concentrated location. Although generally not haute cuisine, these places are sometimes worth it for the sheer simplicity.

Street Food—*Yatai* are small moving carts equipped with a stove and counter. Serving *yakiimo* (roasted sweet potatoes), *yakitori*, *oden*, *rāmen*, *okonomiyaki*, *yakisoba* or *takoyaki*, the stalls are always set up at festival sites, and on weekends and holidays at the major parks. At night they're found in busy night club areas like Ginza, Roppongi, Akasaka and Shinjuku.

Fast Food—Aside from McDonalds and its various Japanese spin-offs, there are forms of fast food indigenous to Japan. *Tachigui-soba* and *-udon* (stand-up noodle restaurants) are the main ones—for people who want to "slurp and go" on a budget. Another favorite is *kaiten-zushi*, or *sushi* restaurants where a moving belt carries plates of very cheap *sushi* along in front of a counter. Take-out *sushi* shops are also popular.

Hoka-hoka bentō is another recent fast food hit. A "home-made" meal packed by middle-aged women in the shop, it costs only ¥300-400 and is still warm when you get it. A photo display panal will show the variations available. The big customers here are salarymen, students and housewives.

Another common packaged meal is the *ekiben*, a packaged meal available at most train stations. The larger stations, Shinjuku, Tokyo, Ueno and Shinagawa have their own "name brand" *ekiben*.

• **International Cuisine**

Asian Food—Surprisingly enough, just because Japan is close to the Asian continent doesn't mean that non-Japanese Asian food is better here than, say, in New York or Paris. The food is often altered to suit Japanese taste, or a lack of ingredients and proper spices make it simply boring. One of the best kinds is Korean food, especially *yakiniku* (grilled meat).

Western Food—As we already mentioned, it's never quite as good as back home, though a few restaurants do come close.

Districts

While restaurants can be found in every Tokyo neighborhood, they tend to be concentrated in the major commuter train station areas. These are just a few of the most important areas:

Roppongi is the most international dining area of Tokyo. Some of the best Japanese and foreign food is found in this area. Restaurants here tend to stay open later than in other parts of town.

Ginza is one of the traditional places to go for a nice dinner. Many of the oldest and most prestigious restaurants are located here. But with the cost of land being some of the highest in Tokyo, you're helping pay the rent at considerable extra cost attached to the price of your meal.

Akasaka is where you'll find the largest concentration of *ryōtei* in the city. Other Japanese style restaurants cater to the night club and nearby TBS television crowd.

Yūrakuchō is notable mainly for the rows of tiny *yakitoriya* (*nomiya* serving *yakitori*) found along the back streets near the train tracks.

Downtown areas such as Asakusa and Ueno are full of restaurants with a "shitamachi" (downtown) feeling and atmosphere, good food and prices that are very reasonable. The distance is intimidating to most foreigners who keep to the south-western fringes of the city. Surprisingly, once you get there, you begin to wonder why it seemed like such a problem in the first place.

Etiquette

Strict rules of dining etiquette do exist in Japan, but as in the west they are rarely followed in real life. The saying "ignorance is bliss" is doubly true here where as a foreigner you're forgiven for almost any embarrassing breach of etiquette you might unwittingly commit. The best policy is to watch the people around you, but here are a few generalizations:

- The Japanese do not usually put sauces (particularly soy sauce) on their rice.

- Do not rest your chopsticks vertically in your rice. This is associated with death.

- Do not pass food from chopstick to chopstick. At Buddhist funerals, the bones of the cremated deceased person are passed this way.

- Sauces often come with condiments such as sliced green onions, grated radish, etc. which are meant to be mixed in, not eaten separately.

- Sauces are generally intended for dipping, not dunking and soaking the food in. You risk destroying the flavor of the often delicate Japanese cooking.

- When drinking beer or sake, one person will usually pour for the others, who will hold up their glass while the drink is being poured. People take turns, which can sometimes become a bothersome ritual. As the night wears on, and the level of intoxication rises, it's everyone for themselves.
- When starting your meal say "*Itadakimasu*" which means "I receive". As the night wears on, and the level of intoxication rises, it's everyone for themselves.

JAPANESE FOOD
Ordering

Ordering Japanese food can be a rather intimidating job. English menus are rare, and even when you know the main type of food being served (or can at least order by the "show and tell" method), ordering appetizers and side dishes is always difficult. The simplest solution is to order a set menu, called a "*kōsu*" (course) or *teishoku*. Most restaurants will offer some sort of course. Ordering this way also gives you a general idea of how much your meal will cost.

If you want to order à la carte, the general practice is first to order an appetizer (often *sashimi*), then a few side dishes, followed by the entree, with the soup and rice finishing the meal. We have listed a few common appetizer and side dish menu items, and explained some general cooking terms. Following is a list of seasonal fish.

The restaurants have been divided by type of food. We've included entree menus and listed a few side dishes common to that particular type of cooking. Restaurant prices are as of July 1984. Accepted credit cards are noted by; AX (American Express), D (Diners Club), V (Visa).

- **General Menu**

Kōsu	A full-course meal, just as in western restaurants.
Teishoku	Set menu includes a main dish with rice, soup and pickles. Home-cooking, *tempura*, *tonkatsu*, *unagi* are usually offered this way. *Teishoku* sometimes is offered in three grades: *nami* (regular), *jō* (choice), *tokujō* (deluxe).
Tsumami	Starters and side dishes
Morokyū	Cold cucumber served with a thick *miso* sauce.
Itawasa	Sliced fish cake, served with soy sauce (add *wasabi*—green horseradish, if you wish).
Sashimi	Raw fish

Kimpira	Fried burdock root and carrots in a sauce seasoned with soy, sugar and red pepper.
Hijiki	Seaweed simmered in a soy and sugar sauce.
Hiyayakko	Cold *tōfu* (bean curd) served with chopped leeks, grated ginger and soy sauce.
Gohan	Rice
Onigiri	Rice balls (often triangular in shape) wrapped in dried seaweed. The center will be filled with *ume* (pickled sour plum), *sake* (salty salmon) or *tarako* (cooked cod fish roe).
Yaki-onigiri	*Onigiri* grilled, seasoned with soy sauce.
Ochazuke	A bowl of rice with tea or sometimes fish stock poured over. It comes with *sake* (salmon), *tsukemono* (pickles) or *nori* (dried seaweed).
Kamameshi	Steamed and seasoned rice with vegetables and a choice of chicken, crab, salmon, etc.
Zōsui	Rice that has been boiled in a seasoned soup, with *kani* (crab), *kaki* (oysters), egg and various vegetables mixed in.
Shiru	Soup, usually with chopped leek, bean curd, and seaweed.
Misoshiru	Made with yellow (white) or brown (red) fermented soybean paste.
Osuimono	Clear soup made with dried bonito flakes and *kombu* (seaweed).
Yakimono	Fried or grilled foods
Robata-yaki	Usually, food cooked over an open grill.
Sumibi-yaki	Food grilled over a charcoal hearth.
Teppan-yaki	Food cooked on a flat grill.
Ishi-yaki	Food cooked on hot stones.
Shio-yaki	A grilling method using salt.
Teri-yaki	A grilling method for meat or fish that have been marinated and basted with sweet sauce.
Nimono	Usually fish or vegetables that have been boiled with soy sauce, sugar and sake.
Mushimono	Foods that have been steamed.
Chawan-mushi	Steamed egg with fish stock, similar to a custard.
-don (or *-domburi*)	*Don* means a pottery bowl, and by association any meal served in a bowl with rice. These

	are common lunch meals: *tendon* (*tempura* on rice) or *oyako domburi* (chicken and egg on rice).
-jū	Means food served in a lacquered box, usually a small box with rice and something on top, such as *tenjū* (*tempura* on rice).

• **Seasonal Fish**

Spring
Hirame	Halibut/flounder
Mutsu	Bluefish
Hamachi	Yellowtail (young)
Sayori	Halfbeak
Tai	Sea bream
Shirauo	Whitebait
Nishin	Herring

Summer
Kuruma-ebi	Large prawn
Isaki	Grunt
Aji	Horse mackerel
Kisu	Sillago/Smelt
Awabi	Abalone
Anago	Conger eel
Ayu	River trout
Masu	Trout
Ainame	Rock trout
Ika	Squid
Katsuo	Bonito

Autumn
Saba	Mackerel
Iwashi	Sardine
Samma	Mackerel/pike
Haze	Goby
Sake	Salmon

Winter
Ise-ebi	Spiny lobster/crayfish
Karei	Turbot
Tako	Octopus
Sawara	Spanish mackerel
Kani	Crab
Akagai	Red clam
Kaki	Oyster

Buri	Yellowtail (mature)
Maguro	Tuna
Aoyagi	Round clam
Tara	Haddock/cod

JAPANESE RESTAURANT
Kaiseki-ryōri

When the tea ceremony became popular in Kyōto during the Ashikaga period, *kaiseki-ryōri* was a light meal, of three or four dishes, served to help protect the stomach against the strong green tea. *Kaiseki* literally means a "warm stone on the stomach", a reference to the heated stones monks placed in their robes during meditation to help them forget their hunger pains.

Kaiseki is now served in many restaurants as a full meal of several courses accompanied by rice and soup. Though it can hardly be called "typical" of Japanese cooking, with its concern for form and its close connection to the changing seasons, *kaiseki-ryōri* is the ultimate demonstration of Japanese culinary theory and aesthetics. The food is delicately prepared and subtly seasoned. Portions are small, sometimes minute. But the idea is simply to feast the eyes, and thereby appease the stomach. It usually works.

Asakusa's Tatsumiya. The restaurant's *noren* is hung in front of the door to tell the customers that it's open for business.

Kaiseki is one of the most expensive kinds of Japanese cooking, with haute cuisine prices that can be easily over ¥10,000 per person. Some restaurants do offer less expensive courses, others have a *bentō* box that will give you the general idea of what *kaiseki* is like.

Menu—*Kaiseki* restaurants usually serve a set menu.

How to Order
- Since *kaiseki* usually comes as a set meal, you can order according to the price.
- There is a set of very formal rules for eating *kaiseki-ryōri*, but since even most Japanese don't know them, you should just follow the basic rules we mentioned before.

TAKAMURA 篁 港区六本木3-4-27
3-4-27 Roppongi, Minato-ku. Tel: 585-6600. Hrs: 12 noon-3:30 p.m., 5 p.m.-10:30 p.m., closed Sun. Lunch courses from ¥8,000. Dinner courses from ¥10,000. An absolutely wonderful and very "Japanese" atmosphere, this restaurant looks and feels like a tea house in the mountains. There is a lovely garden and each room has a hearth. (AX, D, V) [M-1]

DAIKON-YA だいこんや 渋谷区猿楽町9-8代官山パークサイド・ヴィレッジ
Daikan-yama Parkside Village B1, 9-8 Sarugakuchō, Shibuya-ku. Tel: 496-6664. Hrs: 11:30 a.m.-1 p.m., 1:30 p.m.-3:30 p.m., 5 p.m.-10 p.m., closed Sun. A good contemporary setting for this traditional cooking, Daikon-ya is the best of the modern *kaiseki* restaurants in Tokyo. They have one course for ¥7,000, menu changes every month. (AX, D, V) [M-20]

TAMURA 田村 中央区築地2-12-11
2-12-11 Tsukiji, Chūō-ku. Tel: 541-1611. Hrs: 12 noon-3 p.m., 5:30 p.m.-10 p.m., daily. This famous restaurant has recently been rebuilt, and is now in a seven story building. On the first floor you can have *kaiseki-ryōri*, at a table with chairs, from ¥5,000. On the second and third floors you can sit on *tatami* mats and have lunch from ¥10,000, and dinner from ¥20,000. (D) [M-22]

HANATEMARI 華手毬 港区六本木3-14-7六本木アロービル
Roppongi Arrow Bldg. B1, 3-14-7 Roppongi, Minato-ku. Tel: 404-0800. Hrs: 5 p.m.-2 a.m. (until midnight Sun. & Hols.), daily. This restaurant doesn't specialize in *kaiseki*, but offers a *kaiseki* course for ¥5,000. (AX, D) [M-1]

MINOKICHI 美濃吉 港区六本木5-5ロアビル
Roi Bldg. B1, 5-5 Roppongi, Minato-ku. Tel: 404-0767. Hrs: 11:30 a.m.-11 p.m. daily. A branch of Minokichi in Kyōto, they serve *kyō-ryōri* (Kyōto-style *kaiseki*). There are various courses, *kyō-bentō* (¥2,200-¥3,500) is recommended. *Kaiseki* courses are from ¥4,000. They also serve *sukiyaki*, *shabu-shabu* and *sashimi* courses. (AX, V, D) [M-1]

MUNAKATA むなかた 中央区日本橋3-1-17広瀬ビル／三井アーバンホテル
Hirose Bldg. B1, 3-1-17 Nihombashi, Chūō-ku. Tel: 281-3288. Hrs: 11:30 a.m.-2 p.m., 5 p.m.-10 p.m. (11:30 a.m.-9.30 p.m. Sat. & Sun.), daily. [M-9] There is also a branch in the Ginza Mitsui Urban Hotel, B1. Tel: 574-9356. [M-8] If you want to try *kaiseki*, they have a "mini" *kaiseki* course (lunch: ¥2,500, dinner: ¥2,800). (AX, D, V)

KISSO (pg. 124) Lunch from ¥800. Dinner from ¥5000.

Shōjin-ryōri

A traditional form of vegetarian cuisine, *shōjin-ryōri* was developed in Buddhist temples where eating meat, fish or any animal products was against the tenets of the religion. The style of cooking was brought from China to Japan by the *Zen* monk Dōgen (1200-1253) after his training in the Chinese monasteries. The meal was rearranged to suit Japanese tastes and is now rather like a humble version of *kaiseki*.

EATING OUT 69

Shōjin-ryōri is served in restaurants or at temples, where it is a special meal for guests. The monks themselves usually eat one bowl of rice (*kayu*) in the morning, a bowl of rice and one of soup for lunch and nothing for dinner.

Menu
- *Shōjin-ryōri* is generally served as a set course of several dishes, plus rice and soup.
- In place of meat and fish, they have devised numerous ways of preparing soybeans, one of the main ones being *tōfu*.

How to Order—Just as for *kaiseki*.

BON 梵 台東区竜泉1-2-11
1-2-11 Ryūsen, Taitō-ku. Tel: 872-0375. Hrs: meals are served in 2 hour-long courses from 12 noon, 3 p.m. & 6 p.m., closed Tue. This is a wonderful restaurant, but slightly out of the way. They offer three courses: ¥5,000, ¥6,000, ¥7,000, all prepared in a style that originated in Mampukuji Temple in China. Tables are all in simple, Japanese style semi-private rooms. [M-43]

SANKŌIN TEMPLE 三光院 小金井市本町3-1-36
3-1-36 Honchō, Koganei-shi. Tel: (0423) 81-1116. Hrs: 12 noon-2 p.m., 2 p.m.-4 p.m., closed Thur, Aug. 1st-31st, and Dec. 25th-Jan. 10 th. (Located a 10 min. walk from the north exit of Musashi Koganei station on the Chūō line.) This convent, built in 1934, is the most famous temple serving *shōjin-ryōri*. Reservations are accepted up to one month in advance, during the busy spring and autumn seasons you should book early. Courses are: *Zen* ¥5,000, *Yuki* ¥3,000, *Tsuki* ¥2,600 and *Hana* ¥2,000. [off Map]

TAKAOSAN YAKUŌIN TEMPLE 高尾山薬王院 八王子市高尾町2177
2177 Takaochō, Hachiōji-shi. Tel: (0426) 61-1115. (Take the Keiō line from Shinjuku station to Takaosan-guchi station. Change there to a cable car next to the station. Get off at Sanjō station and it's a 15 min. walk.) You can stay in this temple and get two meals for ¥6,500, but you must wake up in the morning at 5 a.m. in the summer or 5:30 a.m. in the winter, and work with the monks. If that's too much trouble, you can just go there for a *shōjin-ryōri* lunch for ¥3,000. For lunch or for staying, you must make a reservation. [off Map]

Sushi

A favorite question of the Japanese to the first-time foreigner used to be "Can you eat raw fish?". While about 75% of the answers were a definitive (if not disgusted) *no*, most visitors now look forward to their first real Japanese *sushi* meal. Raw fish has been demystified, and chances are that now you'll be asked "Can you eat *nattō*?"—a sticky kind of fermented soybean that half of the Japanese population won't eat.

During the *Heian* period, a "primitive" form of *sushi* was a favorite delicacy of the aristocracy. Sliced raw fish was soaked in a salt brine that naturally fermented and preserved it. The slightly sour *sushi* became so popular that demand for the fermented fish exceeded supply. The solution was to put fresh sliced fish on vinegared rice. In the *Edo* period the art of *sushi* reached its current form as "*nigiri-zushi*" and became the favorite meal of the city-wise *Edokko*.

Ideally, *sushi* is prepared by thinly slicing only the choicest parts of the freshest of fish, and serving it on a bed of specially prepared and vinegared rice. Sometimes a dab of *wasabi*, green horseradish, is spread between the two. The *sushi* chef trains for years, spending two or three making just the rice balls, before he is considered a master.

Menu—These are the types of fish most commonly served as *sushi*:

Maguro	Tuna
Toro	Tuna belly
Hamachi	Yellowtail (young)
Ika	Squid
Tako	Octopus (boiled)
Anago	Conger eel (cooked & served with a sweet sauce)
Ikura	Salmon roe
Uni	Sea urchin roe
Katsuo	Bonito
Ebi	Shrimp (boiled)
Ama-ebi	Shrimp (raw)
Awabi	Abalone
Akagai	Red clam
Hotategai	Scallop
Tamago	Cooked egg
Norimaki	*Sushi* rolled in *nori* dried seaweed with various fillings
Kappa Maki	*Norimaki* with cucumber
Tekka Maki	*Norimaki* with Tuna
Chirashi-zushi	Raw fish scattered on top of a bowl of rice (good for lunch)
Gari	Pickled ginger served as a *sushi* condiment
Wasabi	Green horseradish, that is mixed in with the soy sauce when eating *sashimi* (use sparingly or you lose the flavor of the fish).

How to Order
- As an hors d'oeuvre, *sashimi* is usually eaten with *sake* (rice wine) before the *sushi*.
- You can order your *sushi* by pointing or naming the fish if you sit at the counter. At a table you can also order piece by piece, but the best and easiest way is to order a set course such as *matsu* (expensive), *take* (medium) or *ume* (inexpensive). If you want more after the course, you can then order more of your favorites.
- When you make an order, the *sushi* will usually come in a pair.

EATING OUT 71

- Certain fish are particularly good at certain times of the year. On page 66 is a list of the seasonal fish, or you can order by asking for "*shun no sakana*".
- To eat the *sushi*, use your hands and dip it fish side down in the soy sauce. Cooked fish such as *anago* shouldn't be dipped since they will already be sauced.

TSUKIJI FISH MARKET go early in the morning and have the freshest fish possible, at one of the many *sushi* shops in the area. [M-22]

FUKUZUSHI 福鮨し 港区六本木5-7-8
5-7-8 Roppongi, Minato-ku. Tel: 402-4116. Hrs: 5:30 p.m.-11 p.m. (5 p.m.-10 p.m. on Sun & Hols), daily. Considered by some to be the best *sushi* restaurant in town. Very good *sushi* and in a sleekly modern setting. ¥8,000-¥15,000 per person. [M-1]

SUSHI SEI 寿司清 中央区銀座8-2-13第7金井ビル／青山ベルコモンズ／港区六本木5 9 20
Ginza: Dainana Kanai Bldg. 1st Fl. 8-2-13 Ginza, Chūō-ku. Tel: 572-4770. Hrs: 12 noon-1:30 p.m., 5 p.m.-10 p.m., closed Sun. & Hols. [M-8] Aoyama: Bell Commons 5th Fl., Tel: 475-8053. Hrs: 11:30 a.m.-2 p.m., 5 p.m.-10:30 p.m. [M-5] Roppongi: 5-9-20 Roppongi, Minato-ku. Tel: 401-0578. Hrs: 12 noon-2 p.m., 5 p.m.-10:40 p.m. [M-1] A reputable, medium range *sushi* restaurant, there are numerous branches throughout the city. The restaurants have good basic *sushi* bar interiors and good food. Try their "*hamaguri*" cooked clam on rice. About ¥4,000 per person.

TSUKIJI EDOGIN 築地江戸銀 中央区築地4-5-1
4-5-1 Tsukiji, Chūō-ku. Tel: 543-4401. Hrs: 11 a.m.-9:30 p.m., closed Sun. This old shop, located near the fish market, is famous for the size of their *sushi* as well as its taste. Their *tamago-yaki* is huge and only ¥200. They buy their fish right off the boat, so it's about as fresh as it can get. (AX, D, V) [M-22]

MATSUKAN まつ勘 港区麻布十番3-4-12
3-4-12 Azabu-Jūban, Minato-ku. Tel: 455-4923. Hrs: 12 noon-2 p.m., 5 p.m.-11 p.m. (Sat.: 12 noon-11 p.m., Sun. & Hols: 12 noon-9 p.m.), closed Mon. The food service and interior is just like a *sushi* bar should be. Cost is about ¥5,000 per person. For a side dish try their "*hotate no shioyaki*" (grilled scallop), or other *shioyaki* style fish. They have a nice sherbet for dessert. [M-1]

MIYAKO 美家古 台東区浅草2-1-16
2-1-16 Asakusa, Taitō-ku. Tel: 844-0034. Hrs: 12 noon- 3 p.m., 5 p.m.-9 p.m., closed Mon. & the 4th Sun. of the month. This shop has been here since 1866 and they still serve the *sushi* the way they used to. Don't miss their *anago*, *tamago-yaki* and *ni-ika*. [M-12]

SAKAEZUSHI HONTEN 栄寿司本店 新宿区新宿3-6-2
3-6-2 Shinjuku, Shinjuku-ku. Tel: 351-2525. Hrs: 11:30 a.m.-1 a.m., closed the 2nd Thur. *Kōhaku-don*, *maguro* and *ika* on the *sushi* rice, is their specialty at ¥600. (AX, D) [M-7]

UOGASHI 魚がし 中央区日本橋2-2-3
2-2-3 Nihombashi, Chūō-ku. Tel: 271-8833. Hrs: 11:30 a.m.-2 p.m., 4 p.m.-10 p.m., closed Sun. & Hols. A great place for *sushi* fans, this restaurant has standing room only, and some of the cheapest and best *sushi* in town. Most *sushi* is ¥50 per piece—and there is always a queue. [M-9]

SUSHI BAR SAI スシ・バー彩 渋谷区神南1-7-5ランブリング・コア・アンドス・ビル
Rambling Core Andos Bldg. 2nd Fl., 1-7-5 Jinnan, Shibuya-ku. Tel: 496-6333. Hrs: 5:30 p.m.-1 a.m. (4 p.m.-10 p.m. on Hols.), daily. A high-tech *sushi* bar, they serve "*California-maki*" dried seaweed wrapped *sushi* with avocado, and *tōfu zushi* (from ¥150) using *tōfu* instead of rice. (AX, V) [M-3]

GENROKUZUSHI 元禄寿司 渋谷区神宮前5-8-5
5-8-5 Jingūmae, Shibuya-ku. Tel: 498-3968. Hrs: 11 a.m.-8:30 p.m., daily. Fast food *sushi* by this chain of *sushi* restaurants. A conveyor belt moves plates of *sushi* along in front of the counter. You just pick out what you want. Cost is ¥100-¥120 per plate. There is a branch of this shop in most major districts. [M-4]

Tempura

While some people claim that tempura was originally a Portugese recipe, others will say that the Portuguese stole the idea from China. Whatever the case, tempura has become one of the mainstays of Japanese cooking. Many tempura fanatics claim the secret to the tempura lies in the oil. The best Tokyo restaurants will use expensive sesame oil, which leaves no aftertaste. In Ōsaka the lighter vegetable oil is preferred. Most tempura restaurants also serve sashimi.

Menu

Teishoku	A set menu that usually consists of: *Ebi* (Shrimp), *Kisu* (Light, white fish), *Ika* (Squid), *Anago* (Conger eel), *Pīman* (Small green peppers), *Kakiage* (Shrimp in balls of batter), Rice, pickles and *miso* soup.
Tendon, Tenjū	These two are usually prawns and vegetables served on rice, with a sauce poured over the top.

You can also order à la carte:

Kaibashira	Shell ligament
Nori	Dried seaweed
Tamanegi	Onion
Shītake	Mushrooms
Shiso	Leaf of a "beefsteak" plant that tastes similiar to mint
Shishitō	A very small green pepper
Nasu	Eggplant
Kabocha	Squash
Satsumaimo	Sweet potato
Tentsuyu	Sauce for *tempura*. Soy sauce mixed with a fish stock base, with grated *daikon* (white radish) and grated ginger added.

How To Order

- You can order the set meal "*teishoku*" and if you want more, then order à la carte. This is the best and cheapest way.
- *Tempura* should be eaten while it's still hot. The *tentsuyu* sauce will be in a small pitcher, pour it into the empty bowl you're given, and mix in the ginger and radish. Dip the *tempura* into the sauce. Don't let it stay there and soak or it will not only lose its taste, but will look disgusting.

TSUNAHACHI つな八　新宿区新宿3-31-8/渋谷区宇田川町23-3第一勧銀共同ビル
Shinjuku: 3-31-8 Shinjuku, Shinjuku-ku. Tel: 352-1011. Hrs: 11:30 a.m.-10 p.m. (11:30 a.m.-10:00 p.m. Sun. & Hols.), daily. [M-7] Shibuya: Daiichi Kangin Kyōdō Bldg. 6th Fl., 23-3 Udagawachō, Shibuya-ku. Tel: 476-6059. Hrs: 11:30 a.m.-11 p.m., daily. [M-3] A reasonably

priced *tempura* restaurant, their *teishoku* set is only ¥990. Try a la carte if you still have room for it: *hashira no norimaki* (shellfish wrapped in seaweed), *tamago no kimi* (egg yolk), or *ice cream* (fried!) for dessert. A la carte cost is from ¥150-¥600. They have over 36 branches in Tokyo. (AX, V)

TEN'ICHI 天一 中央区銀座6-6-5

6-6-5 Ginza, Chūō-ku. Tel: 571-1949. Hrs: 11:30 a.m.-9:30 p.m., daily. One of the best and most famous *tempura* restaurants in Tokyo, Ten'ichi has more than ten branches throughout the city. Lunch is from ¥4,500 (*Isu-seki* course—meaning at a table) to ¥6,000 (*Zashiki* course sitting on *tatami* mats). Dinner from ¥5,500 (*Isu-seki*) and ¥6,000 (*Zashiki*). *Tendon*, served until 4 p.m. is ¥3,000. (AX, D, V) [M-8]

DAIKOKUYA 大黒屋 台東区浅草1-38-10

1-38-10 Asakusa, Taitō-ku. Tel: 844-1111. Hrs: 11 a.m.-8 p.m., 5 p.m.-9 p.m., closed Mon. With no pretentions to elegance, this great "*shitamachi*" restaurant serves terrific *ebi-tendon*—not only are the prawns unusually large, but besides the usual three, you'll find a fourth prawn hidden underneath. It's a definite bargain at ¥1,400. [M 12]

MINOKICHI listed with the *kaiseki* restaurants serves Kyōto style *tempura*. Lunch: ¥700. Dinner: ¥1,500 and ¥2,500 (These are not full courses). [M-1]

YOTARO 与太呂 港区六本木4-11-4

4-11-4 Roppongi, Minato-ku. Tel: 405-5866. Hrs: 11:30 a.m.-2 p.m., 5 p.m.-10:30 p.m., closed Sun. A branch of the famous Ōsaka restaurant, their *tempura* is Ōsaka style. The restaurant has a beautiful, contemporary-Japanese interior, but the prices are a bit expensive, easily ¥8,500 per person. They have a "*Tai-meshi*" course, with *tempura* plus rice cooked in a casserole with a whole *tai* (sea bream) for ¥9,000. (AX) [M-1]

Yakitori

A favorite hangout for the Japanese salaryman on his way home from work, most *yakitori* restaurants are technically not restaurants, but *nomiya*. The art "refined" is found in more sophisticated restaurants for those who find the under-the-tracks *yakitori* spots not quite to their taste. *Yakitori* at its best is skewered bits of chicken, charcoal broiled to the perfect "crispy on the outside, succulent on the inside" stage.

Menu

Sei-niku	Chicken dark meat
Sasami	Chicken breast meat
Negima	Chicken and leeks (other combinations of chicken and vegetables are also served, depending on the restaurant)
Rebā	Chicken liver
Tsukune	Meatballs
Kawa	Skin
Tebasaki	Wings
Pīman	Green peppers
Shītake	Large mushrooms
Negi	Leek
Ginnan	Ginko nuts
Uzura	Quail eggs

Side Dishes:

Oroshi — Grated white radish with a raw quail's egg on top. Mix it up with soy sauce and eat plain, or use as a dip for the *yakitori*. This will often be served at no extra charge.

Nikomi — Stew of pork, tripe, etc.

Kamameshi — Steamed and seasoned rice with vegetables and a choice of chicken, crab, salmon, etc.

How To Order

- Order a side dish to eat while you're waiting for the grilled items.
- The grilled food is usually served meat first and vegetables last. You can usually see what's available since seats tend to be at a counter surrounding the grill.
- Some of the dishes are good with the *tare* (a slightly sweet sauce), others are best with just lemon and salt. There will be a small jar of *shichimi*—a hot combination of seven spices that can be sprinkled at will.
- You can bite the food right off the skewers or slip it off with your chopsticks.

TORIGIN 鳥ぎん　港区六本木4-12-6
4-12-6 Roppongi, Minato-ku. Tel: 403-5829. Hrs: 11:30 a.m.-2 p.m., 5 p.m.-1 a.m., daily. One of the best known *yakitori* restaurants in town, this is just one of a chain of many Torigins spread throughout the city. The restaurants are all comfortably casual, and the food is basic but good. Skewers from ¥120, courses from ¥880. [M-1]

NAMBANTEI 南蛮亭　港区六本木4-5-6/渋谷区渋谷2-21-12
4-5-6 Roppongi, Minato-ku. Tel: 402-0606. Hrs: 5:30 p.m.-11:30 p.m. (until 11 p.m. on Hols.), daily. [M-1] Shibuya branch: 2-21-12 Shibuya, Shibuya-ku. Hrs: 11:30 a.m.-2 p.m., 5 p.m.-11 a.m., daily. [M-3] Lunch from ¥800, dinner course from ¥2,300. Try their *nambanyaki*—beef dipped in hot *miso* and grilled. *Asupara-maki*—is green asparagus wrapped in thinly sliced pork. A set course will run around ¥3,000, single skewers from ¥200. (AX, D)

ISEHIRO 伊勢廣　中央区京橋1-5-4
1-5-4 Kyōbashi, Chūō-ku. Tel: 281-5864. Hrs: 12 noon-2 p.m., 4:30 p.m.-9 p.m., closed Sun. & Hols. In this nearly 60 year-old restaurant, you can eat an entire hen, bit by bit, for ¥3,900. If you can't make it through the whole bird, just say you've had enough, and you'll only pay for what you've eaten. For lunch they serve *Yakitori-don*—yakitori on rice with a sauce poured over, ¥1,000. *Yakitori teishoku* is ¥1,200. (D) [M-9]

TORIDEN 鳥伝　渋谷区神宮前4-31-4
4-31-4 Jingūmae, Shibuya-ku. Tel: 405-9898. Hrs: 11:30 a.m.-2:30 p.m., 5 p.m.-midnight, daily. A slightly more up-market *yakitori* restaurant, catering to the fashionable Harajuku crowd. They have a great salad, and a special dish called *shiso-maki* with *shiso* leaves wrapped in a thin slice of pork. Skewers from ¥170. [M-4]

GANCHAN がんちゃん　港区六本木6-8-23岡上ビル
Okaue Bldg. 1st Fl., 6-8-23 Roppongi, Minato-ku. Tel: 478-0092. Hrs: 6 p.m.-3 a.m. (until midnight on Sun. & Hols), daily. This place can best be described as pure Japanese funk. The interior is "classic *yakitoriya*" style, the music is either *enka* (see pg. 140) or often California surfer tunes. The crew is amicable and casual (it's not often that you'll find the waitress in a place like this wearing a "California" T-shirt). Food is great, course ¥2,000, skewers from ¥150. [M-1]

AJIWAI 味わい 千代田区有楽町2-3-1
2-3-1 Yūrakuchō, Chiyoda-ku. Tel: 573-7084. Hrs: 4 p.m.-11 p.m., daily. This restaurant is in the heart of the Yūrakuchō *yakitori* "district". Their speciality is *tsukune* (with *miso* flavor). Skewers from ¥90. [M-10]

Robata-yaki

Probably the noisiest restaurants in the world, *robata-yaki* restaurants are known for the lively shouting of the staff welcoming the guests and calling in orders. Though some first-time foreigners mistake the shouts for anger, it's all in good fun. *Robata-yaki* is country-style cooking, a variety of mostly seafood and vegetables prepared over a "*robata*" grill. The atmosphere is usually postcard perfect with Japanese decor and the restaurant crew in provincial costume. The food is great, very simple and filling.

Menu—Just about anything can be ordered in a *Robata-yaki* restaurant, but the speciality is the food grilled on the open *robata* in front of the counter.

Sashimi	Raw fish
Yakitori	See page 73
Shio-yaki:	A whole fish grilled with a bit of salt
Nishin	Herring
Karei	Flounder/Turbot
Samma	Pike
Aji	Horse mackerel
Ika	Squid
Shishamo	Smelt
Ebi	Shrimp

Vegetables:

Nasu	Eggplant
Pīman	Green peppers
Negi	Leek
Shītake	Mushrooms
Ginnan	Ginko nuts
Atsu-age	Deep fried *tōfu*
Satsuma-age	Deep fried ground fish

Side dishes:

Niku jaga	A stew of meat & potatoes
Jagabata	Grilled potatoes with butter

How To Order

- Because grilled foods take time to cook, order *sashimi* first, or a couple of side dishes, along with the grilled fish. The fish will all be displayed in front of you so you can just point. Finish the meal with *onigiri* (rice balls) and *oshinko* (pickles).

- There will usually be some special seasonal fish. To order just ask "*Kyō wa nani ga oishii desu ka?*" (What's good today?).
- Eat the grilled fish and vegetables with a bit of soy sauce. *Onigiri* are eaten plain, with your hands.

INAKAYA 田舎屋　港区六本木7-8-4/港区赤坂3-12-7
Roppongi: 7-8-4 Roppongi, Minato-ku. Tel: 405-9866. Hrs: 5 p.m.-5 a.m., daily. [M-1] Akasaka: 3-12-7 Akasaka, Minato-ku. Tel: 586-3054. Hrs: 5 p.m.-11 p.m., daily. [M-6] One of the most "picturesque" *robata-yaki* restaurants in town, the cooks sit on a platform right in front of the counter. The dinner will cost about ¥7,000-¥10,000 per person. (AX, D, V)

OKAJŌKI 陸蒸気　中野区中野5-59-3
5-59-3 Nakano, Nakano-ku. Tel: 388-3753. Hrs: 5 p.m.-11 p.m., daily. A huge hearth and kitchen, surrounded by an equally huge counter, they serve food in appropriately huge portions. A single *onigiri* is enough for two. Cost is about ¥3,000-¥4,000 per person. [M-26]

GONIN BYAKUSHŌ 五人百姓　六本木スクエアビル
Roppongi Square Bldg. 4th Fl., 3-10-3 Roppongi, Minato-ku. Tel: 470-1675. Hrs: 11:30 a.m.-2 p.m., 5 p.m.-11 p.m., (12 noon-10 p.m. Sun. & Hols.) daily. At the entrance you'll find lockers, just like in the public baths—put your shoes in and lock them up. The restaurant is run by a famous *sushi* company called *Kyōtaru*, and they have the usual *robatayaki* menu, plus specialty items like "*chakin-shūmai*"—steamed minced meat wrapped in a thin egg casing. Courses start at ¥3,500, à la carte from ¥450. The name means "the 5 farmers", and the atmosphere is suitably rural. (AX, D, V) [M-1]

I-RO-HA-NI-HO-HE-TO いろはにほへと　渋谷区神南1-19-3日本生命アネックスビル
Nihon Seimei Annex Bldg. B1., 1-19-3 Jinnan, Shibuya-ku. Tel: 476-1682. Hrs: 4:30 p.m.-4 a.m., daily. A huge restaurant serving very fresh fish from Hokkaidō (northern Japan), this place is always packed with students and salarymen. You may have to wait for a seat, but the food is cheap, delicious and definitely worth the time. Try *hokke* (atka mackerel) ¥400, *danshaku* (grilled Hokkaidō potato with butter) ¥200, *ika sōmen* (thinly sliced raw squid) ¥380. Cost should be less than ¥2,000 per person. (AX, D, V) [M-3]

OKAJŪ 岡重　目黒区自由ヶ丘1-26-3
1-26-3 Jiyūgaoka, Meguro-ku. Tel: 717-0781. Hrs: 5 p.m.-2 a.m. (until 11 p.m. on Sun. & Hols.), daily. This shop has some interesting additions to the usual *robata-yaki* menu: *manjū*—minced chicken wrapped with mashed potato and served in a soup, *kintoki-guratan*—a sweet potato gratin, etc. About ¥3,000 per person. (AX, D, V) [M-21]

Kushi-age

Originally an Ōsaka speciality, *kushi* means skewer and *age* means deep fried. Fish, meat or vegetables are skewered, dipped in batter then bread crumbs and deep fried. This is a delicious, but comparatively little known Japanese meal.

Menu

Set Course	Usually consists of salad, 6-10 skewers of *kushi-age*, rice or noodles, *miso* soup, and pickles.
Ebi	Prawn
Kani no tsume	Crab claw
Tori	Chicken
Gyūniku	Beef
Shītake	Mushroom
Asupara	Asparagus

EATING OUT 77

Imo	Potato
Konnyaku	Arrowroot gelatin
Side dishes:	
Soba	Japanese buckwheat noodles
Kayaku gohan	Seasoned rice
Ochazuke	A bowl of rice over which has been poured tea or fish broth.

How to Order
- Ordering the set menu is the easiest and usually cheapest way.
- The chef will tell you if the *kushi-age* skewer needs sauce (*"sōsu de dōzo"*="please use the sauce"), salt (*"shio de dōzo"*="please use salt"") or if it's best plain (*"kono mama de dōzo"*). When you are almost through with your *kushi-age*, the chef will ask *"Gohan to soba no dochira ni shimasu ka?"* or "Will you have rice (*gohan*) or noodles (*soba*)?" You choose.

CHISEN 知仙　港区六本木4-12-5／六本木7-16-5
4-12-5 Roppongi, Minato-ku. Tel: 403-7677. Hrs: 5:30 p.m.-11 p.m., daily. Another branch in Roppongi is at: 7-16-5 Roppongi, Minato-ku. Tel: 478-6241. They have a great course for ¥3,800, then another "flexible" course where you get all of the side dishes, but pay only for as much *kushi-age* as you can eat. (AX, D, V). [M-1]

HIIRAGI 柊　中央区銀座8-2-8京都新聞銀座ビル
Kyōto Shimbun Ginza Bldg. B1, 8-2-8 Ginza, Chūō-ku. Tel: 572-6961. Hrs: 12 noon-2 p.m. (Mon., Wed. & Fri.) 5 p.m.-10 p.m. Mon.-Sat., closed Sun. & Hols. Hiiragiya is a very famous Japanese *ryokan* in Kyōto. In Tokyo they serve Kyōto-style *kushi-age*, with a thin and delicate batter. One skewer from ¥150. They also serve *oden*. Lunch course from ¥650, dinner from ¥2,000. (AX, D, V). [M-8]

KUSHINOBŌ 串の坊　港区赤坂3-10-17
3-10-17 Akasaka, Minato-ku. Tel: 586-7390. Hrs: 11:30 a.m.-2 p.m., 4:30 p.m.-10 p.m., daily. One skewer from ¥130. Try their *"shītake-toriniku-hasami"*—a large mushroom stuffed with minced chicken, or their *"shiso-maki ebi"*—a prawn wrapped in *shiso* leaves. Lunch ¥700. Dinner about ¥3,500 per person. (AX) [M-6]

Tonkatsu

When meat eating became possible during the *Meiji* period, pork and beef were popularly served as "*katsu*" cutlets dipped in flour, egg and bread crumbs, then deep fried. Now, mainly pork is served in this way, the best having a light and flaky crust while the meat is thick, moist and tender. A fairly inexpensive meal, *tonkatsu* is popular both as a lunch and a family dinner. Fish and vegetables are also sometimes served this way.

Menu

Hire-katsu	Fillet cutlets (all lean meat)
Rōsu-katsu	Loin cutlets (some fat meat)
Kushi-katsu	Meat skewered with onions
Ebi-furai	Fried prawns
Korokke	Potato croquette

Tonjiru	Miso soup with pork and vegetables
Akadashi	Red miso soup
Teishoku	You can order any kind of katsu as a teishoku course which will come with rice, miso soup and pickles.
Katsudon	Pork cutlet with egg and onion served on a bed of rice.
Katsujū	Pork cutlet with egg and onion on rice in a lacquered box.

How To Order

- The set *teishoku* meal is most common. *Tonkatsu* is always served on a bed of crisp, shredded raw cabbage.
- *Tonkatsu* is usually eaten with one of two sauces. *Amakuchi*, which is slightly sweet, or *Karakuchi*, which is slightly hot. Both will be on your table.

TONKI とんき 目黒区下目黒1-1-2
1-1-2 Shimo-Meguro, Meguro-ku. Tel: 491-9928. Hrs: 4 p.m.-11 p.m., closed Tue. One of the great Tokyo *tonkatsu* restaurants, you may have to wait a while for a seat here since it's always busy. They dip their *katsu* in the egg and flour batter three times (once is usual) which keeps the pork crunchy on the outside and moist on the inside. *Hire* ¥850, *Rōsu* ¥800, *Katsu teishoku* (with *hire*) ¥1,100. [M-19]

HONKE PONTA 本家ぽん多 台東区上野3-23-2
3-23-2 Ueno, Taitō-ku. Tel: 831-2351. Hrs: 11 a.m.-2 p.m., 4:30 p.m.-8 p.m., closed Mon. The oldest *tonkatsu* restaurant in Tokyo, their *tonkatsu* is also the thickest and most tender. Other special dishes are *ebi* (shrimp) cream croquettes and tongue or beef stew. *Tonkatsu* is ¥2,000. [M-13]

KAWAKIN 河金 台東区西浅草3-15-10
3-15-10 Nishi-Asakusa, Taitō-ku. Tel: 844-1017. Hrs: 11 a.m.-10 p.m., closed Thur. This shop invented *katsu-karē* (curry sauce poured over *tonkatsu* and rice), here it's called "Kawakin-donburi" (¥600). *Katsu-karē* is a popular dish with students. Another hit is a huge *tonkatsu* (375 g) called "Hyakumomme-katsu"—¥1,500. [M-12]

KAZUYA 和也 港区新橋3-9-8宮岡ビル
Miyaoka Bldg. 1st Fl., 3-9-8 Shimbashi, Minato-ku. Tel: 431-0810. Hrs: 11:30 a.m.-2 p.m., 5 p.m.-9 p.m., closed Sun. & Hols. They claim that the jumbo bread crumbs they use are what make their *katsu* so moist and tender. *Hire* ¥1,300, *rōsu* ¥1,200. [M-11]

Sukiyaki and *Shabu-shabu*

Sukiyaki has been a popular meal since meat eating lost its taboo status in the *Meiji* period. A fairly easy dish to prepare, it's often produced in the home. Specialized restaurants have their own "secret" broth that makes the dish particularly good, and most will cook it for you at the burner on your table. The basic ingredient is the beef, sliced paper thin and sauteed for just a few seconds in the hot pan in front of you. A broth is then added, and the beef lightly simmered. The best beef is that from Matsuzaka, where the cattle are pampered and protected—even massaged—to insure the tenderest of meats. After the beef is cooked, a selection of vegetables will be added to the pot.

Shabu-shabu is named for the "shabu-shabu" sound of the thinly sliced beef swishing in the boiling broth. Restaurants often serve both. The major difference between *sukiyaki* and *shabu-shabu* is the broth. For *sukiyaki*, the broth is soy-based, thick and slightly sweet, while the *shabu-shabu* broth is a clear stock, only lightly seasoned.

Menu
- *Sukiyaki*—Set menu: will include the beef (*gyūniku*) and vegetables such as leeks (*negi*), carrots (*ninjin*), mushrooms (*shītake* and *enokidake*), chrysanthemum leaves (*shungiku*), bean-curd (*tōfu*), etc. In addition you'll be served rice, *miso* soup and pickles.
- *Shabu-shabu*— Set menu: similar to that of *sukiyaki*, but at the end of the meal noodles will be added to the broth.

Ordering and Eating
- *Sukiyaki*: the waitress will do most of the cooking for you. Each person is given a bowl with a beaten raw egg in it. Use the egg as a dip for the beef.
- *Shabu-shabu*: the waitress will help cook, but you will cook the meat piece by piece in the boiling pot (it only takes a few seconds). Dip the cooked meat in the ground sesame, chopped green onions, the *ponzu* sauce made with soy and vinegar, or the *goma-dare*—a sauce of ground sesame and fish stock. After the meat is finished, the vegetables will be added to the broth. The waitress will probably do this for you.

CHIN'YA　ちんや　台東区浅草1-3-4
1-3-4 Asakusa, Taitō-ku. Tel: 841-0010. Hrs: 11:30 a.m.-9:30 p.m., closed Wed. A famous restaurant since the *Meiji* period, the current restaurant is in a seven story building (in the basement part you don't have to take off your shoes). *Sukiyaki teishoku* (B1) ¥1,500. *Sukiyaki* from ¥2,500. *Shabu-shabu teishoku* from ¥2,500. (D) [M-12]

ASAKUSA IMAHAN　浅草今半　台東区西浅草3-1-12
3-1-12 Nishi-Asakusa, Taitō-ku. Tel: 841-1114. Hrs: 11:30 a.m.-10 p.m., daily. They have a cheap *sukiyaki* lunch for ¥1,000 or ¥1,300 (until 3 p.m.). In the evening, *sukiyaki teishoku* is ¥4,500, *gyū-don* (*sukiyaki* on rice) is ¥600. [M-12]

HASEJIN　はせ甚　港区麻布台3-3-15
3-3-15 Azabudai, Minato-ku. Tel: 582-7811. Hrs: 11:30 a.m.-10 p.m., daily. A great beef restaurant, they have a "*gyū-kaiseki*" course (beef *kaiseki*) from ¥5,000. The "mini" *gyū-kaiseki* course costs ¥3,500. *Sukiyaki* courses from ¥5,000, steak from ¥4,500 and *shabu-shabu* from ¥5,000. (AX, V) [M-1]

SERINA　瀬里奈　港区六本木3-12-2/新宿区西新宿2-6-1新宿住友ビル
Roppongi: 3-12-2 Roppongi, Minato-ku. Tel: 403-6211. Hrs: 5 p.m.-10:30 p.m., daily. [M-1]
Shinjuku: Sumitomo Bldg. 52th Fl., 2-6-1 Nishi-Shinjuku, Shinjuku-ku. Tel: 344-6761. Hrs: 11:30 a.m.-10 p.m., daily. [M-7] A favorite with visiting foreigners. *Shabu-shabu* course from ¥8,000, *sukiyaki* from ¥7,500, *ishiyaki* (beef steak roasted on hot rocks) from ¥9,500. (AX, D, V)

SHABUSEN　しゃぶせん　中央区銀座5-8-20銀座コアビル
Ginza Core Bldg. B2 & 2nd Fl., 5-8-20 Ginza Chūō-ku. Tel: 572-3806 (B2), 571-1717 (2nd Fl.). Hrs: 11 a.m.-9:30 p.m., closed two days in Aug. & Feb. One of the most inexpensive *shabu-shabu* restaurants in town, they have a course from ¥2,300. (AX, D, V) [M-8]

Soba

Soba is a very serious subject for many Tokyoites. The buckwheat noodles have been popular since the *Edo* period, when more restaurants served *soba* than any other type of food (*sushi* was a close second). Some *Edokko* still have to have their daily *soba* "hit".

But *soba* restaurants are a hotly debated subject, and everyone has their favorite to which they remain stubbornly loyal. Yabu Soba in Kanda is probably the overall winner. The best *soba* are hand-made "*teuchi*" and have a slightly hard and chewy texture. Fast-food *soba* "*tachigui*" served at stand-up noodle stalls is an almost completely different species of noodle. Noodles are served either in a hot soup or cold.

Menu

Soup *soba*:	All come in a hot soy and fish stock soup flavored with finely chopped leeks.
Kake	With leek slices
Kitsune	With *abura-age* (thin fried slices of *tōfu*)
Tanuki	With pieces of fried batter floating on top
Okame	With *kamaboko* (fish cake), *fu* (wheat cakes) and vegetables.
Tempura	Served topped with shrimp *tempura*.
Tsukimi	Or "moon-viewing". The raw egg on top looks like a full moon.
Tamago-toji	With a cooked egg on top.
Kamo-namban	With chicken and leeks.
Tororo	Served with grated Japanese potato.
Cold *Soba*:	
Mori or *Seiro*	Plain noodles.
Zaru	With *nori* (strips of dried seaweed)
Tenzaru	With shrimp and vegetable *tempura*

How To Order

- For lunch most people just have a bowl of noodles. For dinner you will usually start off with *tsumami* (appetizers) such as *itawasa* (sliced fish cake) or *morokyū* (cucumber served with *miso* sauce).
- *Soba* etiquette involves slurping the noodles quickly into your mouth. The Japanese love doing this and claim that the flavor is much better this way.
- For soup *soba*, you can just mix up the ingredients in the bowl (at the end, you can lift the bowl and drink the remaining soup).
- *Zaru* cold *soba* will be served plain, usually in a lacquered box. The sauce will be brought in a small pitcher, along with an extra bowl, and a small dish with grated horseradish (*wasabi*), thinly sliced leeks, and

grated white radish (*daikon*) if you're having *tempura*. The sauce should be poured into the bowl and the other ingredients mixed in as you go along. You eat the *soba* by dipping the noodles into the small bowl, and slurping them quickly into your mouth. When the noodles are finished, a pitcher of hot water called "*soba-yu*" (the stock the noodles were boiled in) will be brought to the table. Mix the water with the remaining sauce in your bowl and drink the soup.

This is only a small selection of the better and more famous *soba* shops.

YABU-SOBA 藪蕎麦 千代田区神田淡路町2-10
2-10 Awajichō, Kanda, Chiyoda-ku. Tel: 251-0287. Hrs: 11:30 a.m.-7 p.m., closed Mon. Perhaps the most famous *soba* restaurant in Tokyo, Yabu-soba is in a beautiful old Japanese-style house. Their speciality is "*tendane*" (a round patty of fried shrimp *tempura*) ¥1,000. You can order the *tendane* with "*seiro*" which makes a great combination of *tempura* and noodles. Another speciality is "*anago-namban*" (soup *soba* with cooked conger eel) ¥1,300. [M-14]

NAGASAKA SARASHINA 永坂更科 港区麻布十番1-8-7
1-8-7 Azabu-Jūban, Minato-ku. Tel: 585-1676. Hrs: 11 a.m.-8 p.m., daily. A favorite of the *shōgun* during the *Edo* period, this is still one of the best *soba* restaurants in town. They have two different sauces: *amakuchi* (slightly sweet) and *karakuchi* (slightly hot). You can choose either. Try their "*gomakiri soba*" (ground sesame added to the noodles) or "*chakiri soba*" (green tea noodles). (D) [M-1]

MAMIANA SOBA 狸穴そば 港区麻布台3-5-6
3-5-6 Azabudai, Minato-ku. Tel: 583-0545. Hrs: 11:30 a.m.-4 p.m., 5 p.m.-8 p.m., closed Sun. & Hols. Located in an old house right in the heart of Roppongi, this restaurant also has a lovely garden. *Zaru soba* ¥600, *tempura soba* ¥1,500. [M-1]

ŌMATSUYA 大松屋 中央区銀座5-4-18銀座I.N.ビル
Ginza I.N. Bldg. 2nd. Fl., 5-4-18 Ginza, Chūō-ku. Tel: 571-7053. Hrs: 11:30 a.m.-2 p.m., 5 p.m.-10:30 p.m., closed Sun. A branch of a restaurant in Yamagata Prefecture, the interior was taken from a 17th century *samurai*'s house in northern Japan. They specialize in "*teuchi*" hand-made *soba*. In the evening they serve "*sumiyaki*" (game meat, fish and vegetables grilled over the charcoal burner at each table). For lunch they serve a choice of "*oyako-domburi*" (a mixture of chicken and egg on a bed of rice) ¥700, or *zaru soba* with fresh *wasabi* (horseradish) that you grate yourself ¥700. *Sumiyaki* (evening only) from ¥2,500. (AX, V) [M-8]

Udon

Invented in Ōsaka, *udon* are thick, white wheat noodles served in specialized *udon* restaurants, as well as in most *soba* places. *Udon* are prepared exactly like *soba* and are similarly best when hand-made.

Menu

Kake-udon	With leeks.
Kamo-namban	With chicken and leeks.
Karē-namban	In a curry-flavored soup with pork.
Chikara-udon	With *mochi* (rice cake).
Nabeyaki-udon	With vegetables and shrimp *tempura*, served in a lidded casserole.

How To Order—Basically the same rules apply as for *soba*.

MIMIU 美々卯 中央区京橋3-6-4
3-6-4 Kyōbashi, Chūō-ku. Tel: 567-6571. Hrs: 11:30 a.m.-8:30 p.m. (until 8 p.m. on Sun.),

closed the 3rd Sun. of the month. This shop is originally from Ōsaka. *Udon-suki*—udon boiled in a light broth with a combination of vegetables and chicken (*tori*), shrimp (*ebi*) and clams (*hamaguri*)—was their invention ¥2,800. *Kitsune udon* ¥530, *seiro* ¥480. They also serve *soba*. [M-9]

CHŌTOKU 長徳　渋谷区渋谷1-10-5
1-10-5 Shibuya, Shibuya-ku. Tel: 407-8891. Hrs: 11 a.m.-9:30 p.m., closed the 1st & 3rd Mon. of the month. They serve more than 20 kinds of *udon*—all with hand-made noodles. Their menu is great—with each dish shown in a beautiful color photo. Their *udon* are slightly thicker than usual. *Tori-udon* (chicken) ¥1,200, *tempura-udon* ¥1,200. [M-3]

INANIWA いなにわ　港区西麻布1-8-20
1-8-20 Nishi-Azabu, Minato-ku. Tel: 401-4966. Hrs: 12 noon-2:30 p.m., 5 p.m.-10:30 p.m., closed Sun. & Hols. This shop serves "*Inaniwa-udon*", a type of thin *udon* noodles from Akita prefecture. This is a lovely, small and very "discreet" restaurant. They have a good selection of *sake* (rice wine) from all parts of Japan and numerous items on their menu such as *sashimi*, *tori-wasa* (chicken *sashimi*) and *tempura*. "*Misoniku udon*" (*udon* with minced meat and *miso*) ¥750, *tempura udon* ¥1,500. (D, V) [M-1]

Unagi

Eel is a traditional "health food", believed by the Japanese to restore energy, and improve eyesight and virility. *Unagi no kabayaki*, grilled eel, is a surprisingly popular dish with even the most squeamish of foreigners. The eel is first split open, steamed, then charcoal grilled and basted with a sweet sauce. The resulting fillet is rich and tender, not at all what you would expect of an eel.

Menu

Kabayaki	Basic grilled eel (see above)
Shiroyaki	Steamed eel without the sweet sauce
Kimoyaki	Eel liver, grilled and basted with sweet sauce, and served with ginger.
Kimo-sui	*Suimono* is clear soup. This one is served with eel liver.

Set Meals:

Unajū	*Kabayaki* on rice in a lacquered box with *kimo-sui* and pickles.
Kabayaki teishoku	*Kabayaki* plus rice, *kimo-sui* and pickles.
Unadon	*Kabayaki* on a bowl of rice with sauce poured over, plus *kimo-sui* and pickles.

Ordering and Eating

- *Unajū* is recommended. There are no special rules or tricks to ordering and eating. *Sanshō*—Japanese pepper (spicy but not hot) is good sprinkled on the eel.

NODAIWA 野田岩　港区東麻布1-5-4
1-5-4 Higashi-Azabu, Minato-ku. Tel: 583-7852. Hrs: 11 a.m.-1:30 p.m., 5 p.m.-8 p.m., closed Sun. & Hols. They serve natural eel (as opposed to the usual bred eel) which is naturally sweet and tender. The restaurant is in a lovely old building with *tatami* rooms upstairs. *Kabayaki* ¥4,000, *Unajū* ¥2,000. [M-1]

TAMBAYA 丹波屋　千代田区麹町3-2
3-2 Kōjimachi, Chiyoda-ku. Tel: 261-2633. Hrs: 11 a.m.-8 p.m., closed Sun. & Hols. This

restaurant has been here since the 17th century. The current restaurant is in a modern building, but the taste is still the same. *Kabayaki teishoku* ¥2,000, *Unadon* ¥1,600. [M-6]
KIKUKAWA きくかわ 千代田区神田須田町1-24
1-24 Sudachō, Kanda, Chiyoda-ku. Tel: 251-7925. Hrs: 11:30 a.m.-8 p.m. (11:30 a.m.-7:30 p.m. Sat., Sun. & Hols.), daily. While most *unagi* restaurants use just one eel in their *unajū*, this one uses two. *Unajū* ¥1,500, *kabayaki* ¥1,400. [M-14]
YAKKO やっこ 台東区浅草1-10-2
1-10-2 Asakusa, Taitō-ku. Tel: 841-9886. Hrs: 11:30 a.m.-10 p.m., closed Tue. They serve *Edo* style *unagi* in this 200 year old restaurant. *Unajū* ¥1,300. *Kabayaki* ¥1,200. At lunch time (11:30 a.m.-4 p.m.) they serve *kabayaki teishoku* for ¥1,000. (AX) [M-12]

Fugu-ryōri

Fugu, poison blowfish, is considered a great delicacy in Japan. Fanatics will eat a tiny bit of the poison part, which leaves one with a pleasantly benumbed sensation. Like Russian roulette, it's a rather dangerous game—a famous actor died from the poison a few years back. But since a special licence is required to serve *fugu* to the public, and most restaurants won't serve you the poison part, there is no cause for worry. The fish itself is delicious, though so delicately flavored as to be lost on some palates. *Fugu* is only in season from October through March. The rest of the year, *fugu* restaurants serve normal fish, or sometimes *kaiseki-ryōri*.

Menu
Fugu-sashi	Blowfish, sliced and eaten raw with *ponzu* sauce.
Fugu-chiri	Blowfish thinly sliced and served in a thick vegetable soup.

TENTAKE 天竹 中央区築地6-16-6
6-16-6 Tsukiji, Chūō-ku. Tel: 541-3881. Hrs: 12 noon-10 p.m., closed Sun. (Apr.-Sept.), the 1st & 3rd Wed. of the month (Oct.-Mar.). One of the cheapest *fugu* restaurants in town. *Fugu-chiri* ¥2,300. *Fugu-sashi* ¥2,300, *tempura* ¥600. [M-22]
SANTOMO さんとも 台東区上野6-14-1
6-14-1 Ueno, Taitō-ku. Tel: 831-3898. Hrs: 11:30 a.m.-9:30 p.m., closed the 2nd & 4th Sun. (Apr.-Sept.), and open daily Oct.-Mar. *Sumō* wrestlers are big *fugu* fans, and this is one of the places they frequent. *Fugu teishoku* ¥8,000, à la carte from ¥700. [M-13]

Oden

Originally a street and festival food, *oden* is a Japanese "stew" of various fishcakes, *tōfu* and vegetables simmered in a fish stock soup. The *oden* is usually served with a dab of hot mustard on the side. Sometimes you can order it piece by piece, selecting all of your favorites. Other times it comes pre-selected, as *moriawase* (a combination).

Menu—These are the common *oden* ingredients you can order.
Chikuwa	Tube-shaped fish cake
Hampen	Fish cake made with rice and yam flour.
Yaki-dōfu	Fried bean curd

Konnyaku	Arrowroot gelatin
Fukuro	Chopped vegetables and *mochi*, small pieces of rice cake, wrapped in a case of *abura-age* (fried *tōfu*).
Gammodoki	Fried ground *tōfu* with chopped vegetables.
Daikon	Radish
Kombu	A knot of wide-leafed seaweed

YASUKŌ　やす幸　中央区銀座5-4-6
5-4-6 Ginza, Chūō-ku. Tel: 571-0621. Hrs: 4 p.m.-11 p.m. (4 p.m.-10 p.m. on Sun.), daily, except closed Sun. during July & Aug. This shop turned *oden* from a street food into sophisticated cooking. As *oden* goes, it's rather expensive, but worth a try. *Oden* (with four pieces) ¥1,300, à la carte from ¥150. Try *aji no tsumire* (horse mackerel meatball). [M-8]

MARUTA-GŌSHI　丸太ごうし　台東区浅草2-32-11
2-32-11 Asakusa, Taitō-ku. Tel: 841-3192. Hrs: 5 p.m.-10 p.m., closed Sun. A very lively "*shitamachi*" downtown atmosphere. À la carte from ¥50, *nabe-mono* (several pieces of *oden* in a pot of soup) for two ¥1,300. [M-12]

Tōfu-ryōri

Tōfu, soybean curd, is a high-protein, low calorie, vegetarian food that has long been a staple part of the Japanese diet. There are a few specialized *tōfu* restaurants that serve a variety of *tōfu* dishes, many similar to those served in *shōjin-ryōri*. *Tōfu* restaurants are not strictly vegetarian however. Many serve small dishes of chicken or fish along with the *tōfu*.

The restaurants themselves are also similar in atmosphere and service to *shōjin-ryōri* restaurants. Most offer their food in set courses which makes ordering easy.

GOEMON　五右ェ門　文京区駒込1-1-26
1-1-26 Komagome, Bunkyō-ku. Tel: 811-2015. Hrs: 5 p.m.-10 p.m., (3 p.m.-8 p.m.), closed Mon. You'll feel like you're in Kyōto in this lovely restaurant. Most of the rooms open up in the summer and overlook the garden with it's trickling waterfall. Slightly out of the way, this restaurant is definitely worth the trip. Courses cost from ¥3,500. Try to reserve one of the small rooms right next to the garden. [M-32]

SASANOYUKI　笹乃雪　台東区根岸2-15-10
2-15-10 Negishi, Taitō-ku. Tel: 873-1145. Hrs: 11 a.m.-9 p.m., closed Mon. A famous *tōfu* restaurant since the *Edo* period, *Sasanoyuki* prepares *tōfu* in more ways than one would believe is possible. Courses are divided by how many dishes come along with the rice, *miso* soup and pickles, ¥900 (3 dishes), ¥2,100 (6 dishes), ¥2,750 (8 dishes). À la carte from ¥200. A nice, rather understated, traditional interior. [M-13]

Okonomiyaki

Often called "Japanese pizza", *okonomiyaki* is a cheap food that originated in Ōsaka (Ōsaka people, by the way, are considered "cheap" by most Tokyo-ites). *Okonomiyaki* is made from a pancake-like batter to which is added egg, meat or fish, shredded cabbage and other vegetables. You can cook it yourself, or a chef will cook it in front of you. *Okonomiyaki* is also served by street vendors.

Menu
Gyūniku-ten   *Okonomiyaki* with beef
Butaniku-ten   With pork
Ebi-ten   With shrimp
Ika-ten   With squid
Mikkusu   A "mix" of all the above
Yakisoba   Chinese-style fried noodles with vegetables and pork.

How To Order

- You should order some vegetables or a salad to go along with the meal. A combination of *okonomiyaki* and *yakisoba* is nice.

- If you're cooking the *okonomiyaki* yourself, here are the rules: it will come in a small cup, so stir up the ingredients and pour it out like pancake batter on the hot grill in front of you (be sure the grill has been oiled). When the center starts to solidify, flip the patty and pat it soundly. When cooked, move the patty to the side of the grill, spread on the sauce, add the toppings and cut it up like a pizza with the side of the spatula.

- There are two kinds of sauce: *amakuchi* (slightly sweet) and *karakuchi* (hot). There will also be seaweed flakes, shaved dried fish (both delicious), and sometimes mayonnaise—all to go as toppings on the "pizza".

TAMBO 田甫 台東区浅草2-27-8
2-27-8 Asakusa, Taitō-ku. Tel: 841-8402. Hrs: 5 p.m.-9 p.m., closed Mon. You do it yourself here in a *tatami* room in this home-style restaurant. *Okonomiyaki* with cheese "*Chīzu-ten*" ¥500, with rice cake "*mochi-ten*" ¥500. [M-12]

WAKATSUKI 若月 中央区銀座4-13-6
4-13-16 Ginza, Chūō-ku. Tel: 541-6730. Hrs: 12 noon-9:30 p.m., closed Sun. & Hols. Another do-it-yourself place, this shop also has *tatami* rooms. *Ika-ten* ¥600, *buta-ten* ¥650 and courses from ¥2,400. [M-8]

MOTOMACHI モトマチ 目黒区自由ヶ丘2-9-5
2-9-5 Jiyūgaoka, Meguro-ku. Tel: 723-9477. Hrs: 5 p.m.-2 a.m. (3 p.m.-11 p.m. Sun. & Hols), closed Mon. The cook prepares your meal here. Try their "*motomachi okonomiyaki*" ¥650, "*chāhan*" (fried rice) ¥650, and "*yasai-yaki*" (fried vegetables) ¥700. They also have *teppan-yaki* and Kōbe steak. (AX, D, V) [M-21]

BOTEJŪ ほてぢゅう ベルビー赤坂
Belle Vie Akasaka 7th Fl. Tel: 588-5102. Hrs: 11 a.m.-11 p.m., daily. A new branch of the biggest chain of *okonomiyaki* restaurants in Tokyo, they use ketchup and mayonnaise as a sauce. "*Buta no rōsu, tamago ire*" (pork with egg) ¥550, "*ika-tamago*" (squid with egg) ¥550, and "*modan yaki*" (*okonomiyaki*+*yakisoba*, with two eggs fried sunny-side up) ¥800. [M-6]

Rāmen

These Chinese noodles are one of the most popular kinds of "fast food" in Japan. *Rāmen* shops are not known for their decor, but with prices that range from a mere ¥270-¥600, who cares.

Menu

Rāmen	Noodles in chicken soup with leek, sliced bamboo shoot and green vegetables.
Chāshūmen	With sliced, roasted pork.
Wantanmen	With wantan (square pockets of a noodle-dough filled with pork and vegetables).
Gomoku soba	With various ingredients (sliced pork, vegetables, etc.).
Miso rāmen	With miso soup.
Gyōza	Minced pork and vegetables in a crescent shaped Chinese pastry and fried.
Chāhan	Fried rice with meat and vegetables.

How To Order

- People will usually order a bowl of rāmen and a side order of gyōza. As with other noodles, slurp at will.
- Pepper and chilli oil are usually provided to spice up the soup if you so please.

HAGOROMO 羽衣　渋谷区渋谷1-12-22第1ソシアルビル
Daiichi Social Bldg. B1, 1-12-22 Shibuya, Shibuya-ku. Tel: 409-4664. Hrs: 4 p.m.-11 p.m., closed Sun. & Hols. Known for their "hagoromo rāmen", gyōza and paozu (similar to gyōza but round, and steamed). [M-3]

NAOKYŪ 直久　中央区銀座5-2-1東芝ビル
Tōshiba Bldg. B2, 5-2-1 Ginza, Chūō-ku. Tel: 571-0957. Hrs: 11 a.m.-9 p.m., daily. On the 16th of every month from 11 a.m. they serve their rāmen for ¥50. [M-8]

DAIHACHI 大八　港区六本木7-12-1
7-12-1 Roppongi, Minato-ku. Tel: 405-0721. Hrs: 5:30 p.m.-1 a.m., closed Sun. & Hols. [M-1]

SUSUKINO 薄野　港区赤坂5-3-10
5-3-10 Akasaka, Minato-ku. Tel: 582-8080. Hrs: 11:30 a.m.-9 p.m., closed Sun. & Hols. Good miso rāmen. [M-6]

CHARLIE HOUSE チャーリーハウス　渋谷区神南1-15-11
1-15-11 Jinnan, Shibuya-ku. Tel: 464-5552. Hrs: 11:30 a.m.-2:30 p.m., 4:30 p.m.-8:30 p.m., closed Sun. They serve hand-made thin noodles. The soup noodles and toppings come separately here. [M-3]

Katei-ryōri

Basic, good food just like mom used to make, katei-ryōri or home-cooking is usually served in restaurants with a functional Japanese decor and a friendly atmosphere. Many of the dishes listed on our general restaurant menu are served in these restaurants. Others are listed below. This kind of restaurant is found in every neighborhood.

Menu

Yasai no nitsuke (nimono)	Cooked seasonal vegetables in a sugar and soy sauce
Nattō	Fermented soybeans, usually served with raw egg, sliced leek and soy sauce. The mixture is usually poured over rice.

Tori no kara-age	Fried chicken
Yaki-zakana	Grilled fish
Buri no teriyaki	Yellowtail broiled *teriyaki* style
Ohitashi	Boiled green vegetables served in a small bowl and seasoned with soy sauce and dried bonito flakes.

KAPPA かっぱ 港区六本木4-10-7エルビル
Eru Bldg. 2nd Fl., 4-10-7 Roppongi, Minato-ku. Tel: 408-8696. Hrs: 5:30 p.m.-2 a.m., daily. They have a *kushi-age* course from ¥900. Try their *shūmai* ¥400, and *wafū* (Japanese style) salad ¥700. [M-1]

ANRI 安里 港区西麻布2-8-6
2-8-6 Nishi-Azabu, Minato-ku. Tel: 400-7389. Hrs: 5:30 p.m.-2 a.m., closed Mon. *Niku-jaga* (potato stew) ¥450, potato salad ¥450, and *Aji no Nambanzuke* (fish marinated in vinegar, soy sauce and sliced onion) ¥680. [M-5]

ROPPONGI SHOKUDŌ 六本木食堂 港区六本木3-10-11
3 10-11 Roppongi, Minato-ku. Tel: 404-2714. Hrs: 8:30 a.m.-2 p.m., 4:15 p.m.-7 p.m. (8:30 a.m.-2 p.m. on Sat.), closed Sun. & Hols. A classic "*shokudō*", or cafeteria, you pick out your food at the counter and pay around ¥500-¥600 when you go. [M-1]

Yōshoku

Western food as cooked by the Japanese since the *Meiji* period.

TSUTSUI 津つ井 港区赤坂5-5-7
5-5-7 Akasaka, Minato-ku. Tel: 584-1851. Hrs: 11 a.m.-9 p.m., closed Sun. & Hols. Their *bifuteki-don* (teriyaki beef on rice) is good ¥1,900. *Yōshoku-bentō* (western style lunch with fish, vegetables, croquette, rice, etc. in a lacquered box) from ¥1,500. (AX, D) [M-6]

Osechi-ryōri—festive food for the New Year's holiday packed in a set of lacquer boxes.

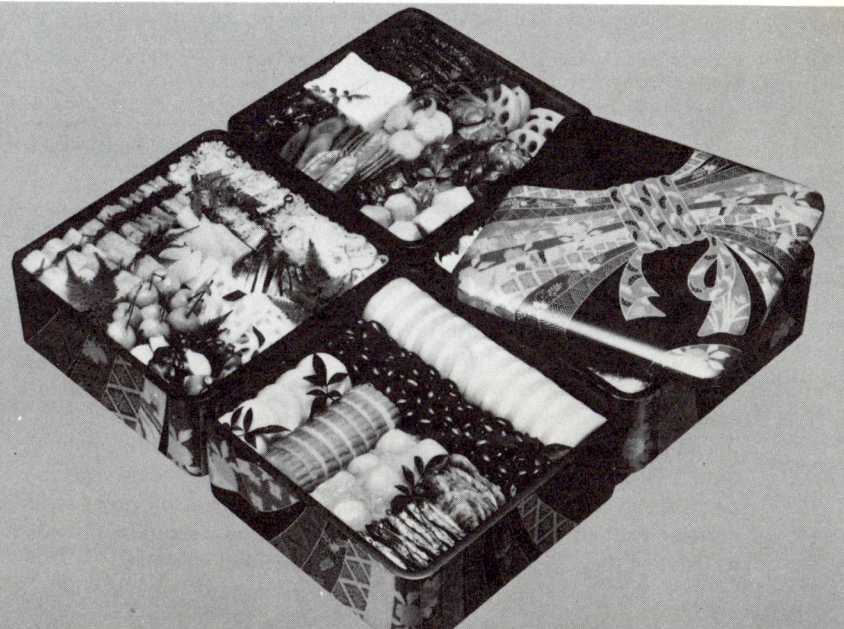

HŌMITEI 芳味亭 中央区人形町2-9-4
2-9-4 Ningyōchō, Nihombashi, Chūo-ku. Tel: 666-5687. Hrs: 11 a.m.-2 p.m., 5 p.m.-9 p.m., closed Mon. In this little house you can eat *yōshoku* in one of seven *tatami* rooms. Beef stew ¥2,300, tongue stew ¥2,000, *shiba-ebi korokke* (shrimp croquette) ¥1,000. [M-23]

SHŌEITEI 松栄亭 千代田区神田淡路町2-8
2-8 Awajichō, Kanda, Chiyoda-ku. Tel: 251-5511. Hrs: 11 a.m.-2:30 p.m., 4:30 p.m.-7:30 p.m., closed Sun. & Hols. Great "*shitamachi*" people and atmosphere, their food is good and cheap. *Yōfū-kakiage* (fried pork and sliced onions with *tempura* batter) ¥550, *korokke* (potato croquette) ¥400, *katsudon* (*tonkatsu* on rice) ¥500. [M-14]

Other Japanese Restaurants

The following restaurants are all great, but don't fit into any of our categories.

DAIKAN KAMADO 代官かまど 港区六本木4-11-4六本木ビル
Roppongi Bldg. 1st Fl., 4-11-4 Roppongi, Minato-ku. Tel: 403-5364. Hrs: 5 p.m.-2 a.m., daily. This is a great seafood restaurant, but they also serve *shabu-shabu* and steak. Their selection of *sake* is impressive. Try à la carte: *hotate no shūmai* (scallop dumpling) ¥700, *ebi-dango* (shrimp ball) ¥900, *dobin mushi* (mushrooms, crabmeat, and soup in a pot) ¥1,100. They have a *shabu-shabu* course for ¥5,500 which includes all these side dishes. (AX) [M-1]

HAYASHI はやし 港区赤坂2-14-1山王会館ビル
Sannō Kaikan Bldg. 4th Fl., 2-14-1 Akasaka, Minato-ku. Tel: 582-4078. Hrs: 11:30 a.m.-2 p.m., 5:30 p.m.-11 p.m., daily. In this lovely country-style restaurant, all tables have *tatami* mat seating and a charcoal grill. The cooking style is called "*sumibi-yaki*", you cook a variety of meat, fish and vegetables over the grill at your table. They have a number of dinner courses: *gyūniku* (beef) course ¥5,000, a "*matsu*" course with a variety of dishes ¥5,000, and a "*ran*" (deluxe) course ¥7,000. Each course has *yakitori*, which you can also order a la carte. For lunch they serve only *oyako domburi* for ¥750. (AX) [M-6]

TATSUMIYA 東南屋 台東区浅草1-33-5
1-33-5 Asakusa. Taitō-ku. Tel: 842-7373. Hrs: 12 noon-2 p.m., 5 p.m.-9 p.m., closed Mon. Like dining in a private home during the *Edo* period, this cozy restaurant full of antiques is located in an old house brought in from Gifu Prefecture in central Japan. The food is home-style cooking and fairly inexpensive. For lunch, try *gyū-rōsu bentō* (teriyaki beef and egg cakes on rice) from ¥800. Dinner courses are ¥2,000 and ¥3,500. [M-12]

KUREMUTSU 暮六つ 台東区浅草2-2-13
2-2-13 Asakusa, Taitō-ku. Tel: 842-0906. Hrs: 4 p.m.-10 p.m., closed Thur. The owner of this restaurant is the brother of Tatsumiya's owner (listed above). This old farm house was also transplanted from the country 18 years ago, but is slightly more eccentric than Tatsumiya. They serve a *kaiseki* course for ¥7000, à la carte *sashimi*, *yakimono*, etc. [M-12]

JIZAKE 地酒 渋谷区道玄坂1-15-8
1-15-8 Dōgenzaka, Shibuya-ku. Tel: 496-5790. Hrs: 5 p.m.-2 a.m., closed Sun. & Hols. This place is best known for its huge selection of *sake* (rice wine) from all over Japan. Their *sashimi* is also particularly good. You can order a course here, with different kinds of cooking styles, from ¥3,500. [M-3]

HEALTH FOOD RESTAURANTS

Because Japanese food was originally based on rice and vegetables, vegetarian restaurants were never really necessary. But with the increased use of chemical feritilizers, artifical ingredients, and pollution, the concern for health has grown. There are a number of good "natural food" restaurants in town. Notable is *shōjin-ryōri*—a traditional vegetarian meal served in temples. Other restaurants serve basically home-style cooking without meat. American style health food restaurants are not as good as they are in America, so we haven't included them.

HEALTHMAGIC ヘルスマジック 新宿区新宿3-16-4
3-16-4 Shinjuku, Shinjuku-ku. Tel: 350-5736. Hrs: 11 a.m.-10:30 p.m. (until 10 p.m. on Sun. & Hols), daily. One of the best known of Tokyo's health food restaurants, Health Magic serves twenty different kinds of pita bread sandwiches, from ¥450. They have a special high protein salad for ¥750, and natural drinks from ¥450. [M-7]

TEMMI 天味 渋谷区神南1-10-6第1岩下ビル
Daiichi Iwashita Bldg. 2nd Fl. 1-10-6 Jinnan, Shibuya-ku. Tel: 496-9703. Hrs: 11:30 a.m.-2:30 p.m., 4:30 p.m.-7:30 p.m. (11:30 a.m.-6 p.m. on Sun. & Hols), closed the 3rd Thur. of the month. Macrobiotic vegetarian food in a Japanese style restaurant. *"Ofukuro no teishoku"* ("Mom's cooking" course) ¥800, *tempura teishoku* ¥1,000, *makunouchi teishoku* (mixed) ¥1,500. Also: seaweed salad ¥800 and natural *sake* ¥400. They have a *kaiseki* course for ¥3,000, but 4-10 people must make the order with you. (AX, D) [M-3]

MANA マナ 新宿区西新宿1-16-5菊水ビル
Kikusui Bldg. B1. 1-16-5 Nishi-Shinjuku, Shinjuku-ku. Tel: 344-6606. Hrs: 11 a.m.-9 p.m. (until 3 p.m. on Fri.), closed Sat., Sun. & Hols. A healthy anomaly in Nishi-Shinjuku, their lunch service is great and only ¥700. In the evening they have a family course for four at ¥12,000. Other items are: western food course ¥3,500, *tempura* course ¥1,800, fried *tōfu* course ¥1,800 and gluten hamburger set ¥1,800. (AX, D) [M-7]

SHIMBASHI KENKŌ SHIZENSHOKU CENTER 新橋健康自然食センター 港区新橋3-26-3
3-26-3 Shimbashi, Minato-ku. Tel: 573-4181. Hrs: 11:30 a.m.-2 p.m., closed Sun. & Hols. A health food shop with a lunch counter in the back and a restaurant upstairs. Their lunch menu changes daily ¥700. Also on the menu are soybean milk yogurt from ¥250, and fresh carrot juice ¥300. [M-11]

TŌJINBŌ 東尋坊 港区新橋2-16-2ニュー新橋ビル
New Shimbashi Bldg. B1, 2-16-2 Shimbashi, Minato-ku. Tel: 580-7307. Hrs: 5 p.m.-11 p.m., closed the 1st & 3rd Sat., Sun. & Hols. This restaurant seats 18, 10 on *tatami* mats, and 8 at their counter. They specialize in fish, fresh from the Japan sea. They also serve *sansai zōsui* (vegetable and rice stew) ¥600, *nattō zōsui* (rice stew with fermented soybeans) ¥600 and *Eiheiji shōjin-ryōri* (a monk's menu from Eiheiji temple) ¥1,000. (V) [M-11]

BODAIJU 菩提樹 港区芝4-3-14仏教伝道センター
Bukkyō Dendō Center Bldg. 2nd Fl., 4-3-14 Shiba, Minato-ku. Tel: 456-3257. Hrs: 11:30 a.m.-2 p.m., 5:30 p.m.-9 p.m., closed Sun. Chinese vegetarian cuisine, using meat substitutes that will fool most people. Multi-course dinners from ¥3,000 (reservations recommended). Lunch courses from ¥800. Other menu items include: *gomoku chāhan* (fried rice) ¥600, *gomoku yakisoba* (fried noodles) ¥600 and curry rice ¥600. (AX, D) [off Map]

OTHER ASIAN FOOD

Korean

Korean barbecue or "*yaki-niku*", is one of the few kinds of Asian food that is very well made in Japan. Most restaurants are smokey and smell of garlic, but the food is great and you get used to the smell after a while anyway. The meat is cooked on a grill at your table and tends to get a little messy—be sure not to wear anything white when you go. The beef they serve has been soaked in *tare* (a marinade of soy sauce, garlic, sugar, etc.).

Menu

Karubi	Fatty meat
Rōsu	Lean meat—comes in grades: *nami* (regular), and *jō* (deluxe).
Tan	Tongue
Yasai	Several kinds of vegetables

Namuru	Korean salad with bean sprouts, mountain vegetables and white radish.
Kimuchi	Very hot Korean pickles
Bibimba	Boiled minced meat and vegetables on a bed of rice.
Yukke	Raw minced beef with raw egg in the center.
Yukke jan sūpu	Very hot red soup with minced beef.
Reimen	Cold noodles with vegetables.

How To Order—Order one or two meat dishes, pickles, a salad, and rice or noodles.

KUSA NO YA 4-6-7 Azabu-Jūban, Minato-ku. Tel: 455-8356. Hrs: 11 a.m.-2 p.m., 5 p.m.-10 p.m. (12 noon-10 p.m. on Sun. & Hols.), daily. One of the best *yaki-niku* spots in town, you may have to wait a while to get a seat. The food is great, the atmosphere is rather "at home". Try their pidento (Korean style *okomomiyaki*) or the Korean Salad. *Karubi* from ¥900, *reimen* noodles ¥700. (AX, D, V) [M-1]

JŪJŪ 3-24-20 Nishi-Azabu, Minato-ku. Tel: 405-9911. Hrs: 11:30 a.m.-4:30 a.m. (11:30 a.m.-2 a.m. on Sun. & Hols.), daily. A very bright, almost antiseptically clean interior, great food. *Karubi* and *rōsu* from ¥750-¥1,800. (AX) [M-2]

YANSANDŌ 6-5-3 Ueno, Taitō-ku. Tel: 831-7333. Hrs: 11 a.m.- 2 a.m. (until midnight on Sun.), daily. The house speciality is *komutan* (vegetables and beef with a bone in soup) ¥800. *Karubi* ¥800, *rei-men* ¥800. For lunch (11 a.m.-2 p.m. except Sun.) try their *yakiniku teishoku* ¥700. (V) [M-13]

JOJOEN Morino bldg. 2nd & 3rd Fls., 7-12-1 Roppongi, Minato-ku. Tel: 478-1446. Hrs: 11:30 a.m.-7 a.m. (i.e. almost 24 hours), daily. This place has a reputation for their high quality meats. *Karubi* ¥900, *rōsu* ¥900, *reimen* ¥700, salad ¥500. [M-1]

TŌKAIEN 1-6-3 Kabukichō, Shinjuku-ku. Tel: 200-2924. Hrs: 11 a.m.-4 a.m., daily. This place has a smokeless roaster, so you won't leave smelling like smoke and garlic. The restaurant has 9 floors all together. 1st-4th Fl. are home-style *yakiniku*, the 6th Fl. has a "Viking" course (which means "all you can eat") with 25 different dishes for ¥1,800. The 7th-9th floors offer a traditional Korean "Royal Family Course" from ¥8,000. À la carte: *rōsu* ¥950, *karubi* ¥950. (AX, D, V) [M-7]

Chinese

HOKKAIEN 2-12-1 Nishi-Azabu, Minato-ku. Tel: 407-8507. Daily. The best Peking style restaurant in the city. Lunch: 11:30 a.m.-2 p.m., from ¥800 (except on Sun. & Hols.). Dinner: 5 p.m.-10:30 p.m. course from ¥5,000 (AX, D) [M-2]

RŌGAIRŌ (SEVENTH HEAVEN) 3-17-7 Roppongi, Minato-ku. Tel: 586-3931. Hrs: 11:30 a.m.-2:30 p.m., 4:30 p.m.-10:30 p.m., daily. The best Shanghai style restaurant in Tokyo. About ¥5,000 per person. (D, V) [M-1]

TOKYO DAI HANTEN 5-17-13 Shinjuku, Shinjuku-ku. Tel: 202-0121. Hrs: 11 a.m.-10 p.m., daily. The biggest Chinese restaurant in Tokyo (12 floors), serves almost every kind of Chinese food. For small groups, go to the 3rd Fl., where you can order lunch for ¥650 and dinner course for ¥5,000. Not the best Chinese restaurant in town, but is one of the few places where dim sum is served all day. (AX, D, V) [M-7]

TONG FŪ 6-7-11 Roppongi, Minato-ku. Tel: 403-3527. Hrs: 6 p.m.-2 a.m., closed Sun. & Hols. Chinese-modern interior and food, this has been a hip place to go for over 6 years. About ¥4,000-¥5,000 per person (AX, D) [M-1]

DAINI'S TABLE 6-3-14 Minami-Aoyama, Minato-ku. Tel: 407-0363. Hrs: 6 p.m.-2 a.m., daily. Chinese nouvelle cuisine served with style in this elegant, rather fashionable restaurant. From ¥8,000-¥10,000 per person. [M-5]

LOTUS CAFE 7-8-4 Minami-Aoyama, Minato-ku. Tel: 407-5891. Hrs: 6:30 p.m.-2 a.m., closed Sun. & Hols. Food is a rather healthy mix of Chinese and Japanese cooking, the atmosphere is sophisticated underground-hip. From ¥3,000-¥4,000 per person. [M-5]

LE CHINOIS Bianca Bldg. B1, 3-1-26 Jingūmae, Shibuya-ku. Tel: 403-3929. Hrs: 6 p.m.-2 a.m., daily. A beautifully designed contemporary interior, the food is similar to Daini's Table, but smaller portions and slightly less expensive. From about ¥5,000-¥8,000 per person. (AX, D, V) [M-5]

KAEN 3-10-12 Moto-Azabu, Minato-ku. Tel: 401-1051. Hrs: 6:30 p.m.-10 p.m., closed Sun. & Hols. Run by a young couple, the restaurant is in an old house near Roppongi. Food is a Chinese-Japanese mix, the atmosphere is casual, almost café-like. From ¥4,000-¥10,000 per person. [M-1]

Taiwanese

REIKYŌ 2-25-18 Dōgenzaka, Shibuya-ku. Tel: 464-8617. Hrs: 12 noon-1 a.m., closed Thur. From ¥2,000-¥3,000 per person. [M-3]

Cambodian

ANGKOR WAT 1-44-12 Yoyogi, Shibuya-ku. Tel: 370-3019. Daily. Lunch: 11 a.m.-2 p.m., from ¥450 (no lunch on Sun. & Hols.). Dinner: 5 p.m.-11 p.m., course from ¥1,800. A *sushi* bar turned Cambodian restaurant, and run by real Cambodians. The food is wonderful and incredibly cheap. A full meal for one—about ¥2,000. [M-28]

Vietnamese

HI LAC NAM 3-9-16 Kita-Shinjuku, Shinjuku-ku. Tel: 369-5431. Daily, except closed Mon., the 2nd Tue. of the month, and the whole month of August. Lunch: 10 a.m.-2 p.m. Dinner 4:30 p.m.-10 p.m., courses from ¥1,540 per person. [M-27]

AO ZAI 5-4-14 Akasaka, Minato-ku. Tel: 583-0234. Hrs: 5 p.m.-10 p.m., closed Sun. & Hols. Slightly sophisticated food and interior. Course from ¥3,800. (AX, D) [M-6]

Indian

MOTI Roppongi Hama Bldg. 3rd. Fl., 6-2-35 Roppongi, Minato-ku. Tel: 479-1939. Hrs: 11:30 a.m.-11 p.m. (10 p.m. last order), daily. A popular restaurant with the foreign residents, they serve basically good, inexpensive Indian food. From about ¥2,000 per person. (AX, D) [M-1]

TAJ 3-2-7 Akasaka, Minato-ku. Tel: 586-6606. Hrs: 11:30 a.m.-2:30 p.m., 5:30 p.m.-10:15 p.m. (12 noon-9 on Sat., Sun. & Hols.), daily. ¥4,000 per person. Slightly more elegant than Moti, the food is also a bit more refined. (AX, D, V) [M-6]

BINDI Apartment Aoyama B1., 7-10-10 Minami-Aoyama, Minato-ku. Tel: 409-7114. Closed Sun. & Hols. Lunch: 11:30 a.m.-2 p.m., dinner: 5:30 p.m.-2 a.m. Home style Indian cooking in this restaurant run by a friendly Indian couple. You can watch Mrs. Menta, an Indian cooking teacher, cook your dinner behind the counter. [M-5]

WESTERN FOOD

French

AUX SIX ARBRES 7-13-10 Roppongi, Minato-ku. Tel: 479-2888. Closed Sun. A charming and rather chic restaurant. Lunch: 12 noon-2 p.m., course ¥1,760 & ¥3,500. Dinner: 6 p.m.-10 p.m., course ¥10,000. (AX, D) [M-1]

QUEEN ALICE 3-17-34 Nishi-Azabu, Minato-ku. Tel: 405-9039. Closed Sun. In a beautiful older house overlooking a small garden. Lunch: 12 noon-2 p.m., course ¥3,600. Dinner: 6 p.m.-9 p.m., course from ¥7,000. (AX, D) [M-2]

LES CHOUX 5-11-28 Roppongi, Minato-ku. Tel: 470-5511. Closed Thur. Casual French elegance, and a small terrace for dining in good weather. Lunch: 12 noon-3:30 p.m., course ¥1,300. Dinner: 5:30 p.m.-10:30 p.m., course ¥5,000. (AX, D, V) [M-1]

BISTROT DE LA CITE 4-2-10 Nishi-Azabu, Minato-ku. Tel: 406-5475. Closed Mon. A cozy, bistro atmosphere. Lunch: 12 noon-2 p.m., courses from ¥1,760. Dinner: 6 p.m.-10 p.m., course ¥6,500. (AX, D) [M-2]

MADAME TOKI'S 14-7 Hachiyamachō, Shibuya-ku. Tel: 461-2263. Closed Mon. In a very elegant older home. Madame Toki herself will greet you at the door. Lunch 12 noon-2:30 p.m., same menu as in the evening. Dinner: 6 p.m.-10 p.m., from ¥10,000-¥15,000 per person. (AX, D, V) [M-20]

L'ORANGERIE DE PARIS Hanae Mori Bldg. 5th Fl. 3-6-1, Kita-Aoyama, Minato-ku. Daily (no dinner on Sun.) Tel: 407-7461. Sister restaurant to l'Orangerie in Paris. The interior is discreetly elegant as is the food. Brunch: 11 a.m.-2:30 p.m. ¥3,000. Lunch: 11:30 a.m.-2:30 p.m., course ¥4,000. Dinner: 5:30 p.m.-10 p.m., course ¥8,000. (AX, D, V) [M-4]

MAXIM'S DE PARIS Ginza Sony Bldg. B3, 5-3-1 Ginza, Chūō-ku. Tel: 572-3621. Just like in Paris. Very elegant and equally expensive. Lunch: 11:30 a.m.-2:30 p.m., course ¥6,000. Dinner: 5:30 p.m.-11 p.m., course ¥18,000. Closed Sun. (AX, D) [M-8]

BOFINGER White Sunnyland Bldg. B1, 3-10-5 Roppongi, Minato-ku. Tel: 479-1123. Daily. Brasserie style decor, the food is slightly Japanese influenced but still great. Lunch: 11:30 a.m.-1:30 p.m., course ¥1,500 & ¥3,000. Dinner: 5 p.m.-10 p.m., course from ¥4,500. (AX, D, V) [M-1]

A TANTÔT Axis Bldg. 3rd Fl. 5-17-1 Roppongi, Minato-ku. Tel: 586-4431. Daily. Contemporary interior design and a great terrace. Lunch: 11:30 a.m.-2:30 p.m., course ¥1,800 & ¥3,000. Dinner 5:30 p.m.-11 p.m., course ¥5,000 & ¥8,000. (AX, D, V) [M-1]

BRASSERIE BERNARD Kajimaya Bldg. 7th Fl., 7-14-3 Roppongi, Minato-ku. Tel: 405-7877. Daily (no lunch on Sun. & Hols.). One of the only "lively" French restaurants in Tokyo, the atmosphere is casual, decor O.K., and the food is good for the price. Lunch: 11:30 a.m.-2 p.m., course ¥1,000 & ¥1,800. Dinner: 5:30 p.m.-1 a.m., course ¥3,000. (AX, D, V) [M-1]

ILE DE FRANCE Com Roppongi Bldg. B1 3-11-5 Roppongi, Minato-ku. Tel: 404-0384. Simple but warm interior, and very good food (the fish soup is fabulous). Lunch: 11:30 a.m.-2 p.m., course from ¥1,200. Dinner: 5 p.m.-10:30 p.m., course from ¥6,000. (AX, D, V) [M-1]

Italian

LA GRANATA TBS Kaikan B1 (in the TBS television Bldg.), 5-3-3 Akasaka, Minato-ku. Tel: 582-3241. Hrs: 11 a.m.-10:30 p.m., daily. A café-like atmosphere, the regulars at this place tend to be the local Italians. Lunch: 11 a.m.-3 p.m. from ¥1,200. Dinner: 5 p.m.-10:30 p.m. Courses from ¥4,000. (AX, D, V) [M-6]

LA PATATA 2-9-11 Jingūmae, Shibuya-ku. Tel: 403-9665. Closed Mon. Simple modern interior and regional Italian cooking. Lunch: 12 noon-2 p.m., course ¥1,600. Dinner: 6 p.m.-11:30 p.m., from ¥5,000 per person. (AX, D) [M-5]

SABATINI DI FIRENZE Ginza Sony Bldg. 7th Fl. Tel: 573-0013. Daily. An average interior but excellent food. Lunch: 12 noon-2:30 p.m., course ¥3,600 & ¥4,500. Dinner: 5:30 p.m.-11:30 p.m., course ¥7,000 & ¥8,000. (AX, D, V) [M-8]

SABATINI AOYAMA Suncrest Bldg. B1, 2-13-5 Kita-Aoyama, Minato-ku. Tel: 402-3812. Daily. Loved or hated for its cheerful, very Italian atmosphere and strolling musicians. Lunch: 11:30 a.m.-2:30 p.m., course ¥3,900. Dinner 5:30 p.m.-11 p.m., course ¥15,000. (AX, D, V) [M-5]

SABATINI AOYAMA/PIZZERIA ROMANA SABATINI Suncrest Bldg. B1, 2-13-5 Kita-Aoyama, Minato-ku. Tel: Main restaurant—402-3812, Pizzeria—402-2027. Daily. The main restaurant is loved or hated for it's cheerful Italian atmosphere and strolling musicians. The Pizzeria next door is good and reasonably priced. Lunch 11:30 a.m.-2:30 p.m., course ¥3,900 (main), ¥1,800 (pizzeria). Dinner 5:30-11 p.m., course ¥15,000 (main). (AX, D, V) [M-5]

CHIANTI Ikura: 3-1-7 Azabudai, Minato-ku. Tel: 583-7546. Hrs: 12 noon-2 a.m., daily. [M-1] A former hang-out of Roppongi celebrities and bohemians, it remains a great casual standby. [M-2] Lunch: 12 noon-2 p.m., from ¥2,500. Dinner will run about ¥6,000-¥8,000. Nishi-Azabu: Goyō Bldg. B1, 3-17-26 Nishi-Azabu, Minato-ku. Tel: 404-6500. Hrs: 12 noon-3 a.m., daily. This new Chianti, opened in June 1984, will probably become as much of a local establishment as the original Chianti. The interior is great, with wall murals by New York artists "Trompe-L'œil". Food is also very good and moderately priced, a full meal running

about ¥3,500-¥5,000. (AX, D, V) [M-2]
AL PORTO 3-24-9 Nishi-Azabu, Minato-ku. Tel: 403-2916. Closed Mon. Supposedly Northern-Italian cuisine, it's closer to Italian nouvelle cuisine. The food is beautiful, as is its setting in a lovely older home. Lunch: 11:30 a.m.-2 p.m., from ¥3,000. Dinner: 5:30 p.m. (5 p.m. on Sun.)-9:30 p.m., course ¥6,000. (AX, D, V) [M-2]
LA BOHEME Harajuku: Jingūbashi Bldg. 2nd Fl., 6-7-18 Jingūmae, Shibuya-ku. Tel: 409-2091. [M-4] Kasumichō: Azabu Palace Bldg. 2nd Fl., 2-25-18 Nishi-Azabu, Minato-ku. Tel: 407-1363. [M-2] Daikan-yama: 16-2 Daikan-yamachō, Shibuya-ku. Tel: 476-4764. [M-20] This is a great "chain" serving inexpensive Japanese influenced Italian food. Interiors are fun. The Harajuku branch is full of antiques, Kasumichō is modern Italian and the Daikan-yama branch is pure deco, with a fireplace downstairs. Lunch: 11:30 a.m.-2 p.m., ¥600-¥950. From 2:30 p.m.-5 a.m. order à la carte, for about ¥2,500-¥4,000 per person. Daily. (AX, V)
LA VERDE Sun's Bldg. 2nd Fl. 1-7-2 Jingūmae, Shibuya-ku. Tel: 470-6498. Hrs: 11:30 a.m.-10 p.m., daily. 43 kinds of inexpensive pasta dishes that cost from ¥650-¥1,200. Decor is typical Italian-funk, atmosphere is very casual. [M-4]

American

SPAGO 5-7-8 Roppongi, Minato-ku. Tel: 423-4025. Hrs: 5 p.m.-11 p.m., daily. Southern Californian haute-cuisine. Good casually L.A. elegant interior. From about ¥6,000 per person. (AX, D, V) [M-1]
VICTORIA STATION Haiyūza Bldg. 1st Fl. & B1, 4-9-2 Roppongi, Minato-ku. Tel: 479-4601. Hrs: 11 a.m.-2 a.m., (until 11 p.m. Sun. & Hols.), daily. An American chain steak house, good for cheap beef, their salad bar and American atmosphere. Prime rib dinners from ¥2,900. Lunch: sets from ¥980. (AX, D) [M-1]
POSH BOY La Mia Bldg. 2nd Fl., 5-1-3 Minami-Aoyama, Minato-ku. Tel: 406-8242. Hrs: 11 a.m.-10:30 p.m., daily. American 50's style diner, serving vaguely American food (i.e. Tuna sandwich with potato chips), refillable coffee at ¥350. Food from ¥700-¥1,000. (AX, D, V) [M-5]
FOX BAGELS 6-15-19 Roppongi, Minato-ku. Tel: 403-7638. Hrs: 9 a.m.-7 p.m., closed Wed. The first bagel manufacturer in town, Fox Bagels is run by an American and his Japanese wife. The shop sells bagels, but also serves bagel with smoked salmon and cream cheese. Other sandwiches and drinks also available. Standing room only. [M-1]

Mexican

MEXICO LINDO Daini Seikō Mansion Bldg., 2-27 Akasaka, Minato-ku. Tel: 583-2095. Closed Sun. Lunch (weekdays only): 11:30 a.m.-2 p.m. Dinner: 5:30 p.m.-11 p.m. (9:30 p.m. last order), courses from ¥3,500. Tokyo's best Mexican food. [M-6]

Russian

SARAFAN Toda Bldg. B1., 3-10-3 Ogawamachi, Kanda, Chiyoda-ku. Tel: 292-0480. Closed Sun. & Hols. Hrs: 10 a.m.-10 p.m. Lunch: 10 a.m.-2 p.m. ¥600, otherwise about ¥2,000 per person. A classic "dive" interior, but very good food cooked by a Russian woman who's lived in Tokyo over 20 years. [M-15]
BALALAIKA Kanda: 1-63 Jimbōchō, Kanda, Chiyoda-ku. 11:30 a.m.-1 a.m., daily. Tel: 291-6737. [M-15] Ginza branch: 5-9-9 Ginza, Chūō-ku. Tel: 572-8388. [M-8] Established in the mid-50's this restaurant has a rather old-world air. Live Russian folk music nightly. (AX, D, V)

DESSERT AND COFFEE SHOPS

There are thousands of coffee and cake shops in Tokyo where people sit for hours nursing a cup of "American" (watered down, weak coffee that Americans are thought to be fond of), or "Blend" (stronger, and usually the better choice of the two). Finding a shop will be no problem. The following list notes a few of the more memorable spots.

Roppongi—Kasumichō

CAPPUCCIO Nogizaka: 9-6-29 Akasaka, Minato-ku. Tel: 403-5193. Hrs: 11:30 a.m.-2:30 a.m., daily. Roppongi: 5-16-8 Roppongi, Minato-ku. Tel: 584-4347. Hrs: 11:30 a.m.-2:30 a.m., daily. Good espresso, cappuccino and some Italian food. [M-1]

KONDITOREI ÖSTERREICH 6-19-47 Akasaka, Minato-ku. Tel: 582-5812. Hrs: 11 a.m.-8 p.m., closed Thur. A beautiful, truly European style coffee shop. Cakes and pastries are Viennese and fabulous. [M-1]

PATISSERIE DE LA TABLE 2-25-26 Nishi-Azabu, Minato-ku. Tel: 498-2131. Hrs: 12 noon-9 p.m., daily. On the 1st Fl. they serve just coffee and tea in a very "modern Italian" room, the 3rd Fl. has a warm, European atmosphere and incredible (and expensive) cakes, ice creams and sherbets. [M-2]

RUELLE DE DERRIÈRE Udagawa Bldg. 1st Fl., 4-3-10 Nishi-Azabu, Minato-ku. Tel: 407-7685. Hrs: 12:30 p.m.-12:30 a.m., closed Mon. An Italian restaurant and café, better for the coffee than the food. Its major attraction is that it opens up to the street in the summer. [M-2]

LA PALETTE 3-13-22 Nishi-Azabu, Minato-ku. Tel: 408-2595. Hrs: 9 a.m.-8 p.m., daily. A tiny shop with coffee and a great selection of ice creams and sherbets. [M-2]

Harajuku—Aoyama

LUSEINE-KAN 1-16-3 Jingūmae, Shibuya-ku. Tel: 470-1852. Hrs: 10 a.m.-8 p.m. from 1 p.m. on Sun. & Hols.), daily. Off on a tiny backstreet behind Harajuku's Takeshita-dōri, this coffee shop with it's spacious European style interior and classical music is a perfect place for a shopping break. Coffee from ¥500. [M-4]

YOKU MOKU 5-3-3 Minami-Aoyama, Minato-ku. Tel: 406-4121. Hrs: 10 a.m.-7 p.m., daily. Great cake and coffee in an incredibly beautiful blue and white tiled building. During the summer have coffee in the courtyard beneath a large cherry tree. [M-5]

STUDIO V COFFEE SHOP 6-31-15 Jingūmae, Shibuya-ku. Tel: 409-6749. Hrs: 11 a.m.-9:30 p.m., daily. A wide selection of teas, good coffee and a nice lunch menu. [M-4]

CAFE DE ROPE 6-1-8 Jingūmae, Shibuya-ku. Tel: 406-6845. Hrs: 10:30 a.m.-2 a.m., daily. They serve passable food and drinks, but this is one of the only true "people watching" street cafés in Tokyo, right in the heart of the Harajuku fashion district. [M-4]

Ginza

BUDŌ NO KI (Maison de Dessert) 5-8-5 Ginza, Chūō-ku. Tel: 574-9779. Hrs: 10 a.m.-10 p.m. (until 8:30 p.m. on Sun.), daily. An elegant, European style coffee and dessert shop with some of the best cakes in the city. The coffee shop is on the 2nd floor. [M-8]

KIMURAYA 4-5-7 Ginza, Chūō-ku. Tel: 561-9947. Hrs: 10 a.m.-9 p.m., daily. This shop, established since the *Meiji* period, is famous for its *ampan*, a cake like dessert with sweet red bean paste in the center. In the 2nd floor coffee shop you can try the *ampan* with a cup of tea or coffee. [M-8]

SATŌ NINGYŌ 7-7-12 Ginza, Chūō-ku. Tel: 574-9891. Hrs: 10 a.m.-1 a.m. (until 11 p.m. on Sat., 11 a.m.-8 p.m. on Sun. & Hols.), daily. A simple modern interior, and good coffee and cakes. [M-8]

Shibuya

CAFE BISTRO McsLord Kasuya Bldg. B1, 2-9 Sakuragaoka, Shibuya-ku. Tel: 496-4495. Hrs: 11:30 a.m.-midnight (2 p.m.-10 p.m. on Sun. & Hols.), daily. Good coffee and vaguely Italian food. Rock music. [M-3]

LAWN 2-3-4 Shibuya, Shibuya-ku. Tel: 409-2329. Hrs: 11 a.m.-7 p.m., closed Sun. This shop serves Tokyo's best pies. [M-3]

Shinjuku

STUDIO V Shinjuku Daini Bldg. 5th Fl., 3-26-2 Shinjuku, Shinjuku-ku. Tel: 354-5225. Hrs: 11 a.m.-9 p.m., daily. This place is near the station, but slightly hard to find. You have to walk through the Hiyoshiya boutique to get to the elevator. It is a refreshing break from Shinjuku's insanity. Have your tea or coffee along with rock music and fashionable waiters. [M-7]

Jimbōchō

RIHAKU 2-24 Jimbōchō, Kanda, Chiyoda-ku. Tel: 264-6292. Hrs: 10 a.m.-8 p.m., closed Sun. & Hols. Classic coffee shop atmosphere, Rihaku is in an old two story house. The serving plates and coffee cups are all antique, and the clientele are mostly elderly gentlemen and students. [M-15]

店
SHOPPING

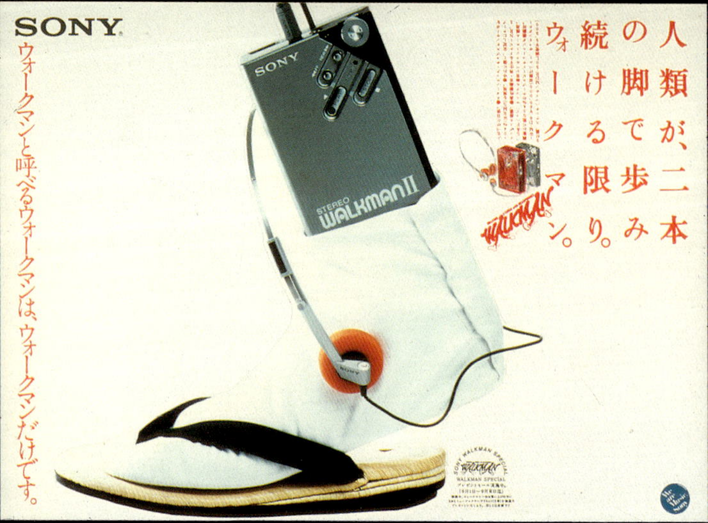

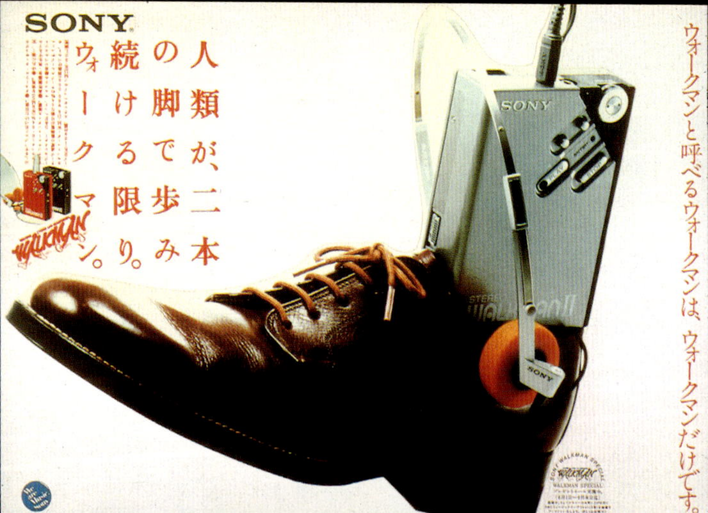

98 SHOPPING

"Walkman, as long as man walks on two legs." The Japanese tradition of fine craftsmanship carries over into the production of contemporary goods with some of the highest quality control standards in the world.

SHOPPING

Contrary to popular opinion, Japan does not survive off its export markets. Consumerism is rampant and shopping a favorite Japanese pastime.

Besides the usual arts, crafts, and antiques, Japan is setting international "shoppers" standards in the fashion, electronics, and camera equipment fields. Don't expect to find many real bargains. Tokyo is an expensive city and even with the discounts given in the Akihabara district on electronics or at the tax-free centers, the merchandise can often be obtained for the same price back home. Still, the quality and quantity of products available in Tokyo is hard to beat.

There are a number of options for where to shop. Tokyo has districts specializing in certain kinds of merchandise such as **Kanda** for books, or **Kappabashi** for wholesale restaurant supplies (where you can buy the wax food models seen in restaurant windows). The department stores are full-service institutions, from the basement food departments to the rooftop playgrounds. There are labyrinthian underground arcades in the basements of major buildings or at the larger train and subway stations, and of course a multitude of small shops and boutiques scattered throughout the city.

Shopping Districts

One of the best and most entertaining ways to shop in Tokyo is to find the district that specializes in what you're looking for and just wander around the neighborhood. Though there is some overlap, and some districts have one of everything, these specialized districts generally have rows of shops that allow you to compare merchandise and prices. Here is a brief description of the major areas.

Akihabara—Electronics paradise with dozens of discount stores.

Aoyama—Fashion in the medium to expensive range, designer boutiques and fashion buildings: BELL COMMONS and FROM 1ST. Also KOTTŌ-DŌRI, a street with numerous antique shops.

Asakusa—Traditional Japanese products, workmen's clothing and wonderfully corny "Japan-esy" souvenirs.

Ginza—One of the most expensive areas in town; there are seven major department stores: MITSUKOSHI, MATSUZAKAYA, MATSUYA, HANKYŪ, WAKŌ, PRINTEMPS, and SEIBU (opened October 1984), numerous "fashion buildings", and scores of exclusive boutiques. Ginza also has some of the oldest and most prestigious shops specializing in traditional Japanese goods.

Harajuku—The best area for youngish fashion, the LA FORET fashion building is a central landmark. TAKESHITA-DŌRI is thick with cheap boutiques. For antiques there's the ORIENTAL BAZAAR and the basement of the HANAE MORI building. For toys there's KIDDYLAND.

Hibiya—Just a few antique shops, the IMPERIAL HOTEL and INTERNATIONAL ARCADES.

Ikebukuro—The main SEIBU department store, branches of PARCO, MITSUKOSHI, and TŌBU department stores, and the multi-purpose SUNSHINE CITY COMPLEX.

Kanda—Lots of books, old and new; antique and old print shops. Martial arts equipment and sporting goods are other specialties.

Nihombashi—The two oldest department stores in Tokyo are here: MITSUKOSHI and TAKASHIMAYA. A good area for old shops specializing in traditional crafts.

Roppongi—Not particularly specialized but has two important new buildings: the AXIS design building and Seibu's WAVE building specializing in audio-visual merchandise.

Shibuya—Has SEIBU and TŌKYŪ department stores and the three part PARCO fashion buildings full of Japanese designer's boutiques.

Shinjuku—Good for cameras and smaller electronic goods. Reasonably priced fashions in TAKANO and the various fashion buildings. ISETAN department store is great, MARUI department store occupies five separate buildings, and the whole of Shinjuku Station building is one enormous arcade called MY CITY.

Ueno—A good place to find discount merchandise is AMEYOKO, an arcade with cheap food, clothing, cosmetics, and toys. For traditional Japanese goods, there is MATSUZAKAYA department store and numerous small shops.

Department Stores

Ask any Japanese where to buy a specific item and the answer will probably be "in a department store". A pivotal institution in Japanese life, in a "depāto" you can buy food, fashion, furniture, fine art, a round-trip ticket to France, or a new home.

Service is a basic part of the system. Japan is probably the only country in the world where department store elevator operators have been trained by the company robot to bow at just the right angle (we suspect that the robot also teaches them to speak in that uniformly falsetto voice).

Most department stores start off with one or two floors in the basement devoted entirely to food. There will be plenty of free samples to ensure that you have the stamina to get through the rest of the building. After shopping your way through the fashion and housewares, you can stop off on the restaurant floor and choose from one of the various eating spots there. Later, take in a bit of culture at one of the art galleries, or if you're in Ikebukuro **Seibu**, you can go to a real museum. Next you can try to find a few bargains on the discount floor, usually located somewhere near the top of the building. On a pleasant afternoon, finish off the day in the rooftop playground or beer garden.

Department stores are good places to shop for traditional Japanese products. The work of well known craftsmen is often on exhibition. Custom orders are generally taken for items such as *kimono* or *byōbu* folding screens.

Some department stores have two or three branch stores, but the main store is usually the best. Department stores are open everyday except one day during the week, which is often a general day-off for the neighborhood. Many stores provide printed English directories at the 1st floor information counter.

MITSUKOSHI: 1-7 Muromachi, Nihombashi, Chūō-ku. Tel: 241-3311. Hrs: 10 a.m.-6 p.m., closed Mon. [M-9] Ginza branch: 4-6-16 Ginza, Chūō-ku, Tel: 562-1111. Hrs: Same as above. [M-8].

The classic Japanese department store, Mitsukoshi opened in 1673 as a *kimono* shop. In the late *Meiji* period it was the first to add a second floor and glass display cases. In competition with the nearby Takashimaya from the beginning, Mitsukoshi kept its number one position until 1982 when a well publicized scandal implicated its president. The scandal surfaced when Mitukoshi sponsored an exhibition and sale of "Persian Art Treasures" that were later proved to be fakes. An investigation followed and the president and his mistress (dubbed the emperor and empress of Mitsukoshi by the press) were charged with embezzling and tax evasion, among other things.

The store hasn't quite recovered, but it remains one of the great examples of a traditional department store. Japanese goods are probably the most interesting, including their large and excellent selection of *kimono* on the 4th floor.

TAKASHIMAYA: 2-4-1 Nihombashi, Chūō-ku. Tel: 211-4111. Hrs: 10 a.m.-6 p.m., closed Wed. [M-9]

A few years older than their rival Mitsukoshi, Takashimaya has a warrant from the Imperial family. In the *Meiji* period Takashimaya was the first department store to hire saleswomen instead of just men, and the first to sell western clothes.

Like Mitsukoshi, Takashimaya is eminently conservative and is perhaps more interesting as a view of daily Japanese life than for its merchandise. They do, however, have a good selection of antiques in the basement.

SEIBU: 1-28-1 Minami-Ikebukuro, Toshima-ku. Tel: 981-0111. Hrs: 10 a.m.-6 p.m., closed Thur. [M-18] Shibuya branch: 23-1 Udagawachō, Shibuya-ku. Tel: 462-0111. Hrs: 10 a.m.-6 p.m., closed Wed. [M-3] Yūrakuchō branch: Tel: 286-0111. closed Thur.

The largest and possibly the best department store in the world, Seibu is also a major sponsor of contemporary arts and cultural events in Tokyo. During their "New York" fair in the fall of 1983, they imported not only New York merchandise, but shipped over around 50 denizens of the city's street scene including break dancers, D.J.'s, rappers, and graffiti artists. There were Japanese kids "breaking" on the streets of Harajuku within the week. Other recent Seibu sponsored events have included concerts by Philip Glass and exhibitions of esoteric Buddhist art.

Seibu carries some of the most interesting merchandise in town. The best Japanese and European designers have boutiques there, and the store is a virtual heaven of new technology. "Studio Tech" on the 9th floor has everything from computers to robots; the 10th and 11th floors have one of the city's best selections of records and books; on the 5th floor is "Studio 200"—a space for contemporary performance and video; on the 12th floor is a contemporary art gallery and the Seibu Museum. The basement food departments are by far the best in Tokyo.

The Shibuya branch is not quite as interesting but still fairly good. In Roppongi they have the "Wave" building.

ISETAN: 3-14-1 Shinjuku, Shinjuku-ku. Tel: 352-1111. Hrs: 10 a.m.-6 p.m., closed Wed. [M-7]

Along the same lines as Seibu, though not quite as good. Oriented to a youngish market, the merchandise is interesting and of good quality. There is a separate building for men's fashion.

MARUI: Fashion Bldg. 3-30-16 Shinjuku, Shinjuku-ku. Tel: 354-0101. Hrs: 10:30 a.m.-7:30 p.m., closed 2nd or 3rd Wed. [M-7]

A training ground for credit card users, Marui is a pioneer in the "buy now, pay later" field of merchandizing in Japan. Credit cards are a relatively new phenomenon here, but Marui alone has issued over 600,000 cards, and continues to grow. The store has numerous branches, most like huge suburban supermarket-department stores, but the Shinjuku branch is an exception. Geared to a young market, there are five separate Marui buildings in the Shinjuku Station area. The most interesting is their new **Fashion** building, with boutiques from known and unknown local designers. Other buildings are: **Young**—for more normal kids' fashion, **Techno**—audio equipment, records, electronics and appliances, **Sports**—for sportswear and sporting goods, and **Interiors**—for furniture and housewares. We have only listed the address of the **Fashion** building, but the others are all located in the same area.

MATSUZAKAYA: 3-29-5 Ueno, Taitō-ku. Tel: 832-1111. Hrs: 10 a.m.-6 p.m., closed Wed. [M-13] Ginza branch: 6-10-1 Ginza, Chūō-ku. Tel: 572-1111. Hrs: Same as above. [M-8]

With a 370 year history, you can imagine how conservative this store is. Most interesting is its famous selection of combs and hair ornaments.

MATSUYA: 1-4-1 Hanakawado, Taitō-ku (Asakusa). Tel: 842-1111. Hrs: 10 a.m.-6 p.m., closed Thur. [M-12] Ginza branch: 3-6-1 Ginza, Chūō-ku. Tel: 567-1211. Hrs: Same as above. [M-8]

The main store is a real downtown working-class institution. Best known for its selection of reasonably priced Japanese products and exhibitions of traditional crafts. The Ginza store is more fashionable and has some interesting boutiques of well known Japanese designers.

TŌKYŪ: 2-24-1 Dōgenzaka, Shibuya-ku. Tel: 477-3111. Hrs: 10 a.m.-6 p.m., closed Thur.

Where your average Japanese shops. Good, basic, and reasonably priced contemporary and traditional merchandise. [M-3]

DAIMARU: 1-9-9 Marunouchi, Chiyoda-ku. Tel: 212-8011. Hrs: 10 a.m.-6 p.m., closed Wed.

Located above Tokyo Station's Yaesu Central Exit, Daimaru is another "basic" department store. Twice a year they have good sales on rental *kimono* and formal wear (See "Bargain Sales") [M-10].

ODAKYŪ: 1-1-3 Nishi-Shinjuku, Shinjuku-ku. Tel: 342-1111. Hrs: 10 a.m.-6 p.m., closed Thur. [M-7]

Not very interesting as a department store but their "Halc" interior division in a separate building next door has a great selection of housewares and furniture.

PRINTEMPS: 3-2-1 Ginza, Chūō-ku. Tel: 567-0077. Hrs: 10 a.m.-6 p.m., closed Wed. [M-8]

Opened in April 1984 by the successful supermarket-department store chain "Daiei", Printemps packs in more trendy fashion per square inch than almost anywhere else in town. Merchandise is geared to young women, and special features include a women's tennis school on the roof and a "Sylvie Vartan Dance Studio" on the 7th floor. A separate wing carries merchandise for interiors.

WAKŌ: 4-5-11 Ginza, Chūō-ku. Tel: 562-2111. Hrs: 10 a.m.-5:30 p.m., closed Sun. & Hols.

Opened by Mr. Hattori of Seikō watch fame, the store features mostly imported and always expensive merchandise. For cheap thrills, check out their window display; it's changed every 40 days at an average cost of ¥2,500,000 (U.S.$9,000). [M-8]

Fashion Buildings

A cross between department stores and arcades, "fashion buildings" are Japan's high-rise answer to the sprawling shopping malls of America. Owned by department stores or real estate companies, boutique space is rented out for a share of the profits. There are hundreds of such buildings in Tokyo, though with most it's a case of "if you've seen one you've seen them all". The best have a certain distinctive character and a good selection of quality merchandise.

PARCO: 15-1 Udagawachō, Shibuya-ku. Tel: 464-5111. Hrs: 10 a.m.-8 p.m., daily.

By far the best of the fashion buildings, Parco comes in three parts: **Part 1** has good cheap boutiques in the basement, **Part 2** offers one-stop shopping for Japanese designers, **Part 3** specializes in interiors. A division of Seibu department store, Parco is predictably innovative. The top floor of Part 1 is **Seibu Theater**, used for plays and performances, in Part 3 is **Space Part 3** for exhibitions. [M-3]

LA FORET: 1-11-6 Jingūmae, Shibuya-ku. Tel: 475-0411. Hrs: 11 a.m.-8 p.m., daily.

Quintessentially Harajuku in spirit, La Foret is the home-away-from-home for thousands of trendy Japanese kids. There's a great selection of moderately priced fashion, and a few boutiques of the big designers. On the top floor is the **La Foret Museum** for events and exhibitions. La Foret has two other "museum" spaces, the **La Foret Īkura 800, 500**, and the **Akasaka La Foret**. Essentially rental halls used for fashion shows and trade exhibitions, there are on occasion interesting contemporary performances and concerts. [M-4]

FROM 1ST: 5-3-10 Minami-Aoyama, Minato-ku. Hours and holidays vary with each shop.

Small and somewhat exclusive, From 1st is an interesting building designed by architect Yamashita Kazumasa. Boutiques include Issey Miyake, Comme des Garçons' Tricot, and Matsuda's Nicole. **Cafe Figaro** on the 1st floor has good cappuccino, and **Le Poisson Rouge** in the basement has inexpensive French food. [M-5]

GINZA TO: 5-4-9 Ginza, Chūō-ku. Tel: 11:30 a.m.-8:30 p.m. daily.

Part of the Ginza "fashion" renaissance, the To building gets points for its fashion merchandise and its fashionable Italianesque interiors. Shops include designer Junko Shimada, and brands Jun and George Sand. On the 5th floor is an aspiring Italian cafe "**it's**" (open from 11 a.m.-11 p.m.)—not haute cuisine but reasonable prices for Ginza. [M-8]

BELL COMMONS: 2-14-6 Kita-Aoyama, Minato-ku. Tel: 475-8111. Hrs: 11 a.m.-8 p.m., daily.

No major surprises in store here. The first floor has a good selection of accessories and hats. On the 8th floor is the **Aoyama Healthy Studio** (Tel: 475-8181) offering classes in yoga, aerobics, and other dance classes, aikidō, tai-chi, etc. The restaurant floor has a branch of **Sushi Sei** [M-5].

BELLE VIE AKASAKA: 3-16 Akasaka, Minato-ku. Tel: 588-5121. Hrs: 11 a.m.-8:30 p.m., closed the 3rd Wed. of Apr. and Oct.

More Japanese designers. Located above Akasaka-mitsuke subway station. [M-6]

STUDIO ALTA: 3-24-Shinjuku, Shinjuku-ku. Tel: 350-5500. Hrs: 11 a.m.-8 p.m., closed the 1st, 2nd, and 3rd Mon. of each month.

Most notable for the huge 11.5 by 8.6 meter video screen built into the front of the building. It could be a scene from "Blade Runner". On the 7th floor is a television studio where the famous comedian "Tamori" films his popular show "Waratte ī to mo". The building is otherwise only marginally interesting. [M-7]

Bargain Sales—Twice a year the department stores and fashion buildings have huge bargain sales to clear the store for the next season's merchandise. The large department stores have major sales in February, August, and December.

PARCO is usually the first fashion building to have a sale. Offering discounts up to 50%, their sale on winter clothes starts the 2nd Friday in January, on summer clothes from the 2nd Friday in July. Both last one week. The other fashion buildings follow.

Rental *kimono* and formal wear are put on sale at DAIMARU Department Store in March and September. This sale is great for cheap wedding *kimono* and funny men's tuxedos.

Special Buildings

Following is a list of special-interest buildings.

AXIS: 5-17-1 Roppongi, Minato-ku. Hours vary with each shop, but most close on Mon.

Subtitled "Living-Design-Concept", the Axis building was opened in 1983 with interior design as a general theme. Includes shops for furniture, lighting, high tech hardware, home accessories, **Nuno** for incredible fabrics, **Kissō** for lacquerware and ceramics (also Japanese food in their small restaurant), **A Tantôt** a French restaurant with a terrace, and four exhibition galleries. [M-1]

WAVE: 6-2-27 Roppongi, Minato-ku. Tel: 408-0111. Hrs: 11 a.m.-9 p.m. daily.

Ostensibly an enormous record, video, and book store, Wave is an extravagant demonstration of the applications of new technology in the search for pleasure and personal satisfaction. The store is a branch of Seibu and a perfect illustration of its parent company's policy of "educating" consumers. Wave is the largest and most automated record store in Tokyo, with a customer access computerized record reference system on the 1st floor, and their **Sound Bank** with 200 top songs on cassettes hooked up to 8 sets of headphones. **Studio Tech** on the 4th floor will custom design audio-visual ambient environments for the home. On the 12th floor is **Art Vivant** for art books, and **Tramart** selling **Tra** magazine and the work of young Tokyo artists and musicians. The top 3 floors are a 48 track recording studio, and computer graphics lab. In the basement is **Cine Vivant**, a movie theater with a late 9 p.m. show (Fri. & Sat.). Check the holographic image of the Buddhist tutelary diety "*Jizō*" by the back door. [M-1]

TŌKYŪ HANDS: 12-18 Udagawachō, Shibuya-ku. Tel: 476-5461. Hrs: 10 a.m.-8 p.m., closed the 2nd and 3rd Wed. of the month.

Eight floors of merchandise for crafts, hobbies, home improvements, etc. The store is almost always crowded. Tōkyū Hands will open a new and larger store in Ikebukuro in fall 1984. [M-3] Ikebukuro branch: Tel: 980-6111. Hrs: 10 a.m.-8 p. m., closed the 2nd and 3rd Thur.

SUNSHINE CITY: 3-1-1 Higashi-Ikebukuro, Toshima-ku. Tel: 989-3331. Hrs: Shops 10 a.m.-8 p.m., daily.

Built on the site of the former Sugamo Prison, Sunshine City is an enormous complex that includes a branch of **Mitsukoshi** department store, **Alpa** fashion building, the **Ancient Orient Museum**, the **Sunshine Theater**, exhibition halls, a culture center for art and sports classes, a branch of the **Tokyo Immigration Office**, a **Prince Hotel**, a planetarium and aquarium, and lots of junk food restaurants. Planned as a cultural focal point for the Ikebukuro area, it's a favorite playground for suburbanites from the north. [M-18]

Arcades

Japan has a rather long history of arcade shopping. In the *Meiji* period, when department stores in the developmental stages were still checking in, and occasionally, losing, hundreds of pairs of shoes a day, arcades were a more convenient way to shop. At one time there were over 20 throughout the city.

There are still a number of arcades in Tokyo, though now most of them have literally gone underground. The basements of major train stations such as **Tokyo Station** (the largest in Asia) and **Shinjuku** have miles of shops serving commuters on the way home. Merchandise is usually a mixed bag of fashion, food, cosmetics, books, and electronics.

Most major hotels have arcades geared to tourists who don't know any better than to buy there. The following three do have some interesting shops:

IMPERIAL HOTEL ARCADE—not to be confused with the new tower full of imported merchandise, this one is in the basement of the old wing. Good shops include **Yaya**—for ceramics and glassware, pearl shops (you can bargain), and two well known but expensive antique shops: **Odawara Shōten**, and **Mayuyama & Co.** Most shops open from 9 or 9:30 a.m. until 7 p.m. daily. [M-10]

HOTEL ŌKURA—Antique shops: **Mildred Warder Ltd.**, and **Yokoyama Inc.**, contemporary prints in **Franell Gallery**. Most shops are open from 9 or 10 a.m. until 6:30 p.m. and close on Sun. & Hols. [M-11]

HOTEL NEW ŌTANI—Various good but expensive arts and antique shops. Most shops open from 10 a.m.-6 p.m. daily. [M-6]

The best arcades are:

AMEYOKO: 4-7-8 Ueno, Taitō-ku. Hours vary with each shop, but most open from 10:30 a.m.-7 p.m., and close on Wed.

The last of Tokyo's post-war black markets, Ameyoko feels more like Hong Kong than Japan. An antiseptic new building houses the spill over from the old shops beneath the train tracks. There are hundreds of shops and it is one of the cheapest places to buy cosmetics and fresh food. Some shops will bargain a bit. [M-13]

INTERNATIONAL ARCADE: 1-7-23 Uchisaiwaichō, Chiyoda-ku. Tel: 591-2764. Hrs: 10 a.m.-7 p.m. Mon.-Sat., 10 a.m.-6 p.m. Sun. and Hols.

A tourist oriented arcade with some good shops including **Hayashi Kimono** for old and new *kimono*. Other shops sell pearls, electronics (tax-free), etc. Most will bargain somewhat. [M-10]

Tax-Free Stores

Most tourist publications, maps, and guide books will direct you to the big tax-free stores around the city. They do a lot of advertising, which they can well afford with the profits they make selling over-priced, shoddy goods to unsuspecting tourists. The definitive "tourist trap", tax-free stores offer only passably acceptable deals on export models of Japanese electronics. But most electronics stores in Akihabara have their own tax-free departments where the prices are usually lower. The worst buys at tax-free centers are the Japanese souvenirs. Why buy a cheap polyester *kimono* there when you can get a beautiful antique silk one for the same price at **Hayashi kimono**, or even cheaper at one of the Sunday flea markets. We recommend you do not shop at these stores.

If you are buying anything tax-free, you must present your passport and fill out a form called a "Record of Purchase of Commodities Tax-Exempt for Export", and then sign a "Covenant of Purchase of Commodities Tax-Exempt of Ultimate Export" form. The store will provide both. Attach the first form to your passport and show the form and article to customs officials when leaving Japan.

Some of the items that can be purchased tax-free are: precious stones, pearls, articles made of precious metal, items plated or coated with precious metal, tortoise-shell, coral ware, amber products, ivory ware, rifles, cameras, projectors, television sets, and other electrical goods.

Wholesale Markets

There are a few specialized wholesale market districts in the city that will also sell retail. Since the shops are generally concentrated along a single street, once you find the area you won't need the names of specific shops. We have given the name of the nearest station and information for which map to use. Most shops open early in the morning through early afternoon and close on Sundays and holidays.

Asakusabashi—Kuramae—between the Sōbu Line and Toei-Asakusa Line's Asakusabashi Stations.

Toys, model kits, party favors, novelties, costumes, and seasonal decorations (e.g. plastic cherry tree boughs). [M-24]

Kappabashi—Tawaramachi Station on the Ginza Line (in the Asakusa area about 5 minute walk from Sensōji Temple).

Plastic and wax restaurant food models, restaurant supplies, including *sushi* chef costumes. [M-12]

Nippori—Nippori Station on the JNR Yamanote Line.

Toys and cheap, unsophisticated kid's sweets and snack foods popular until about ten years ago. Most shops close the 3rd Tue. of the month. The area also has a wholesale fabrics and sewing notions' market. [M-13]

Tsukiji Fish Market—5-2 Tsukiji, Chūō-ku.

Hrs: Outer market from 5:30 a.m.-2 p.m. (some shops close at noon), closed Sun. and Hols.

Tokyo's famous fish market. The general public is not supposed to enter the wholesale market area, but if you act like you belong, you probably won't get stopped. The outer retail market is open to all, and on the 2nd Sunday of the month there is a special morning market for the public with discounts of 20-30%. There are a number of cheap *sushi* restaurants in the area that open from 6 a.m.-1 p.m. to serve the hungry fish buyers. True *sushi* fans shouldn't miss the chance to breakfast on the freshest fish in town. [M-22]

Kanda Fruit and Vegetable Market—4-14-1 Soto Kanda, Chiyoda-ku. Hrs: 6 a.m.-9 a.m., closed Sun & Hols. You can only buy in bulk quantities here. [M-14]

FASHION

Suddenly in the 80's Japan made it on the international fashion map. The *kimono* clad image shifted to an image defined by the work of designers such as Miyake Issey, Kawakubo Rei of "Comme des Garçons" and Yamamoto Yōji of "Y's". Yet Louis Vuitton and Gucci bags are more common than either *kimono* or "Comme des Garçons" and you could probably find at least one of every possible fashion variable somewhere in town. Although fashion is as diverse in Japan as anywhere in the world, there are three major "schools" of fashion thought.

"Trad", a Japanese abbreviation of "traditional", is the dominant fashion faction. The definitive style of *"sararīman"* (salary men), "O.L." (office ladies), and college students, it encompasses everything from plaids to button-down collars, navy blue suits, pleated skirts, designer bags and scarves, as well as those ubiquitous sweatshirts with misspelled, meaningless English.

In second place is the *"kawai-i"* school. Japanese for "cute", the word *"kawai-i"* constitutes a good 50% of the working vocabulary of most high school girls in Harajuku. The "cute" look is predictably pastel, pearls, fuzzy sweaters, gathered skirts, ribbons and lace.

But most interesting is what, for convenience, we'll call the "New Japan Style"—the internationally known Japanese fashion linked to the names of Issey, et. al. While within this group there is considerable diversity, the overall trend is toward unconventional shapes and radical fashion theory.

The international success of the "Japan Style" has spurred incredible creativity in the domestic fashion scene. Selections are great, prices can be either high or low, and quality in even the inexpensive merchandise is exceptional. Size can be a problem however. Shirt sleeves and pants lengths are often too short, and all those terrific cheap shoes are probably too small. There is a size conversion chart in "Appendix".

Designer Boutiques

Following is a selective list of Japanese designers and the locations of their best boutiques. Most boutiques are located in one of the department stores or fashion buildings listed in the previous sections. For boutiques in other locations we have listed the address and opening hours.

108 SHOPPING

• Designers Women's

AKIKO SAKAIZUMI—has a boutique in N.Y. called "Roppongi" that sells her "sono ichi" line. The designs are bright, colorful and fun casuals. Moderately priced.
—In the **Lene** boutiques: La Foret Harajuku B1., Tel: 475-0471. [M-4]

BOUTIQUE YŪYA—by Nagahata Yūya. Contemporary designs made of antique silk *kimono*. Unusual day and evening wear, each piece one of a kind. The boutique is located in the guest house of an old Buddhist temple near Roppongi. Call ahead.
—3-10-12 Moto-Azabu, Minato-ku. Tel: 408-8749. Hrs: 11:30 a.m.-6 p.m. Mon.-Sat., or by appointment. [M-1]

BIGI—by Inaba Yoshie. Designs are a Japanese interpretation of American styles from the 30's and 40's.
—In the Shibuya Parco Part 2, 5th Fl. Tel: 476-2088. [M3]

COMME DES GARÇONS — by Kawakubo Rei. The most unconventional of the major designers, she has four lines: **Comme des Garçons** for women, **Homme** for men, **Robe de Chambre** for lounge and sleepwear, and **Tricot** for knits.
—**Women's**: Shibuya Parco Part 1, 3rd Fl., Tel: 496-2750 [M-3], and From 1st Bldg. 2nd Fl., Tel: 499-4370. [M-5] Hrs: 11 a.m.-8 p.m. daily. **Robe de Chambre**: Axis Bldg. 2nd Fl., Tel: 587-2436. Hrs: 12 noon-7 p.m., closed Mon. [M-1], and Shibuya Parco Part 2, 1st Fl., Tel: 476-2919. **Tricot**: Matsuya Department Store Ginza, 1st Fl. Tel: 567-1211. [M-8]

HALF MOON—the women's line by Tsunoda Yukiko of Men's Bigi. Very trendy, fun clothes.
—La Foret, Harajuku, 3rd Fl. Tel: 403-9450. [M-4]

HANAE MORI—designs haute couture and a prêt à porter line called **Vivid**. Best known for her evening wear. [M-5]
—Hanae Mori Bldg., 3-6-1 Kita-Aoyama, Minato-ku. Tel: 400-3301. Hrs: 10:30 a.m.-7 p.m.

HIROKO KOSHINO—basically European inspired sophisticated casual fashions. Her evening wear often has a more Japanese feeling.
—Daimaru Department Store 3rd Fl., Tel: 212-8011. [M-10]

HIROMI YOSHIDA—Designs a line called **Clove-vs-Cloves**. Nothing extraordinary but nice, feminine, slightly retro ready to wear. [M-2]
—3-21-22 Nishi-Aazabu, Minato-ku. Tel: 403-0857. Hrs: 11 a.m.-8 p.m., closed Sun.

HITOMI ŌKAWA—has two lines: the older line **Milk** belongs the "*Kawai-i*" school, her new line **Obscure Desire of Bourgeoisie** is closer to "Japan Style", loose fitting but somewhat sexy.
—**Obscure Desire of Bourgeoisie**: 6-10-12 Jingūmae, Shibuya-ku. Tel: 409-2674. Hrs: 12 noon-8 p.m. daily. **Milk**: 4-30-10 Jingūmae, Shibuya-ku. Tel: 403-6555. Hrs: 12 a.m.-8 p.m. daily. [M-4]

ISSEY MIYAKE—definitive "Japan Style", his designs border on elegance. His most interesting lines are: women's, men's, **Plantation**, and **Issey Sports**.
—**Women's**: From 1st Bldg., 1st Fl. Tel: 499-6476. Hrs: 12 noon-8 p.m. daily. [M-5] Shibuya Parco Part 2, 3rd Fl. Tel: 464-6626. [M-3] **Issey Sports**: Shibuya Parco Part 2, 6th Fl., Tel: 496-0438 and La Foret Harajuku 1st Fl., Tel: 478-7698. **Plantation**: Tessenkai Bldg. B1 Fl., 4-21-29 Minami-Aoyama, Minato-ku. Tel: 423-1408. Hrs: 12 noon-8 p.m. daily. [M-5]

JUNKO KOSHINO—best known for her knits, designs are sophisticated European style sportswear.
—Ikebukuro Seibu Department Store 3rd Fl., Tel: 981-0111. [M-18]

JUNKO SHIMADA—The only Japanese designer who does truly sexy clothes. She lives most of the year in France. Her brand name is "49th Ave.".
—Aobadai Terasu, 1-1-4 Aobadai, Meguro-ku. Tel: 463-2346. Hrs: 11 a.m.-8 p.m., closed Mon. [M-20], also has small boutiques in the Ginza To Bldg., 4th Fl., Tel: 572-7381 [M-8], and Belle Vie Akasaka 4th Fl., Tel: 588-5049. [M-6]

JURGEN LEHL—Originally a fabric designer, Lehl's work shows a sensitivity to fabric and color. Designs are elegantly casual, very wearable and rather Japanese in feeling. Also has an exquisite line of sheets, towels, and sleepwear called **Tint**.
—Harajuku main shop: 1-13-18 Jingūmae, Shibuya-ku. Tel: 405-9737. Hrs: 12 noon-8 p.m. daily [M-4]. Also Shibuya Parco Part 2, 3rd Fl., Tel: 476-5722. [M-3] **Tint**: Axis Bldg. 2nd Fl., Tel: 587-2404. Hrs: 11 a.m.-7 p.m. closed Mon. [M-1]

SHOPPING 109

KANSAI YAMAMOTO—Colorful and theatrical sportswear with a Japanese twist.
—3-28-7 Jingūmae, Shibuya-ku. Tel: 478-1958. Hrs: 11 a.m.-8 p.m. daily. [M-4]
MADAME HANAI—by Hanai Yukio. Well made sophisticated ready to wear. Beautiful evening wear. Also a line of casual rather "Japan Style" designs called "**Geek**".
—Roi Bldg. 2nd Fl., 5-5-1 Roppongi, Minato-ku. Tel: 404-5791. Hrs: 11 a.m.-8 p.m., closed the 3rd Thur. of the month. [M-1]
MATSUDA—see Madame Nicole
MADAME NICOLE—Designer Matsuda's line goes by his name in New York and Nicole in Japan. The designs have a retro-American influence but with definite Japanese sensibilities.
—Nicole Bldg. 1st Fl., 3-1-25 Jingūmae, Shibuya-ku. Tel: 478-0998. Hrs: 11 a.m.-8 p.m. daily. [M-4]
NICOLE—Shibuya Parco Part 2, 5th Fl., Tel: 476-2133. [M-3]
PINK HOUSE—by Kaneko Isao. Very popular "*kawai-i*" fashions. Lots of storybook prints and pastels.
—La Foret Harajuku 3rd Fl., Tel: 404-5248. [M-4]
STUDIO-V—by Irie Sueo. Colorful, young fashions by this former designer for Kenzō. The clothes are always trendy, often with a playfully sexy twist. Great accessories.
—Shibuya Parco Part 2, 4th Fl. Tel: 476-1620. [M-3]
—Hanae Mori Bldg. 1st Fl. Tel: 406-3177 [M-5]
Y'S—by Yamamoto Yōji. Another big name in contemporary Japanese fashion. Has three interesting lines: **Y's** for men, women and **Workshop**.
—**Y's** super position, 5-3-6 Minami Aoyama, Minato-ku. Tel: 486-5314. Hrs: 11 a.m.-9 p.m. daily. [off Map]
YUKI TORII—sophisticated European style sportswear.
—5-7-16 Ginza, Chūō-ku. Tel: 574-8701. Hrs: 11:30 a.m.-7:30 p.m. [M-8]
TOKIO KUMAGAI—Cederstone Villa B-1, 15-5 Hachiyama-cho, Shibuya-ku. Tel: 477-2613. Hrs: 11 a.m.-8 p.m., daily. One of the best shoe shops in town, there is also a line of mens'

A masked model wears fashions by Miyake Issey

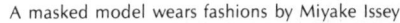

and womens' clothing (often of leather). Designer Tokio is internationally known for his designs for Fiorucci and now has shops in New York and Paris. [M-20]

• Men's Designers and Boutiques

Unfortunately for most men, shopping for fashionable clothes in Tokyo will be somewhat disappointing—the clothes are almost uniformly too small. This is particularly true for "straight" clothes. The wilder designs are often free sized, and easier to fit.

ISSEY MIYAKE MEN Shibuya: Parco Part 2 [M-3] B1. Tel: 476-5720. Aoyama: Tessenkai Bldg. 1st Fl., 4-21-29 Minami-Aoyama, Minato-ku. Tel: 423-1407. Hrs: 12 noon-8 p.m., daily. [M-5]
ISSEY MIYAKE "THE SHIRTS" Hamilton Shirts 3-2-5 Kita-Aoyama, Minato-ku. Tel: 475-1971. Hrs: 11 a.m.-7:30 p.m., closed Mon. [M-5]
"Y'S" FOR MEN by Yamamoto Yōji. Shibuya Parco Part 1 [M-3] 5th Fl. Tel: 496-9459.
COMME DES GARÇONS HOMME by Kawakubo Rei, 5-12-3 Minami-Aoyama, Minato-ku. Tel: 498-0921. Hrs: 11 a.m.-8 p.m., closed Mon. [M-5] Shibuya Parco Part 2 [M-3] B1. Tel: 496-2755. Hrs: 10 a.m.-8 p.m., daily.
MONSIEUR NICOLE by Kobayashi Yukio. Nicole Bldg. 1st Fl., 3-1-25 Jingūmae, Shibuya-ku. Tel: 478-0998. Hrs: 11 a.m.-8 p.m., daily. [M-5]
FICCE UOMO by Konishi Yoshiyuki. Daikan-yama Parkside Village 1st Fl., 9-8 Sarugakuchō, Shibuya-ku. Tel: 464-1722. Hrs: 10 a.m.-9 p.m. Hand knits in natural earth tones. [M-20]
PASHU by Hosokawa Shin. 8-11-37 Akasaka, Minato-ku. Tel: 479-0196. Hrs: 12 noon-7:30 p.m., daily. Very modern, monotone fashions. [M-5]
ARRSTON VOLAJU by Satō Takanobu. 3-24-22 Nishi-Azabu, Minato-ku. Tel: 401-7543. Hrs: 11:30 a.m.-8:30 p.m. Fun, slightly off-beat clothes. [M-2]
TAKEO KIKUCHI 6-6-22 Minami-Aoyama, Minato-ku. Tel: 486-6607. Hrs: 12 noon-8 p.m. Play clothes for grown-ups. (Kikuchi Takeo was formerly designer of "Men's Bigi") [M-5]
GRASS MEN'S by Saitō Jun, Shibuya Parco Part 2 [M-3], B1 Tel: 463-6656. Sophisticated, but not stuffy clothes.
MEN'S TINOLAS Shinjuku Marui "Young" Bldg. [M-7] 5th Fl. Tel: 354-0101. Uni-sex casual wear in your basic Japanese grey.
JUN "MURATA" Jun Murata Bldg. 3rd Fl. 3-3-10 Roppongi, Minato-ku. Tel: 401-8288. Hrs: 11 a.m.-11 p.m., daily. The Murata line designed by Tamura Yumiko is one of the only men's lines manufactured in western sizes. [M-1]
DOMON Shibuya Parco Part 2 [M-3] B1. Tel: 476-4488. Hrs: 10 a.m.-8 p.m., daily.
PERSONS 3-28-8 Jingūmae, Shibuya-ku. Tel: 401-5524. Hrs: 11 a.m.-8 p.m., daily. Casual, colorful clothes. [M-4]
BEAMS Nua Harajuku Bldg., 3-24-7 Jingūmae, Shibuya-ku. Tel: 470-3948. Hrs: 11 a.m.-8 p.m., daily. Some "Trad" styles, some good, basic casual wear. [M-4]

Cheap Fashion

A common misconception of foreign shoppers is that fashion in Japan is outrageously expensive. Nothing could be further from the truth. Expensive fashion is plentiful, some of it, especially imported merchandise, is ridiculously so. But on the other end of the price scale is an abundance of fashion options—in a range of styles and designs far wider, and far better made, than you'll find in the U.S. or Europe.

The major areas for cheap fashion shopping are Shinjuku, Shibuya, and Harajuku. Harajuku is probably the best and most fun. There is a wide selection of clothes that tends to be wild, or inspired by the work of the major designers. The back streets are full of tiny boutiques.

Harajuku's Takeshita-dōri [M-4] is the most famous—the merchandise spills out onto the sidewalks in front of the shops enticing you in. The basement floors of most fashion buildings are another good bargain shopping spot. Most of the shops listed below are best for rather "alternative" fashion. Two large supermarket-department stores Daiē and Seiyū have also been included. Both are located slightly out of town but are very cheap places to shop for food, fashion or furniture.

DAIĒ 4-1 Himon'ya, Meguro-ku. Tel: 710-1111. Hrs: 10 a.m.-7 p.m. closed Wed. (Gakugei-Daigaku station/Tōkyū Tōyoko line.) [off Map]

SEIYŪ 6-27-25 Minami-Ōi, Shinagawa-ku. Tel: 768-1211. Hrs: 10 a.m.-7 p.m. closed Wed. (Ōmori station east exit/Keihin Tōhoku line.) [off Map]

HARAJUKU PLAZA Central Apartment B1, 4-30-6 Jingūmae, Shibuya-ku. Hrs: 11 a.m.-8 p.m., closed the 3rd Tue. A whole collection of odd shops are located here, most sell clothes, but some deal in strange housewares and accessories. [M-4]

BUNKAYA ZAKKATEN 1-9-5 Jinnan, Shibuya-ku. Tel: 461-0985. Hrs: 11 a.m.-8 p.m., closed the 20th of each month. This shop sells a wide range of curios and clothing, much of it pure kitsch and very cheap. There are a number of other shops selling similar goods on either side of Bunkaya (which means literally "culture shop"). [M-3]

GARAGE PARADISE 6-18-17 Jingūmae, Shibuya-ku. Tel: 499-5444. Hrs: 10 a.m.-8 p.m., daily. A favorite shopping spot for Tokyo's James Dean look-alikes, this shop designs original imitation 50's clothing. Their shirts are particularly great. [M-4]

PINK DRAGON 1-23-23 Shibuya, Shibuya-ku. Tel: 498-2577, Hrs: 10 a.m.-8 p.m., daily. By the same company that started Cream Soda (now closed) and Garage Paradise, this shop stocks clothing, housewares, and accessories—all copies of 50's antiques. The building itself is a huge monument to nostalgia, and has a great coffee shop on the 2nd floor. [M-3]

LAST SCENE 1-8-14 Jingūmae, Shibuya-ku. Tel: 404-4866. Hrs: 11 a.m.-8 p.m., daily. A great place to find cheap, almost-knock-offs, of the big designers' work. Women's, some men's. [M-4]

BACK TICK Harajuku Plaza. Tel: 470-5025. Hrs: 12 noon-8 p.m., closed the 3rd Tue. Very "progressive" clothing and accessories, all original designs. This shop is frequented by some of the more outrageous fashion stylists in Tokyo. [M-4]

SURPLUS 6-18-16 Jingūmae, Shibuya-ku. Tel: 409-0258. Hrs: 11 a.m.-8 p.m., daily. Original utility clothing, they say "designed by craftsmen for craftsmen". [M-4]

TOKYO-DŌ Kawaai Bldg. 103, 1-17-9 Jinnan, Shibuya-ku. Tel: 464-3041. Hrs: 11 a.m.-8 p.m., daily. Cheap clothes and kitsch, everything from jumpers (¥500), badges, sunglasses, even mannequins. [M-3]

SABBY GENTEEL Avenue Side 2nd Fl., 3-9 Sarugakuchō, Shibuya-ku. Tel: 461-5029. Hrs: 12 noon-8 p.m. (until 7 p.m. Sun. & Hols.) closed Mon. The shop has mainly merchandise for interiors, but also some clothing, most of which is designed by Ishihara Sachiko. Not extremely cheap, but are reasonably priced, well made casual clothes. Her line is also sold in Base Unit in Parco Part 1 on B1. (This new boutique also stocks design by other interesting new designers.) [M-20]

DEP'T STORE Jingūmae Kōpo B1, 6-25-8 Jingūmae, Shibuya-ku. Tel: 499-2225. Hrs: 12 noon-9 p.m. (Hols. until 7 p.m.), closed the 3rd Fri. of the month. The largest selection of secondhand and antique western-style clothes in Tokyo. [M-4]

ELECTRONICS AND CAMERAS

The field of electronics is one area in which the Japanese have attained undisputed world leadership, much of the well publicized "Japanese miracle" being based on achievements in this area. But while Japanese products are found almost everywhere in the world, nearly 80% of the consumer electronics market is domestic. Competition for a share of this market is relentless, and a company that can survive at home is almost guaranteed success abroad.

Quality control is one of the hallmarks of the Japanese consumer electronics industry. Workers take great pride in their jobs, a hold-over from artisan traditions with a little *samurai* Confucian loyalty ethics thrown in. Domestic success is determined by quality, competitive pricing, and, most importantly, innovation. The Japanese consumer is easily swayed by the attraction of new technology. New, slightly improved models will be snapped up while last year's machine is unceremoniously trashed in perfect running order.

It's worth noting, however, that despite the competition at home, prices for Japanese products here are not much different from those for the same products overseas. Sometimes, they're even higher. Partially due to a chronically under valued yen, another reason is the pervasive Japanese belief that expensive means good. If you're planning on making a major purchase while in Japan, check the prices at home first.

The distribution system is now so advanced that products are almost simultaneously introduced in both domestic and overseas markets. Some products are manufactured solely for domestic use, but since voltage in Japan is different, you should buy only export models of any sophisticated equipment. Most big shops in Akihabara have special export departments that also allow duty-free purchasing. If you're just interested in looking at the latest electronic toys, most manufacturers have showrooms in convenient locations where consumers can go and play.

Showrooms
SONY SHOWROOM Sony Bldg. 3rd & 4th Fl., 5-3-1 Ginza, Chūō-ku. Tel: 573-2371. Hrs: 11 a.m.-8 p.m., daily. Audio, video, and computers. [M-8]
TECHNICS GINZA (National Electronics) Ginza Core Bldg. 7th Fl., 5-8-20 Ginza, Chūō-ku. Tel: 572-3871. Hrs: 11 a.m.-7 p.m., Mon. Audio, video. [M-8]
TŌSHIBA GINZA SEVEN Tōshiba Ginza Seven Bldg. 3rd Fl., 7-9-19 Ginza, Chūō-ku. Tel: 571-5951. Hrs: 11 a.m.-7 p.m., closed Wed. and the 2nd & 4th Tue. Audio, video. [M-8]
HITACHI LO-D PLAZA Yūrakuchō Food Bldg. 1st Fl., 2-2 Nishi-Ginza, Chūō-ku. Tel: 567-8073. Hrs: 10:30 a.m.-8 p.m., daily. Audio, video, and computers. [M-8]
MITSUBISHI DENKI SHOWROOM San'ai Dream Center 5th-7th Fl., 5-7-2 Ginza, Chūō-ku. Tel: 571-9426. Hrs: 11 a.m.-8 p.m., closed Tue. Audio, video. [M-8]
VICTOR VIDEO CENTER Kazan Bldg. 1st Fl., 3-2-4 Kasumigaseki, Chiyoda-ku. Tel: 580-4264. Hrs: 10 a.m.-6 p.m. (until 5 p.m. on Sat.), closed Sun. & Hols. Video. [M-11]

PIONEER SHOWROOM 1-4-1 Meguro, Meguro-ku. Tel: 494-1111. Hrs: 10:30 a.m.-7 p.m., closed Sun. & Hols. Audio and laser disc technology. [M-19]
N.E.C. SHOWROOM Hibiya City, Hibiya Kokusai Bldg. B1, 2-2-3 Uchisaiwaichō, Chiyoda-ku. Tel: 595-0511. Hrs: 10 a.m.-7 p.m., daily. Computers. [M-10]
O.A. CENTER N.S. Bldg. 5th Fl., 2-4-1 Nishi-Shinjuku, Shinjuku-ku. Tel: 348-1128. Hrs: 9:15 a.m.-5:15 p.m., closed Sun. & Hols. Computers, hard & software, from 15 companies. [M-7]
TECHNO CULTURE CENTER MEDIA BUM Shūwa Shiba Park Bldg. 1st Fl., 2-4-1 Shiba-kōen, Minato-ku. Tel: 433-3181. Hrs: 10 a.m.-7 p.m., closed the 4th & 5th Sun. Carries most domestic and foreign computer and audio lines. (We have not misspelled the name) [M-11]

Electronics and Computers
• **Akihabara** [M-14]

Akihabara is famous as the electronics discount district of Tokyo. Though by no means the only area for cheap electrical goods, the vast selection of products laid out in one place makes it the most convenient. Prices quoted by the shops are usually discounted from the manufacturer's suggested retail price. In some shops you can talk the price down even further. If you're making a large purchase, you should insist on it.

The district has a special Electronics Fair from the middle of June through the middle of July and again from the end of November through the middle of January. Prices during the fair are even cheaper than usual.

There are over a thousand shops in Akihabara, most of which offer more or less the same range of merchandise and prices. It's impossible to miss the larger, general stores, but below is a list of some specialty shops that we thought worthy of mention. Access to Akihabara is by Yamanote Line and the Sōbu Line's Akihabara Station (West Exit), Hibiya Line's Akihabara Station (Exit #3).

RAJIO KAIKAN 1-15-16 Soto-Kanda, Chiyoda-ku. Hrs: 10 a.m.-7 p.m., daily. This is a big building with about 50 shops dealing in audio, radio, video, tapes, second hand articles, etc. Many of the shops on the following list are located here.
TOKYO RAJIO DEPĀTO 1-10-11 Soto-Kanda, Chiyoda-ku. Tel: 251-9173. Hrs: 10 a.m.-7 p.m. (depends on the shop). Another building full of parts shops, mostly dealing with radios.
KIMURA MUSEN Rajio Kaikan 4th Fl. Tel: 251-7391. Hrs: 10 a.m.-7 p.m., daily. Everything for audio fans, from cartridges to speakers. They even sell the screws to put together your own cabinets. Cheap second hand Macintosh amps.
SATŌ MUSEN 1-11-11 Soto-Kanda, Chiyoda-ku. Tel: 253-5871. Hrs: 10 a.m.-7 p.m., daily. A very wide selection (over 130 types of headphones alone) with full listening facilities.
SHŌJIN SHŌKAI Rajio Kaikan 4th Fl. Tel: 251-0797. Hrs: 11 a.m.-7 p.m., daily. A first rate secondhand dealer for over thirty years.
HIROSE MUSEN AUDIO CENTER 1-12-1 Soto-Kanda, Chiyoda-ku. Tel: 255-5931. Hrs: 10 a.m.-6:50 p.m., closed Thur. Enormous premises, wide selection.
F. SHŌKAI Rajio Kaikan 7th Fl. Tel: 251-2301. Hrs: 10 a.m.-7 p.m. (until 6:30 p.m. on Sun. & Hols.), daily. Discount video tape and audio cassettes.
ROCKET HONTEN 1-14-1 Sakumachō, Kanda, Chiyoda-ku. Tel: 257-0606. Hrs: 10 a.m.-8 p.m. An electronics superstore.
FUJIONKYŌ "MAIKON" CENTER RAM Rajio Kaikan 7th Fl. 1-15-16 Soto-Kanda, Chiyoda-ku. Tel: 255-7846. Hrs: 10 a.m.-7 p.m. (until 6:30 p.m. on Sun. & Hols), daily. Computer store stocking both domestic brands and Apple.

The following three shops sell parts, mostly for computers, and kits for building IBM and Apple compatible computers.
HONDA TSŪSHŌ Tokyo Rajio Depāto B1. Tel: 251-7611
WAKAMATSU TSŪSHŌ Tokyo Rajio Depāto 4F. Tel: 255-5064
MORI PARTS SHOPS 1-17 Sakumachō, Kanda, Chiyoda-ku. Tel: 251-0381 [off Map]

- **Other Areas**

DYNAMIC AUDIO Villa Bianca 206, 2-33-12 Jingūmae, Shibuya-ku. Tel: 478-5881. Hrs: 11 a.m.-8 p.m., closed Thur. Secondhand audio and video at incredibly cheap prices. Good discounts on new items too. [M-4]
JŌNAN DENKI 2-19-21 Shibuya, Shibuya-ku. Tel: 499-0550. Hrs: 10 a.m.-7 p.m., closed Wed. Claims to have the lowest prices in Japan. If you find something cheaper elsewhere, they will refund the difference. [M-3]
MAICON BASE GINZA 1-8-21 Ginza, Chūō-ku. Tel: 535-3381. Hrs: 10 a.m.-7 p.m. (until 6 p.m. on the 4th & 5th Fl.), closed Wed. A 9 story computer superstore, one of the biggest in town. [M-8]
FLEX JAPAN 3-3-13 Kita-Aoyama, Minato-ku. Tel: 470-3264. Hrs: 10 a.m.-7 p.m. (until 6 p.m. on Sat. & Sun.) Computer specialist, business oriented. Good secondhand bargains. [M-5]

The next two shops deal primarily with wholesale, but will also sell retail, if somewhat reluctantly. Nothing is on display though, so you must check the merchandise elsewhere in advance and bring a note of the maker and the catalogue number.
MARUBOSHI DENKI 3-7-2 Ueno, Taitō-ku. Tel: 833-4541. Hrs: 9 a.m.-6:30 p.m., closed Sun. & Hols. [M-13]
MARUYU SHŌKAI 3-3-2 Taitō, Taitō-ku. Tel: 835-8843. Hrs: 10:30 a.m.-7 p.m., closed Sun. & Hols. [off Map]

Cameras
- **Shinjuku** [M-7]

Like Akihabara for electronics, Shinjuku is known as the discount camera district. Some shops also sell smaller electrical goods.
YODOBASHI CAMERA (Nishiguchi Honten—West Exit Main Store) 1-11-1 Nishi-Shinjuku, Shinjuku-ku. Tel: 346-1010. Hrs: 9:30 a.m.-8:30 p.m., daily. The largest camera shop in the world, stocking just about everything in production. Cameras and videos at 20-50% off.
CAMERA NO DOI (Nishi-guchi Ni-gōten) 1-18-27 Nishi-Shinjuku, Shinjuku-ku. Tel: 348-2241. Hrs: 10 a.m.-9 p.m. daily. Watch for seasonal special bargain sales.
CAMERA NO SAKURAYA 3-17-2 Shinjuku, Shinjuku-ku. Tel: 354-3636. Hrs: 10 a.m.-8 p.m. daily. Six floors of camera and electrical goods at 20-60% discounts. Special bargains in February.
MIYAMA SHŌKAI 3-32-8 Shinjuku, Shinjuku-ku. Tel: 356-1841. Hrs: 10:30 a.m.-8 p.m. (until 7 p.m. on Sun. & Hols.), daily. New and secondhand cameras, lenses, parts exchange. Popular with professional photographers and semi-pros looking for quality equipment.

- **Ikebukuro** [M-18]

BIC CAMERA 1-11-7 Higashi-Ikebukuro, Toshima-ku. Tel: 988-0002. Hrs: 10 a.m.-8 p.m., daily. Cheapest in Japan, will refund the difference if you find the same article cheaper elsewhere. In addition to cameras, they sell video and audio equipment, tapes, computers, even contact lenses.
CAMERA NO KIMURA 1-18-8 Nishi-Ikebukuro, Toshima-ku. Tel: 981-8437. Hrs: 8 a.m.-8 p.m., daily. Great selection of secondhand cameras.

- **Other Areas**

NITTŌ SHŌJI 5-49-6 Nakano, Nakano-ku. Tel: 387-0111. Hrs: 10 a.m.-8 p.m. (until 7 p.m. on Sun. & Hols.), closed Thur. Reputable dealer for cheap, quality secondhand cameras, lenses and other attachments. [M-26]

TRADITIONAL ARTS AND CRAFTS

In a city where fashion and technology sometimes seem to be a form of new religion, it always comes as a relief to find a tiny shop that still produces by hand the same goods the shop has been famous for since the *Edo* period. The reputation of these shops passes down from generation to generation. A true *Edokko*, the rare born and bred Tokyoite, will know these specialty shops, where *zōri* straw sandals are made with the toes squared-off just as they were in *Edo*, where *kabuki* actors and *geisha* buy their cosmetics, where famous architects still have their lamps designed. These shops, often hundreds of years old, preserve the traditions of quality and fine craftsmanship in simple utilitarian products.

Most are proud and will tell stories of fathers and grandfathers, of how things have changed, of concessions to modern technology. *Zōri*, once made with rope soles are now mass-produced in rubber, hand-bent bamboo lamps are now formed by machines that cannot reproduce the craftsman's spirit. Many of the artisans live behind their shops. Asking one when his day-off is, he replies that he hasn't one. Then his wife corrects him from the back room—the next afternoon they'll close for their grandson's wedding. Another shopkeeper says that since their's is the only such shop left, people come from all over Japan. If they close for a day, those people may have to go home empty-handed.

Though prices sometimes seem modest, sometimes exorbitant, considering the work involved, they're clearly justified. These craftsmen do not get rich from their work, but pride prevents them from selling cheap. One craftsman tells a story of how, once, when a customer complained to his grandfather about the price of a bamboo spoon, the old man broke the spoon in two and offered half of the spoon for half-price. It's not the money that's important, but they only want to sell to people who understand the beauty of their work.

Shops like these are usually found in the *shitamachi* old downtown districts, a traditional home of craftsmen. In the shadow of reinforced concrete buildings that have slowly crept up around them, these proud artisans maintain their old wooden shops. Some finally give up and move away. Others have no one to continue the tradition and the skill dies with the last son. A few will survive in spite of, or maybe because of, the advance of modern technology. Even now, Japanese children of the computer generation have begun to look again to their past.

SHOPPING

In the following section we've selected a variety of arts, crafts and traditional products, given short explanations and listed the best shops for each category. Much of the merchandise from the more famous shops can also be found in department stores, but visiting the shops themselves is part of the pleasure.

General Shops

CRAFTS CENTER Plaza 246 2nd Fl., 3-1-1 Minami-Aoyama, Minato-ku. Tel: 403-2460. Hrs: 10 a.m.-6 p.m., closed Thur. Arts and Crafts from around Japan on display and for sale. [M-5]

KYŌTO CENTER "KYŌ-NOREN" Kyōto Shimbun Ginza Bldg. 1st Fl., 8-2-8. Ginza, Chūō-ku. Tel: 572-6484. Hrs: 11 a.m.-7 p.m. (until 6 p.m. on Sat.), closed Sun. & Hols. Arts and Crafts from Kyōto. [M-8]

ORIENTAL BAZAAR 5-9-13 Jingūmae, Shibuya-ku. Tel: 400-3933. Hrs: 9:30 a.m.-6:30 p.m. closed Thur. Slightly touristy but has a good selection of merchandise including old *kimono*, antiques, prints, etc. [M-4]

BLUE AND WHITE 2-9-2 Azabu-Jūban, Minato-ku. Tel: 451-0537. Hrs: 10 a.m.-6 p.m., (1 p.m.-5 p.m. on Sun.) closed Hols. All the merchandise in this small shop is Japanese blue and white. They have a good selection of textiles, some made up into clothing, cushions, napkins, etc. Other items include pottery, paper, and baskets. [M-1]

Mingei—Folkcrafts

Mingei, literally "people's arts" are enjoying something of a boom in Japan. Now more or less thought of as souvenirs, *mingei* are practical things made simply and strongly for use in everyday life. *Mingei* are deeply rooted in local customs and traditions, with a particular item usually made exclusively by a particular region. A broad range of products falls into the folkcrafts category: toys, kitchen utensils, textiles, clothing, and furniture. Besides the several stores that specialize in *mingei*, there is a terrific museum: the Nihon Mingeikan—Japan Folk Art Museum (See "Museums").

TAKUMI たくみ　中央区銀座8-4-2
8-4-2 Ginza, Chūō-ku. Tel: 571-2017. Hrs: 11 a.m.-7 p.m. (until 5:30 p.m. Hols.), closed Sun. [M-8]

ISHIZUKA いしづか　中央区八重州1-5-20
1-5-20 Yaesu, Chūō-ku. Tel: 275-2991. Hrs: 9:30 a.m.-7:30 p.m., closed Sun. & Hols. A great selection of crafts, one of the only places you can find *mompe*—farmer's cotton pants—from Shikoku Island. Upstairs is a pleasant coffee shop with wooden country-style furniture. [M-9]

TSUKAMOTO つかもと　渋谷区道玄坂1-2-2東急プラザ
Tōkyū Plaza 4th Fl., 1-2-2 Dōgenzaka, Shibuya-ku. Tel: 461-4410. Hrs: 10 a.m.-8 p.m., daily. Small, but well stocked. [M-3]

BINGOYA 備後屋　新宿区若松町10-6
10-6 Wakamatsuchō, Shinjuku-ku. Tel: 202-8778. Hrs: 10 a.m.-7 p.m., closed Mon. Recommended by Amaury St. Gilles, author of a great book on folkcrafts titled "*Mingei*". [off Map]

Edo Gangu—Toys

In the *Edo* period, *gangu* were cheap toys made of paper, wood or clay. Popular shapes were puppets, dolls or animals such as tigers and dogs. In this day of techno-toys, *Edo gangu* are primarily bought as souvenirs by nostalgic grown-ups. They are found in most *mingei* shops.

SUKEROKU 助六　台東区浅草2-3-1
2-3-1 Asakusa, Taitō-ku. Tel: 844-0542. Hrs: 10:30 a.m.-6 p.m., closed Thur. Specialist in miniatures of life in the *Edo* period. [M-12]

Tako—Kites

While in the *Nara* period (710-784) kite making was the rage among the court nobility, by *Edo* kites had become popular children's toys, though adults still participated in hotly contested kite competitions that often ended in a huge brawl. Several times the government outlawed the contests because of this. Hand-painted kites made of *washi* (handmade Japanese paper) can still be bought, and kite fanatics still hold contests at the Tama River on New Year's Day, Children's Day (May 5), and Health-Sports Day (October 10). The Japan Kite Association also has a kite museum in Nihombashi.

HASHIMOTO 橋本　台東区東上野2-2-5
2-2-5 Higashi-Ueno, Taitō-ku. Tel: 841-2661. Hrs: 10 a.m.-7 p.m., closed Sun. Hand-painted kites at this shop founded in 1890 will cost from about ¥800. [M-13]

Koinobori—Carp Banners

While in certain parts of America these have become popular porch decorations, in Japan they're hung from tall poles on Boy's Day in May. Originally used as banners by the *samurai*, they came into use for Boy's Festival during the Sino-Japanese War in the late 19th century. Hopefully all little Japanese boys will grow up to be as strong and persistent as the carp that, fearing nothing, climbs the waterfalls up a stream. *Koinobori* can be bought at most shops selling traditional dolls, and on the 2nd floor of the Oriental Bazaar.

MUSASHIYA SHŌTEN むさしや商店　台東区蔵前1-7-1
1-7-1 Kuramae, Taitō-ku. Tel: 851-5817. Hrs: 9 a.m.-6 p.m., closed Sun. & Hols. The *koinobori* are not usually on display, but they have them in stock. If you call ahead, they'll have them ready to show when you arrive. [M-24]

Ningyō—Dolls

Dolls are one of the most common souvenirs given to foreigners. They have black hair styled in traditional coiffures, and wear *kimono* like Japanese are supposed to—clearly the perfect visual aid for explaining the Japanese to overseas visitors.

The earliest dolls in Japan were talismen, made of paper or straw, used to charm away illness and other misfortunes. A carry-over of this custom is seen in festivals where paper-doll shapes are floated down the river. By the *Edo* period, doll making had become quite advanced. The *bunraku* puppet theater dolls were two-thirds life-size and highly mechanized. Wealthy *Edo* families would often order a doll modeled after a beloved child. Dolls are still popular, though less as playthings than as souvenirs or display objects.

The most common type of dolls are the *Hina-ningyō* representing imperial court figures and displayed during the Girl's Festival in March. *Gogatsu-ningyō* are dolls for Boy's Festival dressed in *samurai* costumes. Other dolls representing figures from various periods of Japanese history are also very popular. Collectively known as *Nihon-ningyō*—Japanese Dolls—some are painted, but most are gorgeously costumed. The most famous are those from Kyōto, called *kyō-ningyō*, and from Fukuoka, called *hakata-ningyō*.

Another popular type are called *kokeshi*, which are painted wooden spindle-like dolls that come in various sizes.

In Asakusabashi a number of wholesale and retail doll shops line a street called Edo-dōri. The most famous are Kyūgetsu, Yoshitoku and Kuramae Ningyō-sha.

KYŪGETSU 久月　台東区柳橋1-20-4
1-20-4 Yanagibashi, Taitō-ku. Tel: 861-5511. Hrs: 9 a.m.-6 p.m., daily. This is one of the biggest doll shops in Japan. [M-24]
GALLERY KONOHANA ギャラリー木の花　港区南青山6-3-12
6-3-12 Minami-Aoyama, Minato-ku. Tel: 407-5757. Hrs: 10:30 a.m.-8 p.m., closed Mon. A small but beautiful selection of *kokeshi* dolls. [M-5]

Washi—Paper

For over 1,200 years the Japanese have been making the best handmade paper in the world. Used in a multitude of ways, paper has long been a "basic" material in Japan. Umbrellas, fans, lanterns, toys are only a few of the common paper products. In the arts, paper is used for painting and calligraphy, and even traditional houses, with their expanses of *shōji*, white paper covered windows and doors, are said to be made of paper and wood.

Though machine-made paper is common now, the best papers are still hand-made. Shops specializing in paper products have "files" of hand-made and often hand-printed papers called *chiyogami*. The shops also carry a wide variety of articles made from paper such as wallets, toys, boxes, lanterns, cards, stationery, and *okaeshi*—a kind of tissue paper used in the tea ceremony and by *kabuki* actors.

ISETATSU いせ辰　台東区谷中2-18-9／渋谷区神宮前3-1-24ソフトタウン青山
2-18-9 Yanaka, Taitō-ku. Tel: 823-1453. Hrs: 10 a.m.-6 p.m., daily. A really beautiful little shop. [M-24] They've opened a small branch store in Aoyama: Soft Town Aoyama Bldg. 1st Fl., 3-1-24 Jingūmae, Shibuya-ku. Tel: 497-5305. Hrs: 11 a.m.-7 p.m., closed 1st, 3rd & 5th Sun. [M-5]
HAIBARA 榛原　中央区日本橋2-7-6
2-7-6 Nihombashi, Chūō-ku. Tel: 272-3801. Hrs: 9:30 a.m.-5:30 p.m. (until 5 p.m. on Sat.), closed Sun. & Hols. [M-9]

WASHIKŌBŌ 和紙工房　港区西麻布1-8-10
1-8-10 Nishi-Azabu, Minato-ku. Tel: 405-1841. Hrs: 10 a.m.-6 p.m., closed Sun. & Hols. [M-2]
KYŪKYODŌ (see "Kō—incense")
KURODAYA 黒田屋　台東区浅草1-2-11
1-2-11 Asakusa, Taitō-ku. Tel: 845-3830. Hrs: 11 a.m.-8 p.m., Mon. [M-12]

Fude—Brushes

Fude were brought to Japan from China in the 6th century when the Chinese writing system was introduced. Used now for *sumie*—ink painting, and *shodō*—calligraphy, the brush must be able to produce a line that moves from a deep, intense black through a faint grey, and strokes of varying force, from thick and powerful through fine and feathery. The best brushes are hand-made, the hairs selected, matched and wrapped together in a time-consuming process. The type of hair used differs according to the purpose of each particular brush. Shops selling hand-made brushes also sell less expensive machine-made brushes of good quality.

GYOKUSENDŌ 玉川堂　千代田区神田神保町3-3
3-3 Jimbōchō, Kanda, Chiyoda-ku. Tel: 264-3741. Hrs: 9 a.m.-7 p.m., closed Sun. & Hols. A great selection of *fude* for calligraphy and *sumie*, things for calligraphy, and books. [M-15]
KŌUNDŌ 光雲堂　台東区浅草橋1-30-11
1-30-11 Asakusabashi, Taitō-ku. Tel: 861-4943. Hrs: 9 a.m.-5:30 p.m., closed the 2nd Sat., Sun. & Hols. [M-24]

Tsuzura—Lacquered Bamboo Trunks

Traditionally used for storing *kimono*, *tsuzura* are boxes made of woven bamboo that has been lacquered in bright orange, dark brown or black. The boxes come in three sizes: the largest for *kimono*, medium size for undergarments and footwear, and small ones for stationery and letters. Usually custom ordered, the boxes are painted with the family crest. Small boxes can be found at some stationery stores such as Kyūkyodō in Ginza.

IWAI-SHŌTEN 岩井商店　中央区日本橋人形町2-10-1
2-10-1 Ningyōchō, Nihombashi, Chūō-ku. Tel: 668-6058. Hrs: 8 a.m.-8:30 p.m., closed Sun. & Hols. You can watch the craftsmen at work. [M-23]

Sudare—Bamboo Blinds

In the intense heat of the Japanese summer, the doors and windows of traditional style homes were removed and *sudare*, bamboo blinds, hung. Blinds were also used as room partitions. Another kind of blind, *misu*, are edged in silk binding with two heavy tassels. *Misu* are used in shrines and temples. *Nawa noren* are curtains of twisted rope hung in the entrance way of Japanese-style drinking spots and tea houses.

Most city dwellers no longer remove their doors and windows during the hot summer, but bamboo blinds still appear outside the windows of older apartment buildings in Tokyo. For hand-made blinds, the young bamboo is carefully selected and matched, then tightly laced together. At the smaller shops, blinds are most often custom made. Blinds can also be bought at most department stores.

KAMIYAMA SUDARETEN　神山スダレ店　中央区京橋1-8-8
1-8-8 Kyōbashi, Chūō-ku. Tel: 561-0945. Hrs: 8 a.m.-8 p.m., daily. The blinds must be custom ordered, and usually take three weeks to make. [M-9]

Chōchin—Paper Lanterns

Though *chōchin* are most frequently seen like sign boards outside traditional Japanese drinking spots—*nomiya*, they were originally used for religious services. You can still see strings of lanterns at temples, shrines and festival sites. *Chōchin* can be bought ready-made in various sizes, or you can order one with your name written in a Japanized spelling. Prices start at about ¥3,000.

HANATŌ　花藤　台東区浅草2-25-6
2-25-6 Asakusa, Taitō-ku. Tel: 841-6411. Hrs: 10 a.m.-9 p.m., closed the 2nd & 4th Tue. of the month. [M-12]

KASHIWAYA　柏屋　中央区新富2-3-13
2-3-13 Shintomi, Chūō-ku. Tel: 551-1362. Hrs: 10 a.m.-5 p.m., closed Sun. [M-22]

Interior Lamps

Traditional lamps were wooden-framed floor lamps covered with white paper and lit by a candle. The design has been modified for modern use and a variety of functional and beautiful lamps and lighting fixtures are available. The most beautiful are made from bamboo or unfinished wood frames lined with white paper that softly diffuses the light. Others are collapsible paper lanterns in contemporary designs.

ISHIZUKA SHŌTEN　石塚商店　文京区湯島3-34-10
3-34-10 Yushima, Bunkyō-ku. Tel: 831-0891. Hrs: 7 a.m.-7 p.m., daily. Many famous Japanese architects have their lamps designed at this shop. They specialize in hand-bent bamboo or wood-framed lamps and lighting fixtures. Custom orders are accepted. [M-13]

LIVINA YAMAGIWA　リビナ・ヤマギワ　千代田区外神田1-5-10
1-5-10 Soto-Kanda, Chiyoda-ku. Tel: 253-2111. Hrs: 10 a.m.-7 p.m. (until 7:30 p.m. on Fri. & Sat.) closed the 3rd Wed. of May & Sept. Traditional lamps on 4th Fl. [M-14]

WASHI KŌBŌ (see *Washi* section). A good selection of interior paper lamps. [M-2]

Kasa—Umbrellas

The bamboo ribbed umbrella was, for a long time, one of the inevitable accessories for the Asian girl of the western imagination. Ironically, in *kabuki* the umbrella was often a symbol of masculine virility. Later, to share an umbrella became a mark of lovers. Even now, when school children write their name together with a sweetheart's, it's not inside a heart pierced by an arrow, but beneath an umbrella.

There are two types of traditional umbrella, *bangasa*, a rain umbrella made of oiled paper, and *higasa*, a sun shade made originally of paper but sometimes of cotton or silk. Traditional *kasa* are rather hard to find these days. Stores dealing in traditional footwear sometimes have them. Department stores carry them occasionally. You can usually find them at Nakamise, the shopping street leading to Sensōji Temple in Asakusa.

IDAYA 飯田屋　台東区浅草1-31-1
1-31-1 Asakusa, Taitō-ku. Tel: 841-3644. Hrs: 9 a.m.-8 p.m., daily. *Bangasa* (available all year), fans, etc. [M-12]

HASEGAWA HAKIMONOTEN 長谷川履物店　台東区上野2-4-4
2-4-4 Ueno, Taitō-ku. Tel: 831-3933. Hrs: 8:30 a.m.-8 p.m., closed Sun. This shops sells footwear, but usually has a few umbrellas in stock. [M-13]

Kō—Incense

Incense was brought to Japan with Buddhism in the 6th century. Important in religious ritual, it later developed into a ceremonial esthetic cult called *kōdō*, in a style similiar to the tea ceremony. There are three main types of incense: *kōboku*—smokeless wood chips from naturally scented trees, used in tea and *kōdō* ceremonies; *nerikō*—a smokeless cone of combined wood chips; and *senkō*—smoke producing stick incense used for religious purposes. Most shops selling incense also sell *nioibukuro*—small sachets of fragrant wood chips in tiny brocade bags.

KYŪKYODŌ 鳩居堂　中央区銀座5-7-4
5-7-4 Ginza, Chūō-ku. Tel: 571-4429. Hrs: 10 a.m.-8 p.m. (11 a.m.-7 p.m. on Sun. & Hols.) The store's specialty is incense, but they also stock a wide variety of calligraphy articles, stationery, and small lacquer letter boxes. [M-8]

Cha-dōgu—Tea Ceremony Utensils

For an explanation of the tea ceremony see ''Traditional Arts''. There are five main categories of utensils used in the tea ceremony: vases and scrolls used to decorate the room; the bowl, tea caddies, scoops and whisks used to prepare the tea; the trays and bowls for serving the food; the gong and straw mats placed outside the entrance; and the water jar and charcoal brazier for the washing and preparation area.

RYŪZENDŌ 竜善堂　中央区銀座5-8-6
5-8-6 Ginza, Chūō-ku. Tel: 571-4321. Hrs: 10 a.m.-8 p.m., closed the 3rd Sun. [M-8]

Katana—Swords

Imported from China in the *Heian* period, by *samurai* times the sword had become the tool of the ruling class and its symbol of power. Swords were considered the ''soul'' of the *samurai*, and the best were produced in a semi-religious ceremony where the artisan maintained a state of ritual purity to allow the entrance of ''spirit'' into the blade. The process of sword making developed into a fine art, and required up to several months of tempering to produce a razor sharp edge and a flexible blade of incredible durability. Swords became a major export item—in 1483 over 37,000 were sent to China.

Old swords are hard to come by these days. Highly prized by the Japanese, swords come on the market only rarely, and then at astronomical prices. Sword shops also sell *tsuba* (sword guards), *menuki* (metal sword ornaments) and complete suits of armour.

JAPAN SWORD 日本刀剣　港区虎の門3-8-1
3-8-1 Toranomon, Minato-ku. Tel: 434-4321. Hrs: 9:30 a.m.-6 p.m., closed Sun. New and old swords. [M-11]

Hōchō and *Hasami*—Knives and Scissors

Tightly controlled by the Tokugawa government, *Edo* period Japan settled into over 200 years of peace. As the *samurai* gradually became more of a bureaucrat and less of a soldier, the need for swords declined. With the beginning of the *Meiji* period, the *samurai* lost political control and soon the wearing of swords was outlawed. The swordsmiths turned to knife and scissor making. Produced by the same techniques used in swordmaking, Japanese knives and scissors are the best in the world. The knife capital of Japan is Seki city in Gifu prefecture. For over 700 years the area has been famous for making the bulk of the nation's blades.

KIYA 木屋　中央区日本橋室町1-8
1-8 Muromachi, Nihombashi, Chūō-ku. Tel: 241-0111. Hrs: 10 a.m.-5:30 p.m. (12 noon-5:30 p.m. Sun. & Hols.). [M-9]
UBUKEYA うぶけや　中央区日本橋人形町9-2
9-2 Ningyōchō, Nihombashi, Chūō-ku. Tel: 661-4851. Hrs: 9 a.m.-7 p.m., closed Sun. & Hols. [M-23]

Sashimono—Furniture

The typical Japanese home was (and sometimes still is) furnished sparsely. Rooms were multifunctional: for living by day, at night *futon* were pulled from the closets for sleeping. Furniture was minimal; a *hibachi* for heating, a *tansu* chest for storing clothing, another chest—a *chadansu*—for dishes. Small chests for letters and other personal items were brought out when needed.

The best furniture was made of *kiri*, paulownia wood. Nails were never used, the pieces being jointed and glued. A few shops still make traditional furniture, though even small pieces are quite expensive.

KYŌYA 京屋　台東区上野2-12-10
2-12-10 Ueno, Taitō-ku. Tel: 831-1905. Hrs: 10 a.m.-6 p.m., closed Sun. & Hols. [M-13]
HIRATSUKA 平つか　中央区銀座8-7-6
8-7-6 Ginza, Chūō-ku. Tel: 571-1684. Hrs: 10 a.m.-7 p.m., closed Sun. This shop makes lovely small chests. [M-8]

Oke—Wooden Buckets

Oke are buckets made of cypress wood with copper hoops holding the hand-planed pieces of wood tightly together. Most often seen in *sushi* shops holding large portions of marinated rice, small *oke* called *furo-oke* are used as scoops and wash basins for the bath. *Oke* are generally custom ordered.

ITŌ-OKE-TEN 伊東桶店　墨田区立川2-4-6
2-4-6 Tatekawa, Sumida-ku. Tel: 633-7108. Hrs: 8 a.m.-5 p.m., closed Sun. & Hols. [M-24]

Yōji—Toothpicks

Toothpicks are not normally a terribly exciting subject, but one shop in Tokyo, Saruya, has turned the humble tool into as fine an art as possible. At Saruya, you can buy toothpicks individually cased in brightly printed Japanese paper with a fortune poem wrapped around inside. Also sold are *kashi-yōji*, used for eating Japanese sweets. Hand-cut from pieces of camphor wood, a strip of bark is always retained for artistic effect. Saruya's toothpicks are sold throughout Japan, and can be bought at most major department stores.

SARUYA さるや　中央区日本橋小網町18-10
18-10 Koamichō, Nihombashi, Chūō-ku. Tel: 666-3906. Hrs: 9 a.m.-5 p.m., closed Sun., Hols. & the 3rd Sat. [M-9]

Shikki—Lacquer ware

First imported from China as a technique for making objects of daily use more durable, lacquer ware became a highly refined art in Japan. In very simplistic terms the process involves painting layers of tree sap called *urushi* over a base usually of wood, but sometimes of metal, paper, leather or bamboo. Cloth is sometimes applied, then the lacquer coating reapplied and repolished in a lengthy process which can involve over 100 separate steps. In the final decorative stages, gold, silver, and colors are often applied. The final product is both durable and beautiful. Good lacquer ware is expensive, and requires a certain amount of special care when taken to climates dryer than Japan. Dishes, furniture, small boxes, and trays are a few common lacquer ware products.

INACHŪ JAPAN 稲忠漆芸堂　港区赤坂1-5-2
1-5-2 Akasaka, Minato-ku. Tel: 582-4451. Hrs: 10 a.m.-7 p.m., daily. They have a factory in Wajima city in Ishikawa prefecture. [M-11]
HEIANDŌ 平安堂　中央区日本橋3-10-11
3-10-11 Nihombashi, Chūō-ku. Tel: 272-2871. Hrs: 9 a.m.-6 p.m., closed Sun. & Hols. [M-9]
KUROEYA 黒江屋　中央区日本橋1-2-6黒江屋国分ビル
Kuroeya Kokubu Bldg. 2nd Fl., 1-2-6 Nihombashi, Chūō-ku. Tel: 271-3356 Hrs: 9 a.m.-5 p.m. (until 12 noon on Sat.), closed Sun., Hols., the 1st, 2nd & 3rd Sat. [M-9]

KISSŌ 吉左右 アクシスビル·
Axis Bldg. B1. Tel: 582-4191. Hrs: 11 a.m.-8 p.m., daily. Lacquer ware with a contemporary flair, also some ceramics and Japanese kitchen utensils. The shop is connected to a Japanese *kaiseki* style "café". [M-1]

Tōjiki—Ceramics

The history of ceramics in Japan dates back to Neolithic times, the *Jōmon* period (7,000-300 B.C.) when unglazed earthen ware pots with distinctive rope pattern designs were produced. As an art form, pottery became important during the *Kamakura* period with the development of the tea ceremony. Later, when Japan invaded Korea during the *Momoyama* period, continental potters were brought back to Japan. The new Korean wares and pottery techniques greatly influenced the domestic art. By the *Edo* period, *daimyō* lords were competing for superiority in pottery production, especially for tea ceremony utensils, and pottery centers were developed throughout Japan.

Around 1616, a Korean potter discovered clay suitable for porcelain production in the south of Japan. The Japanese have always prefered pottery over porcelains, but porcelain soon became a major export product. Export wares were adapted to European tastes. Shapes were altered for western table use with bright colors and fancy designs in matched sets of china, a practice never seen in Japan.

The Japanese use unmatched sets of dishes, with each piece selected for its suitability to the dish being served. Most items, if in a set, are in threes or fives, four being considered a particularly unlucky number. For tea ceremony ware, imperfections and irregularities in simple, undecorated pottery are considered aesthetically pleasing. Passed down through history, famous tea bowls are easily worth ¥4-5 million.

Some of the most important types of pottery are *Mino-yaki* (Gifu prefecture), *Karatsu-yaki* (Kyūshū), *Arita-yaki* (formerly called *Imari*, from Kyūshū), *Hagi-yaki* (Yamaguchi pref.), *Raku-yaki* (famous tea master Sen no Rikyū's favorite, from Kyōto), *Kyō-yaki* (Kyōto), *Mashiko-yaki* (Tochigi pref. near Tokyo), *Bizen-yaki* (Okayama pref.), *Kiyomizu-yaki* (Kyōto), *Kutani-yaki* (Ishikawa pref.) and *Satsuma* (Kyūshū).

A good day trip outside Tokyo is a visit to the kilns in Mashiko, a short train ride from the city. Contact TIC for details. For contemporary pottery galleries, see "Contemporary Arts Galleries". Besides the galleries, the following shops are good places to buy.

SAGA TŌEN 嵯峨陶園 港区西麻布2-13-13
2-13-13 Nishi-Azabu, Minato-ku. Tel: 400-3682. Hrs: 10 a.m.-8:30 p.m. (Sun. & Hols. 11 a.m.-7:30 p.m.) [M-2]

TACHIKICHI & CO., LTD. たち吉　中央区銀座6-13
6-13 Ginza, Chūō-ku. Tel: 571-2924. Hrs: 11 a.m.-7 p.m., closed Sun. Kiyomizu-yaki porcelain. [M-8]
ISERYŪ SHŌTEN 伊勢竜商店　中央区日本橋人形町3-8-2
3-8-2 Ningyōchō, Nihombashi, Chūō-ku. Tel: 661-4820. Hrs: 8:30 a.m.-6 p.m., closed Sun. & Hols. Everyday dishes. [M-23]

Ukiyoe—Woodblock Prints

Originally not considered an art form, *ukiyoe* were often advertisements, handbills, or cheap posters produced for mass consumption. The height of *ukiyoe* printing was from the mid to late 18th century when figurative prints were most popular. Famous artists were Utamaro (1753-1806), known for his *bijin-e*, portraits of beautiful women, and Sharaku (active 1794-95), known for his *yakusha-e*, exaggerated actor's portraits. *Ukiyoe* means literally "illustrations of the floating world", an originally Buddhist concept referring to the evanescent and transient nature of the day-to-day world. By the *Edo* period it came to mean the life of the city pleasure quarters, and the courtesans and actors who were its stars. In the 19th century landscape prints grew in popularity. Important artists were Hokusai (1760-1849), known for his "36 Views of Mt. Fuji", and Hiroshige (1797-1858), known for his series "53 Stages of the Tōkaidō".

The prints were considered vulgar by the *samurai* aristocracy, and their low esteem even among the merchant classes was shown by their frequent use as packing materials. The prints eventually found their way to Europe, wrapped around packages of exported tea, where European artists such as Van Gogh and Toulouse Lautrec were the first to recognize the work as art. Even today, some of the best *ukiyoe* collections are outside Japan.

Numerous shops in Tokyo deal in old prints. The best are expensive and should be bought from certified dealers who will guarantee the work. Moderately priced prints (¥5,000-¥30,000), though of lesser quality, can still be good buys. Modern reproductions of the work of famous masters are also available. For contemporary prints see the gallery section.

MATSUSHITA ASSOCIATES, INC. 松下同人社　渋谷区南青山6-3-12
6-3-12 Minami-Aoyama, Shibuya-ku. Tel: 407-4966. Hrs: 10 a.m.-5:30 p.m., closed Sun. & Mon. The shop usually has a good selection of moderately priced work. [M-5]
SAKAI KŌKODŌ GALLERY 酒井好古堂　千代田区有楽町1-2-14
1-2-14 Yūrakuchō, Chiyoda-ku. Tel: 591-4678. Hrs: 10 a.m.-7 p.m. (11 a.m.-7 p.m. on Sun.), daily. This shop has been selling prints for over 100 years. [M-10]
SAIRAKUDŌ 西楽堂　台東区上野1-18-11
1-18-11 Ueno, Taitō-ku. Tel: 832-0024. Hrs: 10 a.m.-5:30 p.m., closed Sun. & Hols. [M-13]
ORIENTAL BAZAAR 2nd Fl., Run by the son of Matsushita. New and old prints. [M-4]

TRADITIONAL INSTRUMENTS
Shamisen

One of the most versatile of Japanese instruments, the *shamisen* was brought to Japan from the Ryūkyū Islands. *Shamisen* music is primarily designed to accompany narrative or lyrical vocal pieces, and is important in all forms of Japanese drama. The instrument has a body made from four pieces of wood (best are of red sandalwood, mulberry or Chinese quince), covered top and bottom with cat skin, or dog skin for less expensive models. The long neck is made of three pieces that can be disjointed. The *shamisen* is played with a large plectrum called a *bachi*.

KIKUYA SHAMISEN-TEN　菊屋三味線店　文京区湯島3-45-11
3-45-11 Yushima, Bunkyō-ku. Tel: 831-4733. Hrs: 9 a.m.-7:30 p.m., closed Sun. & Hols. The least expensive costs ¥55,000. [M-13]
BACHI-EI GAKKITEN　ばち英楽器店　中央区日本橋人形町10-11
10-11 Ningyōchō, Nihombashi, Chūō-ku. Tel: 666-7263. Hrs: 9 a.m.-8:30 p.m., Sun. & Hols. [M-25]

Koto

Popular with the *Heian* court aristocracy, the *koto* remains an instrument, like the western piano, considered one of the genteel accomplishments of a well-bred Japanese. The music is played solo or in ensembles. Made of two pieces of paulownia wood, the instrument has 13 or 17 strings, movable bridges and is at least six feet long. Ivory picks attached to three fingers of the right hand, or sometimes bare hands, are used to pluck the *koto*.

TSURUKAWA GAKKI HONTEN　鶴川楽器本店　中央区京橋1-12-11
1-12-11 Kyōbashi, Chūō-ku. Tel: 561-1872. Hrs: 9:30 a.m.-6 p.m. (Sat. until 5 p.m.), closed Sun. & Hols. [M-9]

Biwa

Imported from China during the *Nara* period, this pear-shaped lute has four strings, four frets, and is played with a small plectrum. *Biwa* playing was an essential skill for the early Japanese courtier, and later became important as the accompaniment to the musical storytelling of itinerant blind priests in the 10th century. The body of the *biwa* is carved from a single piece of wood, a second piece covers the base.

ISHIDA BIWA-TEN　石田琵琶店　港区虎の門3-8-4
3-8-4 Toranomon, Minato-ku. Tel: 431-6548. Hrs: 9 a.m.-7 p.m., closed Sun. & Hols. [M-11]

Shakuhachi

Probably the easiest of Japanese instruments for foreigners to understand, the *shakuhachi* flute was first introduced into Japan during the *Nara* period. The most important *shakuhachi* music is from the *Edo* period. At the time, a group of ex-*samurai* organized themselves as a temple and played on the street corners as beggar priests. They later worked as spies for the Tokugawa government, and their basket hat covering the face became a general method of disguise for anyone wishing to travel incognito. The instrument was also redesigned in a longer and thicker form to serve as a weapon (they were forbidden to wear swords).

The *shakuhachi* is now played solo and in concert with *shamisen* or *koto*. The standard length is 54-55 cm. Most have four holes on top, and one in the back. The mouthpiece is usually of ivory or bone.

CHIKUYŪSHA 竹友社　新宿区三栄町3
3 San'eichō, Shinjuku-ku. Tel: 351-1270. Hrs: 10 a.m.-5 p.m., closed Sun. & Hols. This is a school with a shop attached where the craftsmen make the flutes. [off Map]

Drums

There are two main types of Japanese drums, the large barrel-like *taiko*, and the smaller hour-glass shaped *tsuzumi*. Both come in a variety of sizes capable of producing a range of tones. The drums are used primarily to mark rhythm in folk dance, *kabuki*, and *nō* dramas.

MIYAMOTO UNOSUKE SHŌTEN 宮本卯之助商店　台東区浅草6-1-15
6-1-15 Asakusa, Taktō-ku. Tel: 874-4131. Hrs: 8 a.m.-5 p.m., closed Sun. & Hols. The shop carries festival drums and portable shrines. [M-12]

TRADITIONAL CLOTHING AND ACCESSORIES
Kimono

Apart from a few ceremonial occasions, most young Japanese women no longer wear *kimono*. Most, in fact, are incapable of dressing themselves correctly in one. Special schools will teach them this, as well as the proper way of walking, and appropriate forms of manners and behavior. Beautiful and graceful though they may be, *kimono* are a terribly restrictive form of dress. The pace of modern life in the city makes wearing one wholly impractical. Just watch a *kimono* clad woman climbing the stairs or trying to get into a taxi. Older women, with established social positions, still wear *kimono* for school functions and formal affairs, though whether today's young will do so in the future is hard to say.

The prohibitive cost of *kimono* doesn't exactly serve to encourage its use. A normal everyday, mass-produced *kimono* will cost a minimum of ¥50,000. A hand-dyed silk one, *kimono* haute-couture, will cost from ¥300,000 to over ¥1 million. *Kimono* are a major investment. Parents will give a daughter several, which most of the time stay folded in her closet. When she marries, a wedding *kimono* is usually rented—for at least ¥100,000 a day.

In the *Heian* period, *kimono* were worn in multiple layers of subtly coordinated colors. The inner *kimono* were loosely tied with a low sash-like belt. Taste in *kimono* changed through history, with different patterns, dyes, colors, and embroidery techniques going in and out of fashion. By the *Edo* period, the Tokugawa government, in its efforts to control conspicuous consumption among the merchant class, passed laws restricting the merchants to modest clothing considered more appropriate to their position in the *samurai* social hierarchy. The merchants managed to get around the laws by wearing *kimono* of apparent simplicity, but made from extravagantly expensive hand-dyed and woven silks, or lined with sumptuous fabrics. During the *Meiji* period infatuation with western civilization, western style clothing was slowly adopted, first by men, and very gradually by women, but women continued to wear *kimono* regularly until the 2nd World War.

The rules of taste for *kimono* today are extremely complicated and based on variables such as the wearer's age and the occasion. Colors and patterns considered in good taste follow a concept of coloring totally unlike western ideas of complementary or clashing colors.

Men's *kimono* are less decorative than women's, being usually black, grey or shades of brown, and tied low at the waist with a narrow *obi*. For formal occasions a crested *haori*, the short jacket *kimono*, and *hakama*, culotte-like pants are worn with a black *kimono*.

For informal occasions, after a bath, or at a *ryokan*, cotton *yukata* are worn by both men and women.

The cost of *kimono* will probably keep most non-Japanese from buying new ones. Antique silk *kimono* are a great alternative, and stores selling them are listed later in the Antiques section. The cotton *yukata* are also inexpensive and useful. *Yukata* can be bought at department stores, and the Oriental Bazaar. Listed below are a few *kimono* shops that custom make *kimono*. The fabrics are beautiful, but if you wish to buy the fabric alone, remember the bolts are measured to make exactly one *kimono* each, and you'll have to buy the whole lot.

SHIMAKAME 志ま亀　中央区銀座6-5-15
6-5-15 Ginza, Chūō-ku. Tel: 571-4651. Hrs: 10 a.m.-7 p.m. (12 noon-7 p.m. Sun. & Hols). This shop is originally from Kyōto. [M-8]

MASUDAYA 増多屋　中央区銀座2-8-15
2-8-15 Ginza, Chūō-ku. Tel: 561-3362. Hrs: 10 a.m.-9 p.m., closed Sun. & Hols. *Kimono*, *haori*, and *obi* fabrics. [M-8]

TSUMUGIYA KICHIHEI 紬屋吉平　中央区銀座5-9-20
5-9-20 Ginza, Chūō-ku. Tel: 571-0993. Hrs: 10 a.m.-7 p.m., closed Sun. Famous for their *tsumugi*, hand-spun silks. [M-8]

Obi

Obi are the wide belts worn with *kimono*. Intended as the main attraction of traditional dress, the *obi* is chosen to go with a particular *kimono* and is usually more expensive than the *kimono* itself. The *obi* is wrapped around twice and tied in a bow at the back. There are hundreds of ways to tie it, and for women unable to do it on their own, hairdressers provide the service for a nominal fee. *Obi* can be bought at most shops dealing in *kimono*.

Kimono Accessories

Worn with the *kimono* are various belts and sashes. *Obiage* are wide sashes of soft fabric, often of silk, and dyed in tie-dye like patterns. Colors are usually pastels. The *obiage* is tucked into the top of the *obi*.

Obijime are woven cords tied around the center of the *obi*, and knotted in front.

DŌMYŌ 道明　台東区上野2-11-1
2-11-1 Ueno, Taitō-ku. Tel: 831-3773. Hrs: 10 a.m.-7 p.m. (until 5 p.m. on Sun. & Hols). This shop makes *obijime* and decorative cords for other purposes. [M-13]
KUNOYA くのや　中央区銀座6-9-8
6-9-8 Ginza, Chūō-ku. Tel: 571-2546. Hrs: 10 a.m.-8 p.m., daily. Famous for their *kimono* accessories. [M-8]

Geta and *Zōri*

Though for a time during the *Meiji* period western shoes were popularly worn with *kimono*, now only Japanese style foot-wear is acceptable. The two main types of footwear are *zōri*, leather or straw sandals, and *geta*, wooden clogs. Both are worn with the *tabi* one toed sock. With formal *kimono*, *zōri* must be worn, and *tabi* are required of all but *geisha*. With daily *kimono*, both *zōri* and *geta* are acceptable, but *tabi* must be worn. With *yukata*, *geta* without *tabi* are worn.

HASETOKU 長谷徳　台東区浅草1-18-10
1-18-10 Asakusa, Taitō-ku. Tel: 841-2153. Hrs: 7 a.m.-8 p.m., daily. One of the only places you can find 100% straw *zōri*. [M-12]
YOITAYA 与板屋　中央区銀座5-4-5
5-4-5 Ginza, Chūō-ku. Tel: 572-7580. Hrs: 11 a.m.-7 p.m., closed Sun. *Zōri* and *geta*. [M-8]
HASEGAWA HAKIMONOTEN (see *Kasa*)

Tabi—Socks

Tabi are Japanese socks with one toe sewn separately to fit into the *geta* or *zōri*. *Tabi* evolved from a leather shoe worn by farmers. Its popularity as a sock rose when it became part of the required outfit for tea ceremony participants. The socks are commonly made of cotton, with metal clasps at the ankle. *Jika-tabi* are cotton boots worn by workmen that fasten above the ankle, like high-top tennis shoes. The one toed sock tradition is so strong in Japan that even fishermen's waders come with one toe separated in a strangely frog-like fashion.

MYŌGAYA めうがや　中央区銀座8-6-6
8-6-6 Ginza, Chūō-ku. Tel: 571-3670. Hrs: 11 a.m.-7:30 p.m., closed Sun. & Hols. [M-8]
KIKUYA 喜久家　墨田区緑1-9-3

1-9-3 Midori, Sumida-ku. Tel: 631-0092. Hrs: 9 a.m.-7 p.m., closed Sun. *Tabi* for dancers, *sumō* wrestlers, and tea ceremony wear. [M-24]
ŌNOYA SŌHONTEN 大野屋総本店 中央区新富2-2
2-2 Shintomi, Chūō-ku. Tel: 551-0896. Hrs: 10 a.m.-8 p.m., closed Sun. [M-22]

Sensu—Fans

Originally a symbol of power and authority, fans were used by the emperor and his court, and later as part of *samurai* battle dress. Early fans were often painted by famous masters and were considered very elegant gifts. Lovers often exchanged fans as a sign of intimacy. Fans were one of the few wholly Japanese inventions.

There are two types of fans. The *ōgi*, ornamental folding fan is still an essential accessory for formal occasions. *Ōgi* are also used in traditional dance to symbolize travel, landscapes, etc. *Uchiwa* are flat, round fans used to fan fires and, now, to cool off in the summer.

HŌSENDŌ KYŪAMI 宝扇堂久阿弥 台東区浅草1-19-6
1-19-6 Asakusa, Taitō-ku. Tel: 845-5021. Hrs: 10:30 a.m.-8 p.m., daily. A special store for traditional dance equipment. [M-12]
KYŌSENDŌ 京扇堂 中央区日本橋人形町2-4-3
2-4-3 Ningyōchō, Nihombashi, Chūō-ku. Tel: 666-7255. Hrs: 10 a.m.-8 p.m., closed Sun. & Hols. [M-23]
WAN'YA SHOTEN わんや書店 千代田区神田神保町3-9／中央区銀座8-7-5
3-9 Jimbōchō, Kanda, Chiyoda-ku. Tel: 263-6771. Hrs: 9:30 a.m.-5:30 p.m., closed Sun. & Hols. [M-15] Also in Ginza: 8-7-5 Ginza, Chūō-ku. Tel: 571-0514. Hrs: 10 a.m.-6 p.m. [M-8]
This shop specializes in articles for *nō* drama including scripts (in Japanese), small mask copies, fans, they even sell tickets.
BUNSENDŌ 文扇堂 台東区浅草1-20-2
1-20-2 Asakusa, Taitō-ku. Tel: 844-9711. Hrs: 10:30 a.m.-6 p.m., daily. [M-12]

Kushi and *Kanzashi*—Combs and Hair Ornaments

A comb is one thing you should never give a Japanese until the final *sayonara*; it means you'll probably never see them again. If you break a comb it means bad luck. When breaking up with a lover, one throws away the comb he or she gave as a present.

In the *Heian* period, long hair—preferably trailing a foot or so behind when one walked—was considered a sign of beauty for a woman. From the end of the *Momoyama* period through the *Edo* period hair was knotted up in a variety of elaborate styles that went in and out of fashion with ever increasing frequency. Hair ornaments, used to hold the hair-dos in place, ranged from simple box wood combs to lacquered gold and silver. *Geisha*, *maiko*, and *oiran* prostitutes favored extravagant styles where the ornaments covered the head like pins in a pin cushion. Hair ornaments are now worn on festive occasions. Combs and hair ornaments can be found in various shops along the Nakamise shopping street leading to Sensōji Temple in Asakusa. Matsuzakaya department store is well known for its selection.

YONOYA よのや 台東区浅草1-37-10
1-37-10 Asakusa, Taitō-ku. Tel: 844-1755. Hrs: 10 a.m.-7 p.m., closed Wed. The best shop for natural wood combs, the shop itself is a jewel. [M-12]

Keshōhin—Cosmetics

There is one shop where almost all the kabuki actors, traditional dancers, and geisha go for their make-up—Hyakusuke in Asakusa. Besides cosmetics, the shop carries skin-care products including *uguisu no fun*—politely translated as "nightingale droppings"—a traditional facial mask. They also have a good selection of brushes and hair ornaments.
HYAKUSUKE 百助 台東区浅草2-2-14
2-2-14 Asakusa, Taitō-ku. Tel: 841-7058. Hrs: 11 a.m.-5 p.m., daily. [M-12]

Festival Clothing

Here is a shopping list for those who want to be dressed right for their next neighborhood festival. *Momohiki*—tight-fitting pants that wrap around at the top, often of dark blue cotton. *Shita-shatsu*—a tight-fitting long sleeved cotton shirt. *Haragake*—a type of apron that is worn over the two garments listed above. *Shirushi-banten* or *hanten*—short, cotton *kimono*-like jacket, printed in bright colors with the name of your neighborhood, association, etc. *Sanjaku*—a narrow, cotton, *obi*-like belt. Ta-

Isogai Tetsuo is the fourth generation to run Isogai Tetsuzō Shōten, the family *tabi* and workmen's clothing shop.

bi—one toed socks, and *waraji*—straw sandals. The final touch is a *tenugui* wrapped around your head, or draped casually around your neck.
KIRIYA GOFUKUTEN 桐屋呉服店　台東区浅草2-22-10
2-2-10 Asakusa, Taitō-ku. Tel: 844-4233. Hrs: 9 a.m.-9 p.m., daily. [M-12]
ISOGAI TETSUZŌ SHŌTEN (See Workmen's Clothing)

Workmen's Clothing

A terrific form of alternative fashion, workmen's clothing is well made and reasonably priced. A few of the more useful items are: *shichibuzubon* wool or cotton pants similar to jodhpurs; *shita-shatsu*, like those worn for festivals; *dabo-shatsu*—a loose-fitting shirt worn as a jacket; and *jika-tabi*—cotton and occasionally leather one toed boots.
ISOGAI TETSUZŌ SHŌTEN 磯貝鉄蔵商店　墨田区業平1-10-2
1-10-2 Narihira, Sumida-ku. Tel: 622-2665. Hrs: 8 a.m.-8 p.m., daily. Workmen from all over Tokyo and the surrounding area order their gear from this great shop. [M-47]

Traditional Dance Accessories

Dance *kimono* and costumes, straw hats, umbrellas, fans, wigs, *tenugui*, masks, artificial flowers, dancer's footwear, etc, can all be found at:
HŌSENDŌ (See *Sensu*)

Tenugui—Towels

Tenugui are small cotton towels used in traditional forms of dance and theater, as well as in other towel-like ways. The fashionable *Edokko* had countless ways of tying and wrapping towels around the head. The Japanese buy them now as souvenirs, and at the Kabuki-za you can buy them printed with your favorite actor's crest. The towels are usually white, printed with a blue pattern.
FUJIYA TENUGUITEN ふじ屋手拭店　台東区浅草2-2-15
2-2-15 Asakusa, Taitō-ku. Tel: 841-2283. Hrs: 9 a.m.-8 p.m., closed Thur. [M-12]

Men—Masks

Masks are used in most forms of Japanese dance and drama, except *kabuki*. They range in size from the large and exaggerated *gigaku* dance masks, to the subtly expressive masks of *nō*. Many of the masks are independently considered art objects, and fetch astronomical prices if and when they're offered for sale. Folk dance and festival masks are more affordable. Made of paper or wood, the masks are usually caricatures of typical country bumpkins or animals. Inexpensive copies of *nō* masks can also be bought. Festival masks can be found at most *mingei* shops. Ishizuka and Bingoya usually have a good selection. Copies of *nō* masks can be found at Wanya Shoten.

Martial Arts Clothing and Equipment

There are a number of shops in the Kanda area that specialize in martial arts gear. The following shop is one of the better-known.

YŌMEIDŌ BUDŌGUTEN 陽明堂武道具店　千代田区神田神保町3-1
3-1 Jimbōchō, Kanda, Chiyoda-ku. Tel: 261-4668. Hrs: 10 a.m.-7 p.m. (until 5 p.m. on Sun.), closed Mon. [M-15]

ANTIQUES

Antique Stores

The following list of shops covers only a fraction of the antique stores in Tokyo. We've concentrated on shops for the average buyer. There are two streets famous for antiques shops: Kottō-dōri in Aoyama [M-5] and the street leading from Ikura crossing [M-11] towards Kamiyachō station. We haven't listed all the shops in these areas, but finding them as you walk along should be no problem. In Nihombashi are a number of serious collector's shops.

TOKYO OLD FOLK CRAFT AND ANTIQUE CENTER 1-23-1 Jimbōchō, Kanda, Chiyoda-ku. Tel: 295-7112/7115. Hrs: 10 a.m.-7 p.m., daily. Over 55 dealers in one building, there is a great selection at reasonable prices. [M-15]
GALLERY MEGURO Stork Mansion 2nd Fl., 2-24-18 Kamiōsaki, Shinagawa-ku. Tel: 493-1971. Hrs: 11 a.m.-7:30 p.m., closed Mon. Various dealers have set up shop on one floor of this building. A wide selection, reasonably priced. [M-19]
ART PLAZA MAGATANI 5-10-13 Toranomon, Minato-ku. Tel: 433-6321. Hrs: 10 a.m.-6:30 p.m., closed Sun. & Hols. [M-11]
ORIENTAL BAZAAR Merchandise changes regularly, some good prices. [M-4]
THE GALLERY 1-11-6 Akasaka, Minato-ku. Tel: 585-5019. Hrs: 10 a.m.-6 p.m. (11 a.m.-4 p.m. of Hols.), closed Sun: (Behind the U.S. Embassy). Somewhat expensive, but a good selection of Japanese, Korean, and Chinese antiques. Good for interiors and jewelry. [M-11]
TAKASHIMAYA DEPARTMENT STORE Has a large antique selection in the basement next to the Garden department. [M-9]
HEISANDŌ 1-2-4 Shiba-kōen, Minato-ku. Tel: 434-0588. Hrs: 10 a.m.-5 p.m., closed Sun. & Hols. Famous for its selection of scrolls and screen paintings. [M-11]
MORITA ANTIQUES 5-12-2 Minami-Aoyama, Minato-ku. Tel: 407-4466. Hrs: 10 a.m.-7 p.m., closed Sun. A good assortment of *mingei*, textiles, ceramics, etc. [M-5]
MAYUYAMA & CO., LTD. 2-5-9 Kyōbashi, Chūō-ku. Tel: 561-5146. Hrs: 9:30 a.m.-6 p.m., closed Sun. & Hols. A good shop for collectors. [M-9]
KUROFUNE 7-7-4 Roppongi, Minato-ku. Tel: 479-1552. Hrs: 10 a.m.-4 p.m., closed Sun. & Hols. A good selection of Japanese furniture. Slightly overpriced. [M-1]
KAMMON ANTIQUES 4-3-12 Shibuya, Shibuya-ku. Tel: 406-1765. Hrs: 10:30 a.m.-6 p.m., closed Sun. Chests, *hibachi*, porcelain, screens, paintings. [M-5]

Flea Markets

Flea markets in Tokyo are like sidewalk antique sales. Often held at shrines and temples on designated Sundays, they're a great way to spend a quiet morning or afternoon. Serious antique hunters show up while the dealers are still unpacking at 5-6 a.m., so the best merchandise goes early. The outdoor markets are held weather permitting, and usually last until 4-4:30 p.m.

Some of the merchandise is overpriced, or at least not significantly less expensive than if you went directly to an antique shop. As foreigners make up a large part of the crowd, dealers often figure they can charge tourist prices. Most will bargain somewhat, especially if the crowd hasn't been good that day. The best deals are to be had on not-so-old, but still interesting ceramics, used *kimono*, and Japanese kitsch. If you're looking for high quality merchandise, you should stick to antique shops. In any case, the markets are great fun and shouldn't be missed.

A few markets are held indoors in underground arcades like the Sunshine City Building, though somehow it's not quite as much fun. Also, twice a year (usually spring and autumn) the flea market association sponsors huge indoor markets with dealers from all over Japan. Dealers at the weekly markets will usually have information and flyers printed in English with the dates and locations. The monthly flea market schedule is:

- 1st Sunday: **Tōgō Shrine** (Harajuku) [M-4]
    Arai Yakushi Temple (This temple is not in the book, but is located a short distance on foot from Araiyakushi-mae Station on the Seibu-Shinjuku line). [off Map]
- 2nd Sunday: **Nogi Shrine** (near Roppongi). [M-1]
- 3rd Sat. & Sun.: **Sunshine City** Alpa Shopping Arcade B1 (Ikebukuro). [M-18]
    Hanazono Shrine (Behind Isetan Department Store in Shinjuku). [M-7]
- 4th Sunday: **Tōgō Shrine** [M-4]
- The last Thur. & Fri.: On the steps of the Roi Bldg. in Roppongi. [M-1]

Antique *Kimono*

The real thing is probably too expensive, but secondhand and antique silk *kimono* are one of the truly great bargains to be had in Tokyo. A number of shops carry *kimono* and *obi* ranging from 20 to 50 years old and from ¥1,000 up in price. Genuine antiques are harder to find and much more expensive. Flea markets are another good place to find used *kimono*. Takashimaya and Daimaru department stores have bargain sales on used, rental *kimono* and formal wear about twice a year.

HAYASHI KIMONO International Arcade 1-7 Uchisaiwaichō, Chiyoda-ku. Tel: 591-9826. Hrs: 9:30 a.m.-7 p.m., daily. [M-10]
KONJAKU NISHIMURA Mori Hanae Bldg. B1, 3-6-1 Kita-Aoyama, Minato-ku. Tel: 498-1759. Hrs: 11 a.m.-8 p.m., closed Thur. This shop is originally from Kyōto. [M-4]
ORIENTAL BAZAAR B1 and 2nd Fl. [M-4]
BOUTIQUE YŪYA (See Designers Boutique) This shop mainly custom designs clothing from old *kimono* fabrics, but they also have a stock of *kimono* for sale. [M-1]
AYAHATA 2-21-2 Akasaka, Minato-ku. Tel: 582-9969. Hrs: 11 a.m.-8 p.m., closed Sun. & Hols. Antique *kimono*, *obi*, blue and white textiles, *furoshiki*, *hanten*, etc. [M-6]

Other Secondhand Clothes

There are a few places in town selling a variety of rather junky, but interesting used clothes including *kimono*, old military uniforms and accessories, and *mōningu*—men's black formal suits. One of the best places is in Asakusa, where a number of stalls are set up (weather permitting) on the streets to the left as you approach Sensōji Temple. There are no addresses for these stalls, but you can't miss the rummage sale-like atmosphere. Here are four more shops.

NAKATA SHŌTEN In the middle of the old, under-the-tracks part of Ameyoko Shopping Arcade in Ueno. The shop is famous for carrying old military uniforms and paraphernalia (Japanese and foreign). Tel: 832-8577. [M-13]

SALVATION ARMY 2-21-20 Wada, Suginami-ku. Tel: 384-9114. Hrs: 8:20 a.m.-12:30 p.m. on Sat. (people start queuing at 7 a.m.). A variety of junk including old clothes, furniture, dishes, etc. They will deliver for a small fee. It's a bit out of the way, and not on any of our maps, but once you get to the station it's fairly easy to find. Take the Marunouchi Line to Nakano-fujimichō, west of Shinjuku (sometimes you have to change platforms at Nakano-Sakaue Station). Exit from the station and turn left. At the first light take a right and follow the street as it curves along to the left (there should be a small playground on the right just after you turn). Walk straight about 8 min., the shop is on the right. [off Map]

IWATAYA 3-34 Ebisu, Shibuya-ku. Tel: 441-7588. Hrs: 11 a.m.-7 p.m., closed Thur. Secondhand and dead stock, everything from *kimono*, to formal suits, fur coats, and jeans. [off Map]

DEP'T STORE (see Cheap Fashion). The best western antique clothing store in Tokyo. Huge selection and comparatively reasonable prices. [M-4]

FOOD AND DRINKS
Traditional Sweets

While most westerners have grown accustomed to the idea of eating raw fish Japanese style, few have managed to surmount the conceptual barrier of eating sweet bean and sticky rice cakes for dessert.

Actually, the Japanese don't generally have dessert per se; after meals a small dish of fruit is considered sufficient. But there is a broad range of between meal snack sweets that taste better with a cup of green tea, just as a piece of chocolate cake always seems to call for a cup of coffee.

It's not particularly surprising considering that originally the sweets developed as an accompaniment to the tea ceremony in the *Azuchi-Momoyama* period. The extreme sweetness of the desserts complimented the strong and slightly bitter tea. By *Edo*, the taste had filtered down to at least the urban masses and dozens of specialty shops began developing variations on the basic sweet bean theme.

Many of the *Edo* period shops are still in business. Often in slightly out of the way locations, the famous shops sell out most days by noon. Many have small tea rooms where you can order a cup of green tea and a plate of the house specialty.

• **Namagashi**—one of the most "artistic" kinds of desserts, these sweet bean paste cakes are exquisitely molded and decorated somewhat like fancy marzipan. The shapes and colors are changed with the seasons.

KIKUYA HONTEN　菊家本店　港区南青山5-13-2
5-13-2 Minami-Aoyama, Minato-ku. Tel: 400-3856. Hrs: 9:30 a.m.-6 p.m. closed Sun. This "picture-perfect" little shop handmakes 20 kinds of *namagashi* daily. Each beautiful cake costs from ¥120-¥300. [M-5]

KOTOBUKIDŌ KYŌGASHI-TSUKASA　寿堂京菓子司　中央区日本橋人形町2-1-4
2-1-4 Ningyōchō, Nihombashi, Chūō-ku. Tel: 666-4804. Hrs: 9 a.m.-8:30 p.m., closed the 2nd & 3rd Sun. Established in 1883, the shop is most famous for its *kogane-imo*—cakes made of white beans coated in cinnamon. [M-23]

- ***Dango***—are small rice "dumplings" of steamed or boiled rice. Served usually skewered in threes called *kushi-dango*, *dango* are either broiled and served with soy sauce, or a sweet red bean sauce.

HABUTAE DANGO　羽二重団子　荒川区東日暮里5-54-3
5-54-3 Higashi-Nippori, Arakawa-ku. Tel: 891-2924. Hrs: 9 a.m.-5:30 p.m., closed Tue. When this shop opened in 1819, their famous "kushi-dango" was praised as being as fine as *habutae*—a type of silk fabric. The name was adopted for the shop and became a sort of byword for the *kushi-dango* it produced. The shop has a lovely tea room overlooking a small garden. *Habutae dango* and tea costs ¥320. [M-13]

KOTOTOI DANGO　言問団子　墨田区向島5-5-22
5-5-22 Mukōjima, Sumida-ku. Tel: 622-0081. Hrs: 10 a.m.-6 p.m. closed Thur. *Kototoi dango* was so famous that when the government built a bridge near here they named it *Kototoi* after the shop. The shop sells three kinds of unskewered *dango*. [M-12]

SHIBAMATAYA　柴又屋　葛飾区柴又7-7-5
7-7-5 Shibamata, Katsushika-ku. Tel: 659-8111. Hrs: 10 a.m.-7 p.m., daily. Located in the hometown of the beloved movie character "Tora-San", the shop is full of old posters from his 30 some movies. The restaurant is a rather funky place, with funny waitresses and over 100 kinds of Japanese food on the menu. In front of the shop they make *kusa-dango*, a type of skewered *dango* flavored with the leaves of the *yomogi* plant, a mountain vegetable. [off Map, see Shibamata Taishakuten Temple]

- ***Mochi***—the ingredients and method of preparation are similar to that of *dango*, but *mochi* comes in a much wider variety.

CHŌMEIJI SAKURA-MOCHI　長命寺桜もち　墨田区向島5-1-14
5-1-14 Mukōjima, Sumida-ku. Tel: 622-3266. Hrs: 9 a.m.-5 p.m., closed the 1st & 3rd Mon., 2nd, 4th, & 5th Sun. Hanging in the shop are *ukiyoe* prints that were early advertisements for this famous shop. This shop, named after the nearby Chōmeiji Temple, has been famous since the *Edo* period, for it's *sakura-mochi*—cherry mochi. The *mochi* is baked in thin crepelike rounds, and folded over a filling of sweet bean paste. The *mochi* is then wrapped in three fragrant cherry leaves that have been specially prepared. The leaves are edible. In the shop you can order tea and two *sakura-mochi* for ¥250. The shop is located on the far side of the Sumida River, next to a grove of cherry trees. It's the best place to go for viewing the spring blossoms. [M-12]

- ***Manjū***—is a white or brown unsweetened sponge cake filled with sweet bean paste.

TAKEMURA　竹むら　千代田区神田須田町1-19
1-19 Sudachō, Kanda, Chiyoda-ku. Tel: 251-2328. Hrs: 11 a.m.-8 p.m., closed Sun. & Hols. In a lovely old house, they serve various kinds of desserts such as *oshiruko* (a thick, sweet bean soup with *mochi*). Try their *age-manjū* (fried *manjū*). [M-14]

MIYAGETSUDŌ　宮月堂　江東区富岡1-9-2
1-9-2 Tomioka, Kōtō-ku. Tel: 641-2446. Hrs: 10:30 a.m.-7 p.m., closed the 1st, 2nd & 3rd Wed. Miyagetsudō is on the shopping street that lines the road to Fukagawa Fudō Temple. This shop is on the right hand side. Their *Age-manjū* (¥150) is especially good. [M-25]

- **Kasutera**—a Portugese import that became popular at the beginning of the *Meiji* period, *kasutera* is a sponge cake that caused a minor revolution in the world of Japanese sweets, leading to the development of *dorayaki* and *ningyō-yaki* types of sweets.

USAGIYA　うさぎや　台東区上野1-10-10
1-10-10 Ueno, Taitō-ku. Tel: 831-6195. Hrs: 9 a.m.-6 p.m., closed Wed. This shop is known for its *dorayaki*, small sponge pancakes filled with sweet bean paste. Another specialty is *kisaku-monaka*, a crisp wafer and the inevitable bean paste. [M-13]

SHIGEMORI EISHINDŌ　重盛永信堂　中央区日本橋人形町2-1-1
2-1-1 Ningyōchō, Nihombashi, Chūō-ku. Tel: 666-5885. Hrs: 9 a.m.-8 p.m., closed Sun. (except during the local fairs when they open from 9 a.m.-6 p.m.). *Ningyō-yaki*, this shop's specialty, are small sponge cake cookies filled with bean paste and baked in various shapes. *Ningyō-yaki* are best eaten while still hot. [M-23]

KIMURAYA HOMPO　木村屋本舗　台東区浅草2-3-1
2-3-1 Asakusa, Taitō-ku. Tel: 844-9754. Hrs: 9:30 a.m.-7 p.m., closed Thur. Another specialist in *ningyō-yaki*, especially in statues, pagodas and pigeon shapes. [M-12]

YANAGIYA　柳屋　中央区日本橋人形町2-11-3
2-11-3 Ningyōchō, Nihombashi, Chūō-ku. Tel: 666-1822. Hrs: 10:30 a.m.-9 p.m., closed Sun. Some of the best *taiyaki* in town is made here. *Taiyaki* are made from thin, unsweetened dough filled with sweet bean paste and baked in the shape of a sea bream. The test for quality in *taiyaki* is whether the bean paste fills even the tail. There is almost always a long queue of people in front of the shop waiting to get them while they're hot. [M-23]

Sembei—Crackers

Sembei, Japanese crackers, are the most common snack food in Japan. Most are salty crackers made from rice flour with soy or salt flavoring, often spiced-up with a bit of seaweed (even potato chips in Japan are frequently flavored with seaweed). Sweet *sembei* are made from wheat flour, sugar, and eggs.

Most often found in the downtown districts, *sembei* shops are worth visiting as much for the shops as for the crackers.

IRIYAMA SEMBEI　入山煎餅　台東区浅草1-13-4
1-13-4 Asakusa, Taitō-ku. Tel: 844-1376. Hrs: 10 a.m.-6 p.m., closed Thur. You can watch the shop people facing each other in front of a grill, earnestly turning over dozens of roasting crackers. [M-12]

HINODE SEMBEI　日乃出せんべい　台東区浅草1-26-4
1-26-4 Asakusa, Taitō-ku. Tel: 844-4110. Hrs: 10 a.m.-8 p.m., daily. [M-12]

KIKUMI SEMBEI　菊見せんべい　文京区千駄木3-37-16
3-37-16 Sendagi, Bunkyō-ku. Tel: 821-1215. Hrs: 10 a.m.-7 p.m., closed Mon. [M-13]

MIDORIYA　みどりや　千代田区神田須田町1-13
1-13 Sudachō, Kanda, Chiyoda-ku. Tel: 251-6232. Hrs: 12 noon-7 p.m., closed Sun. & Hols., and sometimes during the week. "*Isono-ishi*"—literally "beach pebbles" are this shop's hit cracker. The shop itself is almost too cute. The shopkeeper sits on a raised *tatami* floor next to rows of round glass pots filled with different kinds of *sembei*. [M-14]

MAMEGEN　豆源　港区麻布十番1-8-12
1-8-12 Azabu-jūban, Minato-ku. Tel: 583-0962. Hrs: 9 a.m.-8 p.m., closed Tue. Their specialty is *mame-gashi*, small crackers wrapped around various kinds of roasted nuts and beans. Their freshly made *age-sembei*, fried *sembei*, is also delicious. [M-1]

Sake

Sake is the general Japanese word for any kind of alcohol. What most foreigners call *sake* is more properly referred to as *nihonshu*, or Japanese *sake*.

Made from fermented rice, there are two main types of *Nihonshu*. *Seishu* became popular after World War II when a shortage of rice led to the production of *sake* by adding alcohol and sometimes sugar to the brew. Most of the less expensive commercial brands are made this way. *Jummaishu*, pure rice wine, is by far the best. Recommended brands are "*Tamano-hikari*", "*Taruhei*", and "*Uragasumi*".

Shōchū is a distilled liquor made from rice or sweet potatoes. A Japanese version of vodka or tequila, it's a cheap, formerly low-class drink, that has recently grown popular with the young and fashionable, no doubt due in part to enormous advertising campaigns by the big liquor companies. *Goma-jōchū*, *shōchū* flavored with sesame, and *kuri-jōchū*, flavored with marron, are also good. *Umeshu* is a plum wine made, often at home, by adding *ume*—Japanese plums—and sugar to *shōchū* then aging the mixture for at least one year.

The easiest place to buy *sake* is in the liquor corner of most department store's food sections. You can usually find a selection of *sake* from all over Japan.

Amazake—literally "sweet *sake*", *amazake* is traditionally made from a mixture of boiled rice and rice malt that has fermented for a few weeks. The resulting drink is a thick, naturally sweet, non-alcoholic beverage. Commonly served at festivals, the *amazake* syrup is mixed with hot water before drinking. The process is often speeded up these days by using a combination of rice kernels left over from making other kinds of *sake*, and sugar instead of malt.

AMANOYA 天野屋　千代田区外神田2-18-1℉

2-18-15 Soto-Kanda, Chiyoda-ku. Tel: 251-7911. Hrs: 9 a.m.-6 p.m., closed Sun. Possibly the only place you can drink the traditional form of *amazake* in Tokyo, this shop has been in business since 1597. They serve it hot in the winter, and cold in the summer. Your drink will come with a small serving of *Hisakata-miso*, another house specialty, made from thick soy bean paste and rice grains. [M-14, 16]

Ocha—Tea

There are six main kinds of *ocha*, Japanese tea. The most popular is *bancha*, an inexpensive, every-day tea made from the tougher tea leaves and stems. *Hōjicha* is a roasted version of *bancha* with a subtle smokey flavor. *Gemmaicha* is roasted *bancha* mixed with kernels of popped brown rice. *Matcha* is a powdered green tea used for the tea ceremony. *Gyokuro*, the most expensive tea, has a mild, slightly sweet taste. *Sencha* is another "better" tea, usually served to guests. In the summer *mugicha*, chilled wheat tea, is also popular. Japanese tea is never served with sugar or milk.

YAMAMOTO-YAMA 山本山 中央区日本橋2-5-2
2-5-2 Nihombashi, Chūō-ku. Tel: 271-3361. Hrs: 9:30 a.m.-6 p.m., daily. Established in 1690, this is the most famous tea shop in all of Tokyo. Their tea is carried by most major department stores. [M-9]

Oshinko (Tsukemono)—Pickles

An essential part of most all Japanese meals, pickles are considered primarily a condiment for the rice. There are thousands of variations, the most common being *daikon*—white radish, *nasu*—eggplant, and *kyūri*—cucumber. In the good old days, people made their pickles at home; now that's only part of country life.

SHUETSU 酒悦 台東区上野2-7-11
2-7-11 Ueno, Taitō-ku. Tel: 831-8156. Hrs: 9 a.m.-7 p.m., daily. Since 1675. Their specialties are: *Fukujinzuke*—a purplish colored cucumber pickle, *Kukiwakame*—seaweed stalks, *Nori no Tsukudani*, and *Homboshi kakoi Takuwan*. [M-13]

Tsukudani

Invented by a fisherman who lived on Tsukuda Island to the south-east of Tokyo, *tsukudani* is a rice condiment made from small fish or seaweed boiled in a soy and sugar sauce.

TEN-YASU 天安 中央区佃1-3-14
1-3-14 Tsukuda, Chūō-ku. Tel: 531-3457 Hrs: 8 a.m.-7:30 p.m. closed the 1st and 3rd Sun. of the month. Since 1837. [M-25]

TANAKAYA 田中屋 中央区佃1-3-13
1-3-13 Tsukuda, Chūō-ku. Tel: 531-2649. Hrs: 8 a.m.-7 p.m., closed the 1st and 3rd Sun. of the month. [M-25]

Grocery Stores

Most Japanese still do their daily shopping on the neighborhood shopping street; at the fruit and vegetable stand, the fish monger, the butcher, etc. Strict zoning regulations have prevented the infiltration of big supermarkets into most areas. For convenience or for western goods, you can shop at one of the big three western-style supermarkets listed below. They charge top prices for their stock but sometimes it's worth it. Department store food departments are also a great place to shop especially for semi-prepared foods.

KINOKUNIYA INTERNATIONAL 3-11-7 Kita-Aoyama, Minato-ku. Tel: 409-1231. Hrs: 9:30 a.m.-8 p.m., daily. The best selection of bread in the city. [M-5]
NATIONAL AZABU SUPERMARKET 4-5-2 Minami-Azabu, Minato-ku. Tel: 442-3181. Hrs: 9:30 a.m.-6:30 p.m. (until 6:45 p.m. on Sun.), daily. You'll feel like you're in suburban America. [M-2]
MEIDIYA (pronounced "Meijiya") Roppongi Store: 7-15-14 Roppongi, Minato-ku. Tel: 401-8511. Hrs: 10 a.m.-10 p.m. daily [M-1]. Hirō Store: 5-6-6 Hirō, Shibuya-ku. Tel: 444-6221. Hrs: 10 a.m.-9 p.m., daily. [M-2]
NATURAL HOUSE 3-6-18 Kita-Aoyama, Minato-ku. Tel: 498-2277. Hrs: 10 a.m.-10 p.m., daily. A large health and natural foods supermarket. [M-5]

RECORDS

While buying records in Japan does not necessarily mean buying domestic releases, this seems as good a place as any for a discussion of the Japanese music business.

To get a good idea of what the Japanese local music scene is all about, turn on the TV any night between nine and eleven. There will undoubtedly be some kind of program featuring middle-aged MC's and either singers in *kimono* performing in a style something like Perry Como, or teenagers looking very, very cute. There are at least a dozen such programs, all rather reminiscent of the Ed Sullivan Show slightly updated. But only slightly.

The bulk of the market (a whopping 32%) is dominated by manufactured teen idols. Best loved are cute, round-faced girls under twenty. With an average popularity life span of approximately two years, you can estimate the length of a star's career by the length of her skirt. The newer, cuter and more adored she is, the shorter the skirt. Fading stars, reaching for a more adult audience, adopt an appropriately sophisticated image. For young boys, things work pretty much the same minus the skirt. Cuteness is definitely the major prerequisite. Coming in a close second would seem to be a total inability to sing or dance. Reigning stars at press time were veteran Matsuda Seiko, who at 21 years old has been at it since 1980, young Nakamori Akina and two former members of the "Tanokin" trio of young boys, arch rivals Toshi and Matchi.

For the mature audience, *enka* is it. Essentially the Japanese equivalent of American traditional country and western music, the *enka* repertoire is formalized and rarely deviates from the pattern. Like country and western there are a few notable singers, some of the best being Miyako Harumi, Mori Shin'ichi, and a group called "Cool Five".

Jazz is another popular genre and a few domestic performers have earned international reputations. Best known are trumpeter Hino Terumasa, saxophonist Watanabe Sadao, and Kondō Toshinori, a trumpet player who performs free music. For jazz fusion, notables are guitarist Watanabe Kazumi and the five member group Cassiopeia.

Most innovative contemporary music is connected, directly or indirectly, with the three members of the now disbanded "Yellow Magic Orchestra." Formed in 1978, the group was the first popular band to produce rock based music geared to an international audience, that wasn't ashamed of being Japanese. At the peak of their popularity in 1980, songs such as "Technopolis" and "Rydeen" played everywhere like theme songs for modern Tokyo. Though the band broke up in the fall of 1983, its three members Hosono Haruomi, Takahashi Yukihiro, and Sakamoto Ryūichi continue to be influencial both domestically and internationally.

Another band of interest is "Sandii and the Sunsetz". Together for over 10 years, the group has attracted more attention internationally than in Japan. Their music is a potent blend of predominantly Asian ethnic sources and western rock-pop traditions.

Yano Akiko is a solo artist whose music is basically sophisticated, well-produced pop. Singer, songwriter, and pianist, her high pitched voice and distinctive singing style make her one of the true Japanese originals.

Another circle of musicians revolves around the former members of a group called the "Plastics". Reformed as "Melon" in 1982, the band is fashionable and fun.

Classical Japanese Music

Recordings by classical musicians can be found in most record shops, but the largest selections are at the Ikebukuro Seibu Department Store, the Wave building in Roppongi and at Ishimaru Denki Honten in Soto-Kanda (all are included in the list of record shops that follows). The best label is CBS-Sony, which releases multi-album sets of excellent quality at exorbitant prices. When buying a record it's best to ask for a recording by one of the artists or groups listed below. Albums go in and out of print but most of these artists continue to produce new recordings.

Shamisen—The basic repertoire consists of narrative works called *katarimono* and lyrical works called *utaimono*. There are three main genres of *shamisen* music, which are better known than the particular artists. The three main genres are: *kiyomoto*, *tokiwazu*, and *shinnai*.

Gagaku—The Imperial Court Orchestra is most representative.

Koto—Most *koto* players also perform on the *shamisen*. The following two artists are designated as "National Living Treasures" by the Japanese government: Nakanoshima Kin'ichi of the *Yamada-Ryū* School, and Yonekawa Fumiko of the *Ikuta-Ryū* School.

Biwa—Most famous player is Tsuruta Kinshi.

Shakuhachi—Yokoyama Katsuya performs classical and contemporary works. Yamaguchi Gorō performs solo and in "*san-kyoku*", a trio of *koto*, *shamisen*, and *shakuhachi*. Aoki Reibō is the most classical of the three and has recorded the entire classical repertoire.

Record Shops

The following list of record stores includes general and specialty shops. Of special interest to collectors are the import shops where you can often find things that you couldn't find at home. There are no discount shops for Japanese records. Price maintenance regulations forbid the practice. As a result, foreign imports are often less expensive.

- **Imported and Domestic**

WAVE The largest record store in Tokyo, carries imports and domestic releases. For new, unknown bands check TRA—a cassette magazine sold on the 4th floor in TRAMART. [M-1]
DISK PORT in the Ikebukuro Seibu Department Store, 10th Fl., is the largest next to Wave. On the 12th Fl., Art Vivant also has a good selection. [M-18]
PIED PIPER HOUSE 5-10-6 Minami-Aoyama, Minato-ku. Tel: 499-1966. Hrs: 11 a.m.-9 p.m., daily. A good place for collectors and for finding interesting contemporary Japanese recordings, the shop is small but well-stocked. [M-5]
ISHIMARU DENKI No. 3 SHOP 1-2-13 Soto-Kanda, Chiyoda-ku. Tel: 257-1300. Hrs: 10 a.m.-7:30 p.m. (until 8 p.m. on Fri. & Sat.), daily. Has a vast selection, all very cheap. [M-14]
ISHIMARU DENKI HONTEN 1-9-14 Soto-Kanda, Chiyoda-ku. Tel: 255-3111. Hrs: 10 a.m.-7:30 p.m. (until 8 p.m. on Fri. & Sat.), daily. Best is the selection of traditional Japanese music on the 3rd and 4th floors. [M-14]

- **Imports**

TOWER RECORDS Village 80 Bldg. 2nd Fl., 39-2 Udagawachō, Shibuya-ku. Tel: 496-3661. Hrs: 10 a.m.-10 p.m., daily. A branch of the California chain, it's usually the first place you can find new U.S. releases and one of the cheapest places to buy them. [M-3]

- **Specialty Shops**

SUMIYA Tōhō Seimei Bldg. 2nd Fl., 2-15-1 Shibuya, Shibuya-ku. Tel: 409-6091. Hrs: 11 a.m.-7:30 p.m., closed the 3rd Wed. of the month. For soundtracks of stage and screen. Lots of oldies. [M-3]
MERURIDŌ Morishita Daini Bldg. 2nd Fl., 2-8 Sakuragaokachō, Shibuya-ku. Tel: 496-1629. Hrs: 12 noon-8 p.m., daily. A large collection of soul and blues. They have their own label for reissues and compilations of material often unavailable elsewhere. [M-3]
DISC UNION 3-31-4 Shinjuku, Shinjuku-ku. Tel: 352-2691. Hrs: 11 a.m.-8 p.m. (until 7 p.m. on Sun. & Hols.), daily. Good for secondhand records and jazz, especially Japanese releases of records out of print elsewhere. [M-7]
WOODSTOCK Oak Plaza Bldg. 1st Fl., 7-9-5 Nishi-Shinjuku, Shinjuku-ku. Tel: 371-5401. Hrs: 11 a.m.-7:30 p.m., daily. Black music, blues, and African. [M-7]
WINNERS Shida Bldg. 1st Fl., 7-16-15 Nishi-Shinjuku, Shinjuku-ku. [M-7] Tel: 371-1999. Hrs: 12 noon-9 p.m. Also: Shibata Yakkyoku Bldg. 3rd Fl., 3-13-8 Roppongi, Minato-ku. [M-1] Tel: 405-8190. Hrs: 12 noon-5 a.m., daily. A wide selection of contemporary black music.
OPUS ONE Ishizuka Bldg. 2nd Fl., 1-31-7 Takadanobaba, Shinjuku-ku. Tel: 200-5040. Hrs: 11 a.m.-8 p.m., daily. Good for reggae and new wave. [off Map]
UK EDISON Sakamoto Bldg. 1st Fl., 7-15-14 Nishi-Shinjuku, Shinjuku-ku. Tel: 369-3708. Hrs: 11 a.m.-9 p.m. (until 8 p.m. on Sun. & Hols), daily. Incredible selection of UK imported and deleted records. Great for collectors of old English bands. [M-7]

BOOKS

There are plenty of bookstores in Tokyo, but only a few that carry English books. All the shops in the following list have a good selection. Some hotels also have bookstores with a good stock of English books, especially books on Japan. The best hotel bookstores are the Hotel Ōkura, the Imperial Hotel, and the Hotel New Ōtani.

General Bookstores
KINOKUNIYA 3-17-7 Shinjuku, Shinjuku-ku. Tel: 354-0131. Hrs: 10 a.m.-7 p.m., closed the 1st & 3rd Wed. of the month. Foreign books on the 5th Fl. [M-7]

MARUZEN 2-3-10 Nihombashi, Chūō-ku. Tel: 272-7211. Hrs: 10 a.m.-6 p.m., closed Sun. Foreign books on the 3rd Fl. [M-9]
JENA (pronounced "Yena") 5-6-1 Ginza, Chūō-ku. Tel: 571-2980. Hrs: 10:30 a.m.-7:50 p.m. (12:30 p.m.-6:45 p.m. Sun.), closed Hols. Foreign books on the 3rd Fl. [M-8]
SANSEIDŌ 1-1 Jimbōchō, Kanda, Chiyoda-ku. Tel: 233-3312. Hrs: 10 a.m.-6 p.m., Dec.-May open daily, June-Nov. closed on Tue. Foreign books on the 5th Fl., 1st Fl. has maps. [M-15]
KITAZAWA SHOTEN 2-5 Jimbōchō, Kanda, Chiyoda-ku. Tel: 263-0011. Hrs: 10 a.m.-6 p.m. closed Sun. 2nd Fl.: Secondhand Books, 1st Fl.: English & American Literature & philosophy. [M-15]
NATIONAL BOOK STORE National Azabu Supermarket 2nd Fl., 4-5-2 Minami-Azabu, Minato-ku. Tel: 442-3181. Hrs: 9:30 a.m.-6:30 p.m., daily. [M-2]

Specialized Bookstores

ON SUNDAYS 3-7-6 Jingūmae, Shibuya-ku. Tel: 478-0809. Hrs: 11 a.m.-10 p.m., closed Mon. Art books, mostly foreign, and great cards. [M-5]
ART VIVANT Ikebukuro Seibu Department Store 12th Fl. [M-18] Also Roppongi Wave Bldg. 4th Fl. [M-1] For Japanese and foreign art books. Tel: 408-0111.
BONJINSHA Kōjimachi Roku-chōme Bldg. 6th Fl., 6-2 Kōjimachi, Chiyoda-ku. Tel: 265-7782. Hrs: 9:30 a.m.-5:30 p.m. (until 2:30 p.m. on Sat.), closed Sun. & Hols. Textbooks on Japan and Japanese Language. [M-31]

English language books can be mail ordered from the following two companies in the U.S. Write for a catalogue.
U.S. BOOK OVERSEAS SERVICE P.O. Box 2066, Great Neck, N.Y., U.S.A., 11022.
THE STRAND BOOKSTORE 828 Broadway, New York, N.Y., USA, 10003

Jimbōchō Book District

Jimbōchō in Kanda is the Tokyo "secondhand book district". Shops here only occasionally carry books in English, but often have an wide stock of items such as *ukiyoe* prints, old magazines, maps, stamps, movie posters, etc. The list below notes only a few of the more interesting shops. Because most shops are concentrated along one street clearly marked on the Jimbōchō/Kanda map [M-15], we have only included the phone numbers here. Shops are open from 10 a.m.-6 p.m., and closed the 1st and 3rd Sunday of the month.

SANCHA SHOBŌ Tel: 291-0453. Literature, *kokeshi* dolls.
ŌYA SHOBŌ Tel: 291-0062. *Edo* period literature, maps, and *ukiyoe*.
TUTTLE BOOK SHOP Tel: 291-7072. Books on Japan and the Far East. Some in English and some secondhand.
MATSUMURA SHOTEN Tel: 291-2410. Art books.
KANDA KOSHO CENTER—This building has seven floors and eleven shops, most of which specialize in one area such as old movie memorabilia, maps and old prints, old magazines, old comic books, etc. You could spend hours here.
HARA SHOBŌ Tel: 261-7444. *Ukiyoe*, books on astrology.
TOKYO TAIBUNSHA Tel: 261-1273. Books and magazines.
TOYODA SHOBŌ Tel: 261-1589. Books on Japanese theater.
HAGA SHOTEN Tel: 263-3956. Pornography.

OTHER SHOPS
Art and Office Supplies
ITŌYA 2-7-15 Ginza, Chūō-ku. Tel: 561-8311. Hrs: 9:30 a.m.-6 p.m. (10 a.m.-6 p.m. on Sun. & Hols.), daily. Established since 1904, this is one of the best supply shops in town, with eight floors of merchandise. On the 5th Fl. is a good stock of Japanese paper. [M-8]
LAPIS Axis Bldg. 3rd Fl. Tel: 583-0861. Hrs: 9:30 a.m.-8 p.m. (10:30 a.m.-7 p.m. on Sun. & Hols), daily. Also Roppongi (next to the Wave Bldg.): Tōnichi Bldg. 1st Fl. 6-2-31 Roppongi, Minato-ku. Tel: 405-2821. Hrs: 9:30 a.m.-8 p.m. (10:30 a.m.-7 p.m. on Sun. & Hols), daily. A well stocked office and art supply store, they have a copy service, and are one of the few places that can do color copies. [M-1]
LEMON 2-6 Surugadai, Kanda, Chiyoda-ku. Tel: 295-4681. Hrs: 10 a.m.-8 p.m., closed the 5th Sun. This shop is best known for its good selection of art supplies. [M-15]
KIYA 3-44-8 Yushima, Bunkyō-ku. Tel: 831-8688. Hrs: 9 a.m.-6:30 p.m., closed Mon. Japanese art supplies; paper, ink, and brushes for *sumie*, etc. [M-13]

Cosmetics

SHŪ UEMURA BEAUTY BOUTIQUE 5-1-3 Jingūmae, Shibuya-ku. Tel: 486-0048. Hrs: 10 a.m.-8 p.m., daily. An absolutely incredible cosmetics boutique, this shop sells make-up artist Uemura Shū's cosmetics in a huge variety of colors. They also have make-up boxes, brushes, etc. There is a testing table in front of a big mirror that's always crowded with Harajuku girls putting on a new face. The boutique has other branches around town, but this one is the largest. [M-4]
ORIENTAL 4-9-9 Roppongi, Minato-ku. Tel: 401-8882. Hrs: 10:30 a.m.-9:30 p.m. (12 noon-8 p.m. on Sun. & Hols.), daily. A good selection of domestic and imported cosmetic lines, brushes, pencils, make-up boxes, etc. Upstairs is a small boutique for lingerie. [M-1]

Discount Shops
The following shops carry a variety of merchandise at discount prices.
KOBUTSU NO DAIMARU 19-17 Maruyamachō, Shibuya-ku, Tel: 462-0781. Hrs: 9 a.m.-7 p.m., closed Sun. Secondhand furniture, appliances, just about everything in this huge shop literally overflowing with bargains. [off Map]
KIMURAYA 2-1 Surugadai, Kanda, Chiyoda-ku. Tel: 294-7531. Hrs: 10 a.m.-8 p.m., daily. 20-30% discounts on electronics, watches, cameras, toys, shoes and socks, bags, etc. This is one of Tokyo's most famous discount shops. [M-15]
SAMPEI STORE 3-22-14 Shinjuku, Shinjuku-ku. Tel: 352-1634. Hrs: 10:30 a.m.-9 p.m., daily. Clothing, food, electronics, etc., at about 20% off. [M-7]
TOKYO HYAKKA FUNABASHIYA 1-17-8 Midori, Sumida-ku. Tel: 634-4541. Hrs: 10:30 a.m.-8 p.m., daily. Furniture, interior goods, food, clothing, sporting goods, etc. [M-24]

Fabrics
Besides the two shops listed below, fabrics can be found in Nippori, a wholesale and retail fabric district. Department stores also have fabric departments, as does Tōkyū Hands.
NUNO "Functional Textile Shop" Axis Bldg. B1, 5-17-1 Roppongi, Minato-ku. Tel: 582-7997. Hrs: 11 a.m.-7 p.m., closed Mon. This shop sells fabrics that Miyake Issey and Kawakubo Rei of Comme des Garçon would love. The fabrics are in natural or neutral shades, a few prints, and amazing weaves. [M-1]
WACOAL FABRICS HOUSE "Linge de Maison" Shibuya Parco Part 1, 1st Fl. [M-3] Tel: 496-9516. Also in Odakyū Halc 6th Fl. [M-7] Interior decorating fabrics, some original Wacoal prints but also European fabrics.

Interiors
AXIS BUILDING 5-17-1 Roppongi, Minato-ku. Most shops close on Mon. This entire building specializes in merchandise for interiors. [M-1]
ODAKYŪ HALC 1-1-3 Nishi-Shinjuku, Shinjuku-ku. Tel: 342-1111. Hrs: 10 a.m.-6 p.m., closed Thur. Halc is Odakyū Department Store's interior section, and is in a building next to the main department store. Halc stands for "Happy Living Center". [M-7]
HABITAT Ikebukro: 1-19-6 Minami-Ikebukuro, Toshima-ku. Tel: 980-0111. Hrs: 10 a.m.-6 p.m., closed Thur. [M-18] Shibuya: Seibu B-kan 5th & 6th Fl. 21-1 Udagawachō, Shibuya-ku. Tel: 462-0111. Hrs: 10 a.m.-7 p.m., closed Wed. [M-3] Licensed from the British Habitat, the designs are the English originals but are made in Japan. There is a good selection of furniture and housewares.
INNOVATOR SHOP 1-4-7 Kita-Aoyama, Minato-ku, Tel: 403-7544. Hrs: 10 a.m.-6 p.m., daily. Furniture, half imported, half made in Japan from Swedish designs. Has a good selection of folding chairs and other pieces suitable for smaller apartments. [M-5]
PARCO PART 3 Shibuya Parco. Various shops selling some domestic, some foreign brands. Furniture and housewares. [M-3]
TŌKYŪ HANDS Good for do-it-yourself interiors and home improvements. [M-3]
DESIGN STUDIO OKAMOTO 4-10-15 Minami Aoyama, Minato-ku. Tel: 423-1937. Hrs: 10 a.m.-6:30 p.m., closed Sun. & Hols. A small shop selling interior accessories and furniture. The Japanese designer for this shop studied in Italy for 6 years. [M-5]
ONE OFF 2-20-11 Jingūmae, Shibuya-ku. Tel: 478-2175. Hrs: 11 a.m.-8 p.m., closed Sun. & Hols. Interior accessories, etc., all made from acrylic materials. [off Map]
MIDGET Marion Bldg. 1st Fl., 3-7-1 Jingūmae, Shibuya-ku. Tel: 404-3271. Hrs: 10 a.m.-8 p.m., closed Mon. Modern, modular and moderately priced furniture and housewares, this shop is great for decorating a tiny Japanese sized apartment. Art direction for the shop is by Yokoyama Tadamasa, a local designer, painter and musician. [M-5]
SABBY GENTEEL Avenue Side Bldg. 2nd Fl., 3-9 Sarugakuchō, Shibuya-ku. Tel: 461-5029. Hrs: 12 noon-8 p.m. (Sun. & Hols. until 7 p.m.), closed Mon. Simple but well designed furniture and housewares. [M-20]

Luggage
Because shopping is so good in Tokyo, most visitors buy far more than will fit into the luggage they brought with them. Luckily, the Japanese also make terrific cheap "carry-all" bags from fabrics, plastics or very good imitation leathers. The best places to find such bags are fashion buildings like Parco (there are a number of shops in Part 1 of the Shibuya branch) or La Foret (Harajuku). Department stores have bags as well as luggage. For cheap suitcases, Ameyoko Arcade in Ueno is good.

Pearls
MIKIMOTO 4-5-5 Ginza, Chūō-ku. Tel: 535-4611. Hrs: 10:30 a.m.-6 p.m., closed Wed. The most famous of Tokyo pearl shops, Mikimoto's merchandise is of high quality with comparably high prices. The main Ginza store is worth stopping by to see the displays of their original designs. [M-8]
MORI SILVER Oriental Bazaar, 2nd Fl. Tel: 407-7010. A reputable local manufacturer and wholesaler of silver, pearls and ivory, the prices at their retail shop are some of the most reasonable in town—you don't pay for a "middleman" here. The pearls are of good quality, as are their ivory, and *netsuke* (both old and new). The shop also accepts custom orders for jewelry. [M-4]

Shoes

The Japanese make terrific, cheap, fashionable shoes; most of which are sized for tiny Japanese feet. A few shops do specialize in large sized shoes, or will have a few in stock.

DIANA Ginza: Kyōdō Bldg. 6-9-6 Ginza, Chūō-ku. Tel: 573-4001. Hrs: 10:30 a.m.-8 p.m., daily (large sizes on the 4th Fl.) [M-8]. Harajuku: 1-8-21 Jingūmae, Shibuya-ku. Tel: 478-4001. Hrs: 10:30 a.m.-8 p.m., daily (large sizes on the 2nd Fl.) [M-4]. A good selection of women's shoes up to size 26 cm. The Harajuku shop is geared to a younger clientele.

WASHINGTON 5-7-7 Ginza, Chūō-ku. Tel: 572-5911. Hrs: 10:30 a.m.-8 p.m., closed the 3rd Wed. of the month. Large sized men's and women's shoes on the 5th Fl. [M-8]

BIG SHOES 3-21-18 Akasaka, Minato-ku. Tel: 586-6234. Hrs: 10:30 a.m.-8:30 p.m. (until 6 p.m. on Sun. & Hols.), daily. Men's and women's large sizes in stock, they also accept custom orders. [M-6]

TOKIO KUMAGAI (see Women's Designers list) Beautiful, sometimes outrageous shoes—and sometimes in larger sizes.

CALZERIA HOSONO Aoyama Elle Bldg. 2nd Fl., 5-1-2 Minami-Aoyama, Minato-ku. Tel: 409-9425. Hrs: 11 a.m.-8 p.m. (12 noon-8 p.m. Sun. & Hols.), daily. This shop doesn't carry large shoes, but accepts custom orders. Sandals from ¥20,000, pumps from ¥24,000. [M-5]

MEDA 5-9-12 Minami-Aoyama, Minato-ku. Tel: 498-3491. Hrs: 11 a.m.-8 p.m., closed Sun. Women's shoes, not so large, but at least up to 25 cm. [M-5]

TELLUS 2-3-1 Dōgenzaka, Shibuya-ku. Tel: 463-7756. Hrs: 11 a.m.-8 p.m., closed one day every 3 months. Most shoes in this shop are sized up to 24.5cm (women) and 26.5cm (men). They occasionally have size 25cm. The shoes are lovely in any case. [M-3]

Sembei displayed in the traditional way (near Shibamata Taishakuten Temple)
©M. YOSHIDA

Toys

KIDDYLAND 6-1-9 Jingūmae, Shibuya-ku. Tel: 409-3431. Hrs: 10 a.m.-7 p.m. (until 8 p.m. on Sat. & Sun.), closed the 3rd. Tues. A favorite hang-out for Harajuku "kids", Kiddyland has a huge selection of toys, and other miscellaneous playthings. [M-4]
TOY PARK Hakuhinkan 2nd-4th Fl., 8-8-11 Ginza, Chūō-ku. Tel: 571-8008. Hrs: 11 a.m.-8 p.m., daily. The largest toy shop in Japan. [M-8]
PLAYTHINGS Axis Bldg. 2nd Fl. Tel: 587-2005. Hrs: 11 a.m.-8 p.m., closed Mon. The shop carries games and toys from around the world. The toy company "Tsukuda" has its showroom here. [M-1]

Miscellaneous Shops

MUJIRUSHI RYŌHIN 5-50-6 Jingūmae, Shibuya-ku. Tel: 407-4666. Hrs: 10:30 a.m.-7 p.m., closed most Thur. A shop selling generic "non-brand" goods made from natural materials, mostly cheaper than elsewhere. Stock includes food, clothing, housewares, accessories, even bicycles. They also have a shop in the Shibuya Seibu B-kan 5th Fl., and at Seiyū on the 1st Fl. [M-5]
DAICHŪ Shibuya: 16-13 Udagawachō, Shibuya-ku. Tel: 463-8756. Hrs: 11 a.m.-9 p.m., closed the 3rd Wed. [M-3] Roppongi: 3-16-26 Roppongi, Minato-ku. Tel: 584-0725, Hrs: 11 a.m.-10 p.m., closed the 3rd Wed. [M-1] A Chinese import store with clothing, baskets, bamboo blinds, and a wide selection of other interesting and amusing merchandise. Not as cheap as you could buy it for in Hong Kong, but still a bargain.

ENTERTAINMENT

In this poster for the Kabuki-za Theater, an aging *kabuki* master actor portrays a beautiful young courtesan. By isolating and abstracting the elements of feminine beauty and behavior, the Japanese believe that a man can successfully project the essence of a woman.

ENTERTAINMENT

TRADITIONAL THEATER

The beginnings of Japanese theater are recorded in the oldest history of Japan, the *Kojiki*. The legend tells how the Sun Goddess, angry with her brother, blocks herself in a cave for revenge. The world is left in darkness, while the other gods try, in vain, to coax her out. When one of the goddesses begins performing a comical, erotic dance, the rest break out in laughter. Not wanting to be left out of the fun, the Sun Goddess peaks out and stays to watch the performance. By the end of the dance, she had forgotten her anger and returned to the heavens. The religious aspects, the dance, the eroticism of this legendary performance, are all important elements of later theater.

The various forms of Japanese theater developed in different periods, under the patronage of different social classes. All became formalized at a certain stage of development and for hundreds of years performance has rigidly preserved the traditions. Japanese theater audiences tend to be older; most young people will confess to having viewed *kabuki*, perhaps once or twice, on television.

The major forms of Japanese traditional theater are covered in the next section. Music and dance, both intregal parts of all Japanese theater, have not been covered independently. They are performed separately throughout the year at various small concert halls and theaters (most often at the National Theater), and can occasionally be seen at festivals. Following the description of the theater forms is information on theater locations and purchasing tickets.

Gagaku and *Bugaku*

The *gagaku* orchestra and the *bugaku* dance performed to *gagaku* music were among the arts imported from the Asian continent during the 7th century. A favorite entertainment of the *Heian* court, by the 11th century the nobility were rewriting the music in a more Japanese style. The decline of the court in the 13th century likewise resulted in a period of decline in these arts that lasted until the *Meiji* Restoration. Possibly the oldest form of orchestral music in the world, *gagaku* music heard today is almost identical to the music performed over 1,000 years ago.

The composition of the *gagaku* orchestra will vary according to the origins of the piece (i.e. from what part of Asia) and whether it is performed as a concert or for the dance. The major instruments are: *hichiriki*—a small oboe that plays the main melody, flutes—of various kinds that play a variation of the *hichiriki* melody, *shō*—a bamboo mouth organ with 17 pipes that provides a harmonic background, *kakko*—a small drum that rests on the floor and is usually played by a senior member of the orchestra who acts as a conductor, *taiko*—a large drum, *shōko*—a small gong, *dadaiko*—a large drum used to mark rhythm in dance pieces, *koto*—a 13 stringed instrument that rests on the floor (not used for dance pieces), *biwa*—a lute used in dance pieces, voice— used only with music of Japanese origin. The Imperial Court Orchestra is the most famous *gagaku* performing group.

Nō

When the warrior class entered Kyōto in the *Muromachi* period (1336-1575), they brought along their taste for the popular *dengaku* field dances and *sarugaku* "monkey music" comic mimes. Under the patronage of the third Ashikaga shōgun, Yoshimitsu, the *sarugaku* performer and writer Kan'ami (1333-84) polished and perfected these early dramatic forms. The resultant theater was called *nō*.

The form of *nō* seen today follows the aesthetic principles laid down by Kan'ami. His son Zeami (1363-1443) is credited with writing most of the extant 250 *nō* plays. Unlike western theater where plot and intellectual experience is important, *nō* is an almost purely aesthetic experience. All aspects of *nō*—the dance, music, chanting and costuming —are painstakingly calculated to achieve this. Action proceeds at a slow and deliberate pace, with movements and gestures carefully measured and stylized. Gorgeous costuming furthers the impact by adding color and pattern to the dance.

The subject matter of *nō* is concerned with the transient nature of this world, the sins of lust and killing, the power of Buddha and the truth of an afterlife. These were problems raised by the political realities of the time. Warfare was endemic and *nō* served as a spiritual release for the warrior class.

All roles in *nō* are performed by men. Make-up is not used, but masks are worn by the principle actor for certain roles. Often created by master craftsmen, the masks themselves are valuable works of art.

An orchestra and chorus of five to eight persons is on stage throughout. The principle role of the chorus is to provide vocal accompaniment to the dance and comments on the action. The orchestra is composed of three kinds of drums and a flute.

Nō was originally performed out of doors on a roofed wooden stage, with a narrow bed of sand or stone separating the audience from the stage while providing the proper visual perspective. Actors enter and exit by a passageway, extending off the back of the stage to the left, that symbolically separates the real from the spirit world. The stage is bare except for a painting of a twisted pine tree on the back wall. Though the scene may change a number of times within the play, concrete expression through backdrops and scenery changes is not given. Rather a symbolic and spiritual atmosphere is sought; the occasional stage prop will be little more than a suggestion—a pine branch will represent an entire forest.

The language used in *nō* is archaic. Even most Japanese need a script to follow the dialogue ridden with ambiguous phrases and allusions to ancient verse. For both Japanese and foreigners alike, *nō* is a profoundly difficult form of art. When Zeami first began to write the plays, he wanted them to be accessible to even the peasants. In the end, however, he admitted that he, alone, could grasp their meaning.

Kyōgen

Kyōgen are short comical "relief" plays performed between *nō* plays. *Ai-kyōgen*, are *kyōgen* performed between the acts of a *nō* play. There are usually two or three actors and no musical or vocal accompaniment. Where *nō* is stately, stylized and symbolic, *kyōgen* is plebeian, realistic and satirical. Nearly one third of the remaining *kyōgen* plays center on the relationship between a *daimyō* feudal lord and his servant Tarōkaja. The *daimyō* is made ridiculous by the servant, but in the end is always proven right (the *daimyō* were, after all, the rulers and patrons of the art). Buddhism, the often corrupt religion of the upper class, was also a major subject of the satires.

Bunraku

Bunraku is the common name for a form of classical drama using puppets. The proper name is *Ningyō Jōruri*, meaning puppet drama with voice and *shamisen* accompaniment. Though it developed into a form of adult theater, its origins were in a children's amusement performed by street puppeteers who manipulated the puppets on top of a box while singing and providing dialogue. Later, the puppeteers combined their skills with those of the *jōruri*, musical storytellers popular in the 14th century.

While early developments in *bunraku* theater were made in Kyōto and Ōsaka, the next stage of development was in Edo (Tokyo). In response to the rather "martial" temperament of the *Edo* population, a puppeteer named Satsuma Jōun introduced a more "heroic" style in the theater. Violent and bombastic action and recitation soon dominated the puppet theater, even affecting the acting styles of humans in the less popular *kabuki*. After the great *Edo* fire of 1657, the theater moved back to Ōsaka and Kyoto.

With the establishment of the Ōsaka Takemoto-za Bunraku Theater in 1685, two major artists, from different fields, combined talents and perfected the art. Takemoto Gidayū (1651-1714) refined the singing and chanting styles. Chikamatsu Monzaemon (1653-1724) wrote some of the greatest masterpieces of Japanese theater. *Bunraku* became immensely popular and flourished through the middle of the 18th century when it was surpassed by *kabuki*.

Bunraku puppets are about one-third human size. Only the head is completely modeled, but the bodies and facial features are fully jointed (even the eyeballs roll). The main puppets are manipulated by three men. The master puppeteer, dressed in formal *kimono*, controls the head and the right arm. The remaining two are dressed in black with their faces covered by hoods. One controls the left arm, the other controls the legs. The *bunraku* stage allows the puppeteers to work in a semi-concealed standing position.

On a platform to the right of the stage sits the *gidayū* singer, accompanied by a *shamisen* player, who supplies the dialogue for all roles. As much actor as singer, the *gidayū*, through an intense range of vocal and facial expression, brings life to the puppets.

Ōsaka continues to be the home of *bunraku*, but it can be seen on occasion at the National Theater in Tokyo.

Kabuki

In the pleasure quarters of the great *Edo* period cities, *kabuki* became the definitive theater form of the masses. Considered vulgar by the military aristocracy, *kabuki* grew through the generous patronage of the wealthy merchant class. After the *Meiji* Restoration *kabuki* became a respectable art form, with the final seal of approval given by an Imperial viewing in 1887. Until twenty or thirty years ago the Kabuki Theater was a favorite place to have the first meeting between the potential partners of a matched marriage (the events of the drama provided an easy subject of conversation for people who had never met).

Kabuki originated in erotic dance-dramas performed by a woman named *Okuni* in the mid-16th century. As her dances grew in popularity, troupes of men and women performers began to tour the country. These early performances served mainly as a cover for prostitution, and eventually women were prohibited from appearing on stage. The performances were continued, but with beautiful young men performing as erotically as had the women. These too were eventually outlawed and *kabuki* was forced to develop a dramatic style that no longer depended solely on erotic appeal. Though men continued to play women's roles, plots became increasingly sophisticated, and acting skills developed into a master art.

While *kabuki* is now considered a serious, "elevated" form of traditional theater, the *Edo* period audiences were a predominately drunk and rowdy crowd. Desperately attempting to gain their attention, the actors used to shout their lines. They eventually found that by suddenly falling silent and striking a dramatic, often cross-eyed, pose, they could effectively shut the audience up for a few moments. The pose has become one of the "trademarks" of *kabuki*.

The *kabuki* repertoire consists of around 350 plays, the last major works written in the late 19th century. Popular plays from the *nō* and *bunraku* repertoire were also adapted for the *kabuki* stage. Drama in *kabuki* often revolves around the struggle between social obligation—*giri*, and personal feelings and emotion—*ninjō*. Evidence of the intensity of social pressures during *samurai* rule, this *giri-ninjō* conflict usually ends in tragedy. Revenge is another common theme. Harm done to one's lord or loved ones must be repaid and often results in death for the avenger.

Music is an essential element in *kabuki*. The combination of instruments and singers will vary according to the kind of play. The major instrumental components are flute, hand drums and *shamisen*. Occasionally used are a big Chinese drum and cymbals. In plays derived from *bunraku*, a *gidayū* singer and a *shamisen* player are visible on a raised platform to the right of the stage.

In both *Edo* and *Meiji* periods, *kabuki* actors had tremendous followings and were fashion trendsetters, starting fads for a certain kind of hair style or *kimono*. Families of actors, some like the Danjirō family established since the early *Edo* period, pass skills from father to son. As an actor's level of artistic achievement rises, he inherits increasingly prestigious family stage names. If a son proves untalented, the names are passed to a talented apprentice or are left unused until an appropriate candidate appears. Certain families specialize in particular types of roles; some families are known for the aragoto style of the strong hero figures (derived originally from the puppet theater), while others are known for onnagata, women's roles. Recently a few actors have begun appearing in other forms of theater. Bandō Tamasaburō, probably the most famous player of women's roles in kabuki, has performed, as a woman, in various western stage and movie productions. Other young actors are regulars in television dramas.

Kabuki has changed little in the past hundred years. Repertoire, acting styles, costumes and staging follow precedents established long ago. There are few real surprises for the audience, but actors continue to be a source of freshness. Within the strict conventions of the theater, the actor is still able to interpret a part in a new way. An extreme example is the well-known actor Ichikawa Ennosuke who once, pulling out a pair of dark glasses and a microphone, began performing a rock and roll song in the middle of a traditional play. During high points of the performance, true fans in the audience will shout their approval—calling out the actor's family name, or the name of a famous actor of the past for comparison.

Kabuki is perhaps the most accessible form of classical Japanese theater for contemporary audiences. In Tokyo the main theater is the Kabuki-za, where performances are given every month except in July and August. There are matinées and evening programs. Each program consists of three or four separate works, usually ending with a dance piece. Any one of them can be missed if the whole program is too long for your attention span. There are short intermissions between each play, sometimes between acts, and one longer break for lunch or dinner. Bring your own food, or eat in one of the theater restaurants. English programs are available as are small translating radios, which are helpful in explaining background, symbolism or action in the play.

Shimpa

Shimpa started as a form of political theater organized by a liberal political party in response to the rigid Meiji period government's ban on party meetings. Originally a strictly amateur theater, the level was gradually raised to professional.

Though men continued to play women's roles, for the first time since the beginning of the Edo period, women appeared on stage. An attempt at realism was made, but acting in shimpa was still influenced by the styles of kabuki. The major difference between the two lay in shimpa's concern with events contemporary in the Meiji era. Another area of divergence was the use of actors not connected with the traditional established families of actors. Shimpa developed little after 1910, and though considered modern drama, it serves more as a transitional phase between classical and modern forms of theater.

Rakugo

There is even a traditional form of comic monologue in Japan, called *rakugo*, this "art of talking" has a history of over 400 years. It is still performed today in small variety halls called *yose*, but its biggest audiences are on television and radio.

The *rakugo* storyteller wears a *kimono* and sits in front of the audience on a *tatami*-matted stage. For props he carries a fan and a small *tenugui* towel. These two props become anything from chopsticks to calculators in his hands.

The predecessors of *rakugo* were street entertainers, popular even before the *Edo* period. But the fashionable *Edo* public loved the fast talking and sophisticated jokes of these storytellers. Many of jokes they told hundreds of years ago have become part of the language, almost like proverbs, although most people are unaware of their *rakugo* origins.

While there is a standard repertoire of old jokes and dialogues, young *rakugo* artists cover contemporary events such as the Lockheed scandal, Paul McCartney's drug bust, or humorous incidents of daily life. As in *kabuki* and *nō*, the storytellers belong to families and spend long years in training. The art of the Japanese comedian is not to be taken lightly.

Geisha

The *geisha* remains a misunderstood symbol of the more exotic aspects of Japan and Japanese history. The question most often asked by foreigners is an unimaginative "does she, or doesn't she". Basically she doesn't, at least that isn't her main role. Prostitution was rather the work of the *oiran*, who was last in line after the client was entertained in the tea houses by the accomplished *geisha*.

The *geisha* was first and foremost an entertainer, the highest class being so accomplished in a variety of arts, so perfectly mannered and attired—that she came as close to a human work of art as is possible.

In the licensed pleasure quarters of the *Edo* period, the *geisha* kept company with some of the wealthiest and most influential men of the time. Now, aside from big business men and politicians who can afford the nearly $500 a head it costs, few people ever see a *geisha* in action. While the steepness of the price has cut down on the clientele, the rigours of the training, in an art with rules as fixed as those of all forms of traditional theater, has diminished the numbers of women willing to undertake it. In their place the hostesses in hundreds of bars, nightclubs and cabarets entertain businessmen by chatting mixing endless *mizu-*

wari (whiskey and water) and occasionally dancing with them to nostalgic music played by the club's live band. Now people always want to know "do the hostesses, or don't they". The answer is some do, but some, in fact most, don't.

Unless you're willing to pay the nearly $500 a head it will cost to see *geisha* at work in a *ryōtei*, your opportunities to see one are rather limited. The *geisha* do make an appearance at two local festivals, where they parade down the street in all their finery. The two are the Sanja Matsuri in Asakusa on the 3rd Sat. & Sun. of May, and the Autumn *Oiran* Parade which happens annually at an unfixed date in the Fall. They also perform traditional dances twice a year. At the end of April *geisha* perform the "*Asakusa Odori*" at the Kabukiza in Ginza, and at the end of May they perform the "*Azuma Odori*" at the Shimbashi Enbujō. Both performances are given for about three days only.

You can see an "*oiran* and folkdance" performance at Matsubaya in the old Yoshiwara pleasure quarters. Formerly a famous *oiran* house, they now cater to tourists and provide a show (with English commentary) that is by no means authentic but about as close as you'll get to the real thing.

MATSUBAYA 4-33-1 Senzoku, Taitō-ku. Tel: 874-9401. Show plus one bottle of beer or *sake* ¥2,000. From 9:20 p.m. (for 40 min.). You can also have a *sukiyaki* or *tempura* dinner before the show for ¥7,700. Daily.

Tickets, Theaters and Information

While both *kabuki* and *nō* are regularly performed at specialized theaters, other traditional theater arts are performed on occasion at any number of halls around the city. Tickets can generally be purchased at Playguides or at the theater (in advance or sometimes on the day of the performance). Tickets, or at least the best seats, sell out early.

Information on current events can be found in the tourist publications, at TIC or from the TIC Teletourist service.

Geijutsu-sai is an annual competition for performing and fine arts held from the beginning of October through mid-November. Sponsored by the Bunka-chō (Culture Division) of the Ministry of Education, artists are invited to perform and compete for a prize. The result is an incredible amount of artistic activity around this time, when various artists perform in Tokyo in hopes of gaining an invitation to participate in the event. Performances range from concerts of traditional music, dance and theater to contemporary and avant-garde works. Western art forms are also presented.

Information on the various events is rather hard to find. The schedule for the offical *Geijutsu-sai* events can be obtained from TIC.

ENTERTAINMENT

- **General theaters**
NATIONAL THEATER 4-1 Hayabusachō, Chiyoda-ku. Tel: 265-7411. [M-6]
SHIMBASHI EMBUJŌ 6-18-2 Ginza, Chūō-ku. Tel: 541-2211. [M-8]

- **Nō**—The best way to purchase tickets for *nō* is to go directly to the theater. *Nō* tickets are also sold at **Wan'ya Shoten** but they tend to sell out quickly. Tickets cost between ¥2,500-¥10,000.

KANZE NŌ THEATER 1-16-4 Shōtō, Shibuya-ku. Tel: 469-5241. The Kanze school of *nō* is the oldest, and closest to the original form. [M-33]
HŌSHŌ NŌ THEATER 1-5-9 Hongō, Bunkyō-ku. Tel: 811-4843. Hōshō school. [M-30]
YARAI NŌ THEATER 60 Yaraichō, Shinjuku-ku. Tel: 268-7311. Yarai school. [off Map]
KITA ROKUHEITA KINEN THEATER 4-6-9 Kami-Ōsaki, Shinagawa-ku. Tel: 491-7773. Kita school. [off Map]
NATIONAL THEATER NŌ HALL 4-18-1 Sendagaya, Shibuya-ku. Tel: 423-1331. This theater was opened in the fall of 1983. [M-29]
GINZA NŌ THEATER Ginza Nōgakudō Bldg. 9th Fl., 6-5-15 Ginza, Chūō-ku. Tel: 571-0197. [M-8]
UMEWAKA NŌ THEATER 2-6-14 Higashi-Nakano, Nakano-ku. Tel: 363-7748. [off Map]
TESSENKAI NŌGAKU KENSHŪJO 4-21-29 Minami-Aoyama, Minato-ku. Tel: 401-2285. The Tessenkai group performs monthly on the 2nd Fri. [M-5]

- *Kabuki*
KABUKI-ZA 4-12 Ginza, Chūō-ku. Tel: 541-3131. This is the main *kabuki* theater. Tickets are sold at the theater, in advance or on the day of the show. Prices range from ¥7,000-¥10,000 for first floor seats, *tatami* matted box seats cost ¥11,000-¥12,000. Balcony seats are ¥3,000 (recommended—try to get seats near the front), and ¥1,500. You can see just one of the plays for ¥600-¥800. If you decide you want to stay and watch more, there is a ticket booth on the fourth floor. [M-8]

- *Gagaku* and *Bugaku*—The *gagaku* music is performed more regularly than is the *bugaku* dance. Concerts are held two or three times a year at the **National Theater**, and occasionally at the local shrine festivals. You can watch *gagaku* practice at **Onoterusaki Shrine** (2-13-14 Shitaya, Taitō-ku. Tel: 872-5514) every month except January and August, on the 6th from 7:30 p.m.-8:30 p.m. You don't need to make any arrangements, just show up.

A group called the **Jūnionkai**, young musicians from the Imperial Court Orchestra, hold performances twice a year at the **Tokyo Bunka Kaikan**, usually in June and sometime in the Autumn. Call the theater for the next date.

- *Rakugo*—*Rakugo* is performed at a number of variety halls called *yose*. Tickets can be bought in advance or on the day of the show.

HOMMOKUTEI 2-6 Ueno, Taitō-ku. Tel: 831-6137. The only theater in Tokyo with all *tatami* seating. [M-13]
SUEHIROTEI 3-6-12 Shinjuku, Shinjuku-ku. Tel: 351-2974. [M-7]
SUZUMOTO ENGEIJŌ 2-7-12 Ueno, Taitō-ku. Tel: 834-5906. [M-13]
ASAKUSA ENGEI HALL 1-43-12 Asakusa, Taitō-ku. Tel: 841-6545. [M-12]
IKEBUKURO ENGEIJŌ 1-23-7 Nishi-Ikebukuro, Toshima-ku. Tel: 971-4545. [M-18]
ASAKUSA MOKUBATEI 2-7-5 Asakusa, Taitō-ku. Tel: 844-6293. [M-12]

CONTEMPORARY THEATER

Contemporary theater in Japan can be basically divided into main stream *shingeki* and underground theater. *Shingeki*, or the "new drama movement" started early in the century and was initially an attempt to create a modern theater for Japan. European classics were favored and companies using non-traditional methods of training actors were formed. The best known *shingeki* troupes are the Haiyūza and Bungakuza. Both perform western and Japanese drama, though the Haiyūza's performances are generally of western works.

The **Haiyūza** has its own theater in Roppongi where performances are regularly given when the troupe is not on tour. The main actor is Nakadai Tatsuya, who appeared in Kurosawa's movie "*Kagemusha*", as the character Takeda Shingen, and his double.

The **Bungakuza** doesn't have a regular venue, but will occasionally give performances at the troupe's rehearsal theater in Shinanomachi. Otherwise they perform at theaters such as Kinokuniya Hall. The principal actress of this troupe is Sugimura Haruko, whose career is almost as long as the history of *shingeki* itself.

The third major *shingeki* troupe is **Gekidan Shiki**, best known for their productions of musicals such as "Cats" and "West Side Story". The director is Asari Keita and their usual venue is the Nissei Gekijō.

There are also a number of underground, or avant-garde, theater troupes in Tokyo. Most perform in short runs, two or three times a year. The plays are usually original, and unlike the *shingeki* troupes, which generally perform well-known plays, the stories will be totally unfamiliar and dialogue, naturally, in Japanese. This is not, however, a major problem. Like *kabuki* and *nō*, avant-garde theater tends to be very visual, with less concern for plot and story line. Here is a list of the more important troupes. Information on performances can be had by calling the telephone numbers listed for each.

JŌKYŌ GEKIJŌ Director: Kara Jūrō. Tel: 391-2745. The troupe is nicknamed *Aka Tento* or "Red Tent"—for the red tent they usually perform in outdoors. Plays tend to be on political themes.
WASEDA SHŌGEKIJŌ Director: Suzuki Tadashi. Tel: 988-3980. Suzuki now lives in Toyama prefecture, and is responsible for the annual Toga International Arts Festival.
TENJŌ SAJIKI This troupe was directed by the late Terayama Shūji, one of Japan's foremost avant-garde theater directors. The future of the group is uncertain, and performances have currently been discontinued.
GEKIDAN SANJŪ-MARU Director: Watanabe Eriko. Tel: 469-6472.
DAISAN BUTAI Director: Kōgami Shōji. Tel: 207-7488.
TENKEI GEKIJŌ Director: Ōta Shōgo. Tel: 582-9738.
NOISE Director: Kisaragi Koharu. Tel: (0423) 21-7085.
BURIKI NO JIHATSU-DAN Director: Ikuta Man. Tel: (0423) 95-5458.
YUME NO YŪMINSHA Director: Noda Hideki. Tel: 493-6511.

• **Other Troupes**
TAKARAZUKA KAGEKIDAN A huge 500 strong all-girl troupe, the Takarazuka Kagekidan is enormously popular with teenage girls and middle-aged housewives. The performances

ENTERTAINMENT 161

are extravagantly staged and costumed, often musical revues with song, dance, and a classic chorus line. Most interesting is that in Takarazuka women play all the male roles, just as in traditional theater men play the women (see below).
ALBION-ZA One of the more popular foreign theater troupes in Tokyo, the Albion-za is best known for its comic "Our Japan" series. The series follows adventures in the life of the "Watanabe" average Japanese family—and is a great introduction for newcomers to Japan. They regularly perform in their own theater the Albion-za (see below).

Concert Halls and Theaters

ABC KAIKAN HALL 2-6-3 Shiba-kōen, Minato-ku. Tel: 436-0430. [M-11]
AKASAKA LA FORET Akasaka Twin Tower 1st Fl., 2-17-22 Akasaka, Minato-ku. Tel: 582-9255. [M-6]
ALBION-ZA 20-2 Ichibanchō, Chiyoda-ku. Tel: 234-6871. [M-6]
ASAKUSA KŌKAIDŌ 1-38-6 Asakusa, Taitō-ku. Tel: 844-7941. [M-12]
GAS HALL Ginza Gas Hall Bldg. 7th & 8th Fl., 7-9-15 Ginza, Chūō-ku. Tel: 573-1871. [M 8]
HAIYŪZA GEKIJŌ 4-9-2 Roppongi, Minato-ku. Tel: 470-2880. [M-1]
HAKUHINKAN GEKIJŌ Hakuhinkan Bldg. 8th Fl., 8-8-11 Ginza, Chūō-ku. Tel: 571-1003. [M-8]
HIBIYA KŌKAIDŌ 1-3 Hibiya-kōen, Chiyoda-ku. Tel: 591-6388. [M-10]
HONDA GEKIJŌ High Town 2nd Fl., 2-10-15 Kitazawa, Setagaya-ku. Tel: 460-0005. [M-34]
IKURA LA FORET 800/500 #39 Mori Bldg. 2-45 Azabu-dai, Minato-ku, Tel: 433-6801. [M-11]
INO HALL 2-1-1 Uchisaiwaichō, Chiyoda-ku. Tel: 506-3251. [M-10]
JEAN JEAN (pronounced "Jan Jan") Yamate Church B1, 19-5 Udagawachō, Shibuya-ku. Tel: 462-0641. [M-3]
KINOKUNIYA HALL Kinokuniya Bldg. 4th Fl., 3-17-7 Shinjuku, Shinjuku-ku. Tel: 354-0131. [M-7]
KOKURITSU GEKIJŌ (NATIONAL THEATER) 4-1 Hayabusachō, Chiyoda-ku. Tel: 265-7411. [M-6]
KUDAN KAIKAN HALL 1-6-5 Kudan-minami, Chiyoda-ku. Tel: 261-5521. [M-17]
LA FORET MUSEUM Harajuku La Foret 6th Fl. Tel: 475-0411. [M-4]
MEIJIZA 2-31-1 Hamachō, Nihombashi, Chūō-ku. Tel: 667-5151. [M-23]
NAKANO SUN PLAZA 4-1-1 Nakano, Nakano-ku. Tel: 388-1151. [M-26]
NHK HALL 2-2-1 Jinnan, Shibuya-ku. Tel: 465-1111. [M-3]
NIHON BUDŌKAN 2-3 Kitanomaru-kōen, Chiyoda-ku. Tel: 216-0781. [M-17]
NIHON SEINENKAN HALL 15 Kasumigaokachō, Shinjuku-ku. Tel: 407-0101. [M-5]
NISSEI GEKIJŌ 1-1-1 Yūrakuchō, Chiyoda-ku. Tel: 503-3111. [M-10]
SEIBU GEKIJŌ Shibuya Parco Part 1, 9th Fl., 15-1 Udagawachō, Shibuya-ku. Tel: 477-5858. [M-3]
SHIBUYA KŌKAIDŌ 1-1 Udagawachō, Shibuya-ku. Tel: 463-5001. [M-3]
SHINJUKU KOMA GEKIJŌ 1-19-1 Kabukichō, Shinjuku-ku. Tel: 202-0131. [M-7]
SŌGETSU HALL Sōgetsu Kaikan B1, 7-2-21 Akasaka, Minato-ku. Tel: 405-0246. [M-5]
SPACE PART 3 Shibuya Parco Part 3, 8th Fl., 14-5 Udagawachō, Shibuya-ku. Tel: 477-5905. [M-3]
STUDIO 200 Ikebukuro Seibu Department Store 8th Fl., 1-28-1 Minami-Ikebukuro, Toshima-ku. Tel: 981-0111. [M-18]
SUNSHINE GEKIJŌ Sunshine City Bunka Kaikan 4th-6th Fl., 3-1-4 Higashi-Ikebukuro, Toshima-ku. Tel: 987-5281. [M-18]
TEIKOKU GEKIJŌ (IMPERIAL THEATER) 3-1-1 Marunouchi, Chiyada-ku. Tel: 213-7221. [M-10]
THEATER APPLE 1-19-1 Kabukichō, Shinjuku-ku. Tel: 209-0222. [M-7]
THE SPACE Mori Hanae Bldg. 5th Fl., 3-6-1 Kita-Aoyama, Minato-ku. Tel: 407-5171. [M-4]
TOKYO BUNKA KAIKAN 5-45 Ueno-kōen, Taitō-ku. Tel: 828-2111. [M-13]
TOKYO KŌSEINENKIN KAIKAN 5-3-1 Shinjuku, Shinjuku-ku. Tel: 356-1111. [M-7]
TOKYO TAKARAZUKA GEKIJŌ 1-1-3 Yūrakuchō, Chiyoda-ku. Tel: 591-1711. [M-10]
TORANOMON HALL 3-2-3 Kasumigaseki, Chiyoda-ku. Tel: 580-1251. [M-11]

YAKULT HALL 1-1-19 Higashi-Shimbashi, Minato-ku. Tel: 574-7255. [M-11]
YOMIURI HALL Sogō Department Store 7th Fl., 1-11-1 Yūrakuchō, Chiyoda-ku. Tel: 231-0551. [M-10]
YŪBINCHOKIN HALL 2-5-20 Shiba-kōen, Minato-ku. Tel: 433-7211. [M-11]

Ticket Outlets

Here is a list of a few of the more convenient places to buy tickets for various performances and events.

GINZA: KYŪKYODŌ TICKET SERVICE Kyūkyodō Bldg. 1st Fl. Tel: 571-0401. Hrs: 10 a.m.-8 p.m. Mon.-Sat. (11 a.m.-7 p.m. Sun. & Hols.) [M-8]
SHINJUKU: ISETAN PLAYGUIDE Isetan Department Store 6th Fl. Tel: 352-4080. Hrs: 10 a.m.-6 p.m., closed Wed. [M-7]
SHIBUYA: AKAGIYA PLAYGUIDE Seibu Department Store B-Kan B1 (It's in the building next to the main Seibu). Tel: 462-0111. 10 a.m.-6 p.m., closed Wed. [M-3]
HARAJUKU: THE PLAYGUIDE LA FORET La Foret Harajuku 1st Fl. (It's to the right just before the main entrance). Tel: 401-9395. 11 a.m.-9 p.m., daily. [M-4]

SPORTS
Sumō

Officially speaking, *sumō* is not a sport, but Japan's *kokugi*, or national skill. Dating back at least 2,000 years, many of the colorful *sumō* rituals derive from *Shintō* religious beliefs. Before a match salt is sprinkled by the wrestlers in a purification ceremony; the *chikaramizu* (lit. "strength water"), given to the pair of wrestlers about to compete, was a farewell symbol to warriors setting out to risk their lives for lord and country.

The rules of *sumō* are fairly simple: the loser is the first wrestler to touch the ground with any part of his body except the soles of his feet, or to be propelled outside the *dohyō*, or ring. Touching of an opponent's hair or "private parts" and punching are prohibited, though slapping is acceptable. A slap in the face from a *sumō* wrestler would break the average person's neck. Despite their superficially flabby appearance, these men are probably the hardest in the world. Standard training for *sumō* wrestlers includes throwing their not inconsiderable body weight hands first into wooden pillars and a lot of the stamping ("*shiko*"), that you see prior to a bout, which develops incredible strength in the back and legs.

Sumō wrestlers tend to be tall, in general over six feet. Weight varies from about 220 lbs. up to double that in a few exceptional cases. There are no weight classes, so obviously the heavier wrestlers have an advantage, but there are always a few clever small "*sumōtori*" (wrestlers) who avoid close combat and specialize in leg trips or other tricks from the rich *sumō* vocabulary.

There are six tournaments yearly, each lasting 15 days. They take place in odd numbered months, usually beginning on the second Sunday. The January, May and September tournaments are held in Tokyo at the Ryōgoku Kokugikan near Asakusa. Opened in January 1985, the new Kokugikan ("national skill hall"), has an enormous solar panelled roof designed to supply all the hot water for the wrestler's baths.

   Sumō is tremendously popular in Japan, and unfortunately the best seats at the tournaments are bought per season by large corporations, or friends and patrons of the wrestlers themselves. Balcony seats are usually available on the day of the match. Try to get *shōmen* (north side) or *mukō-jōmen* (south side) seats for a good overall view of the wrestlers exiting and entering from the east and west sides.

   The wrestlers are divided into classes, starting from the bottom with **jonokuchi**, **jonidan**, **sandamme**, **makushita** and **jūryō**. The top *makuuchi* class has five ranks: **maegashira**, **komusubi**, **sekiwake**, **ōzeki** and **yokozuna**. At any one time there are usually between two and four *yokozuna*, or grand champions, at the top. Once attained, the *yokozuna* title is held until retirement, though wrestlers below *ōzeki* rise and fall in rank and class depending on how many bouts they won in the previous tournament.

   Sumō is well worth a visit for the pageantry alone. If you want to know what it's all about and have a portable radio, the Far East Network (FEN—U.S. Forces radio) on 810 kHz gives simultaneous English broad-

Sports Newspaper

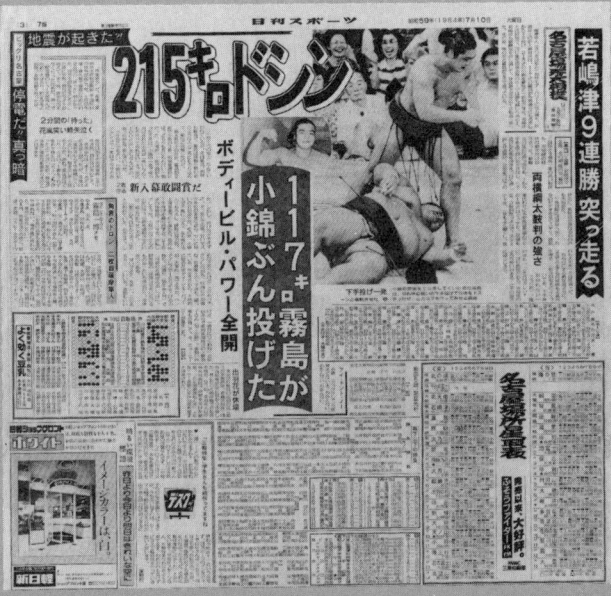

casts of the matches. There is also the English "Sumō World" magazine, available at most bookshops, which provides helpful commentary and information.

Each day's bouts start at noon, with the bottom ranked "jonokuchi" wrestlers proceeding through the lower classes up to the makuuchi. The top two classes jūryō and makuuchi are where the color and ritual start, usually from about 3 p.m. Until then, the house lights are dim, the wrestlers wear only murky grey loincloths, and the gyōji (referees) are dressed in unexciting kimono. But because the bulk of the spectators don't arrive until later in the afternoon (makuuchi starts at about 4 p.m. and finishes at 6 p.m.), if you go around lunch time, you can take your pick of vacant ringside seats, at least until some ex-sumō wrestler heaves you out.

There is a restaurant in the stadium where you can eat surrounded by the wrestlers, and an arcade of chaya (tea houses) where snacks and drinks are sold.

Balcony seats cost ¥1,000. It is probably worth investing some extra money on a pair of binoculars or opera glasses to allow a closer view of the action. Rear box seats, toku-ha, downstairs are sometimes available on the day of the performance, but are cripplingly cramped for the average westerner.

Sumō is televised daily during tournaments on NHK (Channel 1) from about 3:30 or 4 p.m. until the close of the day's events. From 11:15 p.m. TV Asahi (Channel 10) broadcasts a digest of the makuuchi bouts. Though you miss the atmosphere of the real thing, television provides slow motion replay of the fast and furious action (most bouts average under a minute, some only 10-15 seconds).

KOKUGIKAN 1-20 Yokoami, Sumida-ku. Tel: 866-8700.Tickets are sold from around one month before the tournament, but can also be bought on the day at the stadium. Some ticket outlets sell sumō tickets, or you can contact the box office of the stadium. Types of seats available are: sajiki or masu—a four person box at ¥8,500, ¥7,500, ¥6,500 per person (these are almost impossible to get). Isu—single balcony seats at ¥6,000 and ¥4,000. Bench seats (recommended) ¥1,000. You can stand in the very back for ¥500. [M-24]

If you're interested in seeing a sumō practice session, you can visit one of the local stables on the following list. The best time to visit is just before the Tokyo tournaments are held, and from around 8 a.m., so you can get a good place in the visitor's section. If you call ahead, you can find out who is practicing when.

KASUGANO-BEYA 1-7-11 Ryōgoku, Sumida-ku. Tel: 631-1871. [M-24]
KOKONOE-BEYA 1-16-1 Kamezawa, Sumida-ku. Tel: 621-1800. [M-24]
TAKASAGO-BEYA 1-22-5 Yanagibashi, Taitō-ku. Tel: 861-4600. [M-24]
FUTAGOYAMA-BEYA 3-25-10 Narita Higashi, Suginami-ku. Tel: 317-0018. [off Map]

Martial Arts

Martial arts, *bujutsu*, developed with the rise of the *samurai* military class in the *Kamakura* period (12th-14th century). Early arts such as *kenjutsu*—sword art, *iaijutsu*—sword drawing art, *kyūjutsu*—art of archery, *jūjutsu*—the art of unarmed combat, were gradually formalized and by the *Edo* period (17th century) had been organized into a number of schools. After the second World War, the arts were banned by the Occupation authorities because of their military implications. In 1950 the ban was revoked and the "arts" were revived as "sports".

Most of these "sports" remain a form of spiritual education. With the exception of *karate*, all of the currently practiced arts end with the "*dō*" —the way of—suffix attached to many *zen* related arts. *Aikidō*, *kendō*, *jūdō*, *kyūdō* are all, in *zen* terminology, considered a path to enlightenment. The arts, like meditation, develop powers of concentration and build physical, mental and spiritual discipline. Training involves a total mastery of technique, through endless practice and repetition, until the body, without conscious effort, is capable of performing with absolute accuracy. But even more important than learning technique, is to learn the "spirit" or "truth" and thereby reach a state of identity and harmony with the universe.

The actual relationship between the martial arts and *zen* Buddhism is questionable. Many martial arts practitioners would claim that the relationship is a distant one. But while the Japanese are rarely overtly religious, *zen* conceptions of life remain a powerful, if unconscious, cultural substructure. Martial arts are not generally considered spectator sports, though competitions are sometimes held. Classes are given at numerous schools, but some knowledge of Japanese is often required, and short-term students are rarely accepted. For further information, contact the appropriate general organization for each.

• *Aikidō*

Literally translated as "the way of the harmonious spirit", *aikidō* is a non-violent self-defense technique. The art was originated by Minamoto Yoshimitsu, a member of the Minamoto family that founded the Kamakura shogunate. From 1922 to 1942 Ueshiba Morihei reorganized the skill as *aikidō*, combining techniques from other martial arts. The emphasis is on blocking and neutralizing an attack by using wrist throws or "pain" holds to pin down or throw an opponent.

INTERNATIONAL AIKIDŌ FEDERATION 102 Wakamatsuchō, Shinjuku-ku. Tel: 203-9236.

• *Jūdō*

Jūdō was organized as a school in 1882 by Kanō Jigorō, who selected techniques from various schools of *jūjutsu*—a traditional method of unarmed combat that had developed from *sumō* wrestling skills. Basic *jūdō* training teaches a student to use the strength of the opponent to one's advantage. Techniques include falling and throwing methods, strangles and pin holds.

ALL-JAPAN JŪDŌ FEDERATION c/o Kōdōkan, 1-16-30 Kasuga, Bunkyō-ku. Tel: 811-7151.
KŌDŌKAN 1-16-30 Kasuga, Bunkyō-ku. Tel: 811-7151. This is a *jūdō* hall that offers lessons, but also has a spectators' gallery that is open to the public during practice hours. [M-30]
METROPOLITAN POLICE BOARD, P.R. CENTER 3-5-1 Kyōbashi, Chūō-ku. Tel: 561-8251. Hrs: 6 p.m.-7:30 p.m. on odd numbered Tue., Wed. and Fri.; 5 p.m.-7 p.m. Sat., Sun. and Hols. Free instruction. [M-9]

• **Karate**

Originally practiced in China during the T'ang Dynasty, *karate* was introduced to Japan from Okinawa in the 1920's, where it had long been practiced as a form of unarmed combat during the Japanese occupation of the islands. Techniques of jabbing, hitting and kicking are practiced with a partner, or alone in exercises called *kata*, based on the motions of actual combat.

WORLD UNION OF KARATE-DŌ ORGANIZATION Sempaku Shinkōkai Bldg. 4th Fl., 1-15-16 Toranomon, Minato-ku. Tel: 503-6637.

• **Kyūdō**

Of all the martial arts, *kyūdō*—the way of archery—was the most closely related to *Zen*. Now, archery is almost invariably associated with *Shintō* shrines and involves an initial prayer and special ritualized behavior. *Hakama*, a part of traditional formal dress, is worn for practice. The bow measuring over 2 meters in length is made of bamboo and mulberry wood, the arrows of bamboo shafts.

Yabusame, archery on horseback, is occasionally performed at shrines during festivals.

AMATEUR ARCHERY FEDERATION OF JAPAN Kishi Memorial Hall 4th Fl., 1-1-1 Jinnan, Shibuya-ku. Tel: 467-7949.

• **Kendō**

A Japanese form of fencing *kendō*—the way of the sword—is practiced, these days, with bamboo staves and protective clothing. *Kendō* developed from *kenjustu*—"the art of swordsmanship" that was a crucial part of *samurai* basic training. One of the best places to see and practice *kendō* now is at the Metropolitan Police Station where you can fight with the Tokyo police free of charge.

JAPAN KENDŌ FEDERATION c/o Nippon Budōkan, 2-3 Kitanomaru-kōen, Chiyoda-ku. Tel: 211-5804/5.
METROPOLITAN POLICE BOARD, P.R. CENTER (see jūdō)
Hrs: 6 p.m.-7 p.m. on even numbered Tue., Wed., Fri.; 1:30 p.m.-3:30 p.m. Sat., 10 a.m.-12 noon Sun. Free instruction. [M-9]

Baseball

In a contest for who were the more rabid of baseball fans, Japan and the United States would be fighting it out bitterly to the end. First introduced from the U.S. in 1873, baseball is the only western team sport that has captured the popular imagination.

The system is similar to that of the U.S. There are two professional leagues, the Central and the Pacific, playing from April through October, then the top teams from each league meet in the play-offs. In 1982 and 1983, Pacific League headliners the Seibu (a railway company) "Lions" won the title. Their competition is the Central League's Yomiuri (a newspaper company) "Giants". The teams are not associated with cities, but with major corporations, such as Nihon Ham (a food company) "Fighters", the Lotte (a confectionery company) "Orions", or the Kintetsu (a railway company) "Buffalos".

Besides the pro games, the annual high school baseball tournament is closely and emotionally followed by the entire country. Less a sport than a display of youthful purity, the ideology of high school baseball has grown curiously close to that of the traditional martial arts. The high school baseball tournaments are held in Ōsaka, and receive extensive television coverage.

At the Kōrakuen Stadium in Tokyo, you can watch a *"naitā'*—a night game, where there's lots of beer and *sake* drinking on the clean astroturfed seating area surrounding the field.

The three major baseball stadiums in Tokyo are:
MEIJI-JINGŪ KYŪJŌ (Meiji-jingū Outer Gardens) 13 Kasumigaoka, Shinjuku-ku. Tel: 404-3130. [M-5].
KŌRAKUEN KYŪJŌ (near Kōrakuen Amusement Park) 1-3 Kōraku, Bunkyō-ku. Tel: 811-2111. [M-30]
SEIBU KYŪJŌ 2135 Kami-yamaguchi, Tokorozawa-shi, Saitama-ken. Tel: 0429-25-1151 (Seibu Kyūjō-mae station on the Seibu Ikebukuro line). [off Map]

MOVIES

For fans of Japanese movies, a visit to Japan won't necessarily prove to be a rewarding experience, at least in terms of movie viewing. Foreign language subtitles are not supplied here. And even if they were, aside from the classics, the percentage of interesting films produced by the domestic industry is negligible. In 1983, 70% of all movies produced were soft porn (called *"roman poruno"* here). The films produced by internationally known directors such as Kurosawa, Ōshima and Mizoguchi, or by interesting new directors, are the handful of exceptions to the rule, and these will usually find their way subtitled into your local theater.

Foreign films are the big draw here. They arrive sometimes as late as six months after their original release and the big crowd pullers remain for months—the same three or four roadshows playing at all the big theaters around town. There are always the smaller theaters (often in slightly inconvenient locations) that play revivals, and an increasing number of new theaters running more artistic films that would never make it into the major theater distribution network.

Movie theaters tend to be centralized in certain districts, the Shinjuku Kabukichō area having probably the most. In Shibuya, around the station area, are a dozen or so, and the Hibiya-Yūrakuchō station areas have about the same numbers. We haven't listed the major theaters. There are hundreds of these, most of which can be easily found. Movie schedules and theater locations are given in all tourist publications and the English daily papers. One of the best is in the Weekender (all addresses are listed in both English and Japanese). We have supplied a list of smaller theaters, showing films other than those in the major theater networks.

Movie tickets can be bought in advance. "Reserved" seats are usually available. These are the best seats and are generally supplied with clean white covers. They cost around ¥2,200. Normal seats are generally ¥1,500. On Saturdays and Sundays the theaters are often unbelievably crowded (you might want to buy tickets in advance), and when all seats are sold out tickets are sold for standing room only. Be sure to check that you're actually getting a seat. The last show for most theaters starts around 7-7:30 p.m.

ACT MINI THEATER Waseda-dōri Bldg. 2nd Fl., 3-14-2 Nishi-Waseda, Shinjuku-ku. Tel: 208-4733. Western classics, some Japanese. Programs change daily. [off Map]

ATHÉNÉE FRANÇAIS 2-11 Surugadai, Kanda, Chiyoda-ku. Tel: 291-4339. You must fill out a membership card (cost: ¥500) which is good for one year. This can be done on the day of the show, at the 4th Fl. office just outside the theater entrance. Tickets for the movies cost ¥400-¥500. [M-15]

BUNGEIZA 1-43-4 Higashi-Ikebukuro, Toshima-ku. Tel: 971-9422. Second run and classic western films. Movies run all night on Sat. [M-18]

CINE VIVANT ROPPONGI Wave Bldg. B1, 6-2-27 Roppongi, Minato-ku. Tel: 403-6061. First run art films. They have a late night show at 9 p.m. Programs change monthly. [M-1]

CINEMA SQUARE TŌKYŪ Shinjuku Tōkyū Bunka-Kaikan 3rd Fl., 1-29-1 Kabukichō, Shinjuku-ku. Tel: 232-9274. First run "better" movies. It's one of the few cinemas in Tokyo that doesn't allow standing. Late show on Fri. & Sat. from 9:20 p.m. [M-7]

FILM CENTER 3-7-6 Kyōbashi, Chūō-ku. Tel: 561-0823. Japanese and western classics. Programs change daily with shows at 3:15 p.m. and 6 p.m. Mon.-Fri. (1:30 p.m. on Sat.), closed Sun. & Hols. Tickets cost ¥250. [M-9]

GINZA NAMIKIZA Miki Bldg. B1., 2-3-5 Ginza, Chūō-ku. Tel: 561-3034. Japanese cinema classics. [M-8]

HAIYŪZA CINEMA TEN Haiyūza Bldg., 4-9-2 Roppongi, Minato-ku. Tel: 442-0438. Art films, mainly European, with one show daily from 10 p.m. Programs run for an average of six weeks. [M-1]

IWANAMI HALL Iwanami Jimbōchō Bldg. 10th Fl., 2-1 Jimbōchō, Kanda, Chiyoda-ku. Tel: 262-5252. European art movies. [M-15]

SHINJUKU ROYAL 3-18-5 Shinjuku, Shinjuku-ku. Tel: 352-7004. Second-run, usually action, movies, but cheap (¥500) and consistently good programming. [M-7]

SAMBYAKUNIN-GEKIJŌ 2-29-10 Hon-Komagome, Bunkyō-ku. Tel: 944-5451. Often have special programs such as retrospectives of western and Japanese classics. [off Map]

EURO SPACE Tōbu Fuji Bldg. 24-4 Sakuragaoka, Shibuya-ku. Tel: 461-0212. [M-3]

NIGHT LIFE

"As tantalizing as its fragrance is delicate." Nightlife in Tokyo is not always so delicate...

NIGHTLIFE

Theater, cinema and concerts end early in Tokyo, most by 9 p.m., about the same time as many traditional restaurants close for the night. After that, nightlife is limited to just a few districts: Roppongi, Akasaka, Shibuya, Shinjuku and Ikebukuro.

The evening scene tends to be casual. When the working day is done, the millions of Tokyo workers disperse into thousands of tiny bars and *nomiya* where, as "regulars", they have the comfort of being known. Discos are also popular with the post-office crowd, and are packed between 6 p.m. and 8 p.m. with students, young salarymen, and O.L.'s. After a few drinks, and possibly a few songs at a *karaoke* bar, the crowds hurry off to the suburbs, making sure to catch the midnight train. But enough people miss the trains, intentionally or not, to keep plenty of places packed until sunrise.

Tokyo nightlife is not as sophisticated, glamorous, or intense as that of New York or Paris. "Being seen" is not a major activity, at least for the people most interesting to see, and most tend to return to the same, quiet bars.

DISTRICTS
Roppongi—just as for restaurants, this is the most international nightlife district. Though Shinjuku and Ginza outstrip Roppongi in numbers of night spots, the high density of bars and discos in a relatively small area makes the activity seem that much more intense.

Kasumichō—a Roppongi spill-over area, with lots of small, hip bars and restaurants.

Ginza—Shimbashi—specializing in hostess bars and Japanese restaurants for expense account Japanese businessmen, most places in this area close before midnight. Near Shimbashi, the refined air of Ginza gives way to a more "average salaryman" clientele.

Yūrakuchō—best known for its rows of cheap *nomiya* beneath the railroad tracks.

Akasaka—somewhere between Ginza and Roppongi on the scale of nightlife activity, Akasaka claims hundreds of hostess bars and numerous glamorous cabarets, most of which date from the late 50's (or at least look as if they do).

Harajuku—Aoyama—strict zoning regulations keep this fashionable daytime area from becoming a full-fledged nightlife district, but interesting bars and clubs are scattered through the neighborhood.

Shibuya—a favorite area for students and young salarymen, the area has a wealth of cheap bars and *nomiya*.

Shinjuku—the latest of late night districts, this is where people go when they're ready to leave the sophistication of Roppongi, Akasaka, and Ginza behind. Much of the nightlife here borders on sleaze, which can admittedly be rather refreshing at times. The area near Ni-chōme is known for its concentration of gay clubs. Gōruden-gai near Kabukichō has hundreds of tiny *nomiya*. Kabukichō itself is the sleaze center.

Ikebukuro—similar to Shinjuku, but not as interesting.

BARS

Bars open and close in Tokyo about as fast as you can say "dry vodka martini with a twist". In recent years, ever more stylishly designed, ever more elegant and expensive bars have been sprouting up in all neighborhoods of the city. The hippest places invariably wane in hipness as they rise in popularity, but the best mellow into a comfortable maturity.

Traditional drinking places are the *nomiya*. There are thousands of these places still serving drinkers on a budget. In Yūrakuchō you'll find them under the train tracks, while in Shinjuku there is a great stretch near the west exit of the station called *shomben yokochō* or "Piss Alley". Hostess bars are the businessman's favorite form of nightlife. Though conceptually intriguing, they are of little real interest for most foreigners (we've listed a few below). A recent trend is not to call a bar a "bar", but a "café bar", which basically translates as a trendy, modern interior with a fashionable (or an aspiringly so) crowd, some food, coffee, and cocktails. Other bars cater to foreigners which, depending on your personal point of view, can be either an attraction or a reason to avoid the place at all costs.

Most newer places often add a cover charge to your drink bill that runs from ¥500-¥800. Since few Japanese drink enough to pay for the expensive interiors of such places, the charge helps to make up the difference.

General Bars

RADIO BAR Villa Gloria B1, 2-31-7 Jingūmae, Shibuya-ku. Tel: 405-5490. Hrs: 12 noon-4 p.m., 7 p.m.-2 a.m., closed Sun. & Hols. This place is "professional" from its wide selection of liquors, to its battalion of black tuxedoed bartenders, to its great, but expensive cocktails. The interior is contemporary and one of the best in Tokyo, with natural wood and rusting iron inlaid walls, and tiny Tiffany lamps on the bar which seats about a dozen serious drinkers. Cocktails average ¥1,000. [M-4]

EX Jūnikagetsu Bldg., B1, 1-18-7 Jinnan, Shibuya-ku. Tel: 464-8699. Hrs: 5 p.m.-2 a.m. (until 11:30 p.m. on Sun. & Hols), daily. The stunning interior of this cavernous "Brasserie" was designed by the famous Takashi Sugimoto. Better for drinks than food, they also have an extensive wine list. Drinks from ¥600. (AX, D, V). [M-3]

RED SHOES Azabu Palace Bldg. B1., 2-25-18 Nishi-Azabu, Minato-ku. Tel: 499-4319. Hrs: 8 p.m.-6 a.m., daily This small club with an intensely red interior opened in 1981 and for a while was the scene of post concert parties by numerous Japanese bands. Though past its prime as a truly hip spot, it's still a good entry on your nightlife agenda Drinks from ¥600, charge ¥300. [M-2]

MINT BAR Casa Grande Miwa Bldg. B1., 7-5-11 Roppongi, Minato-ku. Tel: 403-1537. Hrs: 7 p.m.-4 a.m., daily. After Red Shoes, Mr. Matsuyama opened Mint—a small pale green bar that has also hosted some great parties. It still goes now and again. Located right across the hall from Matsuyama's live club Ink Stick, it's a convenient stop before or after seeing a concert. Drinks from ¥800, charge ¥600. [M-1]

MONKBERRY'S Chisan Bldg. B1 & B2, 6-12-15 Jingūmae, Shibuya-ku. Tel: 409-1191. Hrs: 6 p.m.-2:30 a.m., closed Sun. A fashionable Harajuku wine bar (B1) and "member's club" (B2) where dancing is a matter of course, despite regulations prohibiting discos in this residentially zoned neighborhood. They'll let almost anyone into the club. The crowd is young and energetic, the music progressive and very danceable. Drinks from ¥600, charge (B2) ¥2,000. [M-4]

DICK'S BAR Nishi-Azabu Pioneer Bldg. 1st Fl., 4-2-10 Nishi-Azabu, Minato-ku. Tel: 499-5423. Hrs: 7 p.m.-4 a.m. (until 2 a.m. on Sun. & Hols.), daily. You won't find a Dick behind the bar here, but like a rash of new local drinking spots, a foreign name has been applied for exotic appeal. A good place for a quiet cocktail, the interior is slickly designed in kelly green and black. Drinks from ¥800. [M-2]

VAL'S BAR 2-13 Nishi-Azabu, Minato-ku. Tel: 403-8757. Hrs: 8 p.m.-5 a.m. (until 2 a.m. on Sun. & Hols.). That's right, there's no Val here. But there are lots of fairly interesting, young-ish patrons and rock music. The atmosphere and interior are unpretentious—which makes one wonder why this "under-designed" spot manages to attract such steady crowds with all those gorgeous café-bars around. Drinks from ¥800. [M-2]

KAY'S BAR 2-6-8 Shibuya, Shibuya-ku. Tel: 400-8885. Hrs: 7 p.m.-2 a.m., closed Sun. & Hols. A predictably well designed contemporary interior, fashionable clientele, and modern music. Drinks from ¥700. [M-3]

CHIANTISSIMO Goyō Bldg. B1, 3-17-26 Nishi-Azabu, Minato-ku. Tel: 404-6500. Hrs: 12 noon-3 a.m., daily. Connected to the new branch of Chianti, this bar is a small but a great place for an early evening or late night drink and hors d'oeuvre. Drinks from ¥600, Italian wine by the glass ¥400. [M-2]

NIGHT BAR Healthy Bldg. B1, 3-34-5 Jingūmae, Shibuya-ku. Tel: 470-0373. Hrs: 7 p.m.-3 a.m. Mon.-Sat.; 5 p.m.-11 p.m. Sun., closed the 2nd Sun. Another great small bar, this one too has the regulation modern interior. The crowd tends to be fashionable, youngish and fairly interesting. Drinks from ¥850. [M-4]

TABAC Pacific Nogizaka Bldg. B1, 9-6-29 Akasaka, Minato-ku. Tel: 403-5193. Hrs: 6 p.m.-3 a.m. (until 11 p.m. Sun. & Hols.), daily. A large, simply furnished room, this is one of the few places in town where you can play pool and backgammon. The place is casual with a fashionable edge to it. Drinks from ¥800 (AX, D, V). [M-1]

OYSTER BAR Kaneko Bldg. 2nd Fl., 7-11-4 Minami-Aoyama, Minato-ku. Tel: 499-5648. Hrs: 6 p.m.-2 a.m., closed Sun. & Hols. This small cafe-bar has a separate art exhibition space showing the work of young artists. A curving opaque glass wall divides the space. Drinks and Japanese-modern snacks are served. Drinks from ¥600. (AX). [M-5]

BAR DE SAVEY Inō Bldg. 3rd Fl., 2-18 Daikan-yama, Shibuya-ku. Tel: 461-8991. Hrs: 7 p.m.-2

a.m., daily. A real drinker's bar, they serve 250 kinds of cocktails. Contemporary interior. Drinks from ¥900. [M-20]
SHIRIN 1-11-10 Nishi-Azabu, Minato-ku. Tel: 403-1318. Hrs: 8 p.m.-4 a.m. (until 5 a.m. on Sat.), closed Sun. A grey and black Japanese "minimal" interior. Music is strictly environmental (i.e. Brian Eno, etc.), and the atmosphere relaxed but not sleepy. Drinks from ¥600, charge ¥800. [M-2]
PIDGEON Kokubu Bldg. 3rd Fl., 1-4-49 Nishi-Azabu, Minato-ku. Tel: 403-2962. Hrs: 7 p.m.-3 a.m., closed Sun. & Hols. A virtual memorial to Bob Marley, Pidgeon is a tiny, reggae-only club, right in the heart of trendy Roppongi. In the palm tree shaded interior you can watch reggae video, and play the house bongos to your heart's content. Drinks from ¥600. [M-1]
69 Daini Seikō Bldg. B1, 2-18-5 Shinjuku, Shinjuku-ku. Tel: 341-6358. Hrs: 12 noon-6 p.m. (no alcohol), 6 p.m.-3 a.m., daily. On a recent trip to Tokyo a woman from New York visited 69, a gay bar and favorite underground-hip hang-out 5 years earlier. She commented that it was like going to a formerly hip place in Manhattan, only to find it taken over by the "bridge and tunnel people" (i.e. not real Manhattanites, but people from Brooklyn, or elsewhere, who come over the bridges and through the tunnels to play in the city on weekends). 69 is, however, still a dive, and still maintains that special charm of places where all sorts of people somehow end up. The place is tiny, music tends to be reggae, and the crowd friendly, if somewhat peculiar. Drinks from ¥600 (¥1,000 on Sat.). [M-7]
KAMIYA BAR 1-1 Asakusa, Taitō-ku. Tel: 841-5400. Hrs: 11:30 a.m.-9 p.m., closed Tue. The oldest western style bar in Tokyo, the Kamiya bar was established in 1880 by Mr. Kamiya who also started the first brandy distillery in Japan. [M-12]
MON 28-13 Udagawachō, Shibuya-ku. Tel: 461-9417. Hrs: 6 p.m.-2 a.m., daily. Another older Japanese interpretation of a western bar, Mon is a real family business run by a father and his three sons. They serve over 300 kinds of cocktails to nostalgic 50's and 60's Japanese music. [M-3]

PUB CARDINAL Sony Bldg. B1, 5-3 Ginza, Chūō-ku. Tel: 573-0011. Hrs: 9 a.m.-2 a.m. (until midnight on Sun. & Hols.), daily. A comfortable, slightly elegant British-style pub. [M-8]
TRADER VIC'S New Ōtani Hotel, New Tower 4th Fl. Tel: 265-1111. Hrs: 11:30 a.m.-1 a.m., daily. Tropical drinks in a tropical atmosphere. Drinks from ¥1,200. [M-6]
HEALTH ANGELS Marugen Bldg. No. 25 B1, 8-6-23 Ginza, Chūō-ku. Tel: 574-9100. Hrs: 5 p.m.-2 a.m., closed Sun. & Hols. Right in the middle of the Ginza hostess club district is this odd club run by a Japanese motorcycle gang called the Health Angels. Actually not all of the "gang" ride motorcycles (some have 50 cc bikes), but all wear the uniform black leather jackets, and look far tougher than they are. The bar plays good contemporary music, and has a slightly funky but relaxed interior. Crowd is mixed. [M-8]
OH GOD Jingūbashi Bldg. B1, 6-7-18 Jingūmae, Shibuya-ku. Tel: 406-3206. Hrs: 6 p.m.-6 a.m., daily. A movie restaurant and bar, showing recent releases or oldies. Shows at 9 p.m., midnight, 3 a.m. Food and drinks from ¥650. [M-4]

Expatriates' Hang-outs

EX Roppongi Maisonette 1st Fl. 7-7-6 Roppongi, Minato-ku. Tel: 408-5487. Hrs: 5 p.m.-4 a.m., closed Sun. & Hols. A German style pub with a good selection of beer and German food that even Germans like. The place is small, friendly and predictably jolly. [M-1]
MAGGIE'S REVENGE Takano Bldg. 3-8-12 Roppongi, Minato-ku. Tel: 479-1096. Hrs: 6:30 p.m.-4 a.m., daily. Run by an Australian woman, this pub has reasonably priced food, live music and lots of honestly friendly patrons. This is one of the better places for single women to go for a drink when they don't want to be hassled but don't mind a friendly chat. Drinks from ¥500. [M-1]
HENRY AFRICA'S Hanatsubaki Bldg. 2nd Fl., 3-15-23 Roppongi, Minato-ku. Tel: 403-9751. Hrs: 6 p.m.-2 a.m. (until 4 a.m. on Fri. & Sat.), daily. Quasi-tropical motif, pin-ball machines, popcorn hors d'oeuvres, and tropical drinks. Drinks from ¥500. [M-1]
CHARLESTON 3-8-11 Roppongi, Minato-ku. Tel: 402-0372. Hrs: 6 p.m.-6 a.m., daily. Popular with some resident foreigners, the place can be fun, but late at night tends to border on the degenerate. Cocktails average ¥700. [M-1]

MR. STAMP'S 4-4-2 Roppongi, Minato-ku. Tel: 479-1390. Hrs: 5 p.m.-11 p.m., closed Sun. & Hols. Wine bar and restaurant run by Mr. Al Stamp, a resident American. Food is good, with reasonably priced steaks and fondues. Drinks from ¥350. [M-1]
LORNE'S PLACE 7-10-22 Roppongi, Minato-ku. Tel: 402-7468. Hrs: 5:30 p.m.-1 a.m., daily. Happy hour from 5:30 p.m.-8 p.m. A jovial "boy's" bar. Drinks from ¥600. [M-1]
BERNI INN Daisan Gotō Bldg. 2nd Fl., 3-13-14 Roppongi, Minato-ku. Tel: 405-4928. Hrs: 4 p.m.-2 a.m. (Sat. & Sun. 12 noon-1 a.m.), daily. British style pub, with an atmosphere similar to Lorne's Place but with older "boys". Drinks from ¥350. [M-1]

Gay Bars

The Ni-chōme area of Shinjuku is the main gay bar center of Tokyo. There are dozens of clubs in the neighborhood, and one will just lead to another. Here are a few to start with.

PETER PAN Kōa Bldg. B1, 2-13-6 Shinjuku, Shinjuku-ku. Tel: 354-5877. Hrs: 10 p.m.-5 a.m., closed Sun. two live shows nightly from about 12:30 a.m. and 3:30 a.m. The sign for this place is not in English, but it is a real find if you can locate it. The interior is rather elegant, as is the bevey of beauties who perform a live, topless cabaret show. Between shows they act as hostesses. Charge: cover ¥7,000, drinks from ¥1,000. [M-7]
KOKUCHŌ NO MIZUUMI (BLACK SWAN LAKE) Arao Bldg. B2, 2-25-2 Kabukichō, Shinjuku-ku. Tel: 205-0128. Hrs: 6 p.m.-4 a.m., closed Sun. Live shows at 8 p.m., 10 p.m. and 12:30 a.m. Another gay cabaret, this one is pretty innocent and at times simply comical. Drinks from ¥400. [M-7]
SAMBIKI NO KOBUTA (THREE LITTLE PIGS) 2-12-15 Shinjuku, Shinjuku-ku. Tel: 341-9434. Hrs: 10:30 p.m.-5:30 a.m., closed Mon. Three chubby gays perform a show and entertain you at your table in this tiny club. Charge: ¥3,000, drinks from ¥1,000. [M-7]
SAZAE Ishikawa Bldg. 2nd Fl., 2-18-3 Shinjuku, Shinjuku-ku. Tel: 354-1745. Hrs: 10 p.m.-6 a.m., daily. Right around the corner from 69, a half gay, half straight bar (see "BARS"), Sazae is famous among fashion business locals for its fashionably low-life atmosphere. [M-7]
REGENT BAR 2-18-3 Shinjuku, Shinjuku-ku. Tel: 352-3037. Hrs: 6:30 p.m.-1 a.m. (until 2 a.m. on Fri. & Sat.), closed Sun. & Hols. A more serious, straightforward gay bar. [M-7]

BEER HALLS AND BEER GARDENS

The first beer hall in Japan opened on the fourth of July 1899 in celebration of the end of the unequal treaties with western powers. Since then beer has become as much a part of Japanese life as green tea. At the top of the beer popularity chart, Kirin Beer has maintained its number one position for years. Serious beer drinkers frequent any one of the many beer halls found throughout the city. The beer is cheap, but the atmosphere is usually not as interesting as you'd hope it to be. There are a few older establishments worth visiting. In the summer, beer gardens sprout up on the rooftops of department stores, hotels, office buildings, etc. Easily recognized by the rows of red lanterns and Christmas tree lights strung around the edge of the roof, beer gardens are open from about mid-June through late August.

AZUMABASHI BEER HOUSE 1-23 Azumabashi, Sumida-ku. Tel: 622-0530. Hrs: 1 p.m.-9:30 p.m. (12 noon-8:30 p.m. on Sun. & Hols.), daily. One of the few beer halls that hasn't received a modern face-lift, the atmosphere here is pure *"shitamachi"*. The beer hall is connected to the Asahi Brewery in Asakusa. [M-12]
PILSEN 6-8-7 Ginza, Chūō-ku. Tel: 571-2236. Hrs: 12 noon-10 p.m. (until 9 p.m. on Sun.

& Hols.), daily. On the 1st floor of the Kōjunsha building, Pilsen at least tries to maintain a faintly "German" atmosphere. [M-8]

KUDAN BEER GARDEN Top of the Kudan Kaikan Hotel. Tel: 261-5521. Open mid-May through late August, from 5 p.m.-9 p.m., closed on rainy days. Rather elegant as beer gardens go, this one also has a great view and occasionally live music. [M-17]

DISCOS

Disco activity is concentrated in the Roppongi and Shinjuku area. The Roppongi Square Building alone claims seven. Tokyo discos tend to be casual. There are no real admission problems, except occasionally for men alone or in large groups.

TSUBAKI HOUSE Teatoru Bldg. 5th Fl., 3-14-20 Shinjuku, Shinjuku-ku. (Behind Isetan department store). Tel: 354-3236. Hrs: 5 p.m.-11:30 p.m., daily. Five years ago, this was the only hip disco in Tokyo. By no means elegant, Tsubaki House is still a respected institution and continues to draw crowds of the more outrageous kids in town. They have a series of special "theme" nights each week. "Heavy Metal Night" (often Monday) is as hysterically funny as it is sociologically revealing. Charge: ¥3,000. [M-7]

CLUB D Villa Bianca B1, 2-33-12 Jingūmae, Shibuya-ku. Tel: 423-1471. Hrs: 7 p.m.-4 a.m., daily. Young Japanese trendies pack this disco run by veteran restauranteur Daini of the popular DAINI'S TABLE and Mr. Satō, former TSUBAKI HOUSE manager. Charge ¥3,000; ¥3,500 on Sat. and pre-holiday evenings, (free drink & food). (D). [M-4]

NEO JAPANESQUE Roppongi Forum Bldg. B2, 5-16-5 Roppongi, Minato-ku. Tel: 586-0050. Hrs: 7 p.m.-midnight, closed Sun. & Hols. In its advertisements, this disco promises to "make up any deficiencies in your nightlife". We wouldn't go that far, but the place is good as a slightly sophisticated but not stuffy standby. The crowd is about half foreigners, half Japanese. The rules say no entry in jeans. Charge: ¥4,000 (men), ¥3,000 (women). (AX, D, V). [M-1]

VIETTI Roppongi Plaza Bldg. 4th Fl., 3-12-6 Roppongi, Minato-ku. Tel: 401-7478. Hrs: 6 p.m.-midnight, daily. Italianesque interior and snack menu sets the tone for this popular new club with good, modern, dance music. Charge: Men ¥3,000, Women ¥2,000 (includes drink & food tickets). [M-1]

TOKIO Aizawa Bldg. B1, 5-9-12 Minami-Aoyama, Minato-ku. Tel: 407-1085. Hrs: 6 p.m.-4 a.m. (until 5 a.m. on Fri.), daily. Since Tokio's opened in 1982, it has been a major hang-out for people in the fashion business. Music is good, the crowd is young, energetic, and heavy on the foreign models (who get in free incidentally). Charge: ¥3,000 (with free drink & food tickets). (AX, D, V). [M-5]

CLEO PALAZZI Shadai Bldg. B1, 3-18-2 Roppongi, Minato-ku. Tel: 586-8494. Hrs: 8 p.m.-6 a.m., daily. Brought to you by the same team as Tokio, Cleo's is best as an after-hours club. The place is small which makes for lots of interesting interaction and uninhibited behavior by the usually well-tanked-up crowd. Charge: ¥2,000 (for 3 food and drink tickets). [M-1]

LEXINGTON QUEEN Daisan Gotō Bldg. B1, 3-13-14 Roppongi, Minato-ku. Tel: 401-1661. Hrs: 6 p.m.-midnight (though this varies sometimes), daily. Opened in 1980, the Lexington Queen was the most glamorous place to go for about two years. Still a good standby, the disco is frequented by foreigners, and regularly throws parties for visiting rock stars, actors, actresses, and other assorted celebrities. The man in charge is local celebrity Bill Hersey, writer of the "Weekender" social column. Charge: ¥3,000 (includes free drink and food ticket). [M-1]

RAJAH COURT Ibis Hotel 4th Fl., 7-14-4 Roppongi, Minato-ku. Tel: 479-5555. Hrs: 6 p.m.-5 a.m., daily. A few years ago Rajah Court tried to be an elegant adult disco with an "Arabian" theme. New management reopened the club in late 1983 and the place has become popular with a younger, hipper crowd. Music is contemporary and fairly good. Charge: ¥1,000 (includes food and drink tickets). [M-1]

MUGEN 3-8-17 Akasaka, Minato-ku. Tel: 584-4481. Hrs: 6:30 p.m.-2 a.m., daily. In the late 60's when discos were first born in Tokyo, this club, along with its neighbor Byblos, was the place to go. Not a very trendy place these days, it is, however, the best place for black music, and has live soul or funk bands nightly. Charge: ¥2,800 (men), ¥1,800 (women), includes one drink. [M-6]

SAMBA CLUB Hotel Century Hyatt 1st Fl., 2-7-2 Nishi-Shinjuku, Shinjuku-ku. Tel: 342-8877/8. Hrs: 5:30 p.m.-2 a.m., daily. Shinjuku is full of discos, most of which cater to kids. You won't have any trouble finding such a place in the neighborhood, but if you want a more elegant or sophisticated atmosphere, this club is probably the best. It's not, however, anything to write home about. Charge: ¥5,000 (includes 2-3 drinks). [M-7]

LIVE MUSIC

Tiny live clubs featuring all sorts of music can be found in Tokyo: jazz, country & western, samba, contemporary, heavy metal, there is even one club where an imitation Beatles group performs songs we all know the words to. A word of advice—those interested in searching out the underground music scene, what's really underground is rarely any more interesting or avant-garde than what hits the main modern music clubs.

Rock and Modern Music

INK STICK Casa Grande Miwa Bldg. B1, 7-5-11 Roppongi, Minato-ku. Tel: 401-0429. Hrs: 7 p.m.-4 a.m. (until 5 a.m. on Fri. & Sat.), daily. One of the best places in town for modern Japanese music, Ink Stick has shows on most Friday and Saturday nights at 10 p.m. and 1 a.m. The rest of the week it's a great place for a relatively quiet drink. The interior of the club is in high-tech Japanese elegance, there is a large video screen, and a Japanese restaurant attached. Drinks from ¥600, charge ¥600 (¥1,000 on Fri. & Sat.). Live charge: usually ¥3,000 (includes three drink tickets). [M-1]

LOFT Daini Mizota Bldg. B1, 7-5-10 Nishi-Shinjuku, Shinjuku-ku. Tel: 365-0698. Hrs: 4:30 p.m.-4 a.m., daily. Shows from 6:30 p.m. The Loft has been a rock music institution for about as long as anyone can remember. Still one of the best places in town to see new rock bands, the club serves its music heavy on the rock and light on interior decor. Charge: ¥1,300-2,000 (includes 1 drink). [M-7]

CROCODILE New Sekiguchi Bldg. B1, 6-18-8 Jingūmae, Shibuya-ku. Tel: 499-5205. Hrs: 6 p.m.-6 a.m., live from 8 p.m.-midnight, daily. Featuring live samba, soul, reggae, blues, and rock bands, Crocodile's music programming is as eclectic as is its fairly "underground" interior. Charge: ¥1,000. [M-3]

THE LIVE INN Ekimae Kaikan 8th Fl., 1-3-1 Dōgenzaka, Shibuya-ku. Tel: 464-8381. Hrs: 6 p.m.-10 p.m. (depends on performance), daily. A good basic live club, this one is larger than most. Music ranges from soul, blues, jazz to rock, and sometimes features overseas bands. Charge: ¥2,000 (includes 1 drink). The price increases with well-known acts. [M-3]

SUSY'S BAR Shinjuku Suzuya B1, 3-26-14 Shinjuku, Shinjuku-ku. Tel: 356-3454. Hrs: café from 10 a.m.-4 p.m.; bar from 5 p.m.-11 p.m.; live from 7 or 9 p.m. on Fri. & Sat., daily. Opened in 1983, this club features a selection of young bands or other stage acts. The high-tech pop interior attracts a late-teens, young 20's crowd. Charge: ¥500. [M-7]

HOT CO-ROCKET Daini Ōmasa Bldg. B1, 5-18-2 Roppongi, Minato-ku. Tel: 583-9409. Hrs: 7 p.m.-3 a.m., daily. Four live shows nightly from 8:30 p.m. This club probably shouldn't be in this section—since the music is strictly Brazilian samba, or (rarely) reggae. The club lives up to the "hot" half of its name. Decor is on a tropical theme, atmosphere is friendly. Charge: ¥1,000, drinks from ¥400. [M-1]

CAVERN CLUB Roppongi Hōshō Bldg. 3rd Fl., 7-14-1 Roppongi, Minato-ku. Tel: 405-5207. Hrs: 6 p.m.-2:30 a.m. (until midnight on Sun.), daily. This is the club where that imitation Beatles band performs nightly. Sweet memories live here forever. Charge: ¥1,000, drinks from ¥500. [M-1]

KENTO'S Fukuyama Bldg. B1, 4-10-3 Roppongi, Minato-ku. Tel: 401-5755. Hrs: 6 p.m.-2:30 a.m. (until midnight on Sun. & Hols.), daily. Almost as funny as the fake Beatle's club, the house band here plays nostalgic 50's and 60's rock'n roll. Charge: ¥1,400. [M-1]

Jazz

SHINJUKU PIT INN YK Bldg. B1, 3-16-4 Shinjuku, Shinjuku-ku. Tel: 354-2024. Hrs: 11:30 a.m.-11 p.m.; live shows from 12 noon, 3 p.m., 7:30 p.m., daily. The most famous jazz club in Tokyo, the Pit Inn is large and features both Japanese and some overseas acts. Charge: ¥500 (1st show), ¥800 (afternoon show), ¥2,000 (evening). [M-7]

ROPPONGI PIT INN Shimei Bldg. B1, 3-17-7 Roppongi, Minato-ku. Tel: 585-1063. Hrs: 6:30 p.m.-11 p.m. (until 3 a.m. on Sat. & Sun.); live shows from 7:30 p.m., daily. The Roppongi branch of the reputable Shinjuku Pit Inn, this one tends to have more fusion bands, and occasionally rock groups. Charge: ¥2,000 (includes 1 drink). [M-1]

BALLANTINE 2 Roppongi Hōshō Bldg., 4th Fl., 7-14-1 Roppongi, Minato-ku. Tel: 478-5068. Hrs: 6 p.m.-5 a.m., daily. Three live shows nightly from 7 p.m.-midnight. Best known for featuring female jazz vocalists, the club sometimes has fusion, and rarely rock bands. Charge: ¥2,000 (live). [M-1]

BODY AND SOUL German Bakery Bldg. 3rd Fl., 7-14-12 Roppongi, Minato-ku. Tel: 408-2094. Hrs: 7 p.m.-2 a.m. (until 3 a.m. on Fri.), closed Sun. Live shows from 8:30 p.m. A small but respected local jazz club. Charge: ¥1,500 plus ¥600 for one drink. [M-1]

J Royal Mansion B1, 5-1-1 Shinjuku, Shinjuku-ku. Tel: 354-0335. Hrs: 6:30 p.m.-2 a.m. (until 3 a.m. on Fri. & Sat.), closed Sun. & Hols. Live shows from 7:30 p.m., four shows nightly. A musicians' hang-out, this place is lively especially after concerts held in the Shinjuku area. Local jazz performers often give spontaneous shows. Charge: ¥1,000 plus one ¥500 drink. [M-7]

SATIN DOLL Haiyūza Bldg. 3rd Fl., 4-9-2 Roppongi, Minato-ku. Tel: 401-3080. Weekdays 5:30 p.m.-1 a.m., Sun. & Hols. until midnight. A small, elegant club with three or four live shows nightly. Cover. ¥1,200, drinks from ¥700. [M-1]

AFTER SIX Zonan Bldg. B1, 3-13-8 Roppongi, Minato-ku. Tel: 405-7233. Hrs: 7 p.m.-2 a.m., closed Sun. A small live bar with 50's jazz standards. Charge: ¥2,000 (men), ¥1,500 (women), plus one ¥500 drink. [M-1]

Country and Western

ASPEN GLOW GM Bldg. 6th Fl., 2-28-2 Dōgenzaka, Shibuya-ku. Tel: 496-9709. Hrs: 5 p.m.-2 a.m., closed Sun. Live shows on Wed., Fri. & Sat. from 8 p.m. This club has done just about everything possible to recreate a west coast country & western bar in the center of Tokyo. They've done a pretty good job. Charge: cover ¥600-¥1,000, and a one drink, one dish minimum, drinks from about ¥500. [M-3]

WISHBONE Tōhō Kaikan Bldg. B1, 1-19-2 Kabukichō, Shinjuku-ku. Tel: 200-1173. Hrs: 3 p.m.-3 a.m., daily. Four live shows nightly from 7 p.m. Charge: ¥1,200, plus one ¥400 drink. [M-7]

CHAPS Shimojō Bldg. B1, 3-14-8 Roppongi, Minato-ku. Tel: 479-2136. Hrs: 7:30 p.m.-4 a.m., daily. Live music nightly, usually real American country & western performers. Charge: ¥600. [M-1]

Karaoke

After a few drinks, the normally restrained average Japanese lets loose and heads for a local *karaoke* bar. There, a microphone waits for the customers to take turns singing their favorite songs from the repertoire of classic *enka*, or pop tunes to recorded background music. Song sheets are provided for those who can't remember all the words. The popularity of *karaoke* is phenomenal. Special cassette machines for home *karaoke* are big sellers at the electronics stores, and on television you can even see a program where a famous *enka* singer performs a hit song while the words run across the bottom of the screen. The best part is that only the music is broadcast, so you sing while the famous talent silently mouths the words. *Karaoke* bars can be found in most neighborhoods; just follow the sound of happy voices singing off-key.

MIDORI NO YAKATA Minochi Bldg. 4th Fl., 3-11-8 Roppongi, Minato-ku. Tel: 401-6361. Hrs: 7 p.m.-5 a.m. (until 4 a.m. on Sun. & Hols.), daily. A very "classic" *karaoke* bar, this place is small, rather dingy, with velvet printed seating, lots of knick-knacks, dusty fake grapes hanging from the electrical wires on the ceiling—all in all a very cozy place. Music is from the standard *karaoke* repertoire. [M-1]

SAINT JULIAN Zex Bamu-kan 4th Fl., 3-9-5 Roppongi, Minato-ku. Tel: 403-0817. Hrs: 7 p.m.-4 a.m., daily. This place is a bit more trendy than Midori no Yakata, and attracts a younger generation of *karaoke* fanatics. The resident expert will give you tips on how to improve your *karaoke* style after your performance. They also have two amateur shows from 10 p.m. and 1 a.m. Charge: ¥2,000 (men), ¥1,300 (women). Drinks from ¥500. [M-1]

CHITOSE-TEI Kotohira Bldg. B1 (You Say Plaza), 1-14-1 Toranomon, Minato-ku. Tel: 508-1194. Hrs: 11:30 a.m.-11 p.m., closed Sun. & Hols. A more "up market" *karaoke* bar and restaurant, this one has special video and laser disc background visuals to accompany the songs. Interior is vaguely Art Deco in style, the atmosphere aims at "Internationalism". Charge: one ¥1,000 hors d'oeuvre minimum, drinks from ¥450. Charge: 7 p.m.-9 p.m. ¥2,000, 9 p.m.-midnight ¥2,500, from midnight onward ¥3,000. Drinks from ¥500. [M-11]

CABARETS AND HOSTESS BARS

Cabarets here are like those anywhere in the world. Extravagant, often featuring topless dancers, some are professional clubs while others are technically "pink cabaret". Hostess bars are a Japanese invention, where the modern *geisha* pours drinks, makes conversation, and strokes the Japanese salaryman or executive's ego. Most are shockingly expensive. Charges include a cover averaging ¥10,000, plus a fee per hostess, plus expensive drinks for the two or three of you. The majority are also very straight (i.e. only the ego gets stroked), and generally disappointing for foreign visitors.

Unfortunately Tokyo's best cabaret closed down in early 1985. A major loss to the nightlife scene here was the close of the old MIKADO, an elegant cabaret and hostess bar that seated around 1,700 guests. There were over 800 hostesses on a busy night, and the club boasted the world's largest indoor waterfall.

NEW LATIN QUARTER 2-13-8 Nagatachō, Chiyoda-ku. Tel: 581-1326. Hrs: 6:30 p.m.-1:30 a.m., closed Sun. Show time: 8:30 p.m. and 10:30 p.m. A medium-sized cabaret and hostess bar, the Latin Quarter has a touch of that blend of 1950's elegance and kitsch that made the Mikado such an amazing place. Occasionally on Sundays when the cabaret is closed, the place is rented out by a local promoter for rock concerts. It's somehow incredibly amusing to attend these concerts, where the band plays on a stage obviously intended for cabaret acts, hip young Japanese lounge around on the velvet curtained walls and where the very serious (almost mean) looking and tuxedo-suited club staff are posted around the circular room like elegant bodyguards or secret service men. Charge: ¥6,000. [M-6]

CORDON BLEU 6-6-4 Akasaka, Minato-ku. Tel: 582-7800. Hrs: 6:30 p.m.-2:30 a.m., closed Sun. Show time: 8 p.m., 10 p.m. and midnight. A restaurant theater with French cuisine and topless dancers. Charge: ¥15,000 (includes dinner, table charge, show and service). [M-6]

CASABLANCA 7-15-30 Roppongi, Minato-ku. Tel: 403-6000. Hrs: 6 p.m.-3a.m., closed Sun. A spacious nightclub on a lavish Arabian theme with hostesses (always a few foreigners) and live music nightly. Music is continuous, with some foreign jazz performers, and on Tue. & Fri. a 17 piece orchestra performs "big band" sounds. Dinner or snacks are also served. Jacket required. Cover charge ¥10,000, hostess ¥5,000, drinks from ¥1,500. [M-1]

Nightlife in Shinjuku's Kabukichō.

X-RATED
X-Rated Tokyo

Every city has its sleaze center and in Tokyo Shinjuku's Kabukichō area takes the prize. Of the over 3,000 business establishments in the area, roughly 400 specialize in a variety of risqué, sex oriented entertainments. Recent census statistics puts the residential population at close to 3,000, but the area nightly attracts crowds of up to 500,000 pleasure seekers.

The most notorious stretch of such shops is along "Sakura-dōri" or Cherry Street. The area is one of the few in Tokyo where some caution is advised.

We won't supply the names and addresses of specific shops. Such establishments are typically rather fly-by-night, and besides the signs of whatever shops are currently in operation are almost comically self-explanatory. Here is a list of the variety of naughty places to choose from. Approximate cost and a "pleasure" rating system (pleasure, great pleasure or super pleasure) is also included. Recommended for "Beginners" are numbers 1, 2, 3 and 4. For intermediates, numbers 5 and 7. For the real pro's, numbers 6, 8, 9 and 10. Though most places are for men, a few do cater to women.

1) **Nōpan Kissa** "No-panty Coffee Shop"—Waitresses clad only in a skimpy apron, serve coffee and tea. Mirrored floors are a common feature. Charge incl. coffee ¥2,000-¥3,000. "Pleasure" course ¥3,000-¥8,000.
2) **Nozoki Gekijō** "Peep Show"—Watch a girl through the little hole of your tiny private room. Charge: ¥2,000-¥3,000. "Pleasure" course ¥3,000-¥8,000.
3) **Sutorippu Gekijō** "Strip Show"—Watch a live strip show. Sometimes volunteers from the audience take turns participating on stage. Charge: ¥3,000-¥5,000.
4) **Poruno Rando** "Porn Land"—Just like Disneyland—all the fun in one building. There's no-pan kissa, peep shows, massage, etc. Special "round trip" tickets available. Entrance fee and "pleasure" charge ¥9,000-¥15,000.
5) **Fasshion Massāji** "Fashion Massage"—There is actually nothing fashionable about the massages given here. Entrance fee and "pleasure" charge ¥9,000-¥15,000.
6) **Dēto Kissa** "Date Coffee Shop"—Young women hang out in the coffee shop and wait for a "date" to take them to a hotel. Charge for one drink, hotel and "super pleasure" ¥25,000-¥40,000.
7) **Sōpu Lando** "Turkish Bath"—A rather traditional form of naughty place, the turkish baths have been in operation since prostitution was outlawed in Japan in 1958. Part of what takes place goes on in a bath. Entrance fee ¥3,000-¥5,000, "super pleasure" ¥15,000-¥60,000.
8) **Hotetoru** "Turkish Bath in a Hotel"—Set up through an agency, the "bath" takes place in a hotel. Japanese language ability required. Hotel and "super pleasure" ¥25,000-¥40,000.
9) **Mantoru** "Turkish Bath in an Apartment"—Same as the above, but in a mansion (the Japanese word for a large apartment). Japanese language ability required. "Great pleasure" for ¥25,000-¥35,000.
10) **Pinku Kyabarē** "Pink Cabaret"—Cabaret where more happens off-stage than on. Drink and "pleasure" ¥10,000-¥30,000.

Love Hotels

Love hotels are another slightly "pink" invention of the Japanese. It's pretty easy to guess from the name just what the hotels are intended for. Located in nightlife areas or along the suburban highways, many are readily spotted by their fantasy architecture which often comically resembles the Disneyland castle.

Rooms are lavish and elegant with lots of round beds, velvet couches, and chandeliers. "Theme" decors are also popular. There are jungle rooms, futuristic rooms, boat beds, and even a Mercedes Benz bed. Service is very discreet. The clerk remains hidden throughout the check-in procedure.

Rooms are rented by the hour (with a 2 hour minimum) for ¥3,000-¥8,000. After 10 p.m. you will pay the overnight charge of ¥5,000-¥15,000. Only couples are allowed to check-in, but some rooms do have "swapping" beds. A display panel or brochure at the front will show the range of rooms available.

MEGURO EMPEROR 2-1 Shimo-Meguro, Meguro-ku. Tel: 494-1211. The "king" of local love hotels, the exterior looks a castle. Rooms from ¥5,000 (short stay 8 a.m.-4 p.m.), ¥15,000 (overnight). [M-19]

HOTEL PERRIER 2-7-12 Kabukichō, Shinjuku-ku. Tel: 207-5921. They have rooms with saunas, videos, jukebox, etc. Their special room called "Galaxy" has an illuminated ceiling that turns off and on to the sound of your voice. Rooms from ¥5,800 (short stay), ¥10,000 (overnight). [M-7]

HOTEL ROPPONGI 7-19-4 Roppongi, Minato-ku. Tel: 403-1571. This hotel looks like a residential apartment building from the outside. Typical love hotel rooms, some are Japanese style with gardens. Rooms from ¥5,500 (short stay), ¥9,900 (overnight). [M-1]

On February 13, 1985 a new law regulating sex business shops went into effect. The law requires all such businesses to close at midnight (love hotels, Hotetoru, Mantoru are not included). Touting of customers on the street is also prohibited. Shops open after these hours are best avoided.

Also, due to the protests of a local Turkish gentleman, all bath houses formerly referred to as "Turkish Baths" or "Toruko" are now politely titled "Soapland."

ARTS

This poster for the Seibu Museum advertises an exhibition of the complete works of Tsuki-oka Yoshitoshi, one of the later *ukiyoe* artists. The first people's art in Japan, *ukiyoe* were often produced as advertisements.

ARTS

Like all aspects of Japanese history, the arts have progressed through cycles where foreign models have dominated, been gradually assimilated, and finally reshaped by Japanese sensibilities. Most early influences on Japanese arts were from China, either directly or indirectly via Korea. Early art was usually religious in character, much of it associated with the great temples. From the introduction of Buddhism in 538 A.D., the religion continued to play a major role in the development of the arts until the present century. Changes in aesthetic sensibilities were often tied to the rise and fall in popularity of the various Buddhist sects.

Fluctuations in the political system and relations with the mainland dynasties were often a measure of Chinese influence and domestic artistic confidence. By the *Edo* period, all contact with the outside world was broken and the first people's art, "*ukiyoe*," emerged. When the country was reopened in the late 19th century, western art styles became the ultimate model and remain so today. For a further discussion of the contemporary arts see "Contemporary Art Galleries".

The subject of Japanese art is so vast and involved that anything less than a full-color plate book can never do it justice. We won't even try. A brief chronological table of the major historical and artistic periods is given in the appendix.

MUSEUMS

In recent years, museum building has become something of a fad in Japan. There are museums now for everyone and everything. Some are devoted to special fields of interest, others are little more than rental spaces for rather unimaginative shows sponsored by the major newspapers. There are a number of major public and private museums. The private museums are built around the collections of wealthy families or corporations. The public museums have excellent collections but a serious shortage of funds. The arts are not one of the Japanese government's big priorities, nor have the wealthy proven to be generous patrons. The results are too often beautiful art work in poorly installed exhibitions, or more newspaper sponsored shows.

Be that as it may, there is always something interesting showing at one of the museums in town. Information on current exhibitions is given in the tourist publications, in the **Japan Times** on Saturdays, in the **Mainichi Daily News** on Mondays, and in the **Asahi Evening News** every second Friday. Art works listed as belonging to a particular museum's collection are not always on view.

Museums in Japan tend to be crowded, so it's advisable to visit early in the morning or late afternoon. Note that in most cases you must enter 30 minutes before the listed closing time. Most museums are closed on Mondays, and many close for the New Year's holiday from around December 29, through January 3.

Japanese Traditional Arts
TOKYO NATIONAL MUSEUM—Tokyo Kokuritsu Hakubutsukan
東京国立博物館　台東区上野公園13-9
13-9 Uenokōen, Taitō-ku. (Ueno Park). Tel: 822-1111/7. Hrs: 9 a.m.-4:30 p.m., closed Mon.

Known before the war as the Imperial Household Museum, it is the largest museum in Japan and houses the best collection of Japanese art and archeology in the world. There are three buildings. In the center is the main building for Japanese art. On the right is the **Tōyōkan**, a gallery containing an excellent collection of art and archeology primarily from China and Korea. The **Hyōkeikan**, on the left, houses the Japanese archeological collections and early Buddhist objects. [M-13]

HŌRYŪJI TREASURE HOUSE—Hōryūji Hōmotsuden　法隆寺宝物殿
To the left of the National Museum's **Hyōkeikan** in Ueno Park. Tel: 822-1111 Hrs: Open only on Thurs. (hours same as above), closed when it rains or when humidity within the building exceeds 70%.

An important collection of early Japanese art from the Hōryūji Temple in Nara presented to the Imperial Household in 1876. Most of the work is from the Asuka and Nara periods, includes Buddhist sculpture, masks, textiles, metal work and some paintings. [M-13]

NEZU ART MUSEUM—Nezu Bijutsukan　根津美術館　港区南青山6-5-36
6-5-36 Minami-Aoyama, Minato-ku. Tel: 400-2536. Hrs: 9:30 a.m.-4:30 p.m.; closed Mon., the day after national holiday, and while changing exhibitions.

A beautiful and well-known collection of Japanese paintings including work by Bunchō, Goshun, Kenzan, and Kōrin's famous screen paintings of irises on gold. Also some Chinese paintings, Japanese calligraphy, ceramics, lacquer, metalwork, and sculpture. In the museum's garden are a few tea houses where the tea ceremony and instruction are held. [M-5]

GOTŌ ART MUSEUM—Gotō Bijutsukan　五島美術館　世田谷区上野毛3-9-25
3-9-25 Kaminoge, Setagaya-ku. Tel: 703-0661. Hrs: 9:30 a.m.-4:30 p.m., closed Mon., and while changing exhibitions.

An excellent collection of Japanese and Chinese paintings and calligraphy, also ceramics, sutras, lacquer and archeological objects. Most famous are the **Genji Monogatari** scroll paintings from the Heian period. The museum is in a large garden with a tea house. [M-21]

ARTS

HATAKEYAMA MUSEUM—Hatakeyama Kinenkan 畠山記念館 港区白金台2-20-12
2-20-12 Shiroganedai, Minato-ku (behind the garden of the Hannya-en Restaurant). Tel: 447-5787. Hrs: Apr. 1-Sept. 15: 10 a.m.-5 p.m., Oct. 1-Mar. 15: 10 a.m.-4:30 p.m., closed Mon.

One of the most pleasant museums in Tokyo, the collection includes paintings, calligraphy, sculpture, lacquer, tea-ceremony objects, ceramics, costumes, and some Chinese and Korean works. Especially notable are painting masterpieces by *Sesshū*, *Kōrin*, and *Kenzan*, also tea-ceremony objects by *Kōetsu*, *Chōjirō*, and pieces connected with the tea-ceremony master *Sen no Rikyū*. [M-19]

EISEI BUNKO FOUNDATION—Eisei Bunko 永青文庫 文京区目白台1-1-1
1-1-1 Mejirodai, Bunkyō-ku. Tel: 941-0850. Hrs: 10 a.m.-4 p.m., closed Sat., Sun., Hols. and while changing exhibitions.

A large and unusual collection of paintings, scrolls, masks, ceramics, and costumes housed in a warehouse behind an old western style building. The collection originally belonged to the *Hosokawa* family from *Kyūshū*, who were important vassals of the *Ashikaga shōgun*. The collection includes paintings by *Sesshū*, *Takuan*, *Niten*, *Tessai*, and *Yokoyama Taikan*. Family swords and suits of armour are also shown. [off Map]

IDEMITSU ART GALLERY—Idemitsu Bijutsukan
出光美術館 千代田区丸ノ内3-1-1国際ビル9階
International Bldg. 9th Fl., 3-1-1 Marunouchi, Chiyoda-ku. Tel: 213-3111. Hrs: 10 a.m.-5 p.m., closed Mon. and while changing exhibits.

An excellent collection of paintings, *ukiyoe*, and calligraphy, including the largest collection in the world of work by the Zen monk *Sengai*. Also ceramics, bronzes, and lacquer. Some Chinese, Korean, and Middle Eastern work. [M-10]

SEIKADŌ BUNKO TENJIKAN 静嘉堂文庫展示館 世田谷区岡本2-23-1
2-23-1 Okamoto, Setagaya-ku. Tel: 700-2250. Hrs: 10 a.m.-4 p.m. Mar.-Nov., closed Mon. and while changing exhibits (call ahead).

Open to the public since 1977, the collection was made by the *Iwasaki* "Mitsubishi" family. Chinese and Japanese calligraphy and painting, *ukiyoe*, ceramics, swords, and sculpture. [off Map]

ŌKURA MUSEUM—Ōkura Shūkokan 大倉集古館 港区虎ノ門2-10-3
2-10-3 Toranomon, Minato-ku. Tel: 583-0781. Hrs: 10 a.m.-4 p.m., closed Mon. and while changing exhibits. In front of the Hotel Ōkura.

Originally the collection of Mr. "Hotel" Ōkura, the museum contains important works of painting, sculpture, ceramics, calligraphy, costumes, books, *Nō* masks. Some Chinese, Tibetan, and Indian pieces as well. [M-11]

SUNTORY ART GALLERY—Santorī Bijutsukan
サントリー美術館 港区元赤坂1-2-3東京サントリービル11階
Tokyo Suntory Bldg. 11th Fl., 1-2-3 Moto-Akasaka, Minato-ku. Tel: 470-1073. Hrs: 10 a.m.-5 p.m. (10 a.m.-7 p.m. on Fri.), closed Mon. and during exhibition changes.

A good collection of Japanese lacquer, ceramics, glass, costumes, masks, paintings, and prints. The gallery regularly holds loan exhibitions using the permanent collection as a base. There is also a small reading room, a library, and tea ceremony room. [M-6]

Modern Japanese and Western Art

TOKYO NATIONAL MUSEUM OF MODERN ART—Tokyo Kokuritsu Kindai Bijutsukan 東京国立近代美術館 千代田区北ノ丸公園3
3 Kitanomaru-kōen, Chiyoda-ku. Tel: 214-2561. Hrs:10 a.m.-5 p.m., closed Mon.

Japanese art since the *Meiji* Period is shown in a rotating collection on the three upper floors of the building. On the first floor are held temporary loan exhibitions. [M-17]

CRAFTS GALLERY OF THE MUSEUM OF MODERN ART—Tokyo Kokuritsu Kindai Bijutsukan Kōgeikan 東京国立近代美術館工芸館 千代田区北ノ丸公園1-1
1-1 Kitanomaru-kōen, Chiyoda-ku. Tel: 211-7781. Hrs: 10 a.m.-5 p.m., closed Mon.

Formerly the 19th century home of the palace guards, the museum has a good collection of contemporary crafts. Special exhibitions are usually very well curated and installed. [M-17]

TOKYO METROPOLITAN ART MUSEUM—Tokyo-to Bijutsukan
東京都美術館　台東区上野公園8-36
8-36 Ueno-kōen, Taitō-ku. Tel: 823-6921. Hrs: 9 a.m.-5 p.m., closed Mon., and during exhibition changes.

Shows mainly Japanese art from the last 50 years, but also some western works. The collection includes prints, calligraphy, sculpture, and handicrafts. [M-13]

NATIONAL MUSEUM OF WESTERN ART—Kokuritsu Seiyō Bijutsukan
国立西洋美術館　台東区上野公園7-7
7-7 Ueno kōen, Taitō-ku. Tel: 828-5131. Hrs: 9:30 a.m.-5 p.m., closed Mon., and during exhibition changes.

An impressive collection of western art housed in a building designed by Le Corbusier. The collection includes work from the Renaissance through the 20th century with an especially large number of 19th century works by French artists. [M-13]

HARA MUSEUM—Hara Bijutsukan　原美術館　品川区北品川4-7-25
4-7-25 Kita-Shinagawa, Shinagawa-ku. Tel: 445-0651. Hrs: 11 a.m.-4:30 p.m. (Wed. 11 a.m.-8 p.m.), closed Mon., day after national holiday.

In a lovely Art Deco building and former home of the *Hara* family, the museum has a good collection of contemporary art. Every month they hold an exhibition for new artists. The museum also has a collection of video art and holography. [M-39]

TOKYO METROPOLITAN TEIEN MUSEUM OF ART—Tokyo-to Teien Bijutsukan
東京都庭園美術館　港区白金台5-21-9
5-21-9 Shiroganedai, Minato-ku. Tel: 443-0201. Hrs: 10 a.m.-6 p.m., closed the 2nd and 4th Wed. of the month (if these days fall on a national holiday, then it is closed the following day).

The former home of Prince *Asaka*, this 51 year-old Art Deco building was opened as a museum in the Fall of 1983. Presently without a collection of its own, the museum is holding various loan exhibitions. The building and garden alone are worth a visit. [M-19]

YAMATANE MUSEUM OF ART—Yamatane Bijutsukan
山種美術館　中央区日本橋兜町7-12山種ビル8階
Yamatane Bldg. 8th Fl., 7-12 Kabutochō, Nihombashi, Chūō-ku. Tel: 669-7643. Hrs: 10:30 a.m.-5 p.m., closed Mon., during exhibition changes.

A collection of contemporary Japanese style paintings from the *Meiji* period to the present. There is also a library, and tea room that can be used by appointment. [M-9]

BRIDGESTONE MUSEUM OF ART—Burijisuton Bijutsukan
ブリジストン美術館　中央区京橋1-10-1ブリジストンビル2階
Bridgestone Bldg. 2nd Fl, 1-10-1 Kyōbashi, Chūō-ku. Tel: 563-0241. Hrs: 10 a.m.-5:30 p.m., closed Mon.

Japanese paintings in the western manner and European, mostly French, art. [M-9]

ASAKURA SCULPTURE GALLERY—Asakura Chōsokan　朝倉彫塑館　台東区谷中7-18-10
7-18-10 Yanaka, Taitō-ku. Tel: 821-4549. Hrs: 10 a.m.-4:30 p.m. Sat., Sun., Mon.

Interesting in the study of the history of western art in Japan, the collection consists of about 20 pieces of sculpture by *Asakura Fumio* (1883-1964). [M-13]

SEIBU ART MUSEUM—Seibu Bijutsukan　西武美術館　豊島区南池袋1-28-1西武デパート12階
Seibu Department Store 12th Fl., 1-28-1 Minami-Ikebukuro, Toshima-ku. Tel: 981-0111. Hrs: 10 a.m.-6 p.m. (until 6:30 p.m. on Sat. and Sun.) closed Thur., during exhibition changes.

Changing exhibitions of contemporary Japanese and western art. [M-18]

Specialist Museums

RICCAR ART MUSEUM—Rikkā Bijutsukan
リッカー美術館　中央区銀座2-3-6リッカービル7階
Riccar Bldg. 7th Fl., 2-3-6 Ginza, Chūō-ku. Tel: 571-3254. Hrs: 11 a.m.-6 p.m., closed Mon.

One of the best known collections of *ukiyoe* prints in Japan. Contains around 6,000 prints. There is a room with displays of printmaking techniques and a library for *ukiyoe* studies. [M-8]

ŌTA MEMORIAL MUSEUM OF ART—Ōta Kinen Bijutsukan
太田記念美術館　渋谷区神宮前1-10-10
1-10-10 Jingūmae, Shibuya-ku. Tel: 403-0880. Hrs: 10:30 a.m.-5:30 p.m., closed Mon., and

"People make fools of people", "A young woman with an old face".
Two late Edo period *ukiyoe* by Ichiyūsai Kuniyoshi.

the from the 25th until the end of the month.

A collection of over 12,000 *ukiyoe* prints in a lovely, small Japanese style building. [M-4]

JAPAN CALLIGRAPHY MUSEUM—Nihon Shodō Bijutsukan
日本書道美術館　板橋区常盤台1-3-1
1-3-1 Tokiwadai, Itabashi-ku. Tel: 965-2611. Hrs: 11 a.m.-5 p.m., closed Mon., Tue., day after national holidays, and when exhibition changes.

A collection of over 2,000 works of 20th century calligraphy. A small garden on the grounds is a calligraphy brush burial ground. [off Map]

MUSEUM OF CALLIGRAPHY—Shodō Hakubutsukan　書道博物館　台東区根岸2-10-4
2-10-4 Negishi, Taitō-ku. Tel: 872-2645. Hrs: 10 a.m.-4 p.m., closed Mon., and mid Jun.-mid July.

The history of calligraphy illustrated through inscribed objects such as pottery, stone objects, etc. Chinese pieces dominate but there are some Japanese. [M-13]

JAPAN FOLK CRAFTS MUSEUM—Nippon Mingeikan　日本民芸館　目黒区駒場4-3-33
4-3-33 Komaba, Meguro-ku. Tel: 467-4527. Hrs: 10 a.m.-5 p.m., closed Mon.

In the former home of folk art enthusiast *Yanagi Sōetsu*, the collection includes furniture, textiles, pottery, and ceramics by unknown craftsmen. In November the museum holds a sale of crafts from around the country. [M-35]

SHITAMACHI MUSEUM—Shitamachi Fūzoku Shiryōkan
下町風俗資料館　台東区上野公園2-1
2-1 Ueno-kōen, Taitō-ku. Tel: 823-7451. Hrs: 9:30 a.m.-4:30 p.m., closed Mon., & Hols.

In a new building at the southern end of Ueno Park's Shinobazu Pond, the musuem recreates a street of merchant's shops and homes as they were before the 1923 earthquake. [M-13]

MEIJI UNIVERSITY ARCHEOLOGICAL COLLECTION—Meiji Daigaku Kōkogaku Chinretsukan　明治大学考古学陳列館　千代田区神田駿河台1-1明治大学内
Meiji Daigaku, 1-1 Surugadai, Kanda, Chiyoda-ku. Tel: 296-4432. Hrs; 10 a.m.-4:30 p.m. (Sat. 10 a.m.-1 p.m.), closed Sun., Nat. & Univ. Hols.

Chinese archeological objects from prehistoric periods to the T'ang Dynasty, Japanese objects from pre-*Jōmon* to the *Kofun* period. [M-15]

KOKUGAKUIN UNIVERSITY ARCHEOLOGICAL COLLECTION—Kokugakuin Daigaku Kōkogaku Shiryōkan　国学院大学考古学資料館　渋谷区東4-10-28
4-10-28 Higashi, Shibuya-ku. Tel: 409-0111. Hrs: 9 a.m.-5 p.m., closed Sun., Nat. & Univ. Hols.
　Archeological materials from preceramic to early historical periods. [off Map]

THE ANCIENT ORIENT MUSEUM—Kodai Oriento Hakubutsukan
古代オリエント博物館　豊島区東池袋3-1-4サンシャインシティ7階
Sunshine City 7th Fl., 3-1-4 Higashi-Ikebukuro, Toshima-ku. Tel: 989-3491. Hrs: 10 a.m.-5 p.m., closed Mon.
　Specializes in West Asian archeology. For 10 years they have been excavating in Syria. [M-18]

PAPER MUSEUM—Kami no Hakubutsukan　紙の博物館　北区堀船1-1-8
1-1-8 Horifune, Kita-ku. Tel: 911-3545. Hrs: 9:30 a.m./4:30 p.m., closed Mon., & Hols.
　The largest museum of paper in the world, the museum has displays showing techniques and utensils for "washi" (Japanese paper) production. [M-48]

MEIJI SHRINE TREASURE HOUSE—Meiji Jingū Hōmotsuden
明治神宮宝物殿　渋谷区代々木神園町1-1代々木公園内
Yoyogi Park, 1-1 Kamizonochō, Yoyogi, Shibuya-ku. Tel: 379-5511. Hrs: Mar.-Oct. 9 a.m.-4:30 p.m., Nov.-Feb. 9 a.m.-4 p.m., closed the 3rd Fri.
　A collection of sacred objects and articles related to the Meiji Emperor. [M-4]

TREASURE HOUSE OF THE YASUKUNI SHRINE—Yasukuni Jinja Hōmotsu-ihinkan
靖国神社宝物遺品館　千代田区九段北3-1-1
3-1-1 Kudan-kita, Chiyoda-ku. Tel: 261-8326. Hrs: 9:30 a.m.-4:30 p.m.
　Dedicated to the memory of Japanese war dead, the collection includes swords, helmets, and other arms, a kamikaze plane, a flag painted in blood, and other thought provoking items. [M-17]

WASEDA UNIVERSITY TSUBOUCHI MEMORIAL MUSEUM—Waseda Daigaku Tsubouchi-hakase Kinen Engeki Hakubutsukan
早稲田大学坪内博士記念演劇博物館　新宿区西早稲田1-6-1早稲田大学内
Waseda Daigaku, 1-6-1 Nishi-Waseda, Shinjuku-ku. Tel: 203-4141. Hrs: 9 a.m.-4 p.m. (until 2 p.m. on Sat.), closed Sun., Nat. & Univ. Hols.
　The collection covers oriental and occidental theater. Includes bugaku and nō masks, puppets, nō and kabuki costumes, instruments and stage models. The building was modeled after London's Fortune Theater. [off Map]

COSTUME MUSEUM—Bunka-gakuen Fukushioku Hakubutsukan
文化学園服飾博物館　渋谷区代々木3-22-1
3-22-1 Yoyogi, Shibuya-ku. Tel: 370-3111. Hrs: 10 a.m.-4:30 p.m. (Sat. 10 a.m.-3 p.m.), closed Sun. Hols., the 23rd of June.
　Over 50,000 costumes from Asia, and 18th-19th century Europe and America. [off Map]

SWORD MUSEUM—Tōken Hakubutsukan　刀剣博物館　渋谷区代々木4-25-10
4-25-10 Yoyogi, Shibuya-ku. Tel: 379-1386. Hrs: 9 a.m.-4 p.m., closed Mon.
　A collection of over 6,000 swords, thirty of which are National Treasures. [off Map]

KITE MUSEUM—Tako no Hakubutsukan
凧の博物館　中央区日本橋1-12-10たいめい軒ビル5階
Taimeiken Bldg. 5th Fl., 1-12-10 Nihombashi, Chūō-ku. Tel: 275-2704. Hrs: 11 a.m.-5 p.m., closed Sun., & Hols.
　Run by the **Japan Kite Association**, the museum has kites from Japan and other parts of the world. [M-9]

DAIMYŌ CLOCK MUSEUM—Daimyō Tokei Hakubutsukan
大名時計博物館　台東区谷中2-1-27
2-1-27 Yanaka, Taitō-ku. Tel: 821-6913. Hrs: 10 a.m.-4 p.m. closed Mon., and Jul. 1-Sept. 30.
　88 clocks from the Edo period in an interesting older building. [M-13]

KURITA MUSEUM—Kurita Bijutsukan　栗田美術館　中央区日本橋浜町2-17-9
2-17-9 Hamachō, Nihombashi, Chūō-ku. Tel: 666-6246 Hrs: 10 a.m.-5 p.m., daily.
　The collection of Mr. Kurita, the museum specializes in ceramics, particularly Imari ware produced in the Edo period, and Nabeshima ware. [M-23]

MEIJI UNIVERSITY CRIMINAL MUSEUM—Meiji Daigaku Keiji Hakubutsukan
明治大学刑事博物館　千代田区神田駿河台1-1明治大学内

ARTS

Meiji Daigaku, 1-1 Surugadai, Kanda, Chiyoda-ku. Tel: 296-4431. Hrs: 10 a.m.-4:30 p.m. (Sat. 10 a.m.-12:30 p.m.), closed Sun., Nat. & Univ. Hols.

A guillotine and many other implements of punishment, and tools used in arresting *Edo* period criminals. Also documents of criminal cases and legislation. [M-15]

FURNITURE MUSEUM—Kagu no Hakubutsukan
家具の博物館　中央区晴海3-10JFCビル2階
JFC Bldg. 2nd Fl., 3-10 Harumi, Chūō-ku. Tel: 533-0098. Hrs: 10 a.m.-4:30 p.m., closed Sun. & Hols.

Established with the intention of preserving and exhibiting traditional furniture to the public. [M-22]

TOBACCO AND SALT MUSEUM—Tabako to Shio no Hakubutsukan
たばこと塩の博物館　渋谷区神南1-16-8
1-16-8 Jinnan, Shibuya-ku. Tel: 476-2041. Hrs: 10 a.m.-5:30 p.m., closed Mon. the 2nd Tue. of Jun.

Covers the history of tobacco since Maya. All exhibits are somehow connected with salt and tobacco, sometimes *ukiyoe* showing smoking customs or collections of old smoking utensils. [M-3]

SUMŌ MUSEUM—Sumō Hakubutsukan　相撲博物館　墨田区横網1-3-28
1-3-28 Yokoami, Sumida-ku. Tel: 622-0366. Hrs: 9:30 a.m.-4:30 p.m., closed Sat., Sun. & Hols.

Sumō history and memorabilia. [M-24]

BASEBALL HALL OF FAME AND MUSEUM—Yakyū Taiiku Hakubutsukan
野球体育博物館　文京区後楽1-3-61
1-3-61 Kōraku, Bunkyō-ku. Tel: 811-3600. Hrs: 10 a.m.-5 p.m., closed one week in Feb.

The history of baseball, plus more than 23,000 volumes of Japanese and foreign publications on sports and physical education. [M-30]

NHK MUSEUM OF BROADCASTING—NHK Hōsō Hakubutsukan
NHK放送博物館　港区愛宕2-1-1
2-1-1 Atago, Minato-ku. Tel: 433-5211. Hrs: 9:30 a.m.-4:30 p.m., closed Mon.

Historical developments in radio and TV broadcasting. [M-11]

TRANSPORTATION MUSEUM—Kōtsū Hakubutsukan　交通博物館　千代田区神田須田町1-25
1-25 Sudachō, Kanda, Chiyoda-ku. Tel: 251-8481. Hrs: 9:30 a.m.-5 p.m., closed Mon.

Miniatures of the JNR system and other train displays. Good fun. [M-14]

SCIENCE MUSEUM—Kagaku Gijutsukan　科学技術館　千代田区北ノ丸公園2-1
2-1 Kitanomaru-kōen (park), Chiyoda-ku. Tel: 212-8471. Hrs: 9:30 a.m.-4:50 p.m., daily.

The newest machines, models, and experimental apparatus displayed, with free access and operation for visitors. [M-17]

NATIONAL SCIENCE MUSEUM—Kokuritsu Kagaku Hakubutsukan
国立科学博物館　台東区上野公園7-20
7-20 Ueno-kōen, Taitō-ku. Tel: 822-0111. Hrs: 9 a.m.-4:30 p.m., closed Mon.

A typical science museum. [M-13]

NATIONAL PARK FOR NATURE STUDY—Shizen Kyōiku-en 自然教育園　港区白金台5-21-5
5-21-5 Shiroganedai, Minato-ku. Tel: 441-7176. Hrs: May-Aug. 9 a.m.-5 p.m., Sept-Apr. 9 a.m.-4:30 p.m., closed Mon., and the day after national holidays.

Part of the National Science Museum, contains outdoor exhibitions of wild plants and animals, and some fragments of natural vegetation from *Musashino*, pre-*Edo*, Tokyo that have been designated as "National Monuments". Admissions are restricted to 300 persons at a time. [M-19]

YOKOYAMA TAIKAN MEMORIAL GALLERY—Yokoyama Taikan Kinenkan
横山大観記念館　台東区池ノ端1-4-24
1-4-24 Ikenohata, Taitō-ku. Tel: 821-1017. Hrs: 10 a.m.-4 p.m., closed Mon. Tue. & Wed.

Formerly the home of the well known painter *Yokoyama*, who died in 1958. Only a few paintings and ceramics are shown at a time, but it's worth a visit to see the house and garden. [M-13]

Outside Tokyo
JAPANESE OPEN AIR MUSEUM OF TRADITIONAL HOUSES—Nihon Minka-En
日本民家園　神奈川県川崎市多摩区枡形7-1-1
7-1-1 Masugata, Tama-ku, Kanagawa Prefecture. Tel: 044-922-2181. Hrs: 9:30 a.m.-4 p.m., closed Mon.
  19 traditional homes and buildings preserved in a park-like setting. [off Map]
MOA MUSEUM OF ART—MOA Bijutsukan
ＭＯＡ美術館　静岡県熱海市桃山町26-2
26-2, Momoyamachō, Atami-shi, Shizuoka-ken. Tel: (0557) 81-5785. Hrs: 9:30 a.m.-4 p.m., closed Thurs.
  Opened in 1981, the museum is an extravagant modern building located half-way up a mountain in Atami, about one hour from Tokyo. The initials MOA stand for Okada Mokichi Association, a group connected with the Japanese "Church of World Messianity". The museum houses a distinguished collection of Japanese and Chinese art, including three National Treasures and 53 Important Cultural Properties. Video tapes in both Japanese and English describe the collection's contents. Other features are a replica of Toyotomi Hideyoshi's golden tea room, a nō theater, and a Japanese garden. (Take the bullet train or Tōkaidō Line to Atami station. Then take the bus at the No. 4 Bus stop to the MOA Museum. The bus takes about 8 min., on foot it takes around 25 min.) [off Map]
HAKONE OPEN-AIR MUSEUM—Chōkoku no Mori Bijutsukan
彫刻の森美術館　神奈川県足柄下郡箱根二の平
1121 Ninotaira, Hakone-machi, Ashigara-shimo-gun, Kanagawa-ken. Tel: (0460) 2-1161. Hrs: 9 a.m.-5 p.m., Mar.-Oct., 9 a.m.-4 p.m., Nov.-Feb., daily.
  19th and 20th century sculpture of Japanese and western artists, exhibited in one of several halls, terraces, or in a large park like garden along a hill side. There is also a collection of contemporary Japanese oil paintings. A very interestisng museum. (From Shinjuku station take the Odakyū Line's "Romance Car" to Odawara station, change to the Hakone Tozan Tetsudō Railway, and go to Chōkoku no Mori station. The museum is about a 2 min. walk from there.) [off Map]

CONTEMPORARY ART GALLERIES

While in design fields Japan has been producing internationally recognized work, the contemporary fine arts have lagged considerably behind. That Japanese aesthetic sensibilities have always tended to be graphic and decorative provides a partial explanation. After all, *ukiyoe* were simple advertisements. But the real problems are far more complex. The basic structure of the Japanese art world, the complete lack of government interest or funding, and traditional concepts of art and the artist's role have proven obstinate barriers to the development of a viable contemporary art movement. What is remarkable is that there is any good contemporary art at all.

The art "scene" in Japan is dominated by two categories of art, both fundamentally conservative in nature. The main category is *Nihonga*—ink and watercolor paintings in the traditional manner. The second is work in western styles, often of a French Impressionistic vein. Art in these categories sells. The system here is rather interesting. The price of a painting is calculated on the basis of a measurement about the size of a postcard, called a *"gō"*. Each artist has his rate per *"gō"*. For a new graduate of the prestigious Tokyo Art University (*"Gei-dai"*) the price

"Utsuroi" sculpture by Miyawaki Aiko, from her 1983 exhibition at Gallery Ueda Warehouse. ©Shigeo Anzai

may start at about ¥10,000. For an established artist, the rate can reach upwards of ¥100,000, with a small painting of 4-gō size easily worth over ¥1 million.

Innovative contemporary art has never found a solid foothold within the established scheme of things. The art does not sell. Galleries that will show it are, more often than not, rental galleries where for a one week show the artist pays over ¥200,000 and acts as both host and hopeful salesperson. Artists who can't afford an exhibition will offer to show their work at a friend's home, or simply remain unknown. Others move into commercial design, which is one likely reason for the high level of work produced in the field.

While the Japanese like their pop heroes to be new and fresh-faced, in the arts acknowledged masters have ruled. The individual iconoclastic artist-heroes so admired in the west have never been a part of the Japanese tradition. The arts here have always involved a certain amount of disciplined imitation, whether it was of master by apprentice, or of China by Japanese artists in general. Development in art has remained consistent with some tradition, never daring, never dramatically breaking new ground.

In hindsight, the arts of Japan don't appear to have suffered from this. But the problems the system presents now are well recognized by artists, sympathetic gallery owners, the few progressive museum curators, and an increasingly knowledgeable public.

Still, the entire blame cannot be laid on the system. Artists intending to be innovative, too often produce work that is clearly derivative of New York or European art. Notably absent in most is anything that identifies the work as made in Japan. As though belonging to mutually exclusive categories, Japanese and western traditions have been consciously separated by artists of all fields. Interestingly, international success and domestic confidence in the music and fashion worlds have grown in proportion with the willingness to mix eastern and western sensibilities. There have been such "blends" in the visual arts as well, but always on a minor scale. Perhaps as in other creative fields, a "star" artist with international potential will surface and provide the necessary focal point for the domestic art movement.

Japan is at an interesting stage now. The current vogue for lifestyle consciousness and consumerism among the young has nurtured an interest in contemporary art. Boutiques and cafe-bars all have miniexhibitions, and whiskey advertisements feature images of art works or whiskey in an "art box" for consumer appeal. Although suspiciously "fashionable" at the moment, the rise in public awareness is, nevertheless, encouraging.

Following is a list of galleries chosen with the help of local artists and others involved in the art world. We have selected galleries that show contemporary, predominately Japanese art. Rental galleries have been noted, primarily because the quality of the exhibitions is slightly more variable when the space can be leased by anyone who can afford it.

Exhibitions run for about a week, during which the artist is usually present. Because the majority of galleries are located in the downtown districts, we have arranged the list so that you can do a walking tour, starting at the South exit of Kanda JNR Station and working down through the western end of Ginza. The tour will take about three hours. Use the maps for Kanda/Akihabara [M-14], Nihombashi/Kyōbashi [M-9], and Ginza [M-8]. The tour will provide a quick look at the current state of the arts, but galleries in the other parts of town shouldn't be neglected.

Galleries
• **Nihombashi—Kanda**

TAMURA GALLERY—mostly rental.
Shōtoku Bldg. 2nd Fl., 2 Nishifukudachō, Kanda, Chiyoda-ku. Tel: 254-6517. Hrs: 11 a.m.-7 p.m., daily. [M-9]
G PARELUGON II—mostly rental, very young artists.
Sankei Bldg. 2nd Fl., 12 Mikurachō, Kanda, Chiyoda-ku. Tel: 254-2767. Hrs: 12 a.m.-7:30 p.m., closed Sun. [M-9]

MAKI GALLERY—mostly rental.
Dai-ni Kumaya Bldg. 1st Fl., 4-9 Honchō, Nihombashi, Chūō-ku. Tel: 241-1310. Hrs: 11 a.m.-7 p.m., daily. [M-9]
KOMAI GALLERY—mostly rental.
Komai Bldg. B. 1, 3-1 Muromachi, Nihombashi, Chūō-ku. Tel: 270-3066. Hrs: 11 a.m.-7 p.m., daily. [M-9]
TOKIWA GALLERY—rental only. Shows primarily avant-garde sculpture.
Kyōeiseimei Bldg. 1st Fl., 4-2 Hongokuchō, Nihombashi, Chūō-ku. Tel: 270-8530. Hrs: 11 a.m.-7 p.m., closed Sun. [M-9]

- **Kyōbashi—Ginza**

INA GALLERY
2nd Fl. Ina Showroom, 3-6-18, Kyōbashi, Chūō-ku. Tel: 562-1710. Hrs: 10 a.m.-6 p.m., closed the 1st Tue. of the month. [M-9]
NANTENSHI GALLERY—more established contemporary artists.
Kimura Bldg. 1st Fl., 3-6-5 Kyōbashi, Chūō-ku. Tel: 563-3511. Hrs: 11 a.m.-6 p.m., closed Sun. & Hols. and the first week of August. [M-9]
KANEKO ART GALLERY—specializes in drawings.
3-7-13, Kyōbashi, Chūō-ku. Tel: 564-0455. Hrs: 11 a.m.-6:30 p.m., closed Sun. [M-9]
KANEKO ART G1—Kaneko Art's rental space, mostly young artists.
Takekawagishi Bldg. B. 1, 3-5-3 Kyōbashi, Chūō-ku. Tel: 564-6895. Hrs: 11 a.m.-6:30 p.m., closed Sun. [M-9]
AI GALLERY—rental
Kikuyagofukuten 2nd Fl., 1-8-17 Ginza, Chūō-ku. Tel: 564-0579. Hrs: 11:30 a.m.-7 p.m. (Sat. until 6 p.m.), closed Sun. [M-8]
GALLERY K—half rental
3rd. Fl., 1-9-6 Ginza, Chūō-ku. Tel: 563-4578. Hrs: 11:30 a.m.-7 p.m., closed Sun. [M-8]
G ART GALLERY
Minagawa Bldg. 1st Fl., 1-6-10 Ginza, Chūō-ku. Tel: 562-5858. Hrs: 11 a.m.-6:30 p.m., closed Sun. [M-8]
LUNAMI GALLERY—rental.
Hanashima Camera 2nd Fl., 2-5-2 Ginza, Chūō-ku. Tel: 561-6076. Hrs: 11:30 a.m.-6:30 p.m.. Closed Sun. [M-8]
GALLERY WHITE ART
Taihōkōsan Bldg. 3rd Fl., 2-5-4 Ginza, Chūō-ku. Tel: 567-0089. Hrs: 11:30 a.m.-7:30 p.m., closed Sun. [M-8]
GALLERY KOBAYASHI—mostly rental.
Yokota Bldg. 1st Fl., 2-11-5 Ginza, Chūō-ku. Tel: 543-0083. Hrs: 11:30 a.m.-7:30 p.m., closed Sun. [M-8]
GALLERY YAMAGUCHI—mostly rental.
Yamato Bldg. 3rd Fl., 3-8-12 Ginza, Chūō-ku. Tel: 561-3075. Hrs: 11 a.m.-6:30 p.m. closed Sun., Mon. & Hols. [M-8]
GEKKŌSŌ GALLERY—holographs
Art Center Bldg. 1st Fl., 6-2-3 Ginza, Chūō-ku. Tel: 573-5021. Hrs: 11:30 a.m.-8 p.m., daily. [M-8]
GALLERY MURAMATSU—some rental, often group shows of young artists.
Hirakata Bldg. 2nd Fl., 7-10-8 Ginza, Chūō-ku. Tel: 571-9095. Hrs: 11 a.m.-7 p.m., closed Sun. [M-8]
GALLERY UEDA
Asahi Bldg. B1, 6-6-7 Ginza, Chūō-ku. Tel: 574-7553. Hrs: 10:30 a.m.-6:30 p.m., closed Sun. & Hols. [M-8]
TOKYO GALLERY—one of the best for more established contemporary artists.
Dai go Shūwa Bldg. 2nd Fl., 8-6-18 Ginza, Chūō-ku. Tel: 571-1808. Hrs: 10 a.m.-7 p.m., closed Sun. & Hols. [M-8]
GALLERY TE
Tōsei Bldg. 4th Fl., 8-10-7 Ginza, Chūō-ku. Tel: 574-6730. Hrs: 11 a.m.-7 p.m., closed Sun. [M-8]
GALLERY Q—mostly rental.

Tōsei Bldg. 4th Fl., 8-10-7 Ginza, Chūō-ku. Tel: 573-1696. Hrs: 11 a.m.-7 p.m., closed Sun. [M-8]

• **Roppongi**

UNAC SALON
Azabu Unihouse #112, 1-1-2 Azabudai, Minato-ku. Tel: 585-7069. Hrs: 10 a.m.-6 p.m., closed Sun. & Hols. [M-1]

TOKYO DESIGNERS SPACE—used as a gallery by members of the **Tokyo Designers Association**.
Axis Bldg. 4th Fl., 5-17-1 Roppongi, Minato-ku. Tel: 587-2007. Hrs: 12 a.m.-7 p.m., closed Sun. & Hols. [M-1]

AO GALLERY—some rental.
Axis Bldg. 4th Fl., Tel: 582-8035. Hrs: 11 a.m.-7 p.m., closed Sun. [M-1]

NEWS—used primarily by members of an association of young artists.
A. T. Bldg. 1st Fl., 4-12-2 Roppongi, Minato-ku. Tel: 423-3501. Hrs: 1 p.m.-9 p.m., closed Sun. & Hols. [M-1]

• **Harajuku**

AT GALLERY—some rental.
Ōkura Bldg. 2nd Fl., 1-22-1 Jingūmae, Shibuya-ku. Tel: 401-3189. Hrs: 12 a.m.-7 p.m., closed Sun. [M-4]

• **Shibuya**

GALLERY VIEW—sponsored by Parco. Some rental, mainly graphics and illustration.
Studio Parco 6th Fl., 1-20-9 Jinnan, Shibuya-ku. Tel: 477-5876. Hrs: 10 a.m.-8 p.m. (no set exhibition schedule). [M-3]

• **Other Areas**

SAGACHŌ EXHIBIT SPACE—in a beautiful art deco building that was formerly a rice warehouse. Contemporary arts and events.
Shokuryō Bldg. 3rd Fl., 1-8-3 Saga, Kōtō-ku. Tel: 630-3243. Hrs: 11 a.m.-6 p.m., closed Mon. [M-25]

GATŌDŌ GALLERY TAKEBASHI—another big warehouse space, this one near the water.
Suzue Warehouse #3, 4th Fl., 1-14-24 Kaigan, Minato-ku. Tel: 433-4479. Hrs: 11 a.m.-6 p.m., closed Sun. & Hols. [M-11]

Ceramics and Crafts

AMAURY ST. GILLES-CONTEMPORARY FINE ART—contemporary ceramics and prints in an old pawnbroker's warehouse.
3-2-9 Ōi, Shinagawa-ku. Tel: 775-2040. Hrs: 1 p.m.-6:30 p.m. Wed.-Sat., or by appointment. [M-40]

AKASAKA GREEN GALLERY—ceramics and contemporary crafts.
Itō Bldg. 1st Fl., 4-8-8 Akasaka, Minato-ku. Tel: 401-5255. Hrs: 10:30 a.m.-6 p.m., closed Sun. & Hols. [M-6]

AOYAMA GREEN GALLERY
Itō Bldg. 1st Fl., 5-10-12 Minami Aoyama, Minato-ku. Tel: 407-0050. Hrs: 10:30 a.m.-6 p.m., closed Sun. & Hols. [M-5]

INUI—ceramics and contemporary crafts.
3-9-3 Akasaka, Minato-ku. Tel: 582-9660. Hrs: 11 a.m.-7 p.m., closed: 8, 9, 10, 18, 19, 20, 28, 29, 30 every month. [M-6]

KURODA TŌEN—mostly pottery. The gallery is on the 2nd Fl.
7-8-6 Ginza, Chūō-ku. Tel: 571-3223. Hrs: 10 a.m.-7 p.m., daily. [M-8]

YAYA GALLERY—sells ceramics and glassware and occasionally has exhibitions.
Imperial Hotel Arcade, B1. Tel. 580-8088. Hrs: 10 a.m.-7 p.m., closed Sun. & Hols. [M-10]

Contemporary Prints

AMAURY ST. GILLES (see ceramics above). [M-40]

ARTS

TOLEMAN COLLECTION—in a lovely traditional Japanese house.
2-2-18 Shiba-Daimon, Minato-ku. Tel: 434-1300. Hrs: 11 a.m.-7 p.m., closed Tue. [M-11]
YŌSEIDŌ GALLERY
5-5-15 Ginza, Chūō-ku. Tel: 571-1312. Hrs: 10:30 a.m.-6:30 p.m., closed Sun. & Hols. [M-8]
GREEN COLLECTIONS—prints by foreign and Japanese artists.
Palace Aoyama Bldg. 1st Fl., 6-1-6 Minami Aoyama, Minato-ku. Tel: 400-1182. Hrs: 10 a.m.-7 p.m., closed Sun. & Hols. [M-5]

Photography

ZEIT PHOTO
Yagichō Bldg. 5th Fl., 1-4 Muromachi, Nihombashi, Chūō-ku. Tel: 246-1370. Hrs: 10:30 a.m.-6:30 p.m. (Sat. until 5:30 p.m.), closed Sun. & Hols. [M-9]
NIKON SALON
Matsushima Gankyōten 3rd Fl., 3-5-6 Ginza, Chūō-ku. Tel: 562-5756. Hrs: 10 a.m.-6 p.m., closed Mon. [M-8]
PENTAX FORUM
Shinjuku Mitsui Bldg. 1st Fl., 2-1-1 Nishi-Shinjuku, Shinjuku-ku. Tel: 348-2941. Hrs: 10:30 a.m.-7 p.m., daily. [M-7]

The following galleries show primarily well-known international artists, but also represent a few Japanese artists.

GALLERY MUKAI
Tsukamoto Bldg. 6th Fl., 5-5-11 Ginza, Chūō-ku. Tel: 571-3291. Hrs: 10 a.m.-7 p.m., closed Sun. [M-8]
GALLERY WATARI
3-7-6 Jingūmae, Shibuya-ku. Tel: 405-7005. Hrs: 11 a.m.-7 p.m., closed Sun. & Hols. [M-5]
NISHIMURA GALLERY
4-3-13 Ginza, Chūō-ku. Tel: 567-3906. Hrs: 11 a.m.-7 p.m., closed Sun. & Hols. [M-8]
AKIRA IKEDA GALLERY
2-8-18 Kyōbashi, Chūō-ku. Tel: 567-5090. Hrs: 11 a.m.-6 p.m., closed Sun. [M-9]
KANRANSHA
3-10-1 Kyōbashi, Chūō-ku. Tel: 567-9674. Hrs: 12 noon-7 p.m., closed Sun. & Hols. [M-9]
GALLERY UEDA WAREHOUSE—slightly hard to find but a huge space.
Mitsubishi Warehouse, 1-28-24 Shinkawa, Chūō-ku. Tel: 553-8791. Hrs: 10:30 a.m.-6 p.m. (Sun. 11 a.m.-5 p.m.) closed Hols. [M-25]

Video

While art videos are sometimes shown at the galleries listed in the previous section, the following is a list of places that specialize.

SCAN VIDEO GALLERY 1-12-1 Jingūmae, Shibuya-ku. Tel: 470-2664. This is presently the only gallery in Tokyo that specializes in artists' video. They distribute both internationally and domestically the works of overseas as well as Japanese artists. Two times a year, in spring and autumn, they sponsor a competition for video artists. Exhibitions, curated by Scan, are held once a month for two weeks, with screenings in the evening from between 5-7 p.m., depending on the program. Call ahead for details. [M-4]
HARA MUSEUM—has a collection of videos primarily by international artists, though a few are by Japanese. The videos are shown Tue.-Sun. from 2 p.m.-4 p.m. on the 2nd floor. A different artist's work is shown each day. [M-39]
VIDEO EARTH TOKYO Minami Aoyama Lihaimu #607, 2-29-9 Minami-Aoyama, Minato-ku. Tel: 408-5749. Basically an organization renting video equipment and an editing studio, they also have a machine for transferring European video tape to the Japanese format (discount given to artists). They run a small club called the "Earth Club" whose members are primarily local video artists. The club sponsors video exhibitions twice a month (one week

runs). The club's address is listed below, but for information call the main office. [M-5]
EARTH CLUB Takakuwa Bldg. #408, 3-5-11 Kita-Aoyama, Minato-ku.
VIDEO INFORMATION CENTER Kazan Bldg. 1st Fl., 3-2-4 Kasumigaseki, Chiyoda-ku. Tel: 580-4264. Hrs: 10 a.m.-6 p.m., Mon.-Fri., 10 a.m.-5 p.m., Sat., closed Sun. & Hols. Run by Japan Victor Co., this is mainly a showroom for video equipment. They sponsor the annual Tokyo Video Festival, an international competition open to amateur or professional artists, basically to anyone. For entry forms and further information contact any JVC dealer in Japan or overseas, or write to the address listed above. Winning entries from previous contests can be viewed at the Information Center. Other services include editing facilities, and video classes. [M-11]

TRADITIONAL ARTS

In the west, they would be called hobbies: *ikebana* or *kadō*—flower arranging, *shodō*—calligraphy and *sadō*—tea ceremony. For the Japanese, these are considered both artistic and spiritual pursuits.

The history of each is long and varied. Only *ikebana* is a Japanese invention, the others being originally Chinese imports. Calligraphy is the oldest; in the *Heian* period the ability to write a beautiful hand was a sign of aristocratic taste and breeding.

All three arts were given an added philosophical dimension when *Zen* Buddhism became the dominant religious sect after the *Kamakura* period. The aim of *Zen* was to purge the mind of egoistic intellectualism and thus attain a sense of calm, tranquillity and identity with the universe. *Sadō, shodō, kadō*, all with the suffix "*dō*" meaning "the way of", were a means of establishing harmony between man and nature, and achieving a state of "enlightenment".

Sadō, tea ceremony, was the most important of the three. Tea was first used by *Zen* monks to help keep themselves awake during long meditation sessions. The tea ceremony developed slowly and, as an art, was formalized by the famous tea master Sen no Rikyū (1521-91). The simple, almost rustic, tea room, sparsely decorated with a flower arrangement or an ink painting, was intended as a miniature of the world in harmony. By the *Azuchi-Momoyama* period, the art began to lose it's simplicity and slowly became a ritual devoid of spiritual content, an ostentatious pursuit of the wealthy *daimyō* lords who competed frantically for the most extravagant, famous, and expensive tea bowls and caddies.

The arts are taught today by a number of schools, which have become huge and profitable organizations. The schools teach the rules, rituals and techniques, but this is where most stop. Only a few teachers are capable of taking the training to the next, and most important, step. Using *Zen* terminology: the fundamental purpose is to achieve spiritual harmony with nature through a circular process of creation and self-expression, then reciprocally learning from the creation. As in the martial arts, the *Zen* foundations of these arts are not always consciously acknowledged.

The arts are taught by a number of schools, each of which holds to a variety of methods and theory. The difference is most extreme in *ikebana* where over twenty different schools teach the two main styles known as "*rikka*" or formal style, and "*nageire*" or natural style. The most traditional school is the Ikenobō, the most contemporary is the Sōgetsu.

For people not interested in the *Zen* aspects of these arts, they all make relaxing, somewhat "exotic" hobbies. Demonstrations of the tea ceremony and *ikebana* are given at various locations, and some schools offer instruction for short periods of time. Calligraphy schools generally accept only long term students.

Ikebana

SŌGETSU Sōgetsu Kaikan Bldg. 4th Fl., 7-2-21 Akasaka, Minato-ku. Tel: 408-1126. Classes given in English every Tue. from 10 a.m.-12 noon. Fee: ¥3,000 per lesson, includes flower cost. You must make an appointment by the preceeding Mon. [M-5]

IKENOBŌ 2-3 Surugadai, Kanda, Chiyoda-ku. Tel: 292-3071. Classes given Wed. from 11 a.m.-12:30 p.m. and from 4 p.m.-5:30 p.m. Fee: ¥3,000. You must make an appointment the day before. [M-15]

OHARA Ohara Kaikan 2nd Fl., 5-7-17 Minami-Aoyama, Minato-ku. Tel: 499-1200.They have lessons Mon.-Fri. from 10 a.m.-12 noon. You can join the classes anytime, but must give 2-3 days notice. Fee: ¥1,200 per lesson, plus a flower fee of about ¥800. [M-5]

SAKURA-KAI (Tea Ceremony Service Center) 3-2-25 Shimo-Ochiai, Shinjuku-ku. Tel: 951-9043. Classes given in English every Thur. & Fri. between 11 a.m.-3 p.m., each lesson lasts about 40 min. Appointment necessary. Fee: ¥1,500. [off Map]

IKEBANA INTERNATIONAL Shufunotomo Bldg. 2nd Fl., 1-6 Surugadai, Kanda, Chiyoda-ku. Tel: 293-8188. For any further information contact this organization. [M-15]

Tea Ceremony

SAKURA-KAI (Tea Ceremony Service Center) 3-2-25 Shimo-Ochiai, Shinjuku-ku. Tel: 951-9043. They give tea lessons Thur. and Fri. from 11 a.m.-12 noon and from 1 p.m.-3 p.m. Fee: for observation and a cup of tea and sweets—¥600, for one lesson ¥1,200. You can have tea ceremony and *ikebana* lesson in one day here. [off Map]

TŌKŌ-AN Imperial Hotel 4th Fl. From Mon.-Sat., 10 a.m.-4 p.m. Two or three times a week they are booked full by groups, so call ahead to be sure if you can observe and have a cup of tea. Fee: ¥1,100. [M-10]

CHŌSHŌ-AN Hotel Ōkura 7th Fl. Tea demonstrations given daily from 11 a.m.-12 noon and 1 p.m.-5 p.m. The ceremony is sometimes booked by groups, so call ahead. Fee: observation and a cup of tea with sweets—¥1,000. [M-11]

SEISEI-AN Hotel New Ōtani 7th Fl. Thur., Fri. & Sat. 11 a.m.-12 noon and 1 p.m.-4 p.m. Fee: ¥1,000. [M-6]

Calligraphy

SHO INTERNATIONAL ICS Center Landic Hirakawachō Bldg. 2nd Fl., 2-6-2 Hirakawachō, Chiyoda-ku. Tel: 234-8757. You can observe or have a calligraphy lesson for ¥2,000. They also offer courses for long term students. Call the office for further details and reservations. Tel: 582-5679. [M-6]

SIGHTSEEING

"It's nice to be old. YMO—one in every home". In this photograph, a rather typical tour group from the countryside poses in front of Asakusa's Kaminarimon Gate, a traditional keepsake photo site. What all these people are holding are not the typical souvenirs, but albums by top Japanese contemporary music groups—like YMO, the now disbanded Yellow Magic Orchestra.

SIGHTSEEING

TEMPLES AND SHRINES

Before a Japanese child is born, chances are that the mother will visit a *Shintō* shrine associated with childbirth to pray for a safe delivery. There, she will probably buy a special *hara-maki* (lit. a "belly-wrap" normally worn to warm the stomach) to wear as a protective amulet. After birth, the child will be taken to the shrine and presented to the god.

Shrines are later visited during the various "rites of passage". On *Shichi-go-san*, a festival day for children 3, 5 and 7 years old, and on Adult's Day, when they turn 20, the visits are made to insure continued good health and fortune.

Throughout these years the child will attend a school where Confucian based social ethics are taught: the hierarchy of respect, loyalty and social obligations all important in Japanese society since the feudal period. The Confucian respect for learning has become so deeply instilled that success in the Japanese sense hinges on academic success. From pre-kindergarten through university graduation, the goal is attendance at a series of increasingly élite schools that will virtually guarantee employment by a top Japanese company, and entrance into salaryman heaven.

When it's time for marriage, a fortune calendar will be consulted to find a propitious day (this is also common for other personal and business decisions). The ceremony will be held in a *Shintō* shrine, though western-style church weddings have become a recent vogue.

When the child's parents die, the funeral will be Buddhist. A priest is summoned to read sutras and pray for the safe passage of the deceased to the spirit world. A small altar will be built in the house and the child will continue to show respect for the parents, praying, burning incense and just making sure they know they're not forgotten. Classical literature is full of tales of unhappy or neglected spirits returning to earth to haunt the living.

If this Japanese was asked whether he/she was religious, the answer would probably be no. There is no regular worship as in western religions, and very little conscious thought. For most Japanese, being Shintoist, Buddhist or Confucianist is less a question of believing than of simply being Japanese. What puzzles most foreigners is the casual mixture of religious systems. People are not either Shintoists or Buddhists, but both. Confucianism is not even considered a religion, rather a system of thought and social ethics.

Shintō, the ancient native religion, focuses on the worship of *Kami*, divine spirits of mythical ancestors or natural phenomena. With no set of moral or ethical principles, and a strictly "this worldly" orientation, *Shintō* stresses a sense of continuity between man, nature, and the *Kami*.

Imported from China in 538 (or 552), Buddhism has had a powerful influence on the Japanese world view. With a rich history of scholarship and scripture, the religion is "other worldly" and teaches the transitory nature of this life. For the Japanese this has become the basis of a complex aesthetic system where beauty is more beautiful if it's here today and gone tomorrow, the festivities surrounding the short-lived spring cherry blossoms being a good case in point.

Throughout history, religions have been harnessed by Japanese rulers for blatantly political purposes. The early adoption of Buddhism had as much to do with undermining the *Shintō* based legitimacy of a ruling family as it had with a strong belief in the foreign religion. Buddhism, associated with the well organized Chinese political system, was seen as a powerful tool for social control. For the feudal *samurai* lords, the *zen* sect of Buddhism, with its stress on austerity and action over intellectual process was a perfect form of training for *samurai* warriors. Later, Confucianism provided a solid theory for the feudal political system based on bonds of loyalty and obedience. When *samurai* rule was overthrown during the *Meiji* Restoration, *Shintō* was revived to promote Emperor worship (and the new regime), and develop nationalist sentiments, which carried the country burning with religious zeal straight into World War II. Since the war a number of new religions, mostly spin-off Buddhist sects, have become powerful religious organizations. *Sōkagakkai*, the largest with a membership of over 20 million, has its own political party, the *Kōmei-tō*.

The post war Japanese are, for the most part, extremely casual about religion. Shrines, connected with *Shintō*, and temples, connected with Buddhism, are visited for specific purposes. During *Obon* in the summer, the family temple is visited in honor of one's ancestors. At New

Years, a shrine is visited to pray for good fortune in the coming year. Most temples and shrines are visited otherwise only for specific "requests", and then an appropriate place is chosen, e.g. students will visit the shrine of a famous scholar to pray for a passing exam score.

For both Japanese and foreigners, sightseeing is a major reason for visiting the more famous shrines and temples. *Shintō* shrines are easily recognized by the *torii*, a gate, usually of wood, with two tall posts topped by one or two cross beams. The architecture is usually rather restrained. There are no images, but the *kami* will be represented by an object such as a mirror or sword. Prayer at a shrine starts by waking up the god, by clapping twice. You then bow the head and pray, and clap once more. A large bell or gong is another way of attracting the god's attention. The wooden tablets, *ema*, seen at many shrines are offered by petitioners seeking anything from a healthy baby to a successful business deal. At both temples and shrines one can purchase *omikuji* and *omamori*. *Omikuji* are poetic fortunes written on a piece of paper. After reading the fortune it's tied on a tree in hopes that a good fortune will come true and a bad one will improve. *Omamori* are amulets, usually in a small brocade case, that are for general protective purposes.

Temples are recognized for their Chinese style architecture which is generally more extravagant than that of *Shintō* shrines. Though traditionally there are a number of gates, a main hall, various outer buildings, and a pagoda, in Tokyo many of the temples' outer buildings have been destroyed. Near the entrance to the temple or shrine grounds is a small fountain, where hands are washed in a symbolic purification ceremony. At the incense burner people will "wash" themselves with the smoke in hopes of curing or preventing illness. Prayer style differs according to which sect of Buddhism one adheres to, but a simple bowing of the head and putting the hands together in a moment of silence in front of the main temple image is most common.

Most temples and shrines in Tokyo have been destroyed numerous times throughout the course of history, or simply rebuilt on a regular basis (the most famous *Shintō* shrine, Ise Jingū, is rebuilt every 20 years). The rebuilding usually follows the traditional architecture, but is often of concrete. Few temples in Tokyo remain in their original condition, but for the Japanese it doesn't seem to matter much.

In the following list of temples and shrines, important works of art belonging to the institution have been noted. Many, however, have been placed in museums or are not shown to the general public except on rare occasions. Festivals and *Ennichi* (small monthly fairs) are also listed, some as part of the calendar of events.

Temples

KAN'EIJI—was one of the most important *Edo* period temples. Built to protect *Edo* castle from the dangerous northeast direction (people are still superstitious of this direction), the temple became a *Tokugawa* family mausoleum and six of the fifteen *shōgun* were buried there. The original temple, built in 1625, was destroyed during the battle between *Tokugawa* loyalists and the *Meiji* Restoration army in 1868. The present structure was moved in 1875 from Saitama Prefecture where it was the main hall of Kitain Temple. Kan'eiji is associated with the *Tendai* sect of Buddhism.
- 1-14-11 Ueno Sakuragi, Taitō-ku. [M-13]

SENSŌJI Asakusa Kannon—During the *Edo* and *Meiji* periods the grounds of Sensōji were one of the liveliest areas in the city. Shops, theaters, amusement grounds and performers of various kinds (often freaks or monkeys) gave the area a carnival like atmosphere. To the north was Yoshiwara, the famous pleasure quarter.

The origins of the temple are legendary. One day in 628 local fishermen found in their nets a small golden image of *Kannon*, the Buddhist goddess of mercy. Sensōji was built to enshrine the statue in the 7th century. A larger temple built in 1692 was destroyed during World War II. The present building is a replica dating from 1958.

The other religious buildings in this area are covered in a walking tour of Asakusa.
- Festivals: Feb. 3-4, March 18, Apr. 8, July 9-10, Oct. 18, Nov. 3, Dec. 14-18.
- 2-3-1 Asakusa, Taitō-ku. [M-12]

ZŌJŌJI—Like Kan'eiji in the northeastern quarter of the city, Zōjōji was a *Tokugawa* family temple built to protect the castle from the south, also considered a dangerous direction. Founded in 1393 by the priest Shōsō of the Jōdo sect, the main temple was destroyed in 1873 by arsonists in protest against the temple's mixture of "foreign" Buddhism and "pure" Japanese *Shintō*. It was rebuilt and again destroyed on April Fools Day 1909, in a fire set by a cold beggar. The temple was again destroyed in World War II, and the present building dates from 1974. The imposing main gate—*Sammon*—built in 1605 remains, and is designated an "Important Cultural Property".
- Festivals: Feb. 3-4, Apr. 8.
- 4-7-35 Shiba-kōen, Minato-ku. [M-11]

ZENPUKUJI—this temple was founded in 832 by Kōbō Daishi (774-835), a Buddhist priest who brought the *Shingon* doctrine of Buddhism to Japan from China. Since 1232 it has been associated with the *Jōdo* sect. Destroyed repeatedly by fire, the temple was last rebuilt after World War II. The temple is perhaps most famous as the site of the first American Legation under Townsend Harris, from 1859-1875. A monument to the first American minister to Japan was erected here in 1936.

Fukuzawa Yukichi, a famous *Meiji* period liberal and founder of Keiō University, is buried on the temple grounds. His grave is a popular spot with Keiō students, who believe that visiting the grave will ensure success in university exams. Another attraction is an enormous ginko tree that shades the temple. The oldest such tree in Tokyo, it has been designated a "Natural Monument".
- 1-6-21 Moto-Azabu, Minato-ku. [M-1]

NISHI-ARAI-DAISHI Sōjiji—Built by Kōbō Daishi in 826, by the *Kamakura* period its popularity had grown, and in the *Edo* period was frequented by the 3rd *shōgun* Tokugawa Iemitsu. The temple's reputation and popularity center on the wooden statue of an 11-headed *Kannon* attributed to the priest Kōbō Daishi. Miraculously escaping the numerous fires that destroyed the main hall, the statue of *Kannon* is believed to help protect supplicants from fires and other forms of evil. A painted wood statue of Kōbō Daishi from the *Kamakura* period is designated an "Important Cultural Property". The current temple is a 1971 reconstruction. The temple is also famous for it peony garden.
- Festivals: Feb. 3-4.
- *Ennichi*: 1st & 21st of the month.
- 1-15-1 Nishi-Arai, Adachi-ku (Daishi-mae station/Tōbu Isezaki line from Asakusa). [M-46]

SHIBAMATA TAISHAKUTEN Daikyōji—Founded in 1631 by the priest Nitchū of Hokekyōji Temple in Chiba prefecture, this *Nichiren* sect temple is noted for its wooden statue of *Taishakuten* (a guardian diety) attributed to the sect's founder *Nichiren* (1222-1282). The current building dates from 1934, the Nitenmmon gate from 1901. The street approaching the

temple has a number of *sembei* and sweet shops including Shibamataya a restaurant that was the model for the famous movie character *Tora-san*'s family shop.
- 7-10-3 Shibamata, Katsushika-ku. (Take the Toei Asakusa line to Oshiage station. Change to the Keisei Dentetsu and go five stops to Aoto station. Change there to the Keisei Kanamachi line and take it two stops to Shibamata station.) [off Map]

JINDAIJI—The second oldest temple in the Tokyo area, Jindaiji was founded in 733. The legend of the temple's origins are recorded in a book kept with the other temple treasures. When the daughter of a rich family fell in love with a man of low origin, the parents sent the girl to a faraway island to separate the lovers. The young man prayed to the Buddhist god of water *Jinjadaiō*. The god heard his prayers and sent a giant turtle to carry the boy to the island to save his sweetheart. The two lived happily ever after. The couple's son later built Jindaiji to honor the god that helped his parents. Since that time the temple has been associated with the god of marriage.

The main hall of the temple, reconstructed in 1914, holds a gilt-bronze statue of *Shaka-Nyorai* (the main Buddha) which dates from the Nara period and is designated as an "Important Cultural Property". Behind the temple is the Jindaiji Botanical Gardens. On the way to the temple are several *soba* restaurants serving "*Jindaiji-soba*" which has been famous since the *Edo* period.
- Festivals: Daruma Fair March 3-4
- 2905 Jindaijichō, Chōfu-shi (Take the #21 bus from Tsutsujigaoka station/Keio line from Shinjuku). [off Map]

SENGAKUJI—While the temple itself is not very interesting, Sengakuji is famous as the burial place of the Forty-seven *Rōnin* (masterless *samurai*). The graves are found in a small court to the left of the front gate. The grave of their leader Ōishi Kuranosuke (1659-1703) and that of their avenged Lord, Asano Naganori (1665-1701), is found in the corner of the courtyard covered by a small roof. The head of their victim, *Kira Yoshinaka*, was washed in the temple well before being placed in front of their master's tomb on the night of December 14, 1702.
- Festivals: Apr. 1-7, Dec. 14.
- 2-11-1 Takanawa, Minato-ku. [M-37]

Shrines

MEIJI JINGŪ—Dedicated to the Emperor and Empress *Meiji*, the shrine is a beautiful example of restrained *Shintō* architecture. The shrine was opened in 1920 with extravagant ceremony, and remains one of the most frequently visited shrines in the city. The two large *torii* (gates) at the entrances to the shrine precincts were built of Japanese cypress wood over 1,700 years old. The shrine is enclosed by the extensive Meiji Jingū Gyoen gardens and Meiji Park.
- Festivals: Jan. 15, Oct. 30-Nov. 3.
- 1-1 Kamizonochō, Yoyogi, Shibuya-ku. [M-4]

HIE JINJA Sannō-sama—In the late 15th century Ōta Dōkan (a military commander) built this shrine, dedicated to *Ōyamakuni-no-Kami*, a tutelary deity of *Edo*, on the grounds of the early *Edo* castle. Later patronized by the Tokugawa, it was the most popular *Edo* period shrine, and gave the best festivals in town. The current building dates from 1959, the main gate from 1962.
- Festivals: Feb. 3-4, June 10-16, Early-mid. Aug. "Tokyo Takigi Nō".
- *Ennichi:* 1st & 15th of the month.
- 2-10-5 Nagatachō, Chiyoda-ku. [M-6]

YASUKUNI JINJA—Built in 1869, Yasukuni Shrine is dedicated to the Japanese war dead, and major figures in the *Meiji* Restoration. The shrine architecture is in classic *Shintō* style. The 15 meter high bronze main gate was built in 1887. While classic in shape, the gate has an unusually modern monumental feeling. Since the *Meiji* period the shrine has been a famous spot for snow viewing and for its cherry blossoms in the spring. There is a small memorial museum on the grounds.
- Festivals: July 13-16 (Traditional dance and *nō* performances until 10 p.m.), Aug. 15 (Anniversary of the end of WWII, the prime minister and politicians visit the shrine).
- 3-1-1 Kudan-kita, Chiyoda-ku. [M-17]

KANDA MYŌJIN—This shrine, dating back as far as the 8th century, was originally in

The east gate of Harajuku's Meiji Shrine.

Surugadai. Tokugawa Ieyasu needed the land, and had the shrine moved to its present location, but only after diplomatically naming it the guardian shrine of *Edo*. The shrine was formerly dedicated to an orthodox *shintō* diety, but became associated with a rebel general Taira no Masakado who led a revolt against the emperor Suzaku in 935. When captured and beheaded, according to legend, his head flew off and landed at the site of the *Edo* shrine. The current building is a 1934 replica of the early structure.
• Festivals: May 15.

• 2-16-2 Soto-Kanda, Chiyoda-ku. [M-16]
YUSHIMA TENJIN—Sugawara Michizane (845-903), a famous *Heian* period scholar, is enshrined in Yushima Tenjin. Originally built in the 14th century, it was later restored by Ōta Dōkan. Because of Sugawara's literary reputation, the shrine is popular with students studying for school entrance exams. Before the yearly testing period, hundreds of *ema* (wooden prayer tablets) are hung at the temple by hopeful (or hopeless) students. The shrine has a small but lovely plum garden and a dramatic bridge to the main building.
• Festivals: Plum viewing—mid. Feb. mid. Mar. A major festival is held in even numbered years on Mar. 25.
• 3-30-1 Yushima, Bunkyō-ku. [M-13] [M-16]
SUITENGŪ—Built in 1818, Suitengū in Tokyo is a branch of the Kyūshū Suitengū Shrine. The original shrine was built to pray for the soul of the six year old Emperor Antoku and his mother who jumped into the sea to escape capture during a battle between the *Taira* and Minamoto clans in 1185. The shrine has since been associated with child birth. Expectant mothers come to pray for safe delivery and newborn babies are brought to give thanks. The present shrine was rebuilt in 1967.
• Festivals: May 5-6.
• Ennichi: The 5th of each month.
• 2-4-1 Kakigarachō, Nihombashi, Chūō-ku. [M-23]
ASAKUSA JINJA Sanja-sama—One of the few buildings in this area to escape undamaged from World War II, the shrine building dates from the 13th century when it was built in honor of the three fishermen who found the *Kannon* image now enshrined in the nearby

Sensōji Temple.
- Festivals: May 17-18.
- 2-3-1 Asakusa, Taitō-ku. [M-12]

TŌSHŌGŪ—Dedicated to the first Tokugawa *shōgun* Ieyasu, this shrine erected in 1651 is the only shrine in Tokyo designated as a "National Treasure". The shrine is built in the elaborate and very Chinese *Gongen* style popular in the *Momoyama* and early *Edo* periods, and is second only to the Tōshōgū Shrine in Nikkō (Tochigi pref.) as an example of this type of architecture. The path to the shrine is lined with 200 stone lanterns donated by various *daimyō* when the shrine was built. Following are a number of bronze lanterns donated when the shrine was renovated in 1651. Inside the shrine are four paintings of animals by the well-known Kanō Tan'yū of the *Kanō* school popular in the *Momoyama* period.

The Chinese style gate to the temple attributed to *Hidari Jingorō* a famous artist of the *Edo* period, along with the stone *torii* at the entrance of the shrine are also "National Treasures".
- Festivals: Apr. 17.
- 9-88 Ueno Kōen, Taitō-ku. [M-13]

KAMEIDO TENJIN—Another shrine dedicated to the *Heian* period scholar *Sugawara Michizane* (845-903), this one, founded in 1662, was a *Tokugawa shōgun* favorite. The present building dates from 1961. The shrine is famous for its wisteria vines which bloom in late April.
- Festivals: Jan. 24-25, Mar. 25, Aug. 25, Sept. 25, Dec. 25. Wisteria viewing from mid-Apr.-early May.
- 3-6-1 Kameido, Kōtō-ku. [M-44]

NEZU JINJA Nezu gongen—This shrine dedicated to four *Shintō* dieties and the popular Sugawara Michizane, is thought to have been founded nearly 2,000 years ago. The present building was rebuilt by the fifth Tokugawa *shōgun* Tsunayoshi in 1706. The shrine's main hall (*Honden*), the two story main gate (*Rōmon*), the Chinese gate (*Karamon*), the oratory hall (*Haiden*), and a wooden fence, are all designated as "Important Cultural Properties". The shrine is also famous for its over 3,000 azalea bushes which bloom in late April. On the grounds of the shrine is a small *Otome Inari* Shrine with rows of red *torii*. (off map, see Ueno walking course)
- Festivals: Sept. 21.
- 1-28-9 Nezu, Bunkyō-ku. [off Map]

PARKS AND GARDENS

The best expression of the Japanese self-acclaimed love of nature is the garden. Traditionally planned before the home, the garden was an integral part of the living environment. The Japanese do love nature, but a nature discreetly tamed and controlled in an orderly, balanced miniature of reality. Grand landscapes are reproduced in a garden, mountains, lakes, rivers, but all on a smaller, more human scale. In an abstract *Zen* garden, the meaning of the cosmos is contained in a few symbolic rocks strategically placed in a bed of raked sand or gravel. A tea ceremony garden is planned to create a poetic mood of solitary detatchment from the world.

Where space permits in the city, small gardens are meticulously cultivated and cared for. Where a garden is not possible, potted plants and trees line the pavement in front of a house or shop. Even in the most industrial parts of the city, a watchman will nurse a lush oasis on the back steps of a huge warehouse.

Parks

UENO KŌEN—A major cultural center for the city, Ueno park has the Tokyo National Museum, the Metropolitan Fine Art Gallery, the National Museum of Western Art, the National Science Museum (all in the museum section). There are numerous shrines, temples, a zoo, the Tokyo University of Art, and the large Shinobazu Pond. The park is one of the wildest places for cherry-blossom viewing in Tokyo. We've covered the park and vicinity in a walking tour of Ueno.
• Ueno Kōen, Taitō-ku. [M-13]

HIBIYA KŌEN—Close to the Imperial Palace, the Hibiya Park area was the site of important *daimyō* mansions during the *Edo* period. After the restoration the *daimyō* packed up and left for the provinces and the land became a parade ground for the new western style army. Plans to build a bureaucratic center here were dropped when the ground proved too marshy to support the weight of major buildings, and the land was opened in 1903 as the first western style park in Japan. Fairly basic as parks go, it's noted for its azaleas in April and chrysanthemums in November. There are over 200 species of trees on the 41 acre grounds, including dogwoods sent from Washington D.C. in exchange for a Japanese gift of cherry trees.
• Hibiya-kōen, Chiyoda-ku. [M-10]

KITANOMARU KŌEN—On the north side of the Imperial Palace is Kitanomaru Park, the former home of the Imperial Palace guards. The park was opened to the public in 1969 in honor of the present Emperor's 60th birthday. One small area along the moat, called Chidorigafuchi Park, is famous for its cherry trees. Other attractions include the Tokyo Museum of Modern Art, the Crafts Gallery, and the Science and Technology Museum.
• 1 Kitanomaru-kōen, Chiyoda-ku. [M-17]

MEIJI JINGŪ GAIEN (MEIJI SHRINE OUTER GARDEN)—Also known as the Meiji Olympic Park, the funeral for the Emperor *Meiji* was held here in 1912. The park opened in 1925 after 10 years of work, and is used primarily as an athletic and recreational area. During the 1964 Olympics it was a major site for sports events, and now contains a baseball stadium, rugby field, the National Stadium, tennis courts, a swimming pool, the Nihon Seinenkan concert hall, etc. The Shōtoku Kinen Kaigakan is a small museum on the grounds, that exhibits 80 paintings of events in the life of the Emperor *Meiji* (open 9 a.m.-4:30 p.m., daily).
• Kasumigaoka-chō, Shinjuku-ku. [M-5]

YOYOGI KŌEN—To the left of the Meiji Shrine grounds, Yoyogi park is dominated by the National Indoor Stadium designed by Tange Kenzō for the Olympics. NHK Broadcasting Station headquarters are here, as well as the NHK Concert Hall. After the war the area was called Washington Heights and held the U.S. Army barracks. Now it's a favorite spot for exhibitionist Japanese kids to dance on Sunday afternoons.
• 2 Jinnan, Shibuya-ku. [M-4]

ARISUGAWA KŌEN—Built around a hill in the Azabu residential area near Roppongi, the park has a decidedly neighborhood feeling about it. There are lots of trees, paths, bridges, streams, a lotus pond, plum orchard, wisteria trellises and a flat area on top of the hill with a library. A statue in the middle of the park depicts Arisugawa Taruhito (1835-95) a member of the Arisugawa branch of the Imperial Family.
• 5 Minami-Azabu, Minato-ku. [M-2]

Gardens

KOISHIKAWA KŌRAKUEN—Begun in 1629 by Tokugawa Yorifusa, the garden was completed 30 years later by the 3rd *shōgun* Mitsukuni with the help of the Chinese scholar Chu Sun-Shui. The garden replicates famous scenic spots in Japan and China, and combines design elements from both countries. There are numerous bridges, ponds and rivers full of carp, stones, lanterns, and monuments. Most famous are the stone Full Moon Bridge, and a small temple to *Benten*, the goddess of good luck. The garden is laid out as a strolling garden and has an area of nearly 18 acres. Designated an "Outstanding Scenic Place of Historical Importance".
• 1-6-4 Kōraku, Bunkyō-ku. Hrs: 9 a.m.-4:30 p.m., closed Mon. [M-30]

RIKUGIEN—A favorite strolling garden for the *Edo* period elite, Rikugien was landscaped

in the late 17th century by Yanagisawa Yoshiyasu, a high-ranking feudal lord. The garden recreates 88 well known scenic spots in Chinese and Japanese literature, with rivers, ponds, forests, a small mountain, and a tea house. The land was bought by the Iwasaki Family (founders of the Mitsubishi empire) in the early *Meiji* period, and donated to the city in 1934.
• 6 Komagome, Bunkyō-ku. Hrs: 9 a.m.-4:30 p.m., closed Mon. [M-41]

KIYOSUMI TEIEN—Kiyosumi Garden, built by the Baron *Iwasaki* in 1878 on the former site of a *daimyō* (feudal lord) estate, is best known for its collection of huge rocks from all over Japan (all brought in by Mitsubishi ships). Beautifully landscaped, the garden surrounds a small pond that holds nearly 10,000 carp, the largest being over 1 meter in length. Other features include an island, bridges, a tea house, and a small play area for children along one side. The 12 acre garden was donated to the city in 1924.
• 3 Kiyosumi, Kōtō-ku. Hrs: 9 a.m.-4:30 p.m., closed Mon. [M-25]

HAMARIKYŪ-TEIEN (HAMA DETACHED PALACE GARDEN)—A visit to this former site of a Tokugawa *shōgun*'s villa will give you a good view of what life for the upper class was like during the *Edo* period. The garden centers around a tidal pond and its three bridges covered by wisteria-vine trellises. There are other ponds, an island, a stretch of pine shaded beach, moon-viewing pavilions, and tea houses. The garden was opened to the public after the second world war.
• Hamarikyū teien, Chūō-ku. Hrs: 9 a.m.-4:30 p.m., closed Mon. [M-11] [M-22]

KŌKYO HIGASHI GYOEN (IMPERIAL PALACE EAST GARDEN)—Once the main part of *Edo* castle, the 53 acre park was opened to the public in 1968. The old castle moat surrounds the garden, which contains the Kyū-ninomaru (or just Ninomaru) garden, landscaped in 1630 by the third *shōgun Iemitsu*. In the Kyū-ninomaru garden is a tea house and pond. The main garden has the Imperial Music Hall (1966 by architect Imai Kenji) for performances of *bugaku* and *gagaku* (court music) and a few remains of old castle buildings including the base of the main castle tower. You can enter the garden through three gates, the *Ōte-mon*, the *Hirakawa-mon*, or the *Kita-hanebashi-mon*. When you enter, the guard will give you a ticket that must be returned when you leave.
• 1 Chiyoda, Chiyoda-ku. Hrs: 9 a.m.-3 p.m., closed Mon. & Fri. [M-10]

SHINJUKU GYOEN—One of the largest gardens in the city (nearly 150 acres), the land was formerly the estate of the *Edo* Period Naitō *daimyō* family. The gardens became the property of the Imperial Family, and were opened to the public after World War II. A terrific strolling garden, it contains both a traditional Japanese style garden, a formal French garden, and a green house for tropical and sub-tropical plants (open year-round). The garden is noted for its cherry blossoms in the spring, and chrysanthemum exhibitions in the fall.
• 11 Naitōchō, Shinjuku-ku. Hrs: 9 a.m.-4 p.m., closed Mon. [M-7]

MEIJI JINGŪ GYOEN (MEIJI SHRINE INNER GARDEN)—Encircling the important Meiji Shrine, this garden contains more than 126,000 trees donated from all parts of Japan when the shrine was constructed in 1920. Entering the grounds from the south (near Harajuku station) on the left is the entrance into the iris garden. A favorite garden of the Meiji Emperor and Empress, there are more than 100 varieties of irises that bloom in early summer. Nearby is the South Pond, noted for its water lilies in mid-summer.
• 1 Kamizonochō, Yoyogi, Shibuya-ku. Hrs: 9 a.m.-4:30 p.m., daily. [M-4]

Botanical Gardens

KOISHIKAWA SHOKUBUTSUEN—Part of Tokyo University, the garden claims 6,000 different plants including trees from the late 17th century. The garden was originally the grounds of the 2nd *shōgun*'s detached palace, and was used by later *shōgun* for the cultivation of medicinal herbs. The early buildings are gone, but part of the landscape garden remains.
• 3-7-1 Hakusan, Bunkyō-ku Hrs: 9 a.m.-4 p.m., closed Mon. [off Map]

JINDAIJI SHOKUBUTSUEN (JINDAIJI TEMPLE BOTANICAL GARDENS)—This rather park-like botanical garden was formerly a wild forest area next to the grounds of Jindaiji Temple. Opened to the public in 1961, there is a rose garden, azalea garden, and a special hall for plant exhibitions.
• 2708 Jindaiji, Chōfu-shi. Hrs: 9:30 a.m.-4 p.m., closed Mon. [off Map, see temples]

212 SIGHTSEEING

MUKŌJIMA HYAKKAEN—Located in the Mukōjima area east of Tokyo proper, the name "Hyakkaen" means the "garden of 100 flowers". The garden dates back to 1804 when Sahara Kikuu, a member of the *Edo* period literary crowd, planted 360 plum trees given to him by his friends on a small plot of land. The friends later helped lay out the rest of the garden using seasonal flowers from all over Japan. The garden became a favorite meeting spot for the *Edo* intelligentsia, but by the *Meiji* period had fallen into disrepair. After changing hands several times the garden was given to the city in 1938. Small, but full of flowers, the garden is at its best in spring when the plum and cherry trees blossom. Located near the Sumida River, the garden makes a good addition to a walking course to the temples of the seven gods of good fortune (See Calendar).
• 3-18-3 Higashi-Mukōjima, Sumida-ku. Mrs: 9 a.m.-4:30 p.m., closed Mon. [M-42]

HORIKIRI SHŌBUEN—This iris garden is famous as one of the "48 views of *Edo*" depicted by the well-known *ukiyoe* artist Hiroshige in the late *Edo* period. Opened in 1800, the garden was planted by a farmer who collected seeds from all over Japan. There are over 30 different kinds of irises represented.
• 2-19-1 Horikiri, Katsushika-ku. Hrs: 9 a.m.-4:30 p.m., daily. [M-45]

SHIZEN KYŌIKUEN—see page "Museums".

ZOOS

UENO DŌBUTSUEN—Ueno Zoo's major claim to fame is its pair of pandas. But for true animal lovers, the zoo is likely to be a traumatic experience. Not only are the animals kept in tiny, depressing cages, but on weekends people out number them at least 2 to 1.
• 9 Ueno-kōen, Taitō-ku. Tel: 828-5171. Hrs: 9:30 a.m.-4:30 p.m. (enter by 4 p.m.), closed Mon. [M-13]

TAMA DŌBUTSU KŌEN—Opened in 1958 as a branch of Ueno Zoo, the animals run free in the Tama Zoo's Park like setting. Moats separate man from beast. There is a lion's park that you ride through in a bus. (From Shinjuku take the Keiō line express train. At Takahata Fudō station change to the Keiō line going to Dōbutsu Kōen station, the last stop on the line. On Sun. & Hols. there is a direct line from Shinjuku to the zoo, leaving every 20 min.)
• 300 Hodokubo, Hino-shi. Tel: 0425-91-1611. Hrs: 9:30 a.m.-5 p.m. (enter by 4 p.m.), closed Mon. [off Map]

PLEASURE GROUNDS

Pleasure grounds first became popular in the 20's as the big private railroad companies started diversifying from their usual commuter line and department store business. While many are modeled after the American Disneyland, now that the real Disneyland has come to town, competition is tough. We've listed only a few of the many grounds located in the Tokyo area. Besides these, some parks have small amusement centers, as do department store roof tops.

TOKYO DISNEYLAND—Just like in America. Hrs: 9 a.m.-7 p.m., Mon.-Thur., 9 a.m.-9 p.m., Fri.-Sun. Prices vary according to the type of ticket, and are subject to change. General admission fee is ¥2,500 for adults, ¥1,500 for children. The "Passport" ticket (¥3,900 for adults, ¥2,800 for childen) includes admission and access to all attractions. On Fri., Sat. & Sun. evenings after 4 p.m., there is a "Starlight" ticket (¥2,800/¥1,600) for entrance and 5 attractions. Access: From Nihombashi or Ōtemachi Station take the Tōzai subway line to Urayasu station (15 min.). From the station it's a 5 min. walk to the Disneyland shuttle bus yard. The bus ride takes 20 min. and costs ¥200 for adults, and ¥100 for children. Another route is from Tokyo Station, where direct shuttle buses are operated from a stop behind the Tekkō Building on the Yaesu exit side of the Station. The bus takes 35 min. (50 min. for the return trip), and costs ¥600 for adults, and ¥300 for children.
• Information Tel: 366-5600 or 0473-54-0001. [off Map]

KŌRAKUEN—Close to Kōrakuen Gardens, These pleasure grounds are famous as the site

of the Japan Baseball Series. The amusement center itself is medium sized; the major attractions are its huge roller coaster and the "Circus Train" which follows a circular track that runs up in the air.
• 1-3 Kōraku, Bunkyō-ku. Hrs: 10 a.m.-7 p.m., closed Mon. [M-30]

HANAYASHIKI YŪENCHI—Located next to Sensōji Temple in Asakusa, this is an old style pleasure ground that dates back to the *Edo* period when the temple was visited as much for the amusements it offered as for religious purposes. At the time it featured jugglers, wrestlers, freak shows, puppet shows, performing monkeys, etc. Now it's more like a small time fair, with game booths, goldfish catching games, vendors, and a modest roller coaster.
• 2-28-1 Asakusa, Taitō-ku. Hrs: 10 a.m.-6 p.m., closed Fri. [M-12]

HISTORICAL SITES AND BUILDINGS

KŌKYO (IMPERIAL PALACE)—Located in the heart of the city, the Imperial Palace stands on the former site of *Edo* castle. The largest castle in the land, *Edo* castle was the administrative center for the *Tokugawa* Shogunate. While the city of *Edo* was planned to serve the needs of the castle, for the city of Tokyo the palace is hardly more than an obstruction to smooth traffic flow in the downtown areas. The castle grounds were taken over by the Imperial family after the *Meiji* Restoration, and the Emperor has lived there since.

Most of the original buildings were destroyed during the 1945 air raids. The new palace, completed in 1968, is in Japanese style, but of very unpoetic ferroconcrete. You can enter the inner palace grounds and see the building only twice a year, on New Year's Day and the Emperor's Birthday on April 29th.

Surrounding the palace are the remains of the *Edo* castle moats and three gardens, Higashi-Gyoen (East Garden), Kitanomaru Kōen (park) and the outer garden.
• Chiyoda, Chiyoda-ku. (Only the Imperial Palace has this address "Chiyoda") [M-10]

NIJŪ BASHI BRIDGE—is the main bridge into the inner palace. A copy of Kyōto's Fushimi castle bridge, there are two spans. The first, constructed of stones from the old walls of the castle, the second is made of iron. The bridge is a classic spot for tour group photo sessions.
• Kōkyo Gaien, Chiyoda, Chiyoda-ku. [M-10]

KOKKAI GIJIDŌ (NATIONAL DIET BUILDING)—Large and very official looking the building houses the Japanese Parliament. Completed in 1936 after 18 years of work, the building has a 215 ft. tower and a total floor area of about 13 acres. Entrance into the Diet is almost impossible these days owing to unbelievably strict security precautions.
• 1-7-1 Nagatachō, Chiyoda-ku. [M-6]

YUSHIMA SEIDŌ—A Confucian shrine, Yushima Seidō was connected with a school of Confucian learning for the Tokugawa elite. The shrine, first built in the 17th century, was destroyed during the 1923 Earthquake. The present building of traditional temple architecture dates from 1965 and contains a statue of Confucius. You can enter the main building on Sun. & Hols. from 10 a.m.-4 p.m.
• 1-4 Yushima, Bunkyō-ku. [M-16]

AKAMON (Red Gate)—was originally the gate to the home of the Maeda, an important *daimyō* family during the *Edo* period. The gate was built to celebrate the marriage of one of the Maeda sons to the daughter of the eleventh *shōgun* in 1827. Now classified as an "Important Cultural Property", the gate stands on the grounds of Tokyo University.
• 7-3 Hongō, Bunkyō-ku. [off Map]

NIKOLAIDŌ (NICOLAI CATHEDRAL)—Another "Important Cultural Property", Nicolai Cathedral was founded by and is named after Father Nicolai, the Russian priest who first introduced Greek Orthodox Christianity to Japan. The Byzantine style cathedral was completed in 1891 after seven years of work. The building, extensively damaged in the 1923 Kantō Earthquake, was reconstructed in 1929. Several icons in the church date from the 18th century.
• 4-1 Kanda Surugadai, Chiyoda-ku. [M-15]

TOKYO TOWER—One of the more whimsical aspects of Tokyo's skyline, the Tokyo Tower is a model of the Eiffel Tower in Paris, with 100 extra feet of height. Built in 1958, the 1,089 ft. tower was a huge hit and attracted over 20,000 people a day. It still pulls in daily crowds in the neighborhood of 10,000. There is a broadcasting studio for TV Tokyo on the 5th floor,

a science museum and a wax museum downstairs. In front of the tower is a statue of Andō Takeshi, a sculptor most famous for his statue of Hachikō at Shibuya Station. Next to him is a statue of two more famous dogs—Tarō and Jirō, who went to the South Pole. Like the leaning Tower of Pisa, the Tokyo Tower is slowly, but surely, tilting to the side.
• 4-2 Shiba-kōen, Minato-ku. [M-11]

NIHOMBASHI BRIDGE—In the *Edo* period, all roads led to this bridge, and all distances throughout the country were measured from a spot now marked by an iron post. The bridge was first built in 1603, the year *Tokugawa Ieyasu* took the title of *shōgun*. Twelve men were buried alive in the foundations to give it added strength. The current bridge, built in 1911, is one of the few constructions in the city that survives from the *Meiji* period. Once a favorite subject of *ukiyoe* prints, the bridge is now hidden in the shadows of an elevated expressway.
• 1-1 Nihombashi, Chūō-ku. [M-9]

NIHON GINKŌ (BANK OF JAPAN)—stands on a site formerly occupied by the Tokugawa gold mint. The new bank, completed in 1896, was the first western style building to be designed and built entirely by Japanese. The building, designed by architect Tatsuno Kingo (he also designed Tokyo Station), is in a vaguely renaissance style. As one of the few remaining *Meiji* period buildings, the bank is classified as an "Important Cultural Property".
• 2-2 Hongokuchō, Nihombashi, Chūō-ku. [M-9]

GEIHINKAN—Also known as the Former Akasaka Detached Palace, the building is a copy of Buckingham Palace on the outside and Versailles on the inside. The Geihinkan now serves as a lodging for state guests, but was formerly the home of the Crown Prince who was later to become the *Taishō* Emperor (1912-26). *Katayama Tōyū* (1854-1917), a leading architect of his time, designed the building, which was completed in 1908.
• 2-1-1 Moto-Akasaka, Minato-ku. [M-6]

KYŪ IKEDA YASHIKI ŌTEMON—The former main entrance to the home of the Ikeda family, the gate was built during the late *Edo* period in a grand style allowed to only the most important of the *daimyō*. The gate was originally located in Marunouchi, then moved to Takanawadai and used as the main east entrance to the Imperial Palace. In 1954 it was moved to its present site in Ueno and designated an "Important Cultural Property".
• 13 Ueno-kōen, Taitō-ku. [M-13]

NOGI TEI (GENERAL NOGI'S HOUSE) General Nogi was an important *Meiji* period military leader famous for his role in the Japanese victory during the Russo-Japanese War. When the Emperor Meiji died in September 1912, the General and his wife committed ritual suicide out of loyalty to their former ruler. The general cut his stomach, then his wife slit his throat with her knife before falling on it and dying herself. You can visit the room where this all happened in their former home near Nogizaka (lit. "Nogi Hill"). Next door is the Nogi Shrine, a *Shintō* shrine built in honor of the loyal general.
• 8-11 Akasaka, Minato-ku. [M-1]

KOKUGIKAN—The old *sumō* wrestling hall, the Kokugikan was built in 1954. The building is a mixture of traditional Japanese and stadium architecture, and has a crowd capacity of 11 thousand.
• 2-1-9 Kuramae, Taitō-ku. [M-24]

KŌDŌKAN—The oldest and largest *Jūdō* institute in Japan, the present building was completed in 1958.
• 1-16-30 Kasuga, Bunkyō-ku. [M-30]

NIHON BUDŌKAN—Originally built for the 1964 Olympics martial arts competitions, the Budōkan is perhaps most famous as a stadium for huge rock concerts, many of which are recorded and made into records titled "Live at the Budōkan". The building itself is a modern interpretation of the architectural design of Hōryūji Temple in Nara. Seating capacity is 14,000.
• 2-3 Kitanomaru Kōen, Chiyoda-ku. [M-17]

CEMETERIES

AOYAMA BOCHI—Formerly the estate of the *Aoyama daimyō* family, the area became a municipal graveyard in 1872. One of the famous local spots for contemplating the spring

cherry blossoms, the cemetery has over 100,000 graves. The most famous of the interred are: General Nogi (1912), Hamaguchi Osachi—a former prime minister assassinated by a young nationalist (1930), Inukai Tsuyoshi—another assassinated prime minister (1932) and Ichikawa Danjūro—one of the most famous *kabuki* actors of all time (1903).
* 2-33 Minami-Aoyama, Minato-ku. [M-5]

YANAKA BOCHI—Next to Kan'eiji Temple, Yanaka graveyard occupies the former grounds of Tennōji Temple that was burned during the *Meiji* Restoration Battle in Ueno. The area became a municipal cemetery in 1874 and is famous for its spring cherry blossoms and ginko trees. A few of the more illustrious "residents" are: Tokugawa Yoshinobu—the last *shōgun* (1913), Yokoyama Taikan—a famous painter (1958) and Father Nicolai—founder of Nicolai Cathedral (1912).
* 7 Yanaka, Taitō-ku. [M-13]

CONTEMPORARY ARCHITECTURE

Much of the best work by contemporary Japanese architects is not in Tokyo, but in the provinces, where the buildings are not limited by the cramped landscape of the nation's capital. Following is a guide to some of the more interesting examples of the work by both the famous and the lesser known architects. Concentrations of contemporary work are found in the Aoyama and Daikan-yama areas.

TANGE KENZŌ
  Tokyo Metropolitan Government Offices 1957, 3-1 Marunouchi, Chiyoda-ku [M-10].
  St. Mary's Cathedral 1964. 3-16-5 Sekiguchi, Bunkyō-ku [off Map].
  National Gymnasium 1964. 2-1 Jinnan, Shibuya-ku [M-4].
  Dentsū Advertising Co. 1967. 1-11-10 Tsukiji, Chūō-ku [M-22].
  Shizuoka Press & Broadcasting Offices 1967. 8-3-7 Ginza, Chūō-ku [M-8].
  Sacred Heart International School 1968. 4-3-1 Hirō, Shibuya-ku [M-2].
  Sōgetsu Kaikan 1977. 7-2-21 Akasaka, Minato-ku [M-5].
  Turkish Embassy 1977. 2-33-6 Jingūmae, Shibuya-ku [M-4].
  Hanae Mori Bldg. 1978. 3-6-1 Kita-Aoyama, Minato-ku [M-5].
  Akasaka Prince Hotel 1983. 1-2 Kioichō, Chiyoda-ku [M-6].
TANIGUCHI YOSHIHIRO
  Jōsenji Temple 1965. 10-15 Uguisudanichō, Shibuya-ku [M-20].
  Imperial Theater 1966. 3-1-1 Marunouchi, Chiyoda-ku [M-10].
  Tokyo National Museum, Gallery of Eastern Antiquities 1968. Ueno Park, Taitō-ku [M-13].
  National Museum of Modern Art 1969. 3 Kitanomaru Kōen, Chiyoda-ku [M-17].
MAKI FUMIHIKO
  St. Mary's International School 1972. 1-6-19 Seta, Setagaya-ku [off Map].
  Austrian Embassy 1976. 1-1-20 Moto-Azabu, Minato-ku [M-1].
  Hillside Terrace 1969, 1973, 1977. 29-9 Sarugakuchō, Shibuya-ku [M-20].
  Royal Danish Embassy 1979. 29-6 Sarugakuchō, Shibuya-ku [M-20].
  Mitsubishi Bank, Hirō Branch 1981. 4-1-1 Minami-Azabu, Minato-ku [M-2].
  Keiō University New Library 1981. Keiō University, 2-15-45 Mita, Minato-ku [off Map].
  Toranomon NN Bldg. 1981. 1-21-17 Toranomon, Minato-ku [M-11].
KUROKAWA KISHŌ
  Nakagin Capsule Tower Bldg. 1972. 8-16-10 Ginza, Chūō-ku [M-8, 10].
  Japan Headquarters of the Red Cross Soc. 1977. 1-1-5 Shiba-daimon, Minato-ku [M-17].
  Wacoal Bldg. 1984. 1-1-2 Kōjimachi, Chiyoda-ku [M-6].
ISOZAKI ARATA
  At the Tsukuba "Science city", the site of Expo. 1985, he has designed a Japanese postmodern civic center.
  Glass Art Akasaka 1984. 3-10-13 Akasaka, Minato-ku. [M-6]
MURANO TOGA/MURANO & MORI ASSOCIATED ARCHITECTS

Yomiuri Hall & Sogō Department Store 1957. 1-11-1 Yūrakuchō, Chiyoda-ku [M-10].
Industrial Bank of Japan 1974. 1-3-3 Marunouchi, Chiyoda-ku [M-10].
New Takanawa Prince Hotel 1982. 3-13-1 Takanawa, Minato-ku [M-37].

The following list is by building name.
ICHIBANKAN—Takeyama Minoru, Arch. & United Actions, 1969. 2-20-9 Kabukichō, Shinjuku-ku. [M-7]
SUPREME COURT—Okada Shin'ichi, 1974. 4-2 Hayabusachō, Chiyoda-ku. [M-6]
YOKU MOKU CONFECTIONERS—Gendai Keikaku Architectural & Planning Office, 1978. 5-3-3 Minami-Aoyama, Minato-ku. [M-5]
FROM FIRST BLDG.—Yamashita Kazumasa, Arch. & Assoc., 1975. 5-3-10 Minami-Aoyama, Minato-ku. [M-20]
NOA BLDG.—Shirai Seiichi, Architecture Laboratory, 1974. 2-3-5 Azabudai, Minato-ku. [M-11]
JAPAN CRAFTS MUSEUM, New Annex—Shirai Seiichi, Architecture Laboratory, Yamashita Kazumasa, Arch. & Associ., 1982. 4-3-33 Komaba, Meguro-ku. [M-35]
SHŌTŌ MUSEUM—Shirai Seiichi, Architecture Laboratory, 1980. 2-14-14 Shōtō, Shibuya-ku. [off Map]
STUDIO EBIS—Suzuki Makoto, Arch. & Assoc., 1981. 1-9-2 Ebisu, Shibuya-ku. [off Map]
SANCTUARY & ZEN HALL OF RYŪIN TEMPLE—Takasugu Susumu, 1978. 5-5-5 Hakusan, Bunkyō-ku. [off Map]
IMPERIAL MUSIC HALL—Imai Kenji, 1966. Kōkyo Higashi Gyoen, (Imperial Palace East Garden), Chiyoda-ku. [off Map, Kōkyo Higashi Gyoen]
REIYŪKAI-SHAKADEN—Iwasaki Ken'ichi, 1975. 1-7-8 Azabudai, Minato-ku. [M-11]
NATIONAL THEATER—Takenaka Kōmuten Co., 1966. 4-1 Hayabusachō, Chiyoda-ku. [M-6]
ATHÉNÉE FRANÇAIS—Takamasa+atelier U, 1962, 2-11 Surugadai, Kanda, Chiyoda-ku. [M-15]

GUIDED TOURS

While the purpose of this book is to make the city accessible to individual travelers, there are a few cases in which a guided tour may make things a bit easier. The Japan Travel Bureau offers two such tours. The first is their "Industrial Tokyo" tour which takes you to a selection of factories and laboratories which are inaccessible to individuals (¥9,000). The other is their "Golden Night Tour" which starts with an optional dinner at Suehiro (best skipped), then takes you for a show at the Cabaret Mikado that would cost at least the price of this whole tour if you went on your own, and finally ends with a slightly corny "Geisha Show" at Matsubaya in Asakusa (¥12,000 with dinner, ¥9,000 without).

Japan Travel Bureau has offices all over town, call 276-7777 to find the one closest to where you're staying.

WALKING COURSES

Tokyo is full of great walking districts. Just about any neighborhood has back streets, full of old houses and shops that are interesting for even long-time residents. We've written up four walks through particularly old, historical areas. Shops, restaurants, and museums introduced soley in the walk section have been explained and opening hours given, all other places have been described elsewhere in the text.

Shitamachi Tour
- **Asakusa—Sumida—Kappabashi** [M-12]

There are two ways to get to Asakusa. Most fun is to take the Suijō Bus (a small ferry) from Hama Rikyū Garden. You can start off with a walk through the garden, then catch the boat that leaves from a dock on the east side. The boat normally leaves every 40 minutes (from 10 a.m. until sunset), but departs more frequently on Sundays, holidays, and during the busy season in spring and summer. Tickets cost ¥480 for the 35 min. ride to Asakusa. The other way is to take the Ginza subway line to Asakusa station, the end of the line. Exit by the middle staircase on the platform, and after passing through the ticket booth, turn left and go up the staircase to street level. Cross over towards the ferry dock where Sumida Park begins.

Sumida Park has been a famous spot for viewing the cherry blossoms since the *Edo* period. The park follows the banks of the **Sumida River** on both the east and west banks (you're on the west). Stroll through the park until you reach the **Kototoi Bridge**, then cross to the east side of the river. Off to the left is **Chōmeiji Temple**, a famous *Edo* period spot for snow viewing. The history of the temple is rather obscure, but its reputation rests on the story of how, when the third *shōgun* Tokugawa Iemitsu stopped off at the temple with a stomach ache after a hard day of hunting, the priest gave him a tonic using water from the temple well. The *shōgun*'s stomach ache disappeared and the temple was thereafter called Chōmeiji, meaning "Long Life".

Near the temple are two Japanese sweet shops, **Kototoi Dango** and **Chōmeiji Sakuramochi** both established since the *Edo* period. Stop for tea and cherry *mochi* at Chōmeiji Sakuramochi. If the cherry trees are in bloom, you can sit beneath the pink petals in the park across the street. After finishing the fragrant cherry *mochi* follow the riverside Sumida Park south to the Azuma Bridge. When you cross the bridge you'll find yourself back where you started.

Walk down the right side of the main street that leads from the bridge. The street, called Kaminarimon-dōri, is lined with shops and restaurants and will take you to the front gate of Sensōji Temple. The large gate **Kaminarimon** with its giant lantern is named for the god of thunder, a Buddhist guardian deity whose statue is in the left side of the gate. On the right is the god of lightning. The original gate was lost in the 1867 *Edo* fire and wasn't rebuilt until 1960.

Pass through the gate and you're on **Nakamise-dōri**, a street with over 100 shops catering to temple visitors. The arcade like shops were first built by the city in the mid-*Meiji* period. The buildings were destroyed during the great earthquake (1923), but the rebuilt shops look much the same as the earlier ones. At the end of the shopping arcade is the **Hōzō-mon** "Treasure Storing" gate. The upper rooms of the gate store the temple's sacred library of sutras and Buddhist scriptures that date from the 14th century. The two statues on each side of the gate are Niō, or Deva Kings, another type of guardian deity. This gate was destroyed in the 1867 fire and rebuilt in 1964. To the left is a five story red and gold pagoda "**Gojū-no-tō**" modeled after the 10th century pagoda of Daigoji Temple in Kyōto. The **Sensōji** pagoda was first built in 1639, and rebuilt in 1970. Inside are four wooden statues of Buddha.

After visiting the main hall of Sensōji, stop by the **Asakusa Jinja** shrine to the right. Both the shrine and its gate remain in their original *Edo* period form and are designated "Important Cultural Properties". Go back to where the Nakamise Arcade begins, turn left, then right onto the second narrow street where you will find **Kuremutsu**, a restaurant in a lovely old house, **Hyakusuke**, a traditional cosmetics shop, **Fujiya**, specializing in *tenugui* printed hand-towels, and finally, further down on the left **Tatsumiya**, a restaurant in an old house full of antiques. Stop here for a quiet lunch. When you've finished lunch you can wander around the shopping area, being sure not to miss **Kurodaya**, for paper crafts, **Hasetoku** for traditional shoes, **Bunseidō** for fans.

For a quiet interlude in the afternoon visit the **Dembōin Garden** to the left as you approach the main temple hall. Permission to enter the garden can be obtained at the five story pagoda near the temple, in an office called the *shomuka* located in the left hand side of the tower (3rd door on the left). Ask to see the garden, sign your name and address in the register, and you'll be given a free entry ticket. The garden dates from at least the early 17th century and has a double pond, a tea house, and a large bronze bell cast in 1387. On the way to the garden, there are a number of rummage sale-like stalls set up (weather permitting). The stalls sell a mixture of old *kimono,* old military gear, used suits, etc.

Further to the left you'll reach the theater district where the first movie theater in Japan was built in 1903. Theater had been in the area since *kabuki* was moved from Ginza in 1842, when the government tried to "clean up" the central downtown neighborhoods and reform the pleasure seeking merchant class. In the *Taishō* and early *Shōwa* periods Asakusa was the city's theater center with numerous music halls, cabarets, and movie houses. There are still movie theaters, but the district is best known for its rather seamy side. The famous **Furansu-za**, an old time strip joint, still remains. Traditional variety shows are also presented in a number of theaters including the **Mokubakan**, whose major attraction is the "*Shitamachi-no* (downtown) *Tamasaburō*"—a minor actor who has taken the name of the famous *kabuki* star.

To the north, the shopping area continues. Here you'll find **Kiriya**, a shop selling festival clothing, and **Hanatō** selling paper lanterns. Back towards the temple is **Hanayashiki pleasure grounds** a slightly corny amusement park with a small town fair atmosphere.

Return back through the theater district and the arcade to the main street Kaminarimon-dōri. Turn right and across the street on top of a building you'll see the Jintan tower, a blue building that looks rather like a light house. An advertisement for Jintan breath freshener, the tower is modeled after the Ryōunkaku a twelve story "cloud scraper" that was the modern wonder of mid-*Meiji* period Asakusa. Cross the street towards the tower to **Miyamoto Unosuke Shōten** selling portable shrines and Japanese drums. Take the street between the shop and the police box, turn right at the first crossing, keep going straight until the road dead-ends at the Kappabashi arcade. Turn left and walk through the arcade until you reach the large street called Kappabashi-dōri. Here you'll find the **Kappabashi wholesale market**, an entire district of shops specializing in restaurant supplies (wax food models, *sushi* chef costumes, tableware, etc.).

After wandering around, return to Asakusa for dinner at one of the following restaurants: **Chin'ya** (*sukiyaki*), **Yakko** (*unagi*), **Daikokuya** (*tendon*), **Tatsumiya** (home style *kaiseki*), **Miyako** (*sushi*).

- Ueno—Yanaka—Nezu [M-13]

Access: Ginza line to Ueno station—take the stairs in the middle of the platform, pass the ticket booth, turn right, on the right you'll see the sign for exit #7, turn left and go out to ground level. Hibiya line to Ueno station (ride the last car going towards Kita-Senju)—follow the signs to the Ginza line and look for exit #7 near the Ginza line ticket booth. JNR Yamanote line—take the steps at the end of the platform towards Okachimachi, and use the Shinobazu exit.

Facing the crossing, you'll see a wide stone staircase diagonally to your left on the opposite side,. Climb the staircase, then take the stairs on the right. On the right hand side at the top is a bronze statue of **Saigō Takamori** by Takamura Kōen. The statue was erected in 1892 in honor of this *Meiji* Restoration Army general who negotiated for the bloodless surrender of the Tokugawa Shogunate's capitol *Edo*. The surrender, however, was not quite bloodless. After the city was turned over in April 1868, Tokugawa loyalists retreated to the hills of Ueno and continued to resist. The Restoration Army led an attack a month later that broke the resistance and destroyed most of the buildings on the hill. The **Shōgitai Kinenhi**, a monument to the loyal Tokugawa samurai who died in the battle, was erected close to Saigō Takamori's statue.

Nearby on the left is the **Kiyomizu Kannon** Temple, built in 1698 as

A back alley in Tsukudajima.

a small scale copy of the Kiyomizu Temple in Kyōto. Dedicated to *Kannon*, the Buddhist goddess of Mercy, the temple is frequented by childless parents (the temple festival is Sept. 15, see the calendar). The temple is an "Important Cultural Asset". Down the stairs behind the temple is a black gate, the Kuromon. This Kuromon is a copy of the *Edo* period front gate to Kan'eiji Temple, the main temple of Ueno hill. Pass through the gate, turn right, and keep straight on the main path until you see a large totem pole. Turn left and continue walking. On your left you will see the gate to **Tōshōgū Shrine**, dedicated to Tokugawa Ieyasu.

After visiting the Tōshōgū shrine, stop for Japanese sweets and green tea at the **Uguisu-dango** just to the left of the Shrine's main gate. Order a small dish of *dango*. The shop is open from 10 a.m.—5 p.m., every day but Monday. Continue down the main path, and you will come to **Ueno Zoo** famous for its pandas. The park's four museums are also concentrated in this area: the **Metropolitan Art Museum**, the **Science Museum**, the **Museum of Western Arts** and the **National Museum** (all discussed in the Museum section. The main path ends as it hits the street bordering the north side of the park. Directly in front is the **Kyū-Ikeda-Omotemon**. To the right of the gate is the entrance to the National Museum, housing the largest collection of Japanese art in the world. When you exit from the museum, turn right and follow the main road back past the Omote-mon. Turn right at the first street, then left, where you'll find **Kan'eiji Temple** on the right hand side.

Stop by the temple, then continue down the road until it meets another road in a T (there is a police box on the right), turn left, then right at the next medium sized street (where there is a coffee shop in an old house on the corner). On the right you will soon pass the **Yanaka Cemetery**. The street will then curve around to the left and lead to a local shopping area where several *Meiji* period buildings remain. If you have time, take a short side trip to visit the **Asakura Chōsokan** a small memorial museum in the former home of the famous sculptor Asakura Fumio (1883-1964). To reach the museum, turn right at a corner where there is a "convenience" store called "Yamasaki Store" on the right hand corner, and walk for about 8-10 minutes. The museum will be on your right.

When you've returned from the museum, continue down the street lined with small temples. As the road slopes downwards, on the left you'll pass **Isetatsu** a Japanese paper shop established 1858. Further down on the right is **Kikumi-Sembei**, a cracker shop established in the *Edo* period. Soon after the *sembei* shop is a main intersection. Turn left and follow the main road. After the fourth traffic light is another large intersection with a ten story white building on one corner. Turn right and follow the road as it slopes upwards. Walking on the left hand side of the street you'll pass one *torii* gate, a few buildings, then reach the entrance to **Nezu Shrine**. 3-4 minutes up the hill from the shrine is a noodle shop **Mukyoan** in an older traditional home. Stop here for lunch. The restaurant is open from 11 a.m.—8 p.m., closed Sundays and the 3rd Saturday of the month.

Go back down the hill towards the main street, turn right, and walk towards Nezu station (Chiyoda line). On the way you could take a detour and visit the **Daimyō Clock Museum**. At Nezu station, take the subway to the next stop Yushima (you could walk the distance in about 10 minutes by just continuing down the same road). You should get on the last car of the train, and take the nearest exit on the left as you pass through the ticket booth, which will let you out at a large intersection. Next to the exit is **Ishizuka** a shop that has been making bamboo and wood Japanese style lamps since the *Edo* period. From there, walk straight in the direction of **Shinobazu pond**, a traditional spot for viewing water lilies in the summer. Turn right at the second small street (where there is a coffee shop called "Swing"). The street is the beginning of a shopping street called Nakamachi-dōri, lined with eating and drinking places and small shops. On the right there is a famous *shamisen* shop, **Kikuya**. Nearby is **Kiya** a shop for Japanese art supplies. On the left is **Hōtan Yakkyoku**, one of the first pharmacies in the city, in an amusing early 20th century building. Next, on the left is **Kyōya** a shop specializing in traditional furniture, and then **Dōmyō** a shop whose skill in making silk cords has been designated an "Intangible National Property".

You'll then come to a large street called Chūō-dōri. Turn to the left, cross the street and turn left again. There will be a small entrance to Ueno Park. Enter the gate and on the right is the **Shitamachi Fūzoku Museum** where a pre-earthquake downtown street has been recreated.

Back to the large intersection, cross the street towards a big modern building called "**ABAB**", and turn down the small street on the right hand side. Walk straight towards the railroad tracks where you'll find the **Ameyoko** shopping arcade.

This walk should have taken you all day, in which case you'll be ready for dinner. In the Ueno area, you should try **Ponta** for *tonkatsu*, or **Yansandō** for Korean *Yakiniku*. Or take a short taxi ride to the *tōfu* restaurant **Sasanoyuki** or **Bon** for *shōjin-ryōri*.

• **Fukagawa—Kiyosumi Gardens—Tsukudajima** [M-25]

Access: Take the Tōzai line to Monzennakachō (ride the front of the train going towards Kiba). Exit from the ticket booth, turn left and take the stairs to street level. To the right of the exit is the red gate to **Fukagawa Fudō Temple**. This temple, a branch of the Narita Fudō Temple, was built in 1878 and reconstructed after the war.

Pass beneath the gate and follow the narrow shopping street to the temple. The street is lined with shops selling sweets and crackers. Try the *age-manjū* at **Miyagetsudō**. After visiting the temple, turn left as you leave the grounds and walk straight until you reach the entrance to **Tomioka Hachimangū** Shrine where *sumō* tournaments were held from 1684-1791. Behind the temple and to the right is a huge stone monument to the *yokozuna*, champion *sumō* wrestlers. On the 1st, 15th and 18th of each month the temple and shrine have a joint *ennichi* fair day where everything from fruit to toys to traditional undergarments are sold. The shrine holds a major festival every three years on August 19th.

Walk through the shrine's main gate to Eitai-dōri, where a good *soba* restaurant Hōseian is located across the street and two doors down from an old *sembei* shop. Stop at **Hōseian** for lunch (Hrs: 11 a.m.-3 p.m., 4 p.m.-8 p.m., closed Thur.), their *tempura soba* is great. After lunch start walking towards Kiyosumi Garden by following Eitai-dōri to a big crossing. The cross street is Kiyosumi-dōri which leads straight to the garden. Turn right on Kiyosumi-dōri, walk straight, then cross a bridge and continue walking for about 12 minutes, until you see the thick foliage of the garden behind the wall on your left. Turn left at the next corner after passing a small playground, walk straight to the **Kiyosumi Garden** entrance.

Return to Kiyosumi-dōri after visiting the garden, cross the street and take the #33 bus to **Tsukudajima** Island. Get off the bus at Shin-Tsukudajima, 6 stops from the garden. You'll now be on the other side of the Sumida River.

In the *Edo* period, Tsukudajima was a tiny island, but has grown in size with reclamation projects started after World War II. The island is one of the few areas of town that suffered little damage in the 1923 earthquake and wasn't firebombed during the war. The narrow back alleys remain much the same as they were during the early part of the century. Wander around the streets behind the bus stop. Afterwards, return to the bus stop and walk back, in the direction the bus came, to the first cross walk. Cross the street and go straight until the road dead-ends. Turn left, then right to the **Tsukuda Kohashi**, a small bridge that crosses a swampy canal where old fishing boats are moored, and wooden houses line the banks. Continue straight until you see the tall concrete wall built to protect the island from floods. Just before you reach the wall on the left will be a sign written in Japanese with a red arrow. The sign reads 住吉神社 and directs you to **Sumiyoshi Jinja**, a shrine dedicated to the patron god of this traditional island home of fishermen.

Exiting from the shrine, walk towards the sea wall, turn to the left and you'll come to **Ten'yasu** in an old house with the shop's name written on a square lantern in front. The shop sells *tsukudani* that is famous throughout Japan.

Walking past Ten'yasu, you'll see a large bridge that crosses the river. Walk through the underpass and turn left on the other side. Walk straight along the bridge to the first crossing and turn right, then left at the next street. There will be a school on the right hand side of the next corner, and straight ahead is the Tsukudajima neighborhood shopping arcade. The shopping area has a wonderful small town feeling you won't find anywhere else in Tokyo.

After doing your shopping, or browsing, return to the bridge and cross over to the Tsukiji district. At the end of the bridge turn right and keep straight until you see a beige building marked with a P for parking on the right. On the left hand side, slightly before the parking building, is an orange brick apartment building on a corner. Turn left here. At the next signal turn right again and you'll reach **Teppōzu Inari** Shrine. The shrine, built originally in 841, is famous for its miniature replica of Mt. Fuji built of lava. The "mountain" was, and still is, ascended by those too weak or too poor to ascend the real thing. The shrine's festivals are held in May and July. Leaving from the shrine's main gate, turn left and left again at the next street. Keep straight until you come to the main road, then turn right towards Hatchōbori station on the Hibiya line. From there you can go to Ginza, just a few subway stops away for a great meal (check the restaurant listings next to the Ginza map).

• **Gotō Museum—Todoroki Ravine—Kuhombutsu Temple—Okusawa Shrine—Jiyūgaoka** [M-21]

If you're tired of big city life, take a short train ride to the suburbs for a glimpse at semi-rural Japan. This walking course starts off with a lovely museum. Take the Tōyoko line from Shibuya station to Jiyūgaoka station. Change trains here to the Tōkyū Ōimachi line (you must change platforms, use the center staircase) and take the train to Kaminoge station (four stops from Jiyūgaoka). When you exit from the station, cross the main street and follow a street that is slightly to the left of the traffic light. At the second crossing turn right, and you'll see the white fence surrounding the museum. The **Gotō Museum** is small but has an excellent collection of Asian art. The museum grounds are large and beautiful, with both a natural and landscaped garden, tea houses, a pond, statues, etc.

After the museum, return to Kaminoge station and take the train back to Todoroki station (you could walk the distance in about 10 min.). When you exit from the ticket booth, turn left, then right at the greengrocer. There you'll find a small spiral staircase that leads down to the banks of the Yazawa River in **Todoroki Keikoku** ravine. This is the only ravine in the Tokyo vicinity that has remained in its natural condition. The river itself is small and not particularly beautiful, but as you continue along the 1 km. ravine the view improves somewhat. Across the river is a garden you can reach by a bridge. Further along you'll find a small waterfall called **Fudō no Taki**, where since the *Edo* period ascetics would come to stand beneath the falls and suffer. Nearby is a small stone statue of the young Kōbō Daishi (744-835), the founder of the *Shingon* sect of Buddhism.

Go up the stairs on the right side, of the waterfall, to **Todoroki Fudō** Temple, founded 800 years ago by Kōgyō Daishi.

From there you should return to Todoroki station, and take the train back to Kuhombutsu station. A short walk from the station is **Kuhombutsu** Temple, a branch of Zōjōji Temple in Shiba, built in 1678. In the three halls opposite the main hall are nine statues of Buddha by the priest Kaseki that date from the same period. The temple yard is quiet (this is not a major sightseeing spot) and covered with huge trees.

Go back towards the station, turn left at the first crossing and keep walking straight. You will have to cross two railroad tracks. To find the crossing for the second one, turn to the right when you get to the tracks, and go back to the left again on the other side. Continue straight, and on the left hand side is the **Okusawa Shrine**. A big snake made of straw entwines the gate. The snake is a *Shintō* charm against evil. The original shrine was built in the *Muromachi* period and the present building is a more recent, but faithful reproduction. On the 14th and 15th of September the shrine has a festival in honor of the snake deity.

Finish the walk in **Jiyūgaoka**, a rather hip suburban community with boutiques, restaurants, coffee shops, etc. Have lunch or dinner at **Hana Kyabetsu**, a coffee and pancake shop serving over 30 kind of pancakes (1-7-3 Jiyūgaoka, Meguro-ku. Tel: 724-0310. Hrs: 8 a.m.-11 p.m., daily), **Motomachi** for *okonomiyaki* or *teppan-yaki*, or **Okajū** for *robatayaki*.

Other Walks

In addition to the four walks we have already given, good walking tours can be made in other parts of town. Use the maps listed under each suggested course.

• **Yushima—Kanda:** From Ochanomizu station. See Yushima Seidō Shrine, Amanoya (*Amazake* shop), Kanda Myōjin Temple, Yushima Shrine, Akamon (at Tokyo University), pass Ochanomizu station again, Jimbōchō (secondhand book district), Kanda (old restaurants), Akihabara (electronics district). Maps: [M-15] [M-16]

• **Nihombashi—Ningyōchō:** Starting from either Nihombashi station on the Ginza line, or Ningyōchō station on the Hibiya line. The area is full of old shops and great for wandering around. There is also Suitengū Shrine). Maps: [M-23] [M-9]

HEALTH AND BEAUTY

Two sisters muse about the future and the elusiveness of love, in this bathhouse poster for Parco fashion building. Typical of much of Japanese advertisement, there is no apparent connection between selling Parco's merchandise and the contents of this poster.

HEALTH AND BEAUTY

ASIAN MEDICINE

Though Oriental medicine has long been viewed with skepticism by western health care professionals, the holilistic theories behind these "exotic" methods have found a new level of respectability. Recent studies on the relationship between stress and the increasing rate of illness have questioned the fundamental theories of western medicine, and its increasingly specialized medicinal or surgical treatment for physical disorders.

While in the west the symptoms of a disease are often mistaken for the disease itself, oriental medicine sees the symptoms as a sign of imbalance in the body. Treatment aims at correcting this imbalance by stimulating both the flow of energy and the body's own self-healing powers.

The major types of treatment are *hari* (acupuncture), *shiatsu* (pressure point massage), *kyū* (moxibustion or heat treatment) and *seitai* (a form of chiropractic). Each of the major organs has its own "pulse" showing activity, or lack of such, in that organ. Treatment is applied not only to the ailing organ but to the entire body. By inserting needles, applying heat, or finger pressure to a series of defined "points" on lines of energy called meridians, the body's energy flow is stimulated, blood circulation improved, muscle fatigue, and nervous aches and pains relieved, while internal organs are generally "toned-up".

Treatment is not necessarily immediately effective, and several treatments over a period of time may be advisable. Western skeptics should note that the methods have been proven for over 4,000 years in China.

Hari—Acupuncture
TŌYŌ IGAKU KENKYŪJO (ORIENTAL MEDICAL RESEARCH CENTER) Kitazato Daigaku

Byōin 5-9-1 Shirogane, Minato-ku. Tel: 444-6161. For the first visit you must go between 8 a.m.-10 a.m., Mon.-Sat. Go to the No. 1 reception desk and ask for "hari" (acupuncture). You'll be given forms to fill out. Only a little English is spoken, but the doctors are great. [M-2]
SHIAWASE KENKŌ CLUB Noguchi Bldg. 5th Fl. 3-2 Sakuragaoka, Shibuya-ku. Tel: 496-6422. Hrs: 8:30 a.m.—closing hour not definite. Closed Tue., Fri. & Hols. ¥8,000. This is the clinic of the well known Aoyagi Shūdō. There are over 10 doctors here who can do all kinds of oriental medical techniques. [M-3]
DR. YUKIO KUROSU 1-1-32 Negishi, Taitō-ku. Tel: 841-2595. Hrs: 9 a.m.-3 p.m. Mon., Wed. & Sat.; 9 a.m.-6 p.m. Tue. & Fri.; closed Sun. & Hols. English spoken. By appointment. [M-13]
KŌJIMACHI REBIRTH Kur Haus Bldg. 2nd Fl., 4-2-12 Kōjimachi, Chiyoda-ku. Tel: 262-7561. Hrs: 10 a.m.-9 p.m., closed Sun. Some English. By appointment. Besides acupuncture, they have massage and a sauna. [M-6]
TANI CLINIC 2-24-12 Minami-Aoyama, Minato-ku. Tel: 405-5639. Hrs: 9:30 a.m.-12 noon, 1:30 p.m.-4 p.m., closed Sun. & Hols. First time visitors on Mon., Tue., Wed., Fri., only. Acupuncture and western medicine. [M-5]
DR. UCHI-IKE Sakamoto Bldg. 3rd Fl., 2-16-8 Dōgenzaka, Shibuya-ku. Tel: 464-4766. Hrs: 9 a.m.-6 p.m. Acupuncture and chiropractic. Some English. By appointment. [M-3]

Seitai—Chiropractic

TOKYO CHIROPRACTIC CENTER 3-5-9 Kita-Aoyama, Minato-ku. Tel: 478-2713. Hrs: 9 a.m.-12:30 p.m., 1:30 p.m.-6 p.m., closed Sun. & Hols. English spoken. By appointment. Chiropractic care. [M-5]

WESTERN MEDICINE

We haven't noted prices for the following clinics, but the cost for an initial visit usually runs from ¥6,000-¥7,000.

Clinics

ISHIKAWA CLINIC Azabu-Sakurada Heights 2nd Fl., 3-2-7 Nishi-Azabu, Minato-ku. Tel: 401-6340. Hrs: 9 a.m.-1 p.m., 3 p.m.-7 p.m., closed Sun. & Hols. English speaking. By appointment. They will also make housecalls. [M-2]
INTERNATIONAL CLINIC 1-5 Azabudai, Minato-ku. Tel: 582-2646. Hrs: 9 a.m.-12 noon, 3 p.m.-5 p.m. (9 a.m.-12 noon on Sat), closed Sun. General practice. English, Russian, Chinese spoken. [M-1]
TOKYO MEDICAL AND SURGICAL CLINIC Mori Bldg. 32, 12th Fl., 3-4-30 Shiba-kōen, Minato-ku. Tel: 436-3028. Hrs: 9 a.m.-4:45 p.m. (until 12 noon on Sat.), closed Sun. 24 hour emergency service. General and specialist practice. English speaking. [M-11]
TŌHŌ FUJIN WOMEN'S CLINIC 5-3-10 Kiba, Kōtō-ku (Kiba station/Tōzai line). Tel: 630-0303. Hrs: 12:30 p.m.-6 p.m., closed Sun. & Tue. Inexpensive gynecological care by English speaking woman, Dr. Matsumine. [off Map]
KANDA CLINIC Umeda Bldg. 2nd Fl., 3-20-14 Nishi-Azabu. Tel: 402-0654. Hrs: 9 a.m.-12:30 p.m., 2 p.m.-4:30 p.m. (9 a.m.-12 noon on Sat.), closed Sun Gynecological and obstetrical practice by English speaking Dr. Makabe. [M-2]

Hospitals

NISSEKI IRYŌ CENTER (JAPAN RED CROSS HOSPITAL) 4-1-22 Hirō, Shibuya-ku. Tel: 400-1311. Hrs: 8:30 a.m.-11 a.m. (until 10:30 a.m. on Sat.), closed Sun. & May 1st. [M-2]
SEIROKA BYŌIN (ST. LUKE'S INTERNATIONAL HOSPITAL) 1-10 Akashichō, Chūō-ku. Tel: 541-5151. Hrs: 9 a.m.-12 noon (by 11 a.m. for first time patients), closed Sun. [M-22]
SEIBO BYŌIN (ST. MARY'S INTERNATIONAL CATHOLIC HOSPITAL) 2-5-1 Naka-Ochiai, Shinjuku-ku. Tel: 951-1111. Hrs: 9 a.m.-11 a.m., closed Sun. [off Map]

HEALTH AND BEAUTY

Dental Care
BESFORD DENTAL OFFICE—Mori Bldg. 32, 2nd Fl., 3-4-30 Shiba-kōen, Minato-ku. Tel: 431-4225. Hrs: 8:30 a.m.-3:30 p.m., Mon. & Thur.; 8:30 a.m.-6 p.m., Tue; 8:30 a.m.-12 noon, Wed. & Fri., closed Sat. & Sun. General dentistry and oral surgery by British dentist J.C.P. Besford. [M-11]
MATSUO SHIKA IIN Akasaka: Tama Bldg. 3rd Fl., 1-3-18 Akasaka, Minato-ku. Tel: 585-6480. Hrs: 10 a.m.-1 p.m., 2:30 p.m.-6 p.m. (10 a.m.-1 p.m. on Sat.), closed Sun. & Hols. [M-11] Shibuya: Horiuchi Bldg. 5th Fl., 2-25-6 Dōgenzaka, Shibuya-ku. Tel: 446-1958. Hrs: same as above. [M-3] General practice dentistry with acupuncture instead of an aesthetics. English speaking Dr. Matsuo is in Akasaka on Thur., and in Shibuya on Wed. & Fri. [M-11]
ISHII SHIKA Ōnuki Bldg. 2nd Fl., 4-29-18 Nishi-Gotanda, Shinagawa-ku (Fudōmae station on the Tōkyū Mekama line). Tel: 491-9004. Hrs: 9 a.m.-12 noon, 2:30 p.m.-6 p.m. Mon., Wed. & Fri., 9 a.m.-5 p.m. Thur. & Sat., closed on Sun. and the 1st & 3rd Sat. (if it's open on Sat. then it closes on Tue.) English speaking. By appointment. [off Map]

Optical Care
TOKYO OPTICAL CENTER Sone Bldg. 3rd Fl., 4-8-6 Ginza, Chūō-ku. Tel: 571-7216. Hrs: 10 a.m.-6 p.m., closed Sun. Complete optical care. English spoken. [M-8]
INTERNATIONAL VISION CENTER Kyōwa Gobankan Bldg. 3-3-13 Kita-Aoyama, Minato-ku. Tel: 497-1491. Hrs: 10 a.m.-7 p.m., closed Sun. & Hols. Complete optical care. English spoken. By appointment only. [M-5]
HAKUSAN Shibuya Parco Part 3, 2nd Fl. Tel: 833-8916. Hrs: 10 a.m.-8 p.m., daily. Optical care, no English spoken but they have a good selection of interesting frames.

Pharmacies
AMERICAN PHARMACY Hibiya Park Bldg., 1-8-1 Yūrakuchō, Chiyoda-ku. Tel: 271-4034. Hrs: 9 a.m.-7 p.m., closed Sun. [M-10].
THE MEDICAL DISPENSARY Mori Bldg. 32, 1st Fl., 3-4-30 Shiba-kōen, Minato-ku. Tel: 434-5817. Hrs: 9 a.m.-5:30 p.m. (Sat. 9 a.m.-1 p.m.), closed Sun. [M-11]
NATIONAL AZABU SUPERMARKET PHARMACY 4-5-2 Minami-Azabu, Minato-ku. Tel: 442-3138. Hrs: 9:30 a.m.-6:30 p.m., daily. [M-2]
ISUKURA YAKKYOKU Suns Bldg. 2nd Fl., 1-7-2 Jingūmae, Shibuya-ku. Tel: 478-4382. Hrs: 10 a.m.-8 p.m., closed the 3rd Mon. All kinds of Chinese medicine. Unfortunately no one speaks English. If you can speak Japanese, or have a friend who does and can explain your illness, they will custom mix a medicine for you. [M-4]
NAGAI YAKKYOKU 1-8-10 Azabu-Jūban, Minato-ku. Tel: 583-3889. Hrs: 9 a.m.-8 p.m., closed Tue. Natural Japanese and Chinese medicine. They'll give a consultation and prescribe the medicine. Some English spoken. [M-1]

SENTŌ—PUBLIC BATHS

While a nice hot bath at the end of a long day is an appealing thought for most people, for the Japanese the love of bathing borders on the religious. Until about twenty years ago, most Japanese city dwellers bathed in *sentō*, public bath houses. More than just a place to wash, the *sentō* was a social institution where while scrubbing your neighbor's back you'd catch up on the local gossip. Though on a statistical average more Japanese families have color televisions than private baths, the regular bath house clientele now consists primarily of students and young people living in cheap apartments, or older people who just like the congenial bath house atmosphere. However, the idea of community bathing remains a pleasant one for most. Even now a favorite company or group outing is to go to an *onsen* (hot spring resort), where everyone soaks together in the steaming hot pools.

Public baths are segregated by sex. You enter and pay the fee (usually ¥250) to the attendant who sits on a high platform overlooking both sides and doubles as a lifeguard. In most places you must bring all the bathing essentials: a towel, soap, shampoo, etc. Japanese generally use a small towel, which as the only concession to modesty, is draped nonchalantly in front of one's most private parts. After stripping in the locker room, you will enter the tiled bathroom. Low along the wall will be a series of faucets (and sometimes shower heads). Sitting on one of the small stools, you will thoroughly wash, scrub, and then rinse away every last soap sud (as a foreigner you will always be under suspicion of breaking this rule). Only then do you climb into the communal bath and soak away your cares.

ASAKUSA KANNON ONSEN 2-7-26 Asakusa, Taitō-ku. Tel: 844-4141. Hrs: 6:30 a.m.-6 p.m., daily. ¥400. A really classic bath house, the water is from a sodium bicarbonate hot spring (great for rheumatism, nervous disorders, etc.) and is kept at a steady 45°C. The walls are painted with the standard wall mural, and every morning the "*Asa-yu Kai*", literally the "morning bath association", meets for a friendly soak. The association has 130 members, most of them true bath-loving *Edokko*. [M-12]

AZABU JŪBAN ONSEN 1-5 Azabu-jūban, Minato-ku. Tel: 404-2610. Hrs: 11 a.m.-9 p.m., closed Tue. On the 1st Fl. is a *sentō* with water from a hot spring (¥250). On the 3rd Fl. is another bicarbonate spring pool, a small sauna, a food shop and a large recreation room (¥800, ¥400 for children). [M-1]

TSUBAME-YU 3-14-5 Ueno, Taitō-ku. Tel: 831-7305. Hrs: 6 a.m.-11 p.m., closed Mon. ¥250. This *sentō* also has an "*Asa no Kai*," morning bathers association, that gets together to bathe in the recreated mountain "grotto" setting. [M-13]

OTOMI-YU 2-14-4 Akasaka, Minato-ku. Tel: 583-7424. Hrs: 4 p.m.-11:30 p.m., closed Sun. Right next to the Mikado cabaret, this is an old style bath in a great traditional building. [M-6]

GINZA-YU 1-12-2 Ginza, Chūō-ku. Tel: 561-2550. Hrs: 3 p.m.-11 p.m., closed Sun. A basic public bath. [M-8]

BAIN DOUCHE Lions Mansion Hanzōmon 1st Fl., 1-5-4 Kōjimachi, Chiyoda-ku. Tel: 263-4944. Hrs: 4 p.m.-10:30 p.m., closed Sun. & Hols. This small but new and super clean bath is located 2 min. from the moat of the Imperial Palace. Stop off here for a bath after jogging around the Palace course. [M-6]

PĀRU ONSEN Okazaki Bldg. 2nd Fl., 2-14-13 Shibuya, Shibuya-ku. Tel: 409-4882/3. Hrs: 10 a.m.-11 p.m., closed the 3rd Tue. They have a *chō-ompa* jacuzzi bath (¥1,400), *shiatsu* and massage (¥2,500). For free you'll get two towels to use at the bath and a glass of *kobucha* or calcium water. [M-3]

SAUNA, STEAM BATH AND MASSAGE

Saunas all have large communal baths, which are slightly more elegant than the general public *sentō*. Most supply towels, hair dryers and other amenities.

Saunas

GAIEN 4-23-6 Sendagaya, Shibuya-ku. Tel: 403-3264 (for men), 403-8565 (for women). Hrs:

10 a.m.-11:30 p.m., daily. Sauna ¥1,800 + massage ¥4,300. [M-29]
KŌRAKUEN SAUNA (for men) Isetan-Kaikan Bldg. 4th Fl., 3-15-17 Shinjuku, Shinjuku-ku. Tel: 352-2443. Hrs: 11 a.m.-11 p.m., closed Wed. Sauna ¥2,400+massage (40 min.) ¥5,000, (70 min.) ¥8,500. [M-7]
LADIES SAUNA (same bldg. as Kōrakuen Sauna, but the 5th Fl.) Tel: 356-2734. Hrs: 10 a.m.-8:30 p.m., closed Wed. Sauna ¥2,800 (after 6 p.m. weekdays ¥1,800)+massage ¥6,500. They have a special body treatment with sauna from ¥7,000. [M-7]
DO SPORTS PLAZA Sumitomo Bldg. B1, 2-1-6 Nishi-Shinjuku, Shinjuku-ku. Tel: 344-1971. Hrs: 10 a.m.-10:30 p.m. (until 9 p.m. on Sun. & Hols.), daily. Sauna ¥2,200+massage ¥5,200. [M-7]
GREEN PLAZA SHINJUKU 1-29-3 Kabukichō, Shinjuku-ku. Tel: 207-5411. Open 24 hours everyday except Sun. when they close at 11 p.m. Located in a large capsule hotel, instead of checking into a capsule after a night on the town, you could come here and sweat off the hang-over. Women's sauna—9th Fl., Men's—5th Fl. 9 a.m.-4 p.m. ¥2,000, 4 p.m.-11 p.m. ¥2,300, 11 p.m.-9 a.m. ¥2,800. 40 min. massage ¥2,500. [M-7]
KŌJIMACHI REBIRTH (see acupuncture) Women's sauna ¥2,800. Men's ¥2,500. Massage ¥5,000. [M-6]

Steam Baths
HOTEL ŌKURA STEAM BATH Hotel Ōkura 1st Fl. Tel: 582-0111. Hrs: 10 a.m.-9 p.m., daily. 1 hour massage and steam bath ¥6,200. Reservations required. [M-11]
PINK PEARL Palace Hotel B1. Tel: 211-6975. Hrs: 1 p.m.-7 p.m., closed Sun. 1 hour massage and steam bath ¥5,000, with oil massage ¥7,000. Reservations required. [M-10]

Massage
Many of the saunas listed above also offer massage.
SANWA MASSAGE Imperial Hotel 4th Fl. Tel: 580-5449. Hrs: 10 a.m.-9 p.m., daily. Massage and pressure shower ¥5,500. 50 min. massage ¥4,300. [M-10]
TOKYO ONSEN-DIAMOND SPA Tokyo Onsen 3rd Fl., 6-13-14 Ginza, Chūō-ku. Tel: 541-3021. Hrs: 10 a.m.-9 30 p.m., daily. For men only. This spa is connected with a bath and sauna, neither of which are very nice. They do, however, offer massage and Chinese style "mud-scrubbing" for the body (¥4,500). [M-8]

SPORTS FACILITIES

Health and fitness is a recent fad in Japan that sports facilities haven't quite yet caught up with. There are numerous public and private facilities. The public facilities are inexpensive and overcrowded, the private ones are usually by membership (often worth its weight in gold) and also tend to be on the crowded side. Some of the larger hotels have facilities that can be visited for a fee that usually runs upwards of ¥5,000 per visit.

Health Clubs
CLARK HATCH (men) 2-1-3 Azabudai, Minato-ku. Tel: 584-4092. Hrs: 7 a.m.-10:30 p.m. (8:30 a.m.-8:30 p.m. on Sat., Sun. & Hols.) A fully equipped gym plus sauna. They will supply gym clothes, towels, etc. ¥2,000. [M-1]
SWEDEN HEALTH CENTER (women) Sweden Center 5th Fl., 6-11-9 Roppongi, Minato-ku. Tel: 404-9739. Connected with Clark Hatch. From Oct.-May this is a members only club (registration fee ¥150,000, monthly fee ¥15,000). It's opened to the public from June-Sept. on a monthly basis (¥20,000 per month). They offer dance and exercise courses, and have a gym and sauna. [M-1]
DO SPORTS PLAZA HARUMI 5-6-41 Toyosu, Kōtō-ku. 7 min. by bus from Ginza on their

special bus from the Ginza Tōkyū Hotel. Tel: 531-8221. Hrs: 12 noon-10 p.m., daily. (until 8:30 p.m. on Sun. & Hols.) A huge sports center with swimming pool, gym, squash courts, jogging track, bowling alleys, golf driving range, sauna, massage, etc. They have a membership system (1 year for ¥100,000 plus ¥1,400 per visit), but visitors are allowed and for ¥7,000 a day you can use all the facilities. [off Map]

DO SPORTS PLAZA SHINJUKU In the Sumitomo Bldg. Annex, 2-6-1 Nishi-Shinjuku, Shinjuku-ku. Tel: 344-1971. Hrs: 10 a.m.-10:30 p.m. (7 a.m.-8:30 p.m. Sun. & Hols.), daily. Gym, sauna, diving pool, indoor track. They have the same charge system as the Harumi center listed above. [M-7]

HARAJUKU TRIMM Harajuku Trimm Hotel, 6-28-6 Jingūmae, Shibuya-ku. Tel: 498-2101. Hrs: 1 p.m.-9 p.m. (sauna until 10 p.m.), Mon.-Fri.; 11 a.m.-8 p.m. (sauna until 10 p.m.). On Sat.; 10 a.m.-7 p.m. (sauna until 8 p.m.) Sun. & Hols. A gym (3rd Fl.) and sauna (2nd Fl.), dance and exercise classes. Membership (from 1 p.m.-5 p.m.) ¥10,000 per month, ¥18,000 for 3 months. Visitors: gym & sauna ¥2,700 per day, just sauna ¥1,700. [M-4]

KŌRAKUEN HEALTH CLUB 1-3 Kōraku, Bunkyō-ku. Tel: 811-2111. Hrs: 9:30 a.m.-9:30 p.m., closed Sun. & Hols. (except on the 3rd Sun. when it's opened from 1 p.m.-7:30 p.m.). Gym, sauna and swimming pool (opened only from 6:30 p.m.-9 p.m., and on the 3rd Sun. from 1 p.m.-7:30 p.m.). They have the usual membership system (¥60,000 for membership, plus ¥50,000 for registration, plus ¥400 per visit), visitor's charge is ¥4,000 a day. [M-30]

TOKYO KŌSEINENKIN SPORTS CENTER 4-7-1 Ōkura, Setagaya-ku. Tel: 416-2611. Gym and sauna—¥1,300, just sauna—¥1,100. Hrs: 12 noon-8 p.m. (enter by 7 p.m.), Sat. & Sun.: gym from 10 a.m., and sauna from 11 a.m., daily. (From Shinjuku take the Odakyū line to Seijōgakuen station, then take the #05 bus, which takes about 5 min. Or take the #24 bus from Shibuya station to NHK Gijutsu Kenkyūjo Sports Center-mae bus stop, which takes about 30-40 min.) The outdoor swimming pool is opened in the summer, and costs ¥550 per day. [off Map]

MAINICHI SPORTS PLAZA TOKYO TBR Kioichō Bldg. 2nd Fl., 5-7 Kōjimachi, Chiyoda-ku. Tel: 234-1180. Indoor swimming pool and tennis courts with professional instructors. Also classes for pregnant women and infants. They have an inexpensive school: ¥10,000 for registration and monthly fees of ¥5,500 (once a week), ¥7,500 (twice a week), etc. [M-6]

Swimming Pools

- **Public Pools**—Many of these are so crowded, especially the outdoor pools in the summer, that you can't actually swim. You can, however, get in and splash around. Summer opening dates vary each year.

NATIONAL GYMNASIUM SWIMMING POOL (indoor) 2-1-1 Jinnan, Shibuya-ku (in Yoyogi Park). Tel: 468-1171. There are three pools here, the Olympic pool is opened July 14-Aug. 24 (but closed the 2nd & 4th Wed., and from Aug. 1-5). Hrs: 10 a.m.-8 p.m. (enter by 7 p.m.). Adults ¥450, children ¥350. The smaller sub-pool is open all year. Hrs: 12 noon-5 p.m., Mon.-Fri., 10 a.m.-5 p.m., Sat., Sun. & Hols., closed the 2nd & 4th Tue. Adults ¥450, children ¥350. There is also a small outdoor children's pool opened from July 11-Aug. 26. Hrs: 10 a.m.-5 p.m., ¥350. [M-4]

TOKYO METROPOLITAN GYMNASIUM INDOOR SWIMMING POOL 1-17 Sendagaya, Shibuya-ku (in Meiji Shrine Outer Garden). Tel: 408-6191. Hrs: June-Sept. 10 a.m.-9 p.m. (enter by 7 p.m.), Oct.-May 1 p.m.-9 p.m. (enter by 7 p.m.), closed Mon., if Mon. is a holiday, then closed Tue. Admission: June-Sept. ¥300 for 2 hours. Oct.-May ¥400. [M-29]

MEIJI JINGŪ POOL (outdoor & indoor) 5 Kasumigaoka, Shibuya-ku (in Meiji Shrine Outer Garden). Tel: 403-3456. Open June-Sept. Hrs: June & Sept.: 10 a.m.-5:45 p.m. (enter by 5 p.m.). Mon.-Sat., (from 9 a.m. on Sun.). July 1-15: 10 a.m.-7:15 p.m. (enter by 6:30 p.m.), Mon.-Sat. (from 9 a.m. on Sun.). July 16-Aug. 31: 10 a.m.-8:45 p.m. (enter by 8 p.m.), Mon.-Sat. (from 9 a.m. on Sun.). Admission: Adults ¥1,200 (per day), students ¥1,000, children ¥500. [M-29]

MINATO-KU SPORTS CENTER POOL (indoor) 3-1-19 Shibaura, Minato-ku. Tel: 452-4151. Hrs: 9:30 a.m.-11:30 a.m., 12 noon-2 p.m., 3 p.m.-5 p.m., 6 p.m.-8 p.m. Tue.-Sat.: 9:30 a.m.-11:30 a.m., 12 noon-2 p.m., 2:30 p.m.-4:30 p.m. Sun. & Hols., closed Mon. and Tue.

HEALTH AND BEAUTY 235

morning. Admission: ¥400. [off Map]
POOL OF KUMIN SŌGŌ UNDŌJŌ (outdoor) 4-6-1 Ōkura, Setagaya-ku (Take a #24 bus from Seijō Gakuen station, on the Odakyū line from Shinjuku station. It will take about 15 minutes by express, 30 minutes by local). Tel: 417-4276. Hrs: open July 1-Sept. 15, 9 a.m.-6:30 p.m. (10 a.m.-5 p.m. on Sept.), daily. Admission: for 2 hours ¥200 for adults, ¥50 for children. [off Map]

- **Private Pools**—Most private pools belong to hotels or sports centers (members only). Hotel pools run upwards of ¥4,000 per day, though some offer special evening discounts. During the summer many of the hotels offer a special summer membership for use of their outdoor pools. The following hotels allow visitors: Hotel New Ōtani (indoor & outdoor), Keiō Plaza Hotel (indoor & outdoor), Hotel Century Hyatt (indoor), Miyako Hotel (indoor & outdoor), Capitol Tōkyū (outdoor), Hotel Ōkura (indoor & outdoor), Tokyo Prince Hotel (outdoor), Shinagawa Prince Hotel (indoor), Holiday Inn (outdoor).

Other private pools are found in membership only sports clubs (listed in the health club section above). Membership is usually long term and expensive which won't help most people.

SUN PLAZA INDOOR POOL Sun Plaza Bldg. B2, 4-1-1 Nakano, Nakano-ku (near the North Exit of Nakano JNR station). Tel: 388-1151. Hrs: July & Aug. opened daily, 12 noon-8 p.m. (enter by 7 p.m.) Mon.-Fri.: 10 a.m.-8 p.m. (enter by 7 p.m.) Sat. & Sun. Sept.-June opened Sat. & Sun. 12 noon-7 p.m. Admission: ¥500 for 2 hours. [M-26]
TOKYO SWIMMING CENTER (indoor & outdoor) 5-4-21 Komagome, Toshima-ku (Sugamo station on JNR line). Tel: 915-1012. Hrs: indoor pool open all year, outdoor pool open from mid-July throughout mid-Sept., 12:30 p.m.-8 p.m., Mon.-Sat., 12:30 p.m.-6 p.m. Sun. & Hols. Admission: ¥1,300 per day. [off Map]

Jogging Courses

IMPERIAL PALACE COURSE (about 5 km.) This popular jogging and cycling course takes you around the moats of the Imperial Palace. You can start anywhere in the palace area. The two closest stations are Nijūbashi-mae station on the Chiyoda line, and Hanzōmon station on the Hanzōmon line. [M-10]
YOYOGI PARK COURSE (about 2.4 km.) You can start near Harajuku JNR train station or Shibuya Kōkaidō Concert Hall, then run around the NHK Broadcasting Center and the Yoyogi National Stadium. [M-4]

Cycling Courses

PALACE CYCLING COURSE (2.5 km., opened only Sun. 9 a.m.-5 p.m.) You can borrow a bicycle behind the police box in the Kōkyo-gaien Garden (Imperial Palace Outer Garden. Nijūbashi-mae station/Chiyoda line). The course starts from the Outer Garden and follows the moat of the East Garden to the entrance of Kitanomaru Park. [M-10]
MEIJI-JINGŪ GAIEN CYCLING ROAD (1.5 km., opened on Sun. & Hols.) Borrow a bicycle near Nihon-Seinenkan Hall (Gaien-mae station/Ginza line). The cycling road is lined with trees and goes around the park's sports facilities. [M-5]
TAMAGAWA SEISHŌNEN CYCLING COURSE (18 km., opened daily) This is a great course along the Tama River passing soccer and tennis courts, and parks. Borrow a bicycle at the service station on the other side of Tamagawa Ōhashi (Tamagawa Bridge) from the station. You will need to show your passport. (Take the Tōkyū Mekama line from Meguro to Yaguchi-Watari station, about 30 min.). [off Map]

BEAUTY CARE
Hair Care
MOD'S HAIR La Foret 3rd Fl. Tel: 475-0051. Hrs: 11 a.m.-6:30 p.m., daily [M-4]. Printemps Ginza 2nd Fl., Tel: 564-4848. Hrs: 10 a.m.-8 p.m., closed Wed. [M-8]. Cut & blow dry from ¥5,500. Associated with the Mod's Hair in Paris, the staff at this salon often do the hair for local fashion shows. The salon is run by *Tamura Tetsuya* who speaks English.

BOY Premier Gaien 2nd Fl., 2-7-30 Kita-Aoyama, Minato-ku. Tel: 401-1256. Hrs: 11 a.m.-8 p.m., closed Tue. Cut & blow dry from ¥4,000. Mogi Masayuki, the head stylist, lived and worked for 10 years in a London salon frequented by musicians. The Tokyo salon is decked out with old English antiques. [M-5]

BIJIN 25-8 Sarugakuchō, Shibuya-ku. Tel: 464-3419. Hrs: 11 a.m.-8 p.m., closed Tue., and when the owner Honda Mikio is working for photos or cinema. Cut & blow dry from ¥5,000. Mr. Honda does hair and make-up for many of the hipper Tokyo entertainers (he worked with YMO on their concert tours). [M-20]

ANDRE BERNARD Hōraiya Bldg. 4th Fl., 5-2-1 Roppongi, Minato-ku. Tel: 404-0616. Hrs: 9 a.m.-6 p.m., closed Sun. Cut & blow dry ¥3,600. Probably the easiest place for foreigners to go, they even answer the phone in English. Their work is basic, particularly good for any chemical treatments (perms or coloring). They also do manicures and pedicure. [M-1]

PEEK A BOO Beruea Garden Bldg. B1, 4-2-11 Jingūmae, Shibuya-ku. Tel: 402-8214. Hrs: 10 a.m.-6 p.m., closed Tue. Cut & blow dry from ¥3,500. [M-5]

Skin Care
NAGAI YAKKYOKU HIFU KŌSO BIGANSHITSU 1-8-10 Azabu-jūban, Minato-ku. Tel: 583-1393. Hrs: 10 a.m.-5 p.m., closed Tue. On the 2nd Fl. above the Nagai Yakkyoku Pharmacy. A great place for inexpensive skin care, this shop, connected with the Nagai Yakkyoku pharmacy, specializes in natural treatments for problem skin. It's also a good place to go for making sure your "perfect" skin stays in good condition. [M-1]

STUDIO ARKIS ESTY HARAJUKU STEP IN 1-16-7 Jingūmae, Shibuya-ku. Tel: 423-1071. Hrs: 10:30 a.m.-8 p.m., daily. Facials and skin care all computer calculated. They also have a tanning salon. [M-4]

ANDRE BERNARD (see Hair Care). Facials, waxing, manicures, etc. [M-1]

THE BASICS

"Excuse me your Highness, could you give me a little more space?" One of a series of award-winning posters by the Tokyo Metropolitan Subway System, this poster reminds people to be considerate of their fellow passengers.

THE BASICS

PLANNING
Climate
The climate of Tokyo is somewhat similar to that of New York, only less extreme. All four seasons are clearly distinguished, a matter of great pride to the Japanese who for some reason believe this to be a feature unique to their country. Here are some generalizations:

Spring—pleasant through May. In June begins the month-long rainy season.

Summer—hot and sticky through September. In August and September typhoons are common.

Autumn—Late September through mid-November are pleasant, crisp, and cool.

Winter—lasts from mid-November through March. Generally not too severe, snow falls occasionally and strong winds are common. December and January are cold but clear and sunny.

The best time to visit is in May or mid-October through mid-November. The inside of buildings and travel facilities such as buses and trains are climate controlled. They tend to overdo it here so it's a good idea to carry around a sweater to wear inside during the summer, and in winter be sure you can take off a layer or two of clothing.

When to Travel
Aside from climatic considerations, Japanese domestic tourism patterns are something to think about. The Japanese tourist's reputation precedes him overseas and the stereotype is no less applicable within the country.

The Japanese travel frequently, to see the cherry blossoms bloom in

Kyōto or the turning of maple leaves in the fall. National parks are visited at a yearly statistical average of over twice per person. Throughout the year famous temples and museums are besieged by tour groups of farmers and schoolkids on class excursions who love nothing more than a group photo with a foreign face in the center. During the major holiday seasons and on public holidays that fall next to a weekend, transportation outside of Tokyo is often booked months in advance, as are hotel rooms. If you're planning a trip out of town, try to book your hotel and tickets ahead of time. Major holiday seasons are:

Shōgatsu—the Japanese New Year celebration. Begins a few days before January 1, and lasts about a week. Tokyo closes down for the first three days of the year as most city dwellers return to their home towns.

Golden Week—from the Emperor's Birthday on April 29 through Children's Day on May 5. This is another period of mass exodus from the city to the countryside or overseas destinations.

***Obon* and School Vacations**—the two coincide. Schools let out from mid-June until late August. *Obon* is a three day holiday from August 14-16 when people return to their home towns to honor the spirits of their ancestors.

Mid-February—not exactly a holiday, but during this time high school seniors from all over Japan come to Tokyo to take their college entrance examinations. It is next to impossible to find a hotel room or to extend your stay in a room.

Special Deals—Before You Go

Following is a list of special deals and information sources to check before you leave for Japan.

Japan National Tourist Organization "JNTO"—this is a good source of general information on Japan as well as any specific information you might need—all free of charge. Ask your travel agent or JAL for the address of the nearest JNTO office. In Tokyo their main office is:

Tokyo Kōtsū Kaikan Bldg., 2-10-1 Yūrakuchō, Chiyoda-ku.
Tel: 216-1901. [M-8]

Japan Rail Pass—Foreign tourists visiting Japan for sightseeing purposes can apply for a rail pass at overseas JAL (Japan Air Lines) offices and at authorized travel agencies. The pass is valid for unlimited travel on the Japan National Railways (JNR) system. There are two kinds of passes: Ordinary and Green 1st Class. The passes are for 7, 14, or 21 days. Passes for children aged 6-11 are half price.
- Ordinary Passes: 7 days—¥25,000, 14 days—¥41,000, 21 days—¥53,000
- Green Passes: 7 days—¥35,000, 14 days—¥58,000, 21 days—¥76,000

The passes can only be purchased overseas. At the time of purchase, you will receive vouchers that can be exchanged for passes at designated locations in Japan. In Tokyo at the Yaesu North Exit of Tokyo Station (near the entrance to Daimaru Department store), Tel: 212-4456. [M-9] Also Narita Airport at the Narita Travel Center in the arrival lobby, Tel: 0476-32-8852.

The vouchers must be exchanged within three months from the date of issue. This is a great bargain considering that one round trip "Bullet Train" ticket to Kyōto costs over ¥23,000.

Japan Air Lines—JAL has long been known for its excellent service. They are also a good source of information on Japan and offer a few special deals for their passengers:

- Executive Salon—passengers on JAL have access to the executive salon in the Imperial Hotel with its various services and facilities for traveling businessmen. For a fee they will print bilingual business cards.
- JAL "Room and Rail" Pass—This package combines the rail pass with a set of coupons covering hotel accommodations for 7 or 14 nights (for 21 nights use one of each). Check with JAL for details.

Packing and Supplies

Just about anything your heart desires can be bought in Tokyo. That includes the items on the following list (with the exception of large sized shoes). These are just suggestions given for the sake of preparedness.

Shoes—All smart tourists already know they should pack comfortable walking shoes. In Japan, however, there are a few more considerations. First, sidewalks are often uneven, temple paths are frequently made of gravel and good shoes tend to be quickly destroyed. Also, you'll be taking your shoes off at unexpected times: in some offices, in homes, in temples, shrines, some museums, at the tea ceremony. Shoes that slip easily off and on will save you a great deal of trouble. To avoid unnecessary embarrassment, socks with holes should be left at home. In the winter, thick socks are advisable. Japanese shoe sizes run small, women's shoes up to 24-24.5 (U.S. 7-7.5, British 5.5-6), men's shoes run only slightly larger (U.S. 7.5-8, British 7-8). A few stores carry larger sizes but don't expect to find anything fashionable.

Tissues and/or Hankies—Most Japanese carry hankies or little packages of tissues. They are used to dab off perspiration in the summer, in lieu of toilet paper and towels in public restrooms, and as napkins in many restaurants. Hankies and tissues can be bought at station kiosks.

Flashlight—Lighting in temples and museums is not always what it should be. If you want to see that lovely 8th century Buddha, you may just have to help light it yourself.

Instant Coffee—If you're planning on staying in Japanese style lodgings —*ryokan*, but can't do without a morning cup of coffee, bring a small jar of instant coffee or buy one here. *Ryokan* usually don't have coffee but there will be a jar of hot water in each room for making tea.

Bath Towel—Japanese public baths do not supply towels, and *ryokan* provide only small handtowels. It's not a bad idea to bring an extra one with you.

Visas

Visas are required of citizens from countries that do not have a reciprocal visa exemption agreement with Japan. The visa must be obtained before arriving in Japan.

Visa exemptions for travelers not engaged in commercial activities are granted to citizens of the following countries:

- For 180 days: Austria, Eire, W. Germany, Liechtenstein, Mexico, Switzerland, U.K.
- For 90 days: Argentina, Bahamas, Bangladesh, Belgium, Canada, Chile, Columbia, Costa Rica, Cyprus, Denmark, Dominica, El Salvador, Finland, France, Greece, Guatemala, Honduras, Iceland, Iran, Israel, Italy, Lesotho, Luxembourg, Malaysia, Malta, Mauritius, Netherlands, Norway, Pakistan, Peru, Portugal, San Marino, Singapore, Spain, Surinam, Sweden, Tunisia, Turkey, Uruguay, Yugoslavia.
- For 30 days: New Zealand.

Visas are required of citizens from all other countries, including the U.S.A. and Australia. They can be obtained by writing to or visiting a Japanese embassy or consulate abroad.

Tourist Visa—A "Short-term Stay" visa is good for tourism, conferences, amateur sports, business trips, cultural, religious, or press activities, basically anything that's legal and you don't get paid for in Japan.

Duration—U.S. citizens: for 15-90 days, multiple entry, valid for 5 years. Australian citizens: for 60 days, multiple entry, valid for 12 months.

Extensions—visas can usually be extended twice, giving you a maximum stay of 180 days. Applications must be made at least 10 days before the expiration date of your current visa. You may be required to prove that you can afford the extended stay. You will also need to apply for an **Alien Registration Card** by the 90th day.

Documentation—you will need 2 passport sized photos, your passport, a return ticket, and proof of financial independence, i.e. travellers

checks, money. It usually takes 2-3 days for processing.
- **Other Visas**

Visas for non-tourist purposes or longer stays are many and varied. The procedure is fairly complicated, usually requiring extensive documentation and one to two months of processing. You will normally have to have some kind of sponsoring organization. For further information check with the nearest Japanese consulate or write for one of the pamphlets listed below.

Working in Japan—It is illegal to work in Japan without a working visa. If you arrive in Tokyo and want to find a job, you will have to come on a tourist visa, find a sponsoring company here, then leave the country to make the application at an overseas consulate. You can buy inexpensive open ended plane tickets that will allow you to leave Japan for a nearby country and return. Cheap tickets from Japan to Korea or Hong Kong will cost around ¥40,000—¥60,000.

Alien Registration Cards—If you are planning to stay for more than 90 days, you are required to apply for an **Alien Registration "Green" Card** by the 90th day. Immigration is very strict and failure to obtain your card in a timely fashion can result in deportation. If you run a few days over, they will usually accept your profuse apologies and a written "*Gomen Nasai*"="I am truly sorry" note that explains why you failed to apply. Applications can be made at the Tokyo Immigration Office. You will need 3 passport sized photos, a passport and an address.

- **Tokyo Immigration Offices**—3-3 Kōnan, Minato-ku, Tokyo. Tel: 471-5111.[M-38] / Sunshine City, Ikebukuro, 6th Fl. World Import Mart. Tel: 986-2271 [M-18] From July the above offices will be closed and a new one opened at: Daisan Gōdō Chōsha Bldg. 2nd Fl., 1-3 Ōtemachi, Chiyoda-ku. Tel: 213-8111
- Helpful publications:

  "A Guide to Alien Procedures in Japan"—by the Japan Times Press. At bookstores for ¥300, or write "The Japan Times", 4-5-4 Shibaura, Minato-ku, Tokyo 108, Japan. Japan ¥200, overseas ¥300.

  "Now You Live in Japan"—by the Research Committee for Bicultural Life in Japan. Write: c/o Japan Times Ltd., CPO Box 144, Tokyo, 100-91. Postage cost: in Japan ¥200, overseas ¥300.

ARRIVAL

Arriving at Tokyo's new international airport "Narita" is one of the least pleasant parts of travel to Japan. The airport is located 60km. from the city and protests by radicals and local farmers have resulted in strict security measures such as car searches and baggage checks of all those entering the airport grounds. The old airport "Haneda" now operates

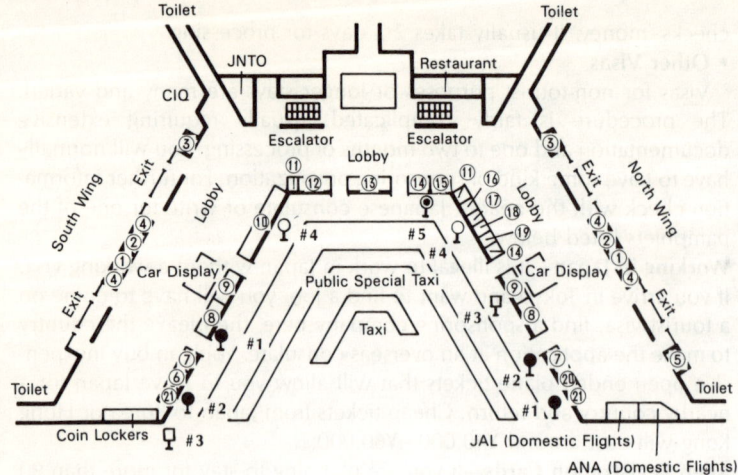

NARITA AIRPORT (Arrival Terminal)

1 Information Counter
2 Traffic Information Center
3 Bonded Baggage Counter
4 Money Changers
5 JAL Baggage Service Counter
6 Airport Express
7 Limousine Bus & Hired Car Counter
8 Hotel Reservation Counter
9 Telephone
10 Airline's Counter
11 Baggage Delivery Service (ABC Counter)
12 Rental Car Counter
13 JNR Ticket Counter
14 Keisei Line Ticket Counter
15 AGS Luggage Service
16 Nippon Express
17 Japan Travel Bureau
18 Limousine Bus Ticket Counter (to Hotels)
19 Limousine Bus Ticket Counter
20 JAL Information Counter
21 Japan National Tourist Organization (JNTO)

Bus Stops
#1 Limousine Bus to TCAT
#2 Limousine Bus to Other Destinations
#3 Hotel Courtesy Bus
#4 Keisei Station Shuttle Bus
#5 JNR Narita Station Shuttle Bus

only domestic flights with the exception of Taiwan's "China Airlines". The People's Republic of China uses Narita. Politics.

Formalities

A visa must be obtained before arrival. You must also fill out a quarantine form and an "Embarkation/Disembarkation" card. Your airline should have these two forms on board.

Customs

Customs inspection on arrival is fast and efficient. Officials are generally easy on foreign travellers, unless of course you've given them reason to act otherwise. There are separate lines for residents and non-residents. Carts are available and can be used to carry your luggage to your transportation.

An oral declaration is sufficient in most cases. Unaccompanied baggage must be declared in writing.

Customs Exempt Items: Personal effects and professional equipment to be used during your stay.

Travelers over 20 years of age can bring in:
- 3 bottles of alcoholic beverages (each bottle approx. 760cc.)
- 500 grams of tobacco (400 cigarettes, 100 cigars)
- 2 ounces of perfume
- Gifts, souvenirs, watches, etc. are given duty-free entry irrespective of their quantity and value, provided that the total market value of all articles brought in other than alcoholic beverages, tobacco products and perfume is not more than ¥100,000 or approx. U.S $450.

If you are planning to live in Japan for over 1 year, household effects including automobiles and boats may be imported. The items must be used and be re-exported upon leaving Japan.

Prohibited Items:
- Narcotic and stimulant drugs, and any utensils for drug use.
- Counterfeit, altered or imitated articles of coins, paper money, banknotes or securities.
- Any books, drawings or items considered damaging to public security or morals (this basically means pornography, they generally draw the line at any portrayal of genitals and pubic hair).
- Articles infringing on patents, trade marks, copyrights, etc.
- Pistols, revolvers and all types of ammunition.

Restricted Items:
- Swords and other types of weapons require special permission.
- Plants and animals must be presented to the quarantine inspector

prior to customs examination.

Currency:
- An oral declaration of currencies in your possesion is requested.
- Up to ¥5,000,000 may be taken out of the country.

Passenger Service Facility Charge

All passengers departing from Narita are subject to a service charge of ¥2,000 per adult, and ¥1,000 for children over 2 and under 12 years of age. The charge is collected at the ticketing counter or before passing through immigration. The charge is not levied on passengers arriving and leaving the same day.

Airport Services
- 24 hour money changers. Try to change your money before exiting from the customs clearance area. If you forget, money changers are also located on the 4th floor.
- 24 hour coin lockers.
- Tourist Information Center—pick up a map of Tokyo, a transit system map and any tourist publications covering events in Tokyo. Hrs: 9 a.m.-12 noon, and 1-8 p.m., weekdays. 9 a.m.-12 noon Saturday. Closed Sundays.
- International calls and telegrams can be made at the KDD office on the 4th floor of the center building. Open 24 hrs.

Transportation to Tokyo

There are a number of ways to get into town from Narita Airport.

Limousine Bus—to TCAT, the Tokyo City Air Terminal. [M-23] This is by far the best way. Tickets can be purchased in the arrival lobby. The bus stops right outside the terminal. There are a number of buses with different destinations so be sure you go to the correct stop. Your bags will be loaded onto the bus, you can reclaim them upon arrival at TCAT. Take a taxi from there to your hotel. Buses from TCAT to Tokyo Station or to some of the major hotels are also available. The closest subway station is Ningyōchō on the Hibiya line, about a 5 min. walk from the terminal.
- Price: ¥2,500. Departure to Tokyo every 10-15 min. (Buses departing from Tokyo to Narita leave at 10-30 min, intervals). Travel time: 1 hour, but varies with traffic.

Limousine Bus to Other Destinations—There are special buses to Yokohama and Haneda Airport, as well as buses making the rounds of major hotels in Tokyo. Prices run from ¥2,000-¥3,100. Departure times are irregular.

Trains—Several trains operate between Tokyo and Narita. All of them require a bus trip from the airport to a train station where there are no porters to help you carry your baggage up and down the stairs. The train is, however, somewhat less expensive. Travel time can also be shorter, but departure times are less frequent.

Keisei Lines—The Keisei private railroad company operates 3 trains from their Keisei-Ueno Station [M-13] to Narita. Buy a ticket at the Keisei counter in the north Wing arrival lobby. A Keisei bus will take you to their airport station (6 min. and ¥170). The trains are differentiated by speed and how many stops are made along the way.

- Keisei Skyliner—Price: ¥1,490. Travel time: 60 min., departures every 30 min.
- Keisei Limited Express—Price: ¥790. Travel time: 70 min., depart. every 40 min.
- Keisei Express—Price: ¥790. Travel time: 85 min., depart. every 40 min.

Japan National Railways "JNR"—The JNR also operates a service to downtown Tokyo, but it requires a 25 min. bus ride to the Narita City Station and from there at least a 63 min. train ride. Compared with the other services this one is inconvenient and not recommended.

Taxi—To central Tokyo the cost is around ¥20,000 and takes 1-1.5 hours depending on traffic.

Hired Car—A car and driver to central Tokyo will cost about ¥29,000. The limousine bus company offers this service. You can order a car at the bus counter in the airport arrival lobby or call (03) 747-0305.

Rental Cars—Driving in Tokyo is one of the cultural experiences we suggest you do not attempt. Streets are narrow, crowded, and confusing. Most signs are in Japanese only. If you need a car, both Hertz and Avis have Tokyo affiliates. The cars can be reserved overseas and you can pick them up at the airport. You will need an international drivers licence or a Japanese one.

- Avis-Nissan Rent-a-Car: 1-5-7 Azabudai, Minato-ku, Tokyo. Landick Ikura Bldg. 6th Fl. Tel: 587-4000
- Hertz-Nippon Rent-a-Car: Jinnan Bldg., 4-3 Udagawachō, Shibuya-ku, Tokyo. Tel: 496-0919.

Cost for rental cars starts at about ¥4,000 for 6 hours.

Haneda Airport

Haneda operates domestic flights and the international flights of Taiwan's China Airlines. The airport is located close to the city and a taxi ride to the center of town takes only 30-40 min. and costs about ¥5,000-¥6,000.

Monorail—The monorail from Hamamatsuchō Station [M-11] in Tokyo to

Haneda is great if you have little baggage or are taking domestic flights from Tokyo. Departures are every 10-20 min. Travel time: 17 min. Price: ¥270. No carts or baggage service available.

DETAILS
Money

The Japanese unit of currency is the yen "¥". Coin denominations are ¥1, ¥5, ¥10, ¥50, ¥100, and ¥500. Bills are ¥500, ¥1,000, ¥5,000, and ¥10,000. Money can be changed at the airport, in banks, or hotels. Exchange rates fluctuate daily. It's a good idea to figure the approximate exchange value of your currency for ¥1,000 which will be your basic bill in Tokyo. ¥1,000 equals about U.S. $4-5.00, or sterling £3.

Japan is essentially a cash society. Although this is changing somewhat, most places will only accept cash ¥. It is illegal to use anything but yen in Japan. Travellers checks should be cashed in. Restaurants will sometimes take only one or two credit cards, if they take them at all.

Japanese banks give excellent but painfully slow service. If you need to transfer money internationally it can take three days to a week. Try to find out if your local bank has a branch or affiliate in Tokyo.

Tipping-Service, Charges-Taxes

There is no tipping in Japan. If you leave your change on the table, the waitress will probably pursue you down the street to return your "*wasuremono*" (literally a "forgotten thing"). Most hotels and restaurants do include a 10-20% service charge on the bill. Taxes are calculated at 10% on hotel rooms when the room rate plus service charge is more than ¥4,000. A 10% tax is also charged on restaurant meals over ¥2,500 per person.

Business Hours

Business is generally done on a 9-5 schedule, but with overtime being a favorite leisure activity of the Japanese, people can often be found in their offices as late as 7 or 8 p.m. Sundays are holidays for all but the major stores, boutiques in busy areas, and some restaurants. Calling ahead is always a good idea. General business hours are:

Banks: 9 a.m.-3 p.m. Mon.-Fri., until 12 noon Sat. Closed the 2nd Sat. of the month, Sun., and holidays.

Government Offices: varies, but basically open from 8:30 or 9 a.m. to 4 or 5 p.m. Mon.-Fri., and Sat. mornings.

Post Offices: Main offices: 9 a.m.-7 p.m. Mon.-Fri, 9 a.m.-5 p.m. Sat, 9 a.m.-12 noon Sun. & Hols. Branches: 9 a.m.-5 p.m. Mon.-Fri., 9 a.m.-12:30 p.m. Sat. Closed Sun. & Hols.

Major Companies: 9 a.m.-5 p.m. Mon.-Fri., some Sat. mornings.
Department Stores: 10 a.m.-6 p.m. daily, except one weekly holiday that varies with each store.
Most Shops: 10 or 11 a.m.-8 p.m. daily.
Japanese Restaurants: lunch: 11:30 a.m.-2 p.m., dinner: 5 p.m.-9 p.m.

Metric

Although the metric system is used in Japan for most things, traces of the traditional system of measurement can still be found. Rooms are commonly measured by how many *tatami* straw mats fill the floor space (6-8 is usual), and *sake* bottles that used to be 1 *shō* are now 1.8 liters. You won't need these traditional measures but for those who don't know the metric system, here is a brief conversion chart:

1 centimeter (cm.) =	4/10 inch	1 inch	= 2.55 cm.
1 meter (m.) =	3.28 feet, 1.1 yds	1 foot	= 0.31 m./
		1 yd	= 0.93 m.
1 kilometer (km.) =	0.62 miles	1 mile	= 1.5 km.
1 gram (g.) =	0.035 oz.	1 oz.	= 28 g.
1 kilogram (kg.) =	35.27 oz., 2.2 lbs.	1 lb.	= 450 g.
1 metric ton (t.) =	1.1 U.S. ton		
1 liter (l.) =	0.26 gal.	1 U.S. gal.	= 3.75 l.

Temperature: an easy formula for changing centigrade (°C) to Fahrenheit (°F) is:
30 °C = (2 × 30 °C) + 30 = 90 °F

Electricity

In Japan the power supply is 100 volts with an alternating current (AC). Eastern Japan including Tokyo is on 50 cycles, western Japan on 60. Most hotels have adapters for small appliances such as shavers and hair dryers.

Food and Drink

In general, standards of hygiene are high and everything is safe to eat and drink. If, however, you're a picky eater, here are a few things to watch:
Water—If you don't like drinking heavily chlorinated tap water, you can find bottled water at most stores and many restaurants. Well known domestic brands are Fuji and Suntory. Imports such as Perrier are also available. Another alternative is club soda but when ordering be sure they understand that you want plain soda, or you might end up with a drink concocted of green sugar syrup and soda water. Ask for "*purein sōda*" or "*tansan*".

Drinks—Cold drinks are usually served pre-sugared. This includes fruit juices, milk, iced coffee and tea. To order without the sugar syrup say "*gamu nuki*". It may not be possible, as often the drinks are bought pre-mixed.

Toast and Sandwiches—Bread almost always comes in inch-thick slices and very white. Brown bread, like brown rice, has not caught on here. Sandwiches are standardized: thin slices of trimmed white bread with a combination of nearly invisible slices of cheese, ham, cucumber, lettuce, tomato, mustard, and mayonnaise. To order minus any ingredient the formula is ____ *nuki*, e.g. "*tomato nuki*".

Vegetarians—in Japanese you're called "*Saishoku-shugi sha*".

Japanese Toilets

Foreigners always laugh at those illustrated "How to use a Western Toilet" signs pasted on almost every western style toilet in Japan. Funny that one would need instructions. It's even funnier when you find tennis shoe tread marks on a public toilet seat (admittedly a rare occurrence). But don't laugh too hard. Foreigners have been known to use Japanese style toilets in all sorts of curious ways (like one woman who used it backwards for two months).

Japanese toilets are essentially small holes sunk in the floor or on a raised platform in the stall. One end of the receptacle will be covered with a small shield. The rules are: facing the shield, stand astride the hole and squat. Men are permitted to stand if they promise to use good aim. Other useful tips:

- Public restrooms are occasionally uni-sex. Just look the other way as you pass the men's urinals on the way to the stalls.
- If there are a number of stalls, queue in front of each door, not in a single line for the first stall opening.
- Toilet tissue and towels are often not supplied in the truly public restrooms. Bring your own.
- To determine if a stall is occupied, do not yank on the door. Give a polite knock. A knock back means it's full.
- In Japanese toilets are called "*toire*".

Safety

Part of Japan's good PR is its low crime rate. Aside from the occasional *Yakuza* (the Mafia) brawl, some white collar crime and family suicides, there's not much trouble. Lost items are usually turned in and women can walk home safely at night. It's all part of the system and one of the best parts of it.

But things are changing. Crime statistics, though far below U.S. standards, are on the rise. Crime and criminals are found in all large cities and tourists make good targets. Don't let your survival instincts relax too far. Here are a few suggestions:
- Have your name and address on your wallet, purse, camera equipment, etc., so it can be turned in if found.
- Carry your passport or Alien Registration Card at all times. The police do not usually stop tourists but if they do and you are without your identification you'll get taken to the police station and kept until someone brings them down for you.
- When crossing the street, look to the right. Also, since pedestrians do not necessarily have the right-of-way, crossing at designated crosswalks is advisable. If you jay-walk in front of a police station they will announce on a loudspeaker that you're doing a no-no.
- For women—if you do get harassed it's probably just an amicably inebriated businessman who wants to practice his English on you. They are easily discouraged.
- If you have problems, the following telephone numbers will put you in touch with emergency services: **Police**—110. **Ambulance:** 119.

COMMUNICATIONS
Mail
Most hotels can handle overseas letters and packages. If you must mail a package internationally or send a registered letter, be sure to find a main post office. Post boxes have two slots, the blue lettered slot on the left is for overseas or out of town mail, the red lettered slot on the right is for Tokyo mail. Restrictions on size and weight of parcels vary with each country, but generally up to 10 kg, and 125 cm. in length is accepted. Most post offices sell boxes in three sizes (small, medium, large) for shipping. **The Tokyo International Post Office** is located at:
2-3-3 Ōtemachi, Chiyoda-ku, Tokyo. Tel: 241-4891. [M-36]
General Delivery—if you don't know where you'll be staying and expect to receive mail, you can have it delivered:
c/o Poste Restante, Central Post Office, Tokyo, Japan. [M-10]

General delivery or Poste Restante is called "*kyoku-dome*" or "*tome-oki*" in Japanese. Your mail will be kept for 30 days, then returned to sender. Most embassies also provide this service.

Telegrams and Cables
Hotels, post offices, telegraph offices, JNR stations and the Bullet Train handle domestic telegrams in English. The phone number for the domestic **Telegraph Office** is: 270-4051.

International telegrams can be sent from your hotel or **KDD** Offices: KDD "Kokusai Denshin Denwa", International Telegraph Office, 1-8-1 Ōtemachi, Chiyoda-ku, Tokyo. Tel: 270-5111. [M-36]

Telephones

Telephones come in a charming range of colors that indicate what kind of service the phone provides.

- Pink Phones—semi-public phones located in shops, restaurants, etc. Take up to six ¥10 coins, for local or short-distance inter-city calls.
- Small Red Phones—public phones located indoors and out. Work like the pink ones.
- Big Red Phones—same as the small ones, but these also take up to four ¥100 coins.
- Blue Phones—Located in street phone booths, work for local and inter-city calls. Small ones take up to six ¥10 coins, big ones—up to 10
- Yellow Phones—for local and domestic long distance, the small ones take up to five ¥10 and four ¥100, large ones can take ten of each.
- Green Phones—these new computerized phones use coins or disposable credit cards sold in denominations of ¥500, ¥1,000, ¥3,000, and ¥5,000. When the card is inserted in the slot, a digital reading tells how many ¥10 units are left—if it reads 50 then you have 50 ¥10's left. The computer subtracts until the card runs out. If your card is on its last yen in the middle of a conversation, you can revert to the primitive coin system. Cards are sold at telephone offices, some station kiosks and a few cigarette stands with green phones nearby.

To use the phones, pick up the receiver, insert your coin then dial. ¥10 pays for 3 minutes on a local call; the rates go up from there according to distance. A warning tone will sound when the time paid for expires. On most phones you can continue the call by inserting more money. It's a good idea to insert more coins than you think you'll need in the beginning, that way you won't be disconnected and the change comes back, though not in fractions of ¥100.

Phone Numbers—a typical Tokyo number is written (03) 456-8913. (03) is the area code which won't be needed when in the city. Long distance, inter-city, and some suburban calls will require the prefix.

Finding a phone number can be difficult. Finding someone's home number is next to impossible. There are English directories but listings are limited. For businesses and restaurants, unless the place is well known, it is essential to know the address. Your hotel front desk can help sometimes. The local directory assistance number is 104, but generally no one speaks English. Although it's not their job, international operators always speak English and will sometimes help. The number is

270-5111. Another possibility is the Tourist Information Center (TIC) 502-1461.

GETTING AROUND
Trains and Subways

Tokyo is blessed with one of the world's best public transportation systems. Trains and subways are fast, clean, convenient, and safe at all hours. Most stations have signs in English and maps of the total system showing all stops and transfer points. Subway and train lines are named and color coded. All systems connect at some point with the Japan National Railway's (JNR) **Yamanote Line** that encircles the city. There are three major systems in Tokyo:

Teitu Rapid Transit Authority—includes the major subway lines: Ginza Line (orange), Hibiya Line (grey), Marunouchi Line (red), Chiyoda Line (green), Yūrakuchō Line (yellow), Tōzai Line (turquoise blue), and the Hanzōmon Line (purple).

Tokyo Metropolitan Subways "Toei"—includes: Toei Asakusa Line (pink), Toei Mita Line (blue), and the Toei Shinjuku Line (chartreuse).

Japan National Railways "JNR"—the nation-wide rail system includes local and long distance lines such as the *Shinkansen* "Bullet" trains. Major lines in Tokyo are:

- Yamanote Line 山手線 (green). The loop train that encircles the inner urban area. The 35km. loop has 29 stops and takes about one hour.
- Chūō Line 中央線 (orange). From Tokyo station this line runs west through Kanda, Ochanomizu, Shinjuku, and ends in Takao. Rapid service trains (marked by a red sign reading 快速 or 特快 "kaisoku" or "tokkai") skip certain stops.
- Sōbu Line 総武線 (yellow). Runs east from Mitaka to Chiba, doubling as a local service for the Chūō Line as far as Ochanomizu.
- Keihin Tōhoku Line 京浜東北線 (blue). From Tokyo station runs north to Ōmiya and south, passing through Yokohama, to Ōfuna.

Tickets—Buy a ticket at the station. Vending machines take ¥10, ¥100 coins, some change ¥1,000 bills. The ticket collector can also change small bills. Destinations are written only in Japanese, but in general the lowest priced ticket will take you 3-5 stops, the next should go 6-8, and so on. Children under 6 ride free, under 12 for half price (use the lower row of buttons). If you are unsure of which is the correct ticket, simply buy the lowest fare (usually ¥100-¥120) and have some change ready to pay the difference when you exit from the ticket booth. Tickets must be turned in as you exit.

Transfers—For transfers within each system the same ticket can be used. For example a JNR Yamanote Line ticket can be used on the JNR Chūō

Line, a ticket for the Toei Mita Line will allow you to transfer to the Toei Shinjuku Line, etc. Inter-system transfers are more complicated. While it is possible to buy special inter-system transfer tickets, everything is written in Japanese. Since all you would save is ¥20-30 and the bother of buying a new ticket, it's probably easier just to buy the second ticket, or, in the case of a transfer that doesn't require exiting from the ticket booth, simply pay the difference when you get off.

Hours—Subways and trains operate from 5 am. to 12 pm. Rush hours are 7:30-9:30 a.m. and 5-7 p.m. If you want to witness the almost terrifying spectacle of thousands of commuters being crushed into trains, visit Shinjuku Station during these hours. If you don't enjoy suffering, avoid rush hour whenever possible.

Stations and Exiting—Stations can be confusing, especially the larger ones and especially during the rush hour sea of commuters. Don't panic. Find a ticket booth and ask slowly. Some stations have numerous exits and the difference in going out one as opposed to another can be drastic. If possible, find out ahead of time which exit you should take. Otherwise ask at the station before exiting from the ticket booth. Landmarks are usually the best thing to ask for. Train station exits are often marked North 北口 (*kita-guchi*), South 南口 (*minami-guchi*), East 東口 (*higashi-guchi*), West 西口 (*nishi-guchi*) and Central 中央口 (*chūō-guchi*). Subway station exits are usually numbered and alphabetized.

Maps—There is a transit map in the back map section. English subway maps are also available at most hotels and at the Tourist Information Center.

Subway and Train Etiquette—Crowd behavior in Japan is sometimes rather curious. A sweet little old lady who just spent five minutes bowing good-bye to her friend on the platform will rush up jabbing her packages or umbrella into your back and scurry on the train to get a seat. Don't take it personally. Like everywhere in the world, women do, occasionally meet an adventurous groper on a crowded train. Try preventive intimidation. If you're next to the door on a crowded train, you might want to step out to avoid being crushed by the stampede of exiting passengers. If you're getting off from the middle of a crowded car, don't be shy and polite—just push, everybody else does. Silver seats are for the elderly and the handicapped.

Lost and Found—If you're lost, ask a platform attendant or go to the nearest ticket booth. Tell them where you want to go. They may not speak English but they should understand the name of the destination. If you lose something, call the appropriate lost and found office listed at the end of this chapter.

Taxis

There are more than 40,000 taxis cruising Tokyo daily. All are equipped with clever automatic doors on the passenger (left) side, some are equipped with coin-operated massage cushions, and recently a few have installed small color televisions—for ¥100 you can watch T.V. till you reach your destination.

To stop a taxi simply wave discreetly. Taxi's do not stop when you whistle or shout "TAXI". Taxi stands are located at most hotels, department stores, and close to major intersections. A red light on the front dashboard of the passenger side indicates the taxi is free, a green light means it's occupied, and no lights or a printed sign means it's off duty.

You won't have much trouble getting a taxi except in bad weather, sometimes during rush hour, late Friday and Saturday nights, and during December. If you get desperate, try holding up two fingers. This is not an obscene gesture but means you are willing to pay double the fare. If that doesn't work, try three fingers. If that doesn't work you may prefer the obscene gesture.

Drivers are generally pleasant, helpful and honest. Rude drivers do exist but contrary to the belief of many foreigners, they're just as rude to Japanese passengers.

Fares—Taxi fares start at ¥470 for the first 2 km. and increase in increments of ¥80 for each additional 370 m. Waiting time is charged at ¥80 per stop over 2.4 min. Between 11 pm. and 5 am. there is an extra charge of 20%. If you need a receipt say "*Ryōshūsho kudasai*".

Giving Directions—See instructions. Some listings in this book have the name and address written in Japanese, and most correspond to a map in the back. Show both to your driver. Remember that if the driver didn't understand you the first time, he probably won't understand you any better if you shout the second time. Check the pronunciation guide in the back and try again.

Buses

If you read some Japanese or have lived here for a while, buses can be great for filling in the gaps of the train and subway system. They are, however, quite confusing and not recommended for the casual tourist. If you want to brave the system here are the general rules for Tokyo bus travel: get on at the front door and deposit your money in the green fare box next to the driver. The average fare is ¥150, though this will soon increase by ¥10-¥20. Children pay half fare. Fare machines can change ¥50 and ¥100 coins but no bills. To stop the bus, push the button located above your seat. Stops are announced by the driver or by a prerecorded message. Exit by the back door. As on trains and subways, silver seats are for the elderly and the handicapped.

Bus Tickets—for a saving in bus fare or simply for convenience, bus tickets can be purchased from the driver or at offices in major bus terminals. In Japanese bus tickets are called "*Kaisūken*".

Bus Routes—Bus routes are extremely complicated and sorry, but we're not giving any. Most buses begin and end at train stations, so if you know the Japanese *kanji* spelling of the stations you can find a bus that at least will end up at a place where you can take other transportation. You can always ask the driver "*Kono basu wa* _____ *e ikimasu ka?* "fill in the blank with your destination.

Getting There

It may sound obvious but the first thing you have to do to get somewhere is to figure out where you're going. With the exception of major buildings, in Tokyo that means first which district, second what is the closest landmark or major crossing, and finally the name and address of the building. Unlike most major cities, Tokyo street names, if they exist at all, are unknown even to most veteran taxi drivers. Addresses alone are not much help either. While in some parts of town the numbering is very systematic, in others numbers seem arbitrarily distributed in a deliberate attempt to induce insanity.

A typical address is written 1-4-7 Roppongi, Minato-ku, Tokyo, 106, or sometimes 4-7 Roppongi 1-chōme, etc. 1 is the "chōme" or sub-district, 4 is the block (or a variation of one), 7 is the building number, Roppongi is the district, Minato-ku is the city ward, Tokyo the city, and 106 is the postal code.

Here is a list of suggestions to get you where you're going:
1. Get the address, phone number and the name of the district. Have someone draw a map.
2. Find out what the nearest landmark or major crossing is and the directions to the place from there.
3. Get a description of the building if possible.
4. If you're traveling by train or subway, find out which exit is closest.

The map section at the back of the book has the major landmarks in each district marked. Use this as a reference. If you need further assistance, someone at your hotel or the staff at the Tourist Information Center can probably help. Instructions written in Japanese are always helpful, but be sure you have them written in English as well, so *you* know where you're going.

Getting Lost

The best place to go for help is a neighborhood police box called a "Kōban". If you can't find one, ask someone on the street. If they don't know, ask someone else. If they do know, ask someone else all the same. People will often give you directions without knowing the place simply to avoid having to say "no" (not considered a nice thing to do in Japan). If two people give you the same directions, there is a good chance that the directions are correct. Shop people or people who look like they belong in the neighborhood are the best bet. 50% of the people on the street commute 1-2 hours to Tokyo and won't know much more than you do. Another possibility is the TIC sponsored English language "Travel Phone" (see below).

Lost and Found

Here is a list of the various Tokyo lost and found offices called "Wasuremono annai-jo" in Japanese.

Metropolitan Police Board—1-9-11 Kōraku, Bunkyō-ku. Tel: 814-4151. Hrs: 8:30 a.m.-4 p.m. Mon.-Fri., until 11:30 a.m. Sat., closed Sun. & Hols. After 3-5 days all lost items go here.

National Railways—Tokyo Station Lost Properties Office—Tel: 231-1880. Ueno Station—Tel: 841-8069.

Teito Rapid Transit Authority (Subways)—Ueno Station Office, Tel: 834-5577.

Tokyo Metropolitan Buses, Streetcars, and Subways—Lost and Found Office of the Metropolitan Government, Kōtsū Kaikan Bldg. 5th Fl., 2-10-1 Yūrakuchō, Chiyoda-ku. Tel: 216-2953.

Taxi—Tokyo Taxi Kindaika Center, Shinseikaikan Bldg., 33 Shinanomachi, Shinjuku-ku. Tel: 355-0300.

TOURIST SERVICES

We've tried to tell you everything you might possibly want to know—but for further information:

Tourist Information Center "TIC"—This is a branch of the Japan National Tourist Organization that acts as an information service for foreigners. The English speaking staff will provide information on touring Tokyo and on travel throughout Japan (all free). They also have information on current cultural events and useful publications like "The Tourists Handbook". Other services are:

- Home Visit System—they will arrange a visit to a Japanese home.
- Travel Phone—provides English travel assistance. In Tokyo call: 502-1461.

- Teletourist Information—recorded information on current cultural events. In English: 503-2911. In French: 503-2926.
- The TIC Tokyo Office is at: 1-6-6 Yūrakuchō, Chiyoda-ku, Tokyo. Tel: 502-1461/2. Hrs: 9 a.m.-5 p.m. Mon.-Fri., until 12 noon Sat., closed Sun. & Hols. [M-10]

Tourist Publications—the following three publications provide information on current events.
- Tour Companion—Free at hotels and TIC.
- Weekender—Free at hotels, TIC, and some foreigners' hang-outs.
- Tokyo Journal—¥300 at certain bookstores, hotels, kiosks and some foreigner's hang-outs. Covers contemporary and traditional events.

Japan Guide Association—will put you in contact with a licensed tour guide. You must then negotiate with the guide over price, etc. Tel: 213-2706.

Japan Travel Bureau—tickets and information on domestic travel at various locations in Tokyo. They recommended their "Foreign Tourist Department" at Nittetsu Nihombashi Bldg. 3rd Fl., 1-13-1 Nihombashi, Chūō-ku. Tel: 276-7771. Hrs: 9:30 a.m.-5:30 p.m., closed Sun. & Hols. [M-9]

Japan National Tourist Organization "JNTO"—For any information on Japan. Tokyo Kōtsū Kaikan Bldg., 2-10-1 Yūrakuchō, Chiyoda-ku. Tel: 216-1901. Hrs: 9:20 a.m.-5:30 p.m. (until 12:30 p.m. on Sat.), closed Sun. & Hols. [M-8]

LANGUAGE

LANGUAGE

Japanese may not be the easiest language to learn for the average English speaker, but it could well be the most gratifying. Where else in the world could just one sentence constructed with merely passable fluency bring such accolades from the natives regarding the speaker's linguistic genius? Despite their self-admitted, though gradually disappearing, complex towards Westerners, many Japanese still remain convinced that their language is impenetrable to *gaijin* (foreigners). Many are the stories one hears of tall blue-eyed Westerners attempting to have conversations with locals in perfect Japanese, only to be rebuffed with "Sorry, I don't understand English".

In fact, in many situations you can get away with using the myriad of English and other foreign words that the Japanese continue to import into their language at an alarming rate. Don't, however, forget that even borrowed words must be pronounced in the Japanese way, or your attempts will simply be met with blank stares.

PRONUNCIATION

Correct pronunciation is the key to being understood, and its importance cannot be stressed too much. Japanese, being purely phonetic, is quite an easy language to pronounce. As an initial guide, you can think of the vowels as being like Spanish, and the consonants Italian.

It is impossible to give correct vowel equivalents in English for Americans, but for speakers of standard British English they go something like this:

Short Vowels

a — as the u in cup
e — as the e in pen
i — as the ee in feet, but clipped shorter
o — as the o in song
u — as the oo in book, but often so short as to be almost unpronounced

Long Vowels

ā — as the a in father
ē — as the ai in air
ī — as the ee in feet
ō — as the ou in thought
ū — as the u in flute

In other words, a long vowel has the same quality as a doubled short vowel. Combinations of vowels also adhere absolutely to the above pronunciation rules. The letter 'y' in Japanese is treated as a consonant, and is never pronounced like the English 'eye', which would be 'ai'.

Consonants

The pronunciation of Japanese consonants never varies. For example, 'g' is always as in game, never as in gin. Most consonants conform fairly well to the same sounds in English, with the following notable differences:

f — halfway between f and h
l/r — as is well known Japanese makes no distinction. In fact the sound is a mixture of the two with a hint of d thrown in for good measure.
v — pronounced b

Because Japanese is a syllabic language, in theory consonants are always broken up by vowels (with the exception of n, which can be followed by another consonant). However, in the spoken language double consonants do exist, and must be given double value. *Motto* (more) should be approached like 'got to' and not 'grotto'.

Non-Existent Sounds

si —	becomes *shi*
ti —	becomes *chi*, or sometimes *tei*
tu —	becomes *tsu*
th —	usually pronounced s (thing=*shingu*) or z (that=*zatto*)
di/zi —	becomes *ji* (also, this=*jisu*)
w —	except *wa*. Otherwise becomes u. Woman=*ūman*
y —	before *i* or *e*, when it becomes i. Yen=*en*; yellow=*ierō*

INTONATION

Unlike English, or most western languages for that matter, Japanese has very little rise and fall in pitch. Its flatness may be disconcerting at first, but as with pronunciation this can be crucial to being understood. Take the word *hashi*, which written with different but identical sounding characters can mean bridge, edge or chopsticks. Of course you don't eat your rice with a bridge, and nine times out of ten context will tell you which meaning is intended, but each of these words is pitched very slightly differently, albeit practically flat. Even in words which combine long and short vowels (e.g. Kyōto), the stress is normally not on the long vowel, but evenly distributed. It is worth noting, though, that the short 'i' and 'u' are all but unpronounced in certain circumstances. For example the famous Japanese percussionist Yamashita Tsutomu used to romanize his name Yamash'ta Stomu. Stomu should probably have been trimmed down to just Stom to give Westerners an accurate idea of the usual Japanese pronunciation.

ORIGIN OF *KANJI*

Kanji, or Chinese characters, were imported in the 6th century, a period when Japan went overboard about mainland culture, including not only Buddhism but also art and music. Used to write a language bearing no similarity to Chinese, most characters have at least two possible readings when used in Japanese. One is an approximation of the original Chinese pronunciation of the 6th century, and one a native Japanese word which was written with that character. This complexity is possibly the biggest obstacle to learning Japanese, and even the locals regularly misread *kanji*. After you have learned several hundred (some 2,000 odd are approved by the government for teaching in school and use in the press) you begin to develop an ability to guess the Chinese derived reading. The native readings, however, just have to be learned by heart.

Taking the numbers one to ten as an example may give you some idea of the difference:

	Chinese derived reading	Native Japanese reading
1	ichi	hitotsu
2	ni	futatsu
3	san	mittsu
4*	shi	yottsu
5	go	itsutsu
6	roku	muttsu
7**	shichi	nanatsu
8	hachi	yattsu
9	ku (or kyū)	kokonotsu
10	jū	to

*often pronounced yon (Japanese way) because shi means death
**often pronounced nana (because shichi is awkward?)

When counting aloud—one, two, three....—the Chinese derived readings are used. If on the other hand you are in a shop and want three of an object whose name you don't know in Japanese, you would point to it and say *mittsu kudasai*. Actually, there are hundreds of different ways to count, using generic numerators indicating the shape or type of thing being counted. However, since these will probably only increase your confusion, they can safely be left out here.

While on the subject of counting, please remember that Japanese has no plural form. Under no circumstances should an 's' ever be tagged on to a Japanese word to indicate more than one. It not only sounds hideous, but is yet another way to invite misunderstanding.

HIRAGANA AND *KATAKANA*

In addition to *kanji*, Japanese has two sets (wouldn't you know it!) of *kana*, or phonetic syllabic signs. In comparison with *kanji* both are almost alphabetic in their simplicity. Although a native script of sorts did exist before the importation of *kanji*, the Chinese characters were used to standardize Japanese writing. However, since it was extremely unwieldy to use this pictorial script to represent sounds in Japanese, a set of angular looking, purely phonetic abbreviations called *katakana* were developed in the early *Heian* period.

Parallel to this, *hiragana*, an identically pronounced but visually more flowing phonetic system, was adapted from the more calligraphic style of *kanji*.

Today *katakana* is used almost exclusively for rendering foreign words into Japanese, as well as for telegrams and governmental edicts. *Hiragana* is much more widely used, for writing common words, and for verb endings etc. (in conjunction with kanji).

The *kana* 'alphabet' when romanized looks like this (H=*hiragana*, K=*katakana*).

	H	K		H	K		H	K		H	K		H	K
a	あ	ア	i	い	イ	u	う	ウ	e	え	エ	o	お	オ
ka	か	カ	ki	き	キ	ku	く	ク	ke	け	ケ	ko	こ	コ
sa	さ	サ	shi	し	シ	su	す	ス	se	せ	セ	so	そ	ソ
ta	た	タ	chi	ち	チ	tsu	つ	ツ	te	て	テ	to	と	ト
na	な	ナ	ni	に	ニ	nu	ぬ	ヌ	ne	ね	ネ	no	の	ノ
ha	は	ハ	hi	ひ	ヒ	fu	ふ	フ	he	へ	ヘ	ho	ほ	ホ
ma	ま	マ	mi	み	ミ	mu	む	ム	me	め	メ	mo	も	モ
ya	や	ヤ				yu	ゆ	ユ				yo	よ	ヨ
ra	ら	ラ	ri	り	リ	ru	る	ル	re	れ	レ	ro	ろ	ロ
wa	わ	ワ	(wi)	ゐ	ヰ				(we)	ゑ	エ	wo	を	ヲ
n	ん	ン												

(*wi*) and (*we*) are in parentheses because, representing sounds that have ceased to exist in Japanese, they have fallen out of usage. The above table includes all the written forms you will need to know to write any sound in Japanese. In addition the *ka*, *sa*, *ta* and *ha* rows can be 'voiced' to produce *ga*, *za*, *da* and *ba* etc., by adding ˝ (e.g. が). Similarly *ha* becomes *pa* by adding ° (ぱ).

Learning *kanji* is obviously a time consuming job, but with a little application *hiragana* and *katakana* can be mastered in the space of a couple of weeks, and they will help you enormously.

RESPECT/POLITE LANGUAGE (*KEIGO*)

Respect language is one of the most difficult aspects of the Japanese language to master. Even young Japanese have a hard time with it. When speaking Japanese, the words you use can differ considerably depending on your relative status and/or familiarity with regard to the person you are talking to.

We don't suggest that you attempt to come to grips with *keigo*, but it is just as well to be aware of its existence. Even between men and women, language can differ greatly, especially when speaking politely.

In Japanese, personal pronouns such as I and you are often omitted, but the range of interchangeable words available is quite astonishing. Normally, I is *watashi* for women, and *boku* or *ore* for men, but when being deferential both become *watakushi*. The verb to go is *iku*, which goes through *ikimasu* and *mairimasu*, to *ukagaimasu*, as you lower your status.

However, don't worry about any of this too much. If anything, err on the impolite side. As long as your pronunciation is good and clear, and your attitude is not patronizing, no one is going to be offended.

As we said at the beginning of this section, you can often get by using English words pronounced in the Japanese way. Just remember that consonants are always to be followed by vowels, and speak slowly. You'll be surprised how often the message will get through. *"Ekusukyūzu mī, ai donto nō hoea ai amu. Kyan yū purīzu teru mī hau tsū fuaindo za posuto ofuisu?* Make any sense? Try this: "Excuse me, I don't know where I am, can you please tell me how to find the post office?" And please don't think that this example is in any way extreme!

COMMON WORDS AND PHRASES
Gairaigo—Imported Words

OK, getting back to those borrowed words from foreign languages, here is a sample list of some of the more frequently used. Have fun!

- **Food/Drink**

hors d'oeuvres	*ōdoburu*
sandwich	*sando-itchi* (*sando* for short)
coffee	*kōhī*
bread	*pan* (from Portuguese)
stew	*shichū*
curry and rice	*karē-raisu*
coke	*kōra* (generic term)
hamburger (with bun)	*hanbāgā*
hamburger (patty)	*hanbāgu* (*sutēki*)
beer	*bīru*
hot chocolate	*kokoa*
on the rocks	*onzarokku* (or just *rokku*)

- **Shopping**

cigarettes	*tabako* (tobacco)
shirt	*shatsu*
radio/cassette player	*rajikase*
radio	*rajio*
television	*terebi*
personal computer	*pasokon*
office computer	*ofukon*
word processor	*wāpuro*
video	*bideo*
record	*rekōdo*
glass (for drinking)	*gurasu*

glass (windows etc.)	*garasu*
panty hose	*pansuto* (panty stockings)

- **Cars**

stall	*ensuto* (engine stop)
flat tyre	*panku* (puncture)
wheel	*hoiru*

- **Names and places**

Hollywood	*Hariuddo*
Beatles	*Bītoruzu*
England/Britain	*Igirisu*
Vienna	*Uīn*
Bach	*Bahha*
Van Gogh	*Gohho*
Russia	*Roshiya*
Prague	*Puraha*
Texas	*Tekisasu*
Graham (man's name)	*Gurahamu*

- **Others**

Women's Lib	*Ūman ribu*
spaghetti western	*makaroni uesutan*
film	*fuirumu*
hotel	*hoteru*
building	*biru*
strike (industrial etc.)	*sutoraiki* (*suto* for short)
wage rise	*bea* (from 'base-up'?!)
bucket	*baketsu*
earth	*āsu*
platform (trains etc.)	*hōmu*
temporary work	*arubaito* (*baito* for short—taken from German 'arbeit')
mass communications	*masukomi*
table	*tēburu*
door	*doa*
center	*sentā*
studio	*sutajio*
artist's studio	*atorie* (from French 'atelier')
petit(e)	*puchi* (!)
stadium	*sutajiamu*
almond	*āmondo*
Almond (chain of coffee shops, of which Roppongi branch is a major meeting place)	*Amando* (remember this to tell taxi drivers)

freebie   sābisu (service)

Basic Vocabulary

Here is a collection of Japanese phrases that you should find useful. Don't forget about pronunciation though, or your efforts may be to no avail.

- **Greetings**

How do you do?	Hajimemashite
Good morning	Ohayō gozaimasu
Good day (from mid morning to late afternoon)	Konnichiwa (often pronounced 'chiwa')
Good evening	Kombanwa
Goodnight	Oyasumi nasai
Goodbye	Sayōnara
Excuse me (I'm sorry)	Gomen nasai or sumimasen
Excuse me (attracting attention)	Sumimasen
Thank you	Arigatō
Thank you very much	Dōmo arigatō
Don't mention it	Dō itashimashite
Please (go ahead)	Dōzo

- **General**

Yes (noting agreement)	Sō desu
Yes please	Onegai shimasu
No thank you	Kekkō desu
I don't want any	Irimasen
I've had enough	Mō ī desu
No (I disagree)	Chigaimasu

*Hai for yes and īe for no are usually given in phrase books, but are actually used mainly in situations where only a yes or no answer is expected. Hai is also used as polite confirmation that you have heard what the speaker is saying (or to indicate acceptance of an order), though not necessarily noting agreement with what has been said.

My name is _____	_____ to īmasu
Do you speak English (Japanese)?	Eigo (Nihongo) wakarimasu ka?
I don't understand	Wakarimasen
I understand	Wakarimasu
Where is _____ ?	_____ wa doko desu ka?
telephone	denwa
Hello (on phone)	Moshi-moshi
Is Fred there?	Fureddo imasu ka?
Just a moment please	Chotto matte (kudasai)

- **Counting** (see previous part for numbers one to ten)
*above 1,000 the next unit is 10,000. After that units proceed in multiples of 10,000

eleven	jūichi
twelve	jūni
(etc. to) twenty	nijū
thirty	sanjū
forty	yonjū
(etc. to) 100	hyaku
200	nihyaku
300	sambyaku
700	nanahyaku
1,000	sen
2,000	nisen
3,000	sanzen
7,000	nanasen
10,000	ichiman
20,000	niman
100,000	jūman
one million	hyakuman
100 million	ichioku

- **Time**

one o'clock	ichi-ji
four o'clock	yo-ji
half past seven	shichi-ji han
9:10 (20)	kuji-jippun (nijippun)
10:15 (45)	jūji-jūgofun (yonjūgofun)

*If you can't be bothered to work it out, just write it down in figures!

What time is it?	Ima nanji desu ka?
daytime	hiruma
night	yoru
now	ima
today	kyō
tomorrow	ashita
the day after tomorrow	asatte
yesterday	kinō
the day before yesterday	ototoi
Sunday	Nichiyōbi
Monday	Getsuyōbi
Tuesday	Kayōbi
Wednesday	Suiyōbi

Thursday	*Mokuyōbi*
Friday	*Kin'yōbi*
Saturday	*Doyōbi*
this week	*konshū*
last week	*senshū*
next week	*raishū*
one week	*isshūkan*
two weeks	*nishūkan*
January	*Ichi-gatsu*
February	*Ni-gatsu*
April	*Shi-gatsu*
July	*Shichi-gatsu*
October	*Jū-gatsu*
December	*Jūni-gatsu*

*Months are quite logical—dates not so. They have been omitted here intentionally.

Later	*Ato de*
I'll come back later	*Ato de kimasu*
an hour ago	*ichiji-kan mae*

- **Shopping**

How much is it?	*Ikura desu ka?*
How much for all these?	*Zembu de ikura?*
Do you have a larger (smaller) size?	*Motto ōkī (chīsai) no wa arimasu ka?*
What other colours do you have?	*Hoka ni, donna iro ga arimasu ka?*
I'll (just) take this	*Kore (dake) kudasai*
Do you have _____ ?	_____ *wa arimasu ka?*

- **Restaurants**

I'd like to make a reservation	*Yoyaku onegai shimasu*
one person	*hitori*
two people	*futari*
three people	*sannin*
four people	*yonin*
five people	*gonin*
six people	*rokunin*
seven people	*shichinin*
ten people	*jūnin*
We'd like the course for ____ yen	____ *en no kōsu de onegai shimasu*
The name is _____	*Namae wa* _____ *desu*
rice wine	*osake*
cold (only for *sake*)	*hiya*

hot (only for *sake*)	*atsukan*
sake flask	*tokkuri* or *ochōshi*
sake cup	*ochoko*
one flask (or bottle for other drinks)	*ippon*
two flasks	*nihon*
one cup (or glass)	*ippai*
two cups	*nihai*
I don't drink	*nomemasen*
May I have some tea (water) please?	*Ocha (omizu) kudasai*
One more flask of *sake*	*Osake mō ippon*
tastes good	*oishī*
tastes bad	*mazui*
The check (bill) please	*Okanjō onegai shimasu*
That was a lovely meal, thank you	*Gochisō-sama*

• **Hotel**

Have you got a room?	*Heya aiteimasu ka?*
How much with tax?	*Zeikomi de ikura desuka?*
Until _____	_____ *made*

• **Travelling**

taxi	*takushī*
airport	*kūkō*
station	*eki*
ticket (train)	*kippu*
ticket (plane)	*kōkūken*
map	*chizu*
Does this train go to Shinjuku?	*Shinjuku wa kore de ī desu ka?*
Which platform for the train to _____ ?	_____ *yuki wa nanban sen desu ka?*
Where is the entrance (exit)?	*Iriguchi (deguchi) wa doko desu ka?*
north	*kita*
south	*minami*
east	*higashi*
west	*nishi*
central exit	*chūō-guchi*
right	*migi*
left	*hidari*

straight on	*massugu*
I want to go here (pointing at map etc.)	*Koko e ikitai*
Can I walk there?	*Aruite ikemasu ka?*

The above is only a small selection, and any selection is going to be inadequate. If you intend to stay you will probably be buying dictionaries and/or textbooks anyway, or even taking a language course. Thousands of foreigners learn Japanese these days, some very well. If your interest is a sincere one you will find that even a superficial knowledge of Japanese will broaden your horizons tremendously. *Gambatte kudasai* (good luck!).

APPENDIX

APPENDIX

CALENDAR

Festivals, or *matsuri*, have been an integral part of Japanese life for centuries. Tied to *Shintō* religious beliefs, festivals are like huge community parties given in honor of the local god. *Matsuri* are multi-function events. The purpose is to give thanks, ask for future favors and protection from misfortune, to celebrate the joy of life and promote group solidarity.

Japan was traditionally an agricultural society, and many festivals were rituals connected with planting and harvest seasons in the spring and autumn. In cities, the major festival time was the summer, being a season of frequent plagues and epidemics in the crowded urban areas. Though the original purpose of most festivals is now often forgotten, *matsuri* are still joyous, occasionally raucous, celebrations. Hundreds of thousands of people turn out for the more famous ones, while the small neighborhood festivals are more casual, family affairs.

Flower viewing seasons have also been included in the calendar. *Edo* period guides to the city listed the best spots for viewing the various seasonal attractions; where to view snow, cherry blossoms, fireflies, or autumn grasses. Much of the *Edo* scenery has disappeared, but a few of the famous sites have survived. We've included as many as possible.

The festivals listed in the calendar represent only a fraction of the hundreds held in and around the city. Because many festivals correspond to the lunar calendar, dates vary from year to year. The local tourist publications and TIC will usually have specific information on such upcoming events. A few of the temples, shrines and gardens listed in this section are not covered elsewhere in the book or on the maps. In such cases we have listed the nearest station, but for further information please ask TIC. All other locations are listed in the Sightseeing

Chapter under the appropriate headings.

January :

1   **Ganjitsu**—New Year's Day (National Holiday).

From the stroke of midnight through the first few days of the year, people visit Buddhist Temples and *Shintō* Shrines to pray for good fortune during the coming year. It's great fun to go at midnight, bonfires are built and stalls sell *amazake*—sweet *sake*, food, astrology books, and *hamaya*—good luck arrows. It's the only night of the year that the trains and subways don't stop.

The most popular places to visit are: **Meiji Shrine, Sensōji Temple, Yasukuni Shrine, Hie Shrine** and **Kanda Myōjin Shrine.**

1-7   **Shichi Fukujin Meguri**—Pilgrimage to the "Seven Gods of Good Fortune". Since the late *Edo* period people have spent the first week of the New Year visiting the shrines of the seven gods of Good Fortune. There are several "courses" you can take, but the most popular is along the Sumida River. Each of the temples customarily gives away a small image of the god.
(1) **Tamonji Temple**—for *Bishamonten*, the god of treasure. (2) **Shirahige Shrine**—for *Jurōjin*, god of longevity. (3) **Mukōjima Hyakkaen Garden**—for *Fukurokuju*, god of wealth and longevity. (4) **Chōmeiji** Temple—for *Benzaiten*, goddess of fortune. (5) **Kōfukuji Temple**—for *Hoteison*, god of good fortune. (6) **Mimeguri Shrine**—for *Ebisu*, god of commerce and wealth, and *Daikokuten*, god of wealth.

2   **Kōkyo Ippan Sanga**—Visit to the Imperial Palace. One of two times during the year that the Emperor and Empress appear before the people in the inner gardens of the palace. Enter by the **Nijūbashi Bridge**. 9 a.m.-3:30 p.m. (Nijūbashimae station/Chiyoda line) [M-10]

6   **Dezomeshiki**—Grand Parade of Fire Brigades. Held since the *Edo* period, men in traditional firefighter's uniforms perform acrobatic stunts on tall ladders. The parade is held in **Chūō-dōri hiroba** in Harumi from 10 a.m.

8   **Dondo Yaki**—A bonfire is built from the pine and straw New Year's decorations in a rite called "*Dondo-yaki*" to pray for good fortune in the coming year. Gathering around the fire, children beat the ground with bamboo stakes shouting "*Dondoya*". When the fire dies down, pounded rice cakes "*mochi*" are roasted on the stakes and eaten to insure good health during the year. Held 12 noon-3 p.m. at **Torigoe Shrine** (Kuramae station/Toei Asakusa line). [M-24]

2nd Sun.   **Kagami-Biraki**—This ceremony brings the New Year's festivities to an end. *Kagami-mochi*, a round two layer rice cake used as an offering to the gods, is cut and eaten in a red-bean soup called "*oshiruko*". This is usually done in people's homes, but a large ceremony is held at the **Kōdōkan Jūdō Hall**. After a *Jūdō* match, a *Shintō* priest cuts an enormous *kagami-mochi* which is then mixed in the *oshiruko* soup and served to the audience. The ceremony starts at 10 a.m. [M-30]

15   **Seijin no Hi**—Adult's Day (National Holiday).

A day to honor all 20 year olds, who are now legally permitted to drink and smoke. It is one of the rare occasions that young women wear *kimono* these days. At **Meiji Shrine** a traditional bow and arrow shooting ceremony is performed by the *Ogasawara* school of "classical" etiquette (based on *Bushi-dō*). The ceremony called *Momoteshiki* is held on the grass near the Hōmotsukan at Meiji Shrine from 1 p.m. [M-4]

Mid Jan.

Hatsubasho—The 1st *Sumō* Tournament of the year is held for 15 days at the new **Kokugikan**. [M-24]

February :
3 or 4

Setsubun—Bean Throwing Ceremony. To purify the home against potential evil, people scatter roasted beans from inside to out shouting *"Oni wa soto"* (Go out, devils!) and from outside in *"Fuku wa uchi"* (Come in good luck). The ceremony is also held at temples and shrines, where famous personalities partake in the festivities. Ceremonies are held at **Kanda Shrine**, **Zōjōji Temple**, **Hie Shrine**. At **Sensōji Temple**, in addition to the bean throwing, a classical dance called *"Fukuju-no-Mai"*—representing the dance of the seven gods of fortune before a treasure ship is also performed. (Ask TIC about time). At **Nishiarai Daishi Temple** a memorial for *Daruma* (see "Daruma Ichi" on March 3-4) that brought good fortune to the owners during the previous year is held where nearly a hundred thousand *Daruma* are burned while Buddhist sutras are chanted. The *Daruma* service starts from 11 a.m., and the bean throwing from 3 p.m.

Early February

Tako-Ichi—Kite Fair. Small kites called *Yakkodako* in the shape of a man, are sold as fire-prevention charms for the home. At **Ōji Inari Shrine** 10 a.m.-7 p.m. (Ōji station/Keihin Tōhoku line).

8

Hari-kuyō—A memorial service for pins and needles used and broken during the previous year. A custom since the *Edo* period, women bring the pins and needles to the shrine and "bury" them in radishes, *tōfu*, etc. Held at Awashimadō in the precincts of **Sensōji Temple**. [M-12]

11

Kenkoku Kinen no Hi—National Foundation Day (National Holiday).

14

Valentine's Day—with an unusual Japanese twist. Only girls give to boys, and only chocolate. A boon for candy manufacturers, the chocolates go on sale at least one month before.

25-Mar.15

Shiraume-Matsuri—Plum blossom viewing Festival. Held at **Yushima Tenjin Shrine**, one of the famous *Edo* period "plum-viewing" spots, the festival includes special ceremonies and entertainment on Saturday and Sunday during this period. [M-13, 16]

Plum blossom viewing is also good at **Jindai Shokubutsuen** (Take 51 or 58 bus from Mitaka station/Chūō line to Jindai Shokubutsuen)

March :
3

Hina-Matsuri—Girl's day. *Hina* dolls representing imperial court figures are displayed on tiered shelves at home and in some public places during this festival for little girls. From mid-Feb. to this day, a *hina* doll fair is held in Asakusabashi on Edo-dōri.

3-4

Daruma-Ichi—*Daruma* Fair. A *daruma* is a legless tumbler doll that is bought with blank eyes. A wish is made and one eye painted in. If the wish comes true, the other eye is painted. The dolls come in a wide range of sizes and are sold on the temple precincts during the festival. Over 200 thousand people usually attend. Held at **Jindaiji Temple** in Chōfu 9 a.m.-7 p.m.

18

Kinryū no Mai—Golden Dragon Dance. A 15 meter long, 75 kg. golden dragon is carried by young men through the temple precincts. The festival celebrates the discovery of the small golden statue of *Kannon* (Goddess of Mercy) by the three *Hinokuma* brothers in the Sumida River in 628 AD. The statue is now in **Sensōji Temple** where this festival is held. The dance is performed two or three times during the day. [M-12]

20   **Shumbun no Hi**—Vernal Equinox Day (National Holiday).

27-28   **Sentaikōjin Matsuri**—Festival for the Kitchen God. **Kaiunji Temple** is dedicated to the God who protects the kitchen. On the festival day, small images of the God in a miniature shrine are given away. It is said that when you receive this charm, you must return home without visiting anyone along the way. The festival is held 6 a.m.-5 p.m. (Aomonoyokochō station/Keihin Kyūkō line.)

April :
Early-Mid Apr.

Ohanami (Sakura)—Cherry Blossom Viewing. A major rite of spring, almost everyone in town turns out to frolic beneath the pink blossoms at one of the famous spots in the city. Festivities often last until late in the evening and involve singing, dancing and lots of *sake* drinking. The famous spots are: **Chidorigafuchi Park** along the palace moat [Map 17], **Yasukuni Shrine**, **Kōrakuen**, **Aoyama Bochi**. The two most lively spots are **Ueno Park** and **Sumida Park** in Asakusa along the Sumida River.

Mid-late Apr.

Ohanami (Yaezakura)—*Yae*-Cherry Blossom Viewing. A late blooming cherry to see if you missed the early ones. At **Shinjuku-Gyoen Garden**. Also *tsutsuji*—Azalea viewing at **Nezu Shrine**.

8   **Hana-Matsuri**—Birthday of Buddha. Commemorative services are held at a number of temples. Entertainment includes a *"Daimyō Gyōretsu"* or parade of Lords. At: **Gokokuji Temple** (Gokokuji station/Yūrakuchō line), **Sensōji Temple**, **Zōjōji Temple** and **Hommonji Temple** (Ikegami station/Tōkyū Ikegami line).

17   **Ueno Tōshōgū Taisai**—Tōshōgū Shrine is dedicated to *Tokugawa Ieyasu*, founder of the *Edo Samurai* Government, who is worshipped as a *Shintō* deity. Traditional music and dance are performed and ceremonies held in his honor. At **Tōshōgū Shrine** in Ueno Park from 10 a.m. [M-13]

29   **Tennō Tanjōbi**—The Emperor's Birthday (National Holiday). The Golden Week holiday starts from this day.

End of Apr.-Beg. of May

Ohanami (Fuji)—Wisteria Blossom Viewing. At **Kameido Tenjin Shrine**. [M-44] **Ohanami (Botan)**—Peony Viewing. At **Nishiarai Daishi Temple**. [M-46]

May :

3   **Kempō Kinembi**—Constitution Memorial Day (National Holiday).

5   **Kodomo no Hi**—Boy's Day (National Holiday).
Theoretically for all children, the emphasis is on the little boys who everyone hopes will grow-up big and strong like the carp. A symbol of strength and manhood, the carp banners *"koinobori"* are flown from homes where little boys live. *Samurai* dolls are also displayed in the house.

5	**Kurayami Matsuri**—This festival dates back over 1,800 years. Starting off with fireworks at 4 p.m., over 300 people carry *mikoshi* (portable shrines) through the streets. Things get pretty wild as people chant and push their way along. Much more energetic than your typical downtown festival, **Ōkunitama shrine** is slightly out of the way but worth the trip. It's 30-40 minutes outside Shinjuku in Fuchū on the Keiō Line.
5	**Suitengū Taisai**—A typical neighborhood type festival. Portable shrines are carried by adults and children. Festival music and dancing are performed, and street stalls set up. The festival is held at **Suitengū Shrine** in Ningyōchō, 8 a.m.-10 p.m. [M-23]
Mid May	**Kanda Matsuri**—The Kanda Festival, one of the three big *Edo* festivals, is held to commemorate the *Tokugawa* victory at *Sekigahara* in 1600. Over 70 portable shrines are paraded through the street, *geisha* perform classical dances, and a "*shishimai*"—a lion's mask dance is performed. The main festival is held every other year, the next one being in 1985. At **Kanda Shrine** for 3-4 days including a Sat. & Sun. near the 14th or 15th. [M-16]
Mid May	**Natsubasho**—The summer *Sumō* Tournament is held for 15 days at the **Kokugikan**. [M-24]
3rd Sat. and Sun.	**Sanja Matsuri**—Another of the three big *Edo* Festivals, this one in honor of the three fishermen who found the image of *Kannon* in the river. Lots of ritual dances, music, over 100 portable shrines, and huge crowds. At **Asakusa Shrine** next to Sensōji Temple. [M-12]
31-Jun.1	**Ofujisan Ueki Ichi**—Mt. Fuji Potted Plant Fair. The summer opening of Mt. Fuji for climbing has been celebrated since the *Edo* period. The mountain has a semi-religious connotation for the Japanese and climbing Fuji was something people tried to do once in their life. But for those with legitimate excuses for not climbing the real thing, a small replica of Fuji-san has been built since 1890 at **Sengen Shrine** in Asakusa to allow a symbolic "climb". Potted plants and flowers are also on sale at over 300 booths. Goldfish, wind chimes, and a good luck snake charm made of straw are other big items. At Sengen Shrine in Asakusa. (Asakusa station/ Ginza line, Toei Asakusa line)
June : **Fri.-Sun. in early Jun.**	**Kappa Matsuri**—A *Kappa* is a legendary water imp that looks something like a turtle with a plate on its head. The plate is full of water, and if the water runs out, the *Kappa*, known for being mischievous, loses his power. In this festival, portable shrines are carried out into the waters of Tokyo Bay by young men. A good show of macho energy. At **Ebara Shrine** from noon on Sunday. (Shimbaba Station/Keihin Kyūkō line)
2nd Sun.	**Torigoe Jinja Taisai**—A night time festival, where the heaviest portable shrine in Tokyo (4 tons) is carried around the streets by lantern light. At **Torigoe Shrine** 7 a.m.-9 p.m. [M-24]
10-16	**Sannō Sai**—Another of the big *Edo* festivals festival. The is somewhat smaller now, with only 50 portable shrines and 200-300 street stalls. There is a "*gyōretsu*" a parade of people in traditional costume, folk dancing, and tea ceremony demonstrations. The "*gyōretsu*" is held on Saturday. At

Hie Shrine 9 a.m.-6 p.m. [M-6]

Mid Jun.   Ohanami (Shōbu)—Iris viewing. Best at **Horikiri Shōbuen** (Horikiri Shōbuen station/Keisei line) [M-45], the **Meiji Shrine Gyoen** and **Kōrakuen**.

July :

1   Suijō Matsuri—Water Festival. A group of festival boats travel down the **Sumida River** from Yanagi Bridge near the Torigoe Shrine to Tokyo Bay. On arriving at the bay, "katashiro", small paper dolls are thrown into the sea by Shintō priests. The katashiro carry away bad luck and misfortune. Held at **Torigoe Shrine**. [M-24]

6-8   Asagao-Ichi—Morning Glory Fair. In Edo, the morning glory was loved for its medicinal properties and for blooming only in the morning. For this fair, over 120 merchants set up stalls, many selling "the morning flower". At **Iriya Kishibojin**. (Iriya station/Hibiya line) [M-43]

7   Tanabata Matsuri—This festival celebrates the only day of the year that, according to ancient Chinese legend, the Weaver Princess (Vega) and her lover the Cowherd (Altair) can cross the Milky Way and meet. People write their wishes on strips of colored paper called tanzaku, hang them on bamboo branches, and float them down a river the next day.

9-10   Hōzuki-Ichi—Ground Cherry Fair. A visit to Sensōji Temple on the 10th of July is equal to 46,000 visits at other times. The main souvenir of the fair is Hōzuki, a ground cherry tree with red lantern-shaped blossoms. At **Sensōji Temple** from early morning to midnight both days. [M-12]

13-14   Tsukuda Bon Odori—A special Buddhist prayer-dance has been held here for 300 years as a memorial service to the spirits of the neighborhood's ancestors. The dance has been designated an "Intangible Cultural Asset." At **Tsukuda Itchōme** from 5:30 p.m. to 9 p.m. [M-25]

13-16   Obon—A summer festival when people return to their hometowns to make offerings and give prayers to the souls of departed ancestors. During this time Bon Odori folk dances can be seen all over town.

Last Sat. of Jul.
    Sumidagawa Hanabi Taikai—Sumida River Fireworks Display. Originally a festival to celebrate the summer "opening" of the river, the fireworks are the main thing today. The best place to watch is from between the **Kototoi Bridge** and the **Shirahige Bridge**, or at the **Komagata Bridge**, all in Asakusa. This is the biggest of Tokyo's fireworks displays, but from the end of July through the beginning of August there are nearly two dozen other displays throughout the city and in nearby suburbs. [M-12]

August :
Early-Mid Aug.
    Tokyo Takigi Nō—Two nō dramas and one kyōgen farce are performed by firelight in a memorial for the souls of those killed in World War II. It has been held since 1970. At **Hie Shrine** 5:30 p.m. to 8:30 p.m. Tickets for the performance are available one month in advance, or may be bought the day of the performance. [M-6]

3 days, including one Sun. near the 7th

Tsukudajima Sumiyoshi Jinja Matsuri—This major festival, held every three years, is famous for preserving *Edo* traditions. There is a dragon dance on the first day, on the second day portable shrines tour the neighborhood, and on the third day the whole neighborhood visits the shrine. The next one will be held in 1986. At **Sumiyoshi Shrine** [M-25].

3 days around the 15th

Fukagawa Hachiman Matsuri—Another the big *Edo* festival, 100 portable shrines are carried by porters who run 8 km. to the shrine while the crowd dashes water on them. *Hommatsuri* (a major festival) is held every three years, the next one in 1986. At **Tomioka Hachimangū Shrine**. [M-25]

16

Omen Kaburi—In a traditional event from the *Edo* period, twenty-five believers in Buddha cross a 65 meter bridge, wearing masks representing various Buddhist saints. The ceremony dramatizes the Buddhist teaching that *Amida* will come with 25 saints to escort the dying to the western paradise. Held every three years, the next one is in 1987. Performances are given three times a day (at 11 a.m., 2 p.m., 5 p.m.) at **Kuhombutsu Jōshin-ji Temple** [M-21].

25

Kameido Tenjin Matsuri—*Hommatsuri* is held every four years to propitiate the shrine's spirit. 200 *Shintō* priests parade in *Heian* costumes by lantern light. The next festival is in 1985. At **Kameido Tenjin Shrine**. [M-44]

September :
10-21

Dara Dara Matsuri—*Dara dara* means "long" in Japanese, this annual festival of the **Shiba Daijingū Shrine**, being unusually long, has been so named. A ginger market is set up and *chikibako* small boxes are special souvenirs. It's said that if you put *chikibako* in a chest of drawers, you will have more *kimono*. The festival is especially popular the 13th-17th. The major festival is held every other year, the next one in 1986. At Shiba Daijingū Shrine from noon to 9 p.m. [M-11]

15

Keirō no Hi—Respect for the Aged Day (National Holiday).

Mid Sep.

Akibasho—Autumn *Sumō* Tournament. The last of the year in Tokyo, held at the **Kokugikan**. [M-24]

21

Nezugongen Matsuri—Another famous *Edo* period festival, a portable shrine from that period is still carried around the neighborhood. *Shintō* music and dance are performed among other things. A very popular festival. The *Edo* period shrine is presented only every other year, next will be 1986. At **Nezu Shrine**.

23

Shūbun no Hi—Autumnal Equinox Day (National Holiday).

25

Ningyō-Kuyō—During this ceremony, childless couples make an offering of dolls to the *Kannon* Goddess of Mercy and pray that the goddess bless them with children. Connected with this ceremony is a memorial service for old and worn-out dolls given to the temple (people don't like to throw them away). The dolls are burned in a huge pile and sutras are chanted for them. At **Kiyomizudō Temple** in Ueno Park 2 p.m.-3:30 p.m. [M-13]

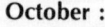

October :
1st Sat. and Sun.

Furusato Tokyo Matsuri—Hometown Tokyo Festival. A huge city-wide festival to celebrate "Metropolitan Citizen's Day" on the 1st of the month. The Miss Tokyo Contest is held at this time, as well as a vast range of traditional cultural events, including folk and *Shintō* dancing, and music. A large market is set up with folkcraft, and food products from all over Japan. At **Hibiya park**, **Ueno park**, **Sensōji Temple** and many other places in Tokyo.

1-Nov.15	**Geijutsu Sai**—A major city-wide cultural festival, see Entertainment section.
1st Sat.	**Kiba no Kakunori**—Young men in *Edo* period worker's costumes perform acrobatic stunts on floating timbers, just like the real lumber workers used to do in the *Edo* period. At **Kurofune Bridge**. (Monzennakachō station/Tōzai line)
1st Sat.	**Fukagawa no Chikaramochi**—Another event from the *Edo* period, this one was for carriers of rice bags and *sake* casks to show their strength and ability. Now, strong young men perform acrobatics to traditional *Edo* music. At **Rinkai Park**. (Monzennakachō station/Tōzai line)
10	**Taiiku no Hi**—Health-Sports Day (National Holiday).
Mid-Late Oct.	**Ohanami (Kiku)**—Chrysanthemum Viewing. Displays of chrysanthemums, many trained in shapes like dolls, are given at various spots around the city. Best are: **Yasukuni Shrine**, **Sensōji Temple**, from the end of October at **Kōrakuen**, from the beginning of November at **Hibiya Park** and **Meiji Shrine**.
11-13	**Oeshiki**—All temples of the *Nichiren* sect of Buddhism hold a memorial service in commemoration of the death of founder *Nichiren*. The main temple Hommonji at Ikegami (where *Nichiren* died in 1282) has the largest festival of all. On the night of the 12th *Nichiren* followers chant prayers and march to the temple carrying lanterns and huge paper flower decorations. At **Ikegami Hommonji Temple**. (Ikegami station/Tōkyū Ikegami line)
16-18	**Kishibojin Sai**—A lighted lantern service is held once a year for *Kishibojin*, the goddess of children. A popular souvenir is a folk toy called "*Susukimimizuku*", a small horned owl made of straw. At **Soshigaya Kishibojin Temple** 9 a.m. to 11 p.m. (Kishibojimmae station/Toden Arakawa line)
27-Nov.3	**Kanda Furuhon-Ichi**—Kanda Secondhand Book Fair. Over a million secondhand books are put on sale at 30% off along the streets of the Kanda old book shop district. At **Jimbōchō** Intersection.
30-Nov.3	**Meiji Reidaisai**—In commemoration of the November 3rd Birthday of the Meiji Emperor, classical court dance and music (*bugaku* and *kagura*), and classic martial arts are performed. Two special archery events are given, one on horseback with the riders in classical costumes. Other events include of *nō* drama and martial arts. At **Meiji Shrine**. [M-4]

November :

3	**Bunka no Hi**—Culture Day (National Holiday).
	Tori no Ichi—Cock Festival. According to legend, the festival started when

a group of samurai who had offered a kumade (bamboo rake) to the shrine, returned to give thanks for their victory. Since that time, the kumade has been considered a bringer of good luck. At the fair, bargaining for the rakes is customary, as is noisy clapping by the two parties when a price is finally agreed upon. At Asakusa **Ōtori Shrine**. [M-43] The date of this fair is determined by the Chinese Calendar and varies each year. Check with TIC for exact dates.

15 Shichi-Go-San—Three-Five-Seven. This is a ceremony for five year old boys and three or seven year old girls. The children, usually dressed in full kimono, are taken to visit the shrines. At: **Meiji Shrine, Yasukuni Shrine, Kanda Shrine, Asakusa Shrine** and **Hie Shrine**.

23 Kinrō Kansha no Hi—Labor Thanksgiving Day (National Holiday).

December :
14 Gishi Sai—A memorial service for the famous 47 Rōnin is performed at the **Sengakuji Temple** where they were buried after being forced to commit seppuku for avenging the death of their master. It was on this day in 1702 that they killed Kira Kōzukenosuke in revenge. At Sengakuji Temple 7 a.m.-11 p.m. [M-37]

15-16 Boro-Ichi—Trash Market. This fair has a history of over 400 years. About 600 booths are set up selling mainly nursery trees and plants, but also New Year's decorations and daily necessities, used clothing, and farm tools. At **Boro-ichi** Street 9 a.m.-10 p.m. (Setagaya station/Tōkyū Setagaya line)

17-19 Hagoita-Ichi—Battledore Fair. Traditional battledores hagoita are sold in a variety of sizes with prices ranging from ¥500 to ¥300,000. At **Sensōji Temple** 8 a.m.-2 a.m. [M-12]

Mid-Late Dec.
Gasa-Ichi—This market sells New Year's decorations made of pine, bamboo, and rice-straw ropes. At **Sensōji Temple** from early morning to midnight. [M-12]

31 Joya no Kane—At the stroke of midnight, on the last day of the year, every temple bell throughout the country begins to toll simultaneously. The bells toll 108 times to clear us of our 108 evil human passions. The general public are allowed to strike the bells at the **Zojōji Temple** and the **Kan'eiji Temple**.

CHRONOLOGICAL TABLE
150,000BC **PRECERAMIC CULTURE**

7,000-300BC **JŌMON PERIOD**—Jōmon unglazed pottery. Hunting and gathering society.

300BC-AD300 **YAYOI PERIOD**—Introduction of rice cultivation, bronze then iron, probably from China via Korea.

APPENDIX 283

AD300-710   **YAMATO PERIOD**—The country is ruled by warring clans. The Yamato clan takes control around AD400. The early Yamato state rulers were the legendary ancestors of Japan's Imperial Family

538 (or 552)   Buddhism and Chinese writing introduced from Korea.
593-622   Imperial regent Prince Shōtoku Taishi promotes Buddhism and Chinese based social and political reforms.
630   1st official embassy to T'ang China
645   Taika Coup D'Etat. The Soga Family, having ruled behind the throne since 587, loses power to a coalition of influential families.

710-784   **NARA PERIOD**—1st permanent capital built in Nara on the Chinese model. Esoteric Buddhism influences the arts. The 1st official histories written: "Kojiki" (Record of Ancient Things, 712), and "Nihon Shoki" (Chronicles of Japan, 720). Poetry is compiled in "Man'yōshū" (759).

781-   Buddhist monasteries become a powerful threat to the Imperial Court, Nara is abandoned.

794-1185   **HEIAN PERIOD**—The capital is moved to Heian-kyō (present day Kyōto) and the great age of Imperial Court culture begins. In the later half of the period, Japanese arts and culture begin to develop independently of the formerly pervasive Chinese influence. Native writing scripts, *hiragana* and *katakana* come into use.

850-1160   The Fujiwara Family (of noble class) dominates the court, through intermarriage with the royal family and a series of "regencies".
941   The court, intent on its pursuit of the arts, gradually loses control of the provinces to increasingly powerful provincial military families.
~1000~   Writing of the "Makura no Sōshi" (Pillow Book) by Sei Shōnagon.
~1013~   Writing of the literary classic "Genji Monogatari" (Tale of Genji) by Lady Murasaki Shikibu.
1167   The provincial Taira Family rises to power. Taira-no Kiyomori, the family head, becomes Grand Minister and dominates the Kyōto Court.
1180-85   Gempei War—started by a dispute over Imperial succession, becomes a struggle between the Taira and Minamoto military families for political control of the country. The Taira are defeated in 1185 by Minamoto forces under their leader Yoritomo.

1185-1333   **KAMAKURA PERIOD**—Minamoto Yoritomo establishes a military (*bushi* or *samurai*) government in Kamakura near Tokyo. Court rule is ended, and Japan enters an age of feudal society. *Bushi* ethics and the "sword cult" become important, Zen Buddhism influences the arts. The tea ceremony rises in popularity.

1192   Title of *Shōgun* granted to Minamoto Yoritomo.
1203   After the death of Yoritomo, the Hōjō Family rules as regents to the shogunate.

1274 & 81	The Mongol Invasions, both repelled by timely typhoons.
1333	A power struggle between the senior and junior branches of the Imperial Family results in the Ashikaga Family's rise to power as supporters of the retired emperor Godaigo (senior branch).
1334	Kemmu Restoration. Godaigo takes Kyōto. The Hōjō Family loses power and the Kamakura Shogunate is ended as Godaigo reestablishes Imperial rule.

1334-95 NAMBOKUCHŌ PERIOD—the succession dispute continues with rival North and South courts.

1392-1573 MUROMACHI PERIOD—Control of the government taken from Godaigo by Ashikaga Takauji, who takes the title of *shōgun* and rules from Kyōto. The central government remains weak and the provinces under the control of constantly warring military rulers. The arts flourish as *bushi* and Court aesthetics are blended. *Nō* and *kyōgen* dramatic forms are developed, Zen and the tea ceremony grow in importance and influence the arts of flower arranging, pottery, calligraphy, etc. *Suibokuga* (monochrome ink painting) becomes popular.

1457	Ōta Dōkan, a minor provincial *daimyō*, builds the first Edo Castle.
1467-77	Ōnin War—over succession in the shogunate splits the Ashikaga following into factions. Fighting levels half the city of Kyōto, and destroys the power of the shogunate. A stage of decentralized feudalism begins, with the country divided into small domains, tightly controlled by provincial military leaders, the later *daimyō* lords. The court in Kyōto loses its source of land income, and sinks into poverty.
1543	The appearance of the Portuguese and the introduction of Christianity and western firearms. As trade develops and the use of firearms increases, the former balance of land-based wealth and power is disrupted. By the 16th century there is a trend towards unification of the country as the powerful *daimyō* begin to expand their territory.

1573-98 AZUCHI-MOMOYAMA PERIOD—Civil war ends the Ashikaga rule. Under a series of powerful military leaders the country is reunified. Throughout Japan urbanized castle towns develop as the provincial *daimyō* consolidate their power. The arts become "Baroque" in style, with palaces adorned in gold, lacquer, and primary colors. Screen painting (often on a gold ground) in the Kanō school style fourishes.

1590	Toyotomi Hideyoshi completes the unification of Japan, rules from Ōsaka. Tokugawa Ieyasu is given the Lands of Musashi (present Kantō province) and Edo castle.
1582-98	Nationwide survey of the land—giving all rights to the overlord and registering the fields in the names of peasant cultivators. The survey institutionalizes the division of peasant and *samurai* and hastens the sepa-

	ration of the *samurai* from the land.
1592 & 97	Invasions of Korea by Hideyoshi. After his death, the troops withdraw from Korea.
1600	Battle of Sekigahara—a struggle for power after Hideyoshi's death, from which Tokugawa Ieyasu emerges victorious.

1603-1867 EDO PERIOD

—The capital is moved to Edo (present day Tokyo), and under the Tokugawa Family rule over 250 years of peace begins. The country is closed to outside influences, and strictly controlled in a division of classes with the *samurai* at the top, followed by the farmer, artisan, and the merchant. The *samurai* role changes from soldier to bureaucrat, the agrarian foundations of feudal society are undermined as the economy becomes money-based, and the merchant class becomes an economic power. Popular culture develops in the city pleasure quarters. *Bunraku, kabuki, ukiyoe* flourish.

1603	Tokugawa Ieyasu takes the title of *shōgun*.
1612	Official mint silver opened in Ginza.
1612-23	Mass persecution of Christians.
1639	Foreigners expelled (except a small colony of Dutch traders isolated on a southern island), the country closed, ban on Japanese travel abroad.
1657	Great Edo Fire.
1783-88	Crop failures throughout Japan lead to a period of great famine.
1804-29	Bunka-Bunsei Period—flourishing of the arts and popular culture in Edo.
1830-44	Tempō Era—domestic political and economic problems become serious, the government tries a series of reforms, but continues to fall into debt while the merchant class prospers.
1853	Arrival of Commodore Perry from the U.S., and the opening of two Japanese ports.
1867	The 15th and last *shōgun*, Tokugawa Yoshinobu, accepts a proposal returning power to the emperor but keeping the position of prime minister within the Tokugawa Family.
1867	The Meiji Emperor, Mutsuhito, is enthroned.

1868-1912 MEIJI PERIOD

—A coalition of powerful *daimyō* and nobility seizes power from the Tokugawa. With the Meiji Restoration administrative power is returned to the Emperor, the shogunate abolished, and the Tokugawa excluded from the new government. The Emperor is moved from Kyōto to Edo, now renamed Tokyo (the eastern capital). With national security threatened by the western powers, a program for rapid modernization and westernization is undertaken.

1868	Meiji Restoration.
1876	The wearing of swords is abolished.
1877	Satsuma Rebellion—*samurai* resistance to the new government is crushed.
1881-85	In preparation for constitutional government, the Diet and Cabinet sys-

	tem are established.
1889	Adoption of the new consitution.
1894-95	Sino-Japanese War—over control of Korea. Japan defeats China and annexes Taiwan.
1899	Treaties with foreign powers revised and extraterritoriality end.
1902	Anglo-Japanese alliance treaty.
1904-05	Russo-Japanese War—Japan wins the southern tip of Manchuria and the Sakhalin Islands.
1910	Annexation of Korea.
1912	Death of the Meiji Emperor.

1912-25   **TAISHŌ PERIOD**—Under the reign of the new Taishō emperor the problems of a rapidly modernizing society emerge. By the 1920's total population over 55 million, Tokyo over 2 million. Japan sides with the Allies during WWI and sits as victor at Versailles.

1914	Japan joins the Allies in WWI.
1923	Great Kantō Earthquake strikes in the Tokyo and Yokohama area, approximately 143,000 persons were killed by the earthquake, and the tidal wave and fires that followed.
1925	Universal Manhood Suffrage Bill made law, the suppressive Peace Preservation Law passed by the Diet.
1925	Death of the Taishō Emperor.

1926-   **SHŌWA PERIOD**—The military grows in power as the country swings from a fascination with the west and nationalist sediments rise. Japan becomes an imperialist power in Asia, and meets growing international disapproval. Siding with the Axis powers in WWII, the defeat and subsequent occupation of Japan by the U.S. forces find the country destroyed, and rebuilding following the pattern of a western capitalist economy.

1931	Manchurian Incident, Japan sets up a puppet state in China.
1933	Japan quits the League of Nations after being admonished for its actions in China.
1937	War with China breaks out again and becomes a part of WWII.
1940	Signing of the Tripartite Alliance with Germany and Italy.
1941	General Tōjō Hideki becomes Prime Minister. Attack on Pearl Harbor in Hawaii.
1945	The U.S. drops atomic bombs on Hiroshima and Nagasaki. Japan surrenders to the Allies.
1946	The Allied Occupation of Japan begins with Gen. MacArthur in charge.
1947	New Constitution made law, the Emperor loses his "divine" status. The Army, navy, and airforce are abolished and Japan renounces war forever.
1951	Peace Conference held in San Francisco. Japan signs a general peace treaty with 48 nations.
1952	Occupation of Japan ends.
1953	U.S.-Japan Security Treaty signed, permitting the U.S. to maintain military bases in Japan.
1956	Japan becomes a member of the United Nations.
1960	Mass demonstrations over the renewal of the Security. Treaty with the

	U.S.
1964	Tokyo Olympic Games.
1970	Ōsaka Expo, and the launching of Japan's first satellite.
1972	The U.S. returns Okinawa Islands to Japan. Winter Olympic Games held in Sapporo. Lockheed Scandal, Prime Minister Tanaka Kakuei resigns.
1983	Former Prime Minister Tanaka found guilty by court of bribery. Charges appealed.

STATISTICS

1) Area (1982)
    Tokyo   2,156.77 km^2
    *One quarter of the area is a national park, and the total includes the Izu and Ogasawara Islands. There are 23 ku (wards), 26 shi (cities), 7 machi (towns), and 8 mura (villages).

2) Population (March, 1984)
    Japan   119,310,000
            (Male 58,810,000/Female 60,500,000)
    Tokyo   11,503,000

3) Average size of households (Japan 1985)
    2.99 persons

4) Average number of children (Japan 1982)
    2.23 persons

5) Average annual earnings of regular employees (Japan 1983)

	Male	Female
Total	4,230,444	2,207,868
Contractural Earnings	3,136,140	1,672,608
Bonus & Premiums	1,094,304	535,260

6) Starting salary (Tokyo 1982)
    Male
        High School Graduates.................................. 107,000 yen
        University Graduates 130,200
    Female
        High School Graduates.................................. 102,300
        Special training school or 2 year university 112,000

7) Average consumption expenditure (worker households, Japan 1983)

Food & beverages 26.5%
　　　Transportation & communication 9.5%
　　　Clothing 6.9%
　　　Utilities 5.8%
　　　Housing 4.8%
　　　Furniture, etc. 4.1%
　　　Education 3.8%
　　　Medical care 2.4%
　　　Reading & recreation 8.6%
　　　Others 27.6%

8) Average monthly propensity to save (Japan 1983)
　　20.9%

9) Average amount of savings (Japan 1983)
　　　6.1 million yen

10) Complete unemployment (Japan 1983)
　　　2.6

11) Marriage rate (Japan 1983)
　　　771,000 couples, once every 41 sec.

12) Divorce rate (Japan 1983)
　　　178,000 couples, once every 2 min. 57 sec.
　　　*Who mentioned it first? .... Wife (60%), Husband (30%)

13) Average money spent for a wedding (Japan 1982)
　　　4,577,000 yen (parents pay 71.6% of it)

14) Owned homes (Japan 1982)
　　　61.1%

15) Per capita estimate of copies published (Japan 1982)
　　　Books　　　　　　　　9.6 copies
　　　Monthly magazines　　14.5
　　　Weekly Magazines　　 11.7

16) Average number of newspapers subscribed (daily, Japan 1982)
　　　1.8 copies per household

17) Elementary school students opinion (Japan 1983)

	Japan (%)	U.S. (%)
Going to school is enjoyable	86.1	53.9
Has their own room	74.5	63.1
Mother doesn't work	27.9	33.8
Living with parents	92.0	77.4
Want to go to university	57.8	84.2

*The most scary thing
    Japan   1. ghost 2. father
    U.S.   1. father 2. evil

18) Status of high school graduates (Tokyo 1982)

Total	148,246
In college or university	34,063
Junior college	17,295
At trade and vocational schools	47,600
Working students	955
Working	41,979
Without occupation	7,272
Dead or unknown	37

19) Number of believers (Tokyo 1981)
    Shintō 13,817,919
    Buddhism 8,921,521
    Christianity 559,668
    Others 1,014,371

20) Number of temples and shrines in Japan (1981)
    Shrines 81,295
    Temples 75,167
    Churches 25,006

SOURCE OF STATISTICS
Bureau of Statistics, Prime Minister's Office, no's: 1, 2, 3, 7, 8, 9, 14, 15, 16
Tokyo Metropolitan Government, no's: 15, 18
Ministry of Public Welfare, no's: 4, 11, 12
Ministry of Labor, no's: 5, 10
Japan Youth Research Institute, no.: 17
Sumitomo Bank, no.: 13
Kyōikusha, no.: 6
Religion Annual, no's: 19, 20

INFORMATION, SERVICES AND REFERENCE
• Airline Reservations

Aeroflot Soviet Airlines (SU)	Tel: 272-5311
Air France (AF)	475-1511
Air-India (AI)	214-7631
Air New Zealand (TE)	287-1641
Alitalia Airlines (AZ)	580-2242
British Airways (BA)	214-4161
Cathay Pacific Airways (CX)	504-1531
Civil Aviation Administration of China (CA)	404-3660
China Airlines (CI)	436-1661
Continental Air Micronesia (CO)	592-1631
CP Air (CP)	281-7426
Egypt Air (MS)	211-4521
Finnair (AY)	504-0915
Garuda Indonesian Airways (GA)	593-1181
Iran Air (IR)	586-2101
Iraqi Airways (IA)	586-5801
Japan Air Lines (JAL)	457-1111
Japan Asia Airways (JAA)	455-7511
KLM Royal Dutch Airlines (KL)	216-0771
Korean Air Lines (KE)	211-3311
Lufthansa German Airlines (LH)	580-2111
Malaysian Airlines System (MH)	432-8501
Northwest Orient Airlines (NW)	433-8151
Pakistan International Airlines (PK)	216-4641
Pan American World Airways (PA)	240-8888
Philippine Airlines (PR)	580-1571
Qantas Airways (QF)	211-4481
Sabena Belgian World Airlines (SN)	585-6151
Scandinavian Airlines System (SK)	503-8101
Singapore Airlines (SQ)	213-3431
Swiss Air Transport (SR)	212-1011
Thai Airways International (TG)	503-3311
United Airlines (UA)	213-4511
UTA French Airlines (UT)	593-0771
Varig Brazilian Airlines (RG)	211-6751

• Business Assistance

While most large companies will have an interpreter, as a 1984 issue of Business Week notes-an interpreter in Japan is worth the high cost. At least you know you're getting the whole story. A number of companies offer interpreting and secretarial services:

TEMPU STAFF Tel: 405-5507. Aoyama Suzuki Garasu Bldg. 5th Fl., 3-5-14 Kita-Aoyama, Minato-ku.
JAPAN CONVENTION SERVICE Tel: 508-1211. Nippon Press Center Bldg. 2-2-1 Uchisaiwai-chō, Chiyoda-ku.
SUMMIT SERVICE Tel: 499-0245. Namikibashi Property 201, 1-32-13 Higashi, Shibuya-ku.

For detailed information, translations, press conference organization, and news releases, a good company is: **Lee & Williams** Gosei Bldg. 3rd Fl., 16-7-5 Minami-Azabu, Minato-ku. Tel: 440-0845.

• Courier Service
DHL Tel: 454-0501. Kōwa Bldg. #38, 5th Fl., 4-12-24 Nishi-Azabu, Minato-ku.
WORLD COURIER Tel: 508-9281. Kawashima Hōshin Bldg. 5th Fl., 2-2-2 Shimbashi, Minato-ku.

• Cultural Organizations
AMERICA-JAPAN SOCIETY, INC. Tel: 201-0780. Marunouchi Bldg. 3rd Fl., 2-4-1 Marunouchi, Chiyoda-ku.
AMERICAN CENTER Tel: 436-0901. ABC Kaikan 2-6-3 Shiba-kōen, Minato-ku.
ASIA CENTER OF JAPAN Tel: 402-6111. 8-10-32 Akasaka, Minato-ku.
BRITISH COUNCIL Tel: 264-3721. 2-1 Jimbōchō, Kanda, Chiyoda-ku.
INSTITUTE FRANCO-JAPONAIS Tel: 260-7224. 15 Funagawarachō, Ichigaya, Shinjuku-ku.
INTERNATIONAL HOUSE OF JAPAN Tel: 470-4611. 5-11-16 Roppongi, Minato-ku.
ITALIAN INSTITUTE OF CULTURE Tel: 264-6011. 2-1-30 Kudan-Minami, Chiyoda-ku.
JAPAN FOUNDATION, THE Tel: 263-4503. Park Bldg. 3rd & 4th Fl., 3-6 Kioichō, Chiyoda-ku.
TOKYO GERMAN CULTURE CENTER Tel: 584-3201. 7-5-56 Akasaka, Minato-ku.

• Directory Assistance
Tokyo .... Tel: 104
International .... Tel: 0051

• Domestic Help and Babysitting
TOKYO DOMESTIC SERVICE CENTER Tel: 584-4769. Palais Royal Akasaka No. 2 Bldg. Rm. 1003, 2-17-54 Akasaka, Minato-ku. Maid and Baby Sitting Service.
TOKYO MAID SERVICE Tel: 291-3595. Nara Bldg. 2nd Fl., 1-54 Jimbōchō, Kanda, Chiyoda-ku. Maid, baby sitting & party help.
BABY ROOM Tel: 265-1111. Baby Sitting Service at the New Ōtani Hotel.

• Economic Organizations
JAPAN CHAMBER OF COMMERCE Tel: 213-8585. Tokyo Kaijō Bldg. 1-2-1 Marunouchi, Chiyoda-ku.
JAPAN CONVENTION BUREAU Tel: 210-1901. Part of the Japan National Tourist Organization. Organizes trade fairs and exhibitions.
JETRO (Japan External Trade Org.) Tel: 582-5511. 2-2-5 Toranomon, Minato-ku.
KEIZAI KŌHŌ CENTER Tel: 201-1415. Japan Institute for Social & Economic Affairs. 1-6-1 Ōtemachi, Chiyoda-ku.

• Embassies
Afghanistan	Tel: 407-7900	Chile	Tel: 400-4522
Algeria	499-2661	China	403-3380
Argentina	592-0321	Colombia	409-0424
Australia	453-0251	Costa Rica	486-1812
Austria	451-8281	Cuba	449-7511
Bangladesh	442-1501	Czechoslovakia	400-8122
Belgium	262-0191	Denmark	496-3001
Bolivia	499-5441	Dominica	499-6020
Brazil	404-5211	Ecuador	499-2800
Bulgaria	465-1021	Egypt	463-4564
Burma	441-9291	El Salvador	499-4461
Canada	408-2101	Ethiopia	585-3151

Finland	Tel: 442-2231	Pakistan	Tel: 454-4861
France	473-0171	Panama	499-3741
E. Germany	585-5404	Papua N. Guinea	454-7801
W. Germany	473-0151	Paraguay	447-7496
Ghana	409-3861	Peru	406-4241
Greece	403-0871	Philippines	496-2731
Guatemala	400-1830	Poland	711-5224
Guinea	499-3281	Portugal	400-7907
Honduras	409-1150	Qatar	446-7561
Hungary	476-6061	Romania	479-0311
India	262-2391	Saudi Arabia	409-8291
Indonesia	441-4201	Senegal	464-8451
Iran	446-8011	Singapore	586-9111
Iraq	423-1727	South Africa	265-3366
Ireland	263-0695	Soviet Union (U.S.S.R.)	583-4224
Israel	264-0911	Spain	583-8531
Italy	453-5291	Sri Lanka	585-7431
Jordan	580-5856	Sudan	406-0811
Korea	452-7611	Sweden	582-6981
Kuwait	455-0361	Switzerland	473-0121
Laos	408-1166	Tanzania	425-4531
Lebanon	580-1227	Thailand	441-1386
Liberia	499-2451	Tunisia	262-7724
Libya	586-1886	Turkey	470-5131
Malaysia	463-0241	U.A.E.	478-0659
Mexico	581-1131	Uganda	469-3641
Mongolia	469-2088	U.S.A.	583-7141
Morocco	478-3271	U.K.	265-5511
Nepal	444-7303	Uruguay	486-1888
Netherlands	431-5126	Venezuela	409-1501
New Zealand	460-8711	Viet Nam	466-3311
Nicaragua	499-0400	Yemen	499-7151
Nigeria	468-5531	Yugoslavia	447-3571
Norway	440-2611	Zambia	445-1041
Oman	402-0877		

- **Emergency**

Police .... Tel: 110
Fire & Ambulance .... Tel: 119

- **Film Processing**

FAR EAST LABORATORY Used by professional photographers in Tokyo.
Ginza: Tel 567-1681. 3-2 Ginza, Chūō-ku.
Aoyama: Tel: 407-4850. 3-11-14 Kita-Aoyama, Minato-ku. [M-5]
Shinjuku: Tel: 346-1681. 3-1 Nishi-Shinjuku, Shinjuku-ku.
TŌKAN Tel: 437-2816. 5-27-3 Shimbashi, Minato-ku. Hrs: 8:30 a.m.-6:30 p.m. (until 4 p.m. on Sat.), closed Sun. & Hols. Overnight service with pick-up at many hotels.
TRYWELL Tel: 585-2855. Tama Bldg. 1st Fl., 1-3-18 Akasaka, Minato-ku. Same day processing, in by 10 a.m., out by 5:30 p.m.

- **Furniture Rental**

INTERFORM Tel: 406-8751. 4-9-10 Higashi, Shibuya-ku. Leases quality furniture (some modern Italian) and offers excellent service.
DAIMARU Tel: 212-8011. 1-9-1 Marunouchi, Chiyoda-ku. Long term leasing (3-6 year) on furniture and electrical goods.

- **Housing**

  For less expensive housing, it's best to check with a real estate agent in the area where you want to live. The Tokyo Journal has listings.
  KEN CORPORATION Tel: 478-3821. Sonic Bldg. 2-12 Nishi-Azabu, Minato-ku. Good for more expensive western style housing.
  SUN REALTY Tel: 584-6171. Homat Royal Bldg. 1-14-11 Akasaka, Minato-ku. Also good for more expensive housing.

- **Libraries**

  NATIONAL DIET LIBRARY Tel: 581-2331. 1-10-1 Nagatachō, Chiyoda-ku. Hrs: 9:30 a.m.-5 p.m., closed Sun., Hols. & the 4th Wed. You must fill in a form to request a book, then wait about 15 min. You must be over 20 years old.
  METROPOLITAN CENTER LIBRARY Tel: 442-8451. 5-7-13 Minami-Azabu, Minato-ku (in Arisugawa Park). Tel: 9:30 a.m.-8 p.m. (until 5 p.m. on Sat. & Sun.), closed Mon., Hols. & the 14th.
  METROPOLITAN HIBIYA LIBRARY lel: 502-0101. 1-4 Hibiya-kōen, Chiyoda-ku. Hrs: 10 a.m.-7 p.m. (until 5 p.m. on Sat.), closed Sun., Hols. & the 14th. If you stay in Tokyo more than one month you can borrow books, but you'll need a certificate from your hotel verifying this.
  MING-YU INTERNATIONAL LIBRARY Tel: 561-1181. 4-8-8 Ginza, Chūō-ku. Hrs: 9 a.m.-5:30 p.m., closed Sun. & Hols. This library is especially good for visual books.
  WORLD MAGAZINE GALLERY Tel: 545-7227. Magazine House Bldg. 3-13-10 Ginza, Chūō-ku. Hrs: 10 a.m.-7 p.m., closed Mon. Magazines from around the world and a large video screen showing news and promotional videos.

- **Lost and Found Offices**—See "The Basics".

- **Printers**—For quick printing of business cards.
  HOTEL ŌKURA EXECUTIVE SERVICE SALON Tel: 586-7400. Hotel Ōkura Main Bldg. 5th Fl., 2-10 Toranomon, Minato-ku. Hrs: 8:30 a.m.-6:30 p.m., closed Sun. & Hols.
  NAGASHIMA INTERNATIONAL PR OFFICE Tel: 504-1111. Imperial Hotel Main Bldg. Mezzanine., 1-1 Uchisaiwaichō, Chiyoda-ku. Hrs: 9 a.m.-5:30 p.m., closed Sat., Sun. & Hols.

- **Professional and Community Service Organizations**

  AA ALCOHOLICS ANONYMOUS Tel: 431-8534.
  AMNESTY INTERNATIONAL Tel: 203-1050. Dai San Yamatake Bldg. 3rd Fl., 2-3-22 Nishi-Waseda, Shinjuku-ku.
  FOREIGN CORRESPONDENTS' CLUB OF JAPAN Tel: 211-3161. Yūrakuchō Denki Bldg. 20th Fl., 1-7-1 Yūrakuchō, Chiyoda-ku.
  INTERNATIONAL FEMINISTS OF JAPAN Tel: 904-2646. CPO Box 1780, Tokyo 100. Hrs: 7 p.m.-10 p.m.
  TOKYO ENGLISH LIFE LINE "TELL" Tel: 264-4347. Hrs: 9 a.m.-1 p.m., 7 p.m.-11 p.m. English language counseling service.
  TOKYO GAY SUPPORT GROUP Tel: 485-0414. CPO Box 1901, Tokyo 100-91. Hrs: 6 p.m.-10 p.m.

- **Repairs**
  Luggage:
  WAKAO BAG Tel: 404-3925. Kobayashi Kōpo 201, 2-3-21 Minami-Aoyama, Minato-ku. Hrs: 9 a.m.-6 p.m., closed Sun. Luggage and leather goods repair.
  Shoes:

MR. MINIT—found at major department stores (Mitsukoshi, Tōkyū, Seibu, Daimaru, etc.). They fix while you wait.
TŌKYŪ BUNKA SHOE REPAIR Tel: 407-7131 (ex. 313). Tōkyū Bunka Kaikan 1st Fl., 2-21-12 Shibuya, Shibuya-ku. Hrs: 10 a.m.-6 p.m., closed Sun.
Electrical:
YAMAMURA MUSEN Tel: 582-0064. 2-12-2 Higashi-Azabu, Minato-ku. Hrs: 9 a.m.-6 p.m., closed Sun. & Hols. English spoken.

• Shipping/Removal
GLOBAL INTERNATIONAL Tel: 707-0471. Haraken Bldg. 3rd Fl., 1-8-1 Tamagawadai, Setagaya-ku. A reliable and efficient company.
NIPPON EXPRESS CO., LTD. Tel: 572-4301. Sankin Bldg. 5th Fl., 8-9-4 Ginza, Chūō-ku. They will ship anything, by sea or air.
PURCELL INTERNATIONAL FORWARDING JAPAN Tel: 666-2981. Yanagi Homes Nihombashi #309, 18-3 Koamichō, Nihombashi, Chūō-ku. Handles everything but mail.
AKABŌ KUMIAI DESPATCH CENTER Tel: 866-8151. A mini truck service for moving in Japan.

• Tailor
RICKY SARANI Tel: 582-9741. 3-3-12 Azabudai, Minato-ku. Hrs: 10 a.m.-7 p.m., closed Sun. & Hols. Tailoring for men and women, also tuxedo rental.
KŌDA YŌFUKU KŌBŌ Tel: 433-4074. 3-24-1 Shimbashi, Minato-ku. Hrs: 10 a.m.-7 p.m., closed Sun. & Hols. Alterations and mending.

• Tourist Services—See "The Basics".

• Travel Agents
TOPPAN TRAVEL SERVICE Tel: 276-8130. Toppan Yaesu Bldg. 2-2-7 Yaesu, Chūō-ku. Hrs: 9 a.m.-5 p.m. (until 12 noon on Sat.), closed Sun. & Hols. English speaking.
TŌZAI TRAVEL Tel: 355-1661. Daini Maejima Bldg. 5th Fl., 1-9 Yotsuya, Shinjuku-ku. Hrs: 9:30 a.m.-5:30 p.m. (until 12 noon on Sat.), closed Sun. & Hols. English speaking, good for cheap tickets.

• Tuxedo and Formal Rental
RICKY SARANI (See "Tailor").
DAIMARU DEPARTMENT STORE 10th Fl. Tel: 212-8011.
TOKYO ISHŌ Tel: 485-6101. 3-21-8 Nishihara, Shibuya-ku.

Instruction

• **Japanese Language**—There are hundreds of language schools in Tokyo. Some are very good, but others are basically unprofessional organizations set up to provide "cultural visas" to supposed students. The entries on the following list have been recommended by the Japan Foundation, and are primarily for serious full-time students. For details concerning prerequisites, course offerings and cost, please contact the schools directly. For other part time schools check listings in the "Tokyo Journal".
SOPHIA UNIVERSITY Department of Comparative Culture, Sophia University, Ichigaya

Campus, 4 Yombanchō, Chiyoda-ku. Tel: 238-4000. They also have a special summer session with various courses on Japan.
INTERNATIONAL CHRISTIAN UNIVERSITY Japanese Dept., Division of Languages, College of Liberal Arts. Admission Office, I.C.U. 3-10-2 Ōsawa, Mitaka-shi. Tel: (0422) 33-3131. Summer Program: (0422) 33-3501.
THE JAPANESE LANGUAGE SCHOOL, THE INTERNATIONAL STUDENTS INSTITUTE 3-22-7 Kita-Shinjuku, Shinjuku-ku. Tel: 371-7265.
THE JAPANESE LANGUAGE DIVISION, ASAHI CULTURE CENTER P.O. Box 22, Sumitomo Shinjuku Bldg., 2-6-1 Nishi-Shinjuku, Shinjuku-ku. Tel: 348-4041.

- **Japanese Arts, etc.**—For courses in tea, *ikebana*, calligraphy, and martial arts, see the corresponding chapters in the main text. A variety of other classes are offered in Tokyo, but most require Japanese language ability. The following schools do accept students who can't speak Japanese.

TERAKOYA CULTURAL HOUSE 2-34-3 Mejiro, Toshima-ku. Tel: 989-9851. Connected with the Intercult Language School, the Terakoya House offers a variety of courses including tea, *ikebana*, *shodō*, *sumie*, cooking and *shiatsu*. The school is in a lovely, older Japanese building.
ASAHI CULTURAL CENTER Sumitomo Bldg. 4th Fl., 2-6-1 Nishi-Shinjuku, Shinjuku-ku. Tel: 344-1941. They have various arts, crafts and language courses. For most classes Japanese language ability is required. The exceptions are pottery and *ikebana*. Minimum enrollment period is three months.

Reference And Recommended Reading
• General
A LOOK INTO JAPAN (Japan Travel Bureau, 1984) A small picture dictionary that covers a wide range of subjects. Information is brief, but well presented.
THE TOURIST'S HANDBOOK: Practical Ways to Relieve Your Language Problems (Japan National Tourist Organization) A free pamphlet that provides language assistance by a clever show and tell method. You point to a question which has been translated into Japanese, and the Japanese person being questioned will point back the answer.
NOW YOU LIVE IN JAPAN: Handbook of Essential Knowledge for Resident Foreigners (Research Commitee, for Bicultural Life in Japan & the Japan Times, 1982).
IMMIGRATION: A Guide To Foreign Residence Procedures in Japan (Immigration Bureau, Ministry of Justice, & The Japan Times, 1982).

• History
JAPAN: The Story of a Nation (Edwin O. Reischauer, New York, Knopf, 1974). A fairly detailed coverage of the subject.
JAPAN: From Prehistory to Modern Times (J.W. Hall, New York, Delacorte, 1970). A good general survey.
A HISTORY OF MODERN JAPAN (Richard Storry, New York, Penguin Books, 1960, revised 1982). From *Meiji* period to the present.

• Society
THE ANATOMY OF DEPENDENCE (Doi Takeo, Tokyo, Kōdansha, 1971). An interesting psychological study of the Japanese.
MIRROR, SWORD & JEWEL: The Geometry of Japanese Life (Kurt Singer, Tokyo, Kōdansha International, 1981). A powerful perspective on Japanese society and character, written by an economist.

A JAPANESE MIRROR: Heroes & Villains of Japanese Culture (Ian Buruma, London Jonathan Cape, Ltd., 1984). A brilliant analysis of Japanese culture via its fantasies.
JAPAN'S MODERN MYTH: The Language Beyond (Roy Andrew Miller, Weatherhill, 1982). Cultural analysis through a study of the language.
THE JAPANESE (Edwin O. Reischauer, Tuttle, 1977). A standard general text on Japan, covers history, current politics and social issues.

• Arts and Culture

THE HERITAGE OF JAPANESE ART (Tanaka Ichimatsu, et al, Kōdansha International, 1982). A beautifully illustrated survey.
HEIBONSHA SURVEY OF ART (31 volumes by various authors, co-published by Heibonsha & Weatherhill, 1976-80). 31 volumes covering specific periods styles, or subjects in the history of Japanese art.
THE JAPANESE PRINT: A Historical Guide (Hugo Munsterberg, Weatherhill, 1982). A good survey of Japanese prints and the history of printmaking.
MINGEI (Amaury Saint-Gilles, San Francisco, Heian International, 1983). A beautifully illustrated guide to Japanese folk crafts.
EARTH 'N' FIRE (Amaury Saint-Gilles, Tokyo, Shufunotomo, 1978). A survey guide to Japanese kilns.
GEISHA (Liza Dalby, Tokyo, Kōdansha International, 1983). American Liza Dalby became a *geisha* in Kyōto as part of an anthropological research project.
THE TEA CEREMONY (Tanaka Sen'ō, Tokyo, Kōdansha International, 1983). Covers the history and philosophy behind the tea ceremony, through the text and numerous photographs.
THE BOOK OF TEA (Okakura Kakuzō, Tokyo, Charles Tuttle, 1956). A translation of a classic text on the tea ceremony, originally published in 1906.
JAPANESE MUSIC & MUSICAL INSTRUMENTS (William P. Malm, Tokyo, Tuttle, 1952). Somewhat outdated, but still the definitive text on Japanese music. Also covers theater. The book is technical but remains entertaining and highly informative.
THE TRADITIONAL THEATER OF JAPAN (Inoura Yoshinobu & Kawatake Toshio, Weatherhill, 1981). A good background study.
THE JAPANESE MOVIE (Donald Richie, Tokyo, Kōdansha International 1966, revised in 1982). By the respected critic and historian of Japanese cinema, the book is informative and lavishly illustrated.
NEW FASHION JAPAN (Leonard Koren, Kōdansha International, 1984) The first book to cover the recent Japanese fashion phenomenon.
MANGA! MANGA! THE WORLD OF JAPANESE COMICS (F.L. Schodt, Tokyo, Kōdansha International, 1983). Japanese pop culture explored through comics in this informative and very fun book.
JAPANESE COOKING FOR HEALTH & FITNESS (Konishi Kiyoko, Tokyo, Gakken, 1983). Some traditional recipes but also new "healthy" variations. Great for diet cooking.
JAPANESE COOKING: A Simple Art (Tsuji Shizuo, Tokyo, Kōdansha, 1980). The last word on standard Japanese cooking.
THE LAYMAN'S GUIDE TO ACUPUNCTURE (Manaka Yoshio, M.D. & Ian A. Urquhart, Ph. D., Weatherhill, 1972). An very good introduction to the subject.

• Religion

SHINTŌ: Japan's Spiritual Roots (Stuart Picken, Tokyo, Kōdansha International, 1980).
BUDDHISM: Japan's Cultural Identity (Stuart Picken, Tokyo, Kōdansha International, 1982). This and the book above, both written by Mr. Picken, are authoritatively written and well illustrated.
(About *Zen*—any books written by Daisetz T. Suzuki are recommended.)

- **Japanese Magazines**—Here is a list of some of the more interesting magazines available in Tokyo.

Women
RYŪKŌ TSŪSHIN "FASHION NEWS" (Ryūkō Tsūshin)—monthly. The most avant-garde fashion magazine in Tokyo. (and the publishers of this book!)
AN AN (Magazine House)—weekly young women's fashion and life-style magazine.
KATEIGAHŌ (Sekai Bunkasha)—A monthly women's magazine with a traditional culture emphasis. Well designed with beautiful photographs.

Men
X-MEN (Ryūkō Tsūshin)—A new magazine by the women's "Fashion News" company.
MR. HIGH FASHION (Bunka Shuppan-kyoku)—Monthly men's fashion magazine.
BRUTUS (Magazine House)—A biweekly men's fashion and lifestyle magazine.
POPEYE (Magazine House)—Same as "Brutus," but for younger men.

Art
BIJUTSU TECHŌ (Bijutsu Shuppansha)- Monthly. Arts information, mainly contemporary.
GEIJUTSU SHINCHŌ (Shinchōsha)—Monthly. Concentrates on a different subject each issue.
GINKA (Bunka Shuppan-kyoku)—Quarterly. Arts and crafts.
ART ANNUAL (Bijutsu Nenkansha)—An annual arts magazine.

Architecture
S.D. (Kajima Shuppan)—Monthly. A beautiful magazine for professional architects.
SHIN KENCHIKU (Shinkenchikusha)—Monthly. Concentrates more on residential architecture and interiors.

Photography and Illustration
NIHON CAMERA (Nihon Kamerasha).
COMMERCIAL PHOTO (Genkōsha)—Covers primarily commercially produced photography.
SHAGAKU (Shōgakukan)—Monthly. Mainly portraits by well-known photographers.
SHASHIN JIDAI (Byakuya Shobō).
ILLUSTRATION (Genkōsha)—Monthly. Concentrates on current illustration work.

Music
MUSIC LIFE (Shinkō Music)—Rock and new music.
AD LIB (Swing Journal-sha)—Fusion, jazz, and rock.
MUSIC MAGAZINE (Music Magazine-sha)—Black and white photo's and lots of text.
TRA (Tra Projects)—A visual magazine with cassette. Music is often of new bands.

General
FOCUS (Shinchōsha)—A weekly scandal magazine with a visual format.

Comics
GARO (Seirindō)—A monthly comic magazine with work by interesting artists.

Information
PIA (Pia)—A biweekly magazine with information on everything happening in Tokyo. It's all in Japanese but you can have someone help you find events.
CITY ROAD (Ekō Kikaku)—Like PIA, but monthly, and with more commentary.

Charts
• Clothing Size Conversion Chart
Women's Dresses & Suits

	Japanese	9	11	13	15	17	19	21
	American	6	8	10	12	14	16	18
	English	32	34	36	38	40	42	44
	Continental	36	38	40	42	44	46	48

Men's Suits, Overcoats & Sweaters

	Japanese	S		M		L		LL
	American	34	36	38	40	42	44	46
	English	34	36	38	40	42	44	46
	Continental	44	46	48	50	52	54	56

Shirts & Collars

	Japanese	36	37	38	39	40	41	42
	American	14	14$\frac{1}{2}$	15	15$\frac{1}{2}$	16	16$\frac{1}{2}$	17
	English	14	14$\frac{1}{2}$	15	15$\frac{1}{2}$	16	16$\frac{1}{2}$	17
	Continental	36	37	38	39	40	41	42

Women's Shoes

	Japanese	23	23$\frac{1}{2}$	24	24$\frac{1}{2}$	25	25$\frac{1}{2}$	26
	American	6	6$\frac{1}{2}$	7	7$\frac{1}{2}$	8	8$\frac{1}{2}$	9
	English	4$\frac{1}{2}$	5	5$\frac{1}{2}$	6	6$\frac{1}{2}$	7	7$\frac{1}{2}$
	Continental	36	37	38	38	38	39	40

Men's Shoes

	Japanese	24$\frac{1}{2}$		26		27$\frac{1}{2}$	28	29
	American	5$\frac{1}{2}$	6$\frac{1}{2}$	7$\frac{1}{2}$	8$\frac{1}{2}$	9$\frac{1}{2}$	10$\frac{1}{2}$	11$\frac{1}{2}$
	English	5	6	7	8	9	10	11
	Continental	39	40	41	42	43	44	45

• Year Conversion Chart
—In the traditional Japanese calendar, year periods are calculated as what year of which Emperor's rule. According to this system, 1984 is Shōwa 59, or the 59th year of Emperor Shōwa's rule (Shōwa is the official name for the current Emperor Hirohito).

Meiji :	1	1868
	10	1877
	20	1887
	30	1897
	44	1911
Taishō :	1	1912
	10	1921
	14	1925
Shōwa :	1	1926
	10	1935
	20	1945
	30	1955
	40	1965
	60	1985

MAPS

300 MAP

TOKYO TRANSPORTATION

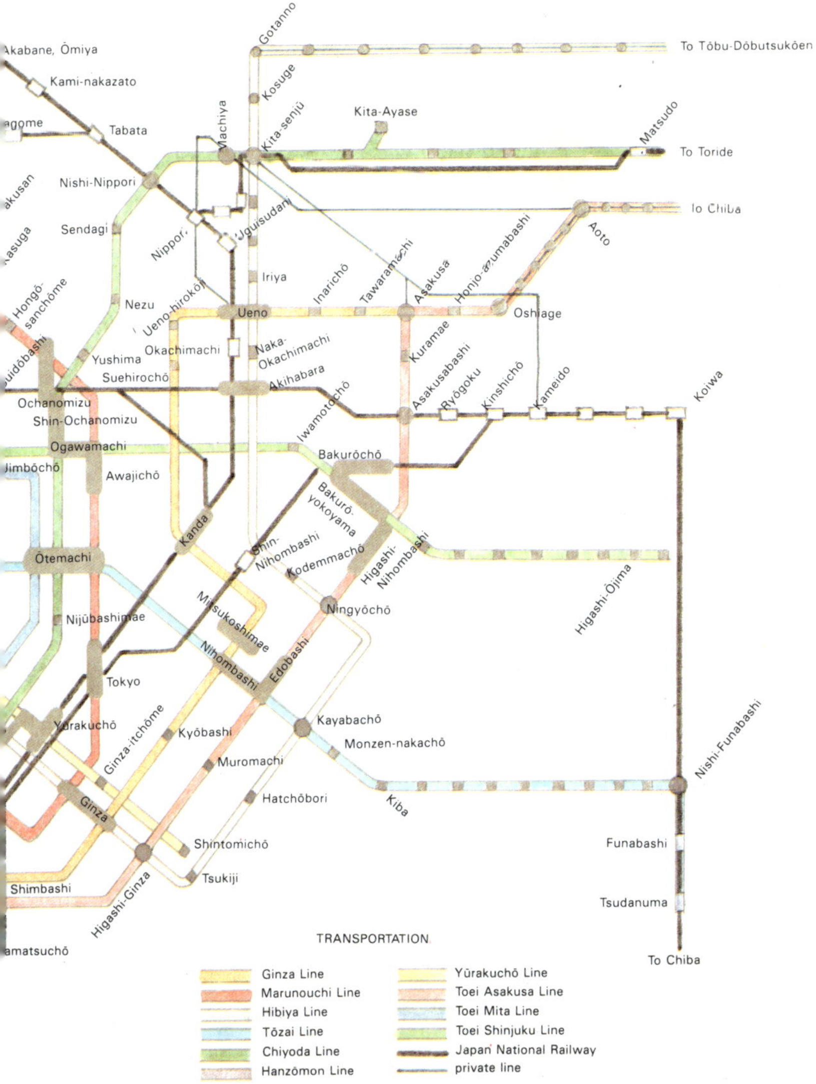
Akabane, Ōmiya
Kami-nakazato
agome
Tabata
Nishi-Nippori
Sendagi
Nippori
Uguisudani
Machiya
Gotanno
Kosuge
Kita-senjū
Kita-Ayase
Matsudo
To Tōbu-Dōbutsukōen
To Toride
To Chiba
Aoto
Hongō-sanchōme
Nezu
Ueno-hirokōji
Iriya
Inarichō
Tawaramachi
Asakusa
Honjo-azumabashi
Ueno
Oshiage
Yushima
Okachimachi
Naka-Okachimachi
Kuramae
Suehirochō
Akihabara
Asakusabashi
Ryōgoku
Kinshichō
Kameido
Koiwa
Ochanomizu
Shin-Ochanomizu
Iwamotochō
Ogawamachi
Jimbōchō
Awajichō
Bakurōchō
Bakurō-yokoyama
Kanda
Ōtemachi
Shin-Nihombashi
Kodemmachō
Higashi-Nihombashi
Higashi-Ōjima
Ningyōchō
Nijūbashimae
Mitsukoshimae
Nihombashi
Edobashi
Tokyo
Kayabachō
Monzen-nakachō
Yūrakuchō
Ginza-itchōme
Kyōbashi
Muromachi
Nishi-Funabashi
Hatchōbori
Kiba
Ginza
Shintomichō
Funabashi
Tsukiji
Shimbashi
Tsudanuma
Higashi-Ginza
amatsuchō
To Chiba
TRANSPORTATION
Ginza Line
Marunouchi Line
Hibiya Line
Tōzai Line
Chiyoda Line
Hanzōmon Line
Yūrakuchō Line
Toei Asakusa Line
Toei Mita Line
Toei Shinjuku Line
Japan National Railway
private line

AREAS

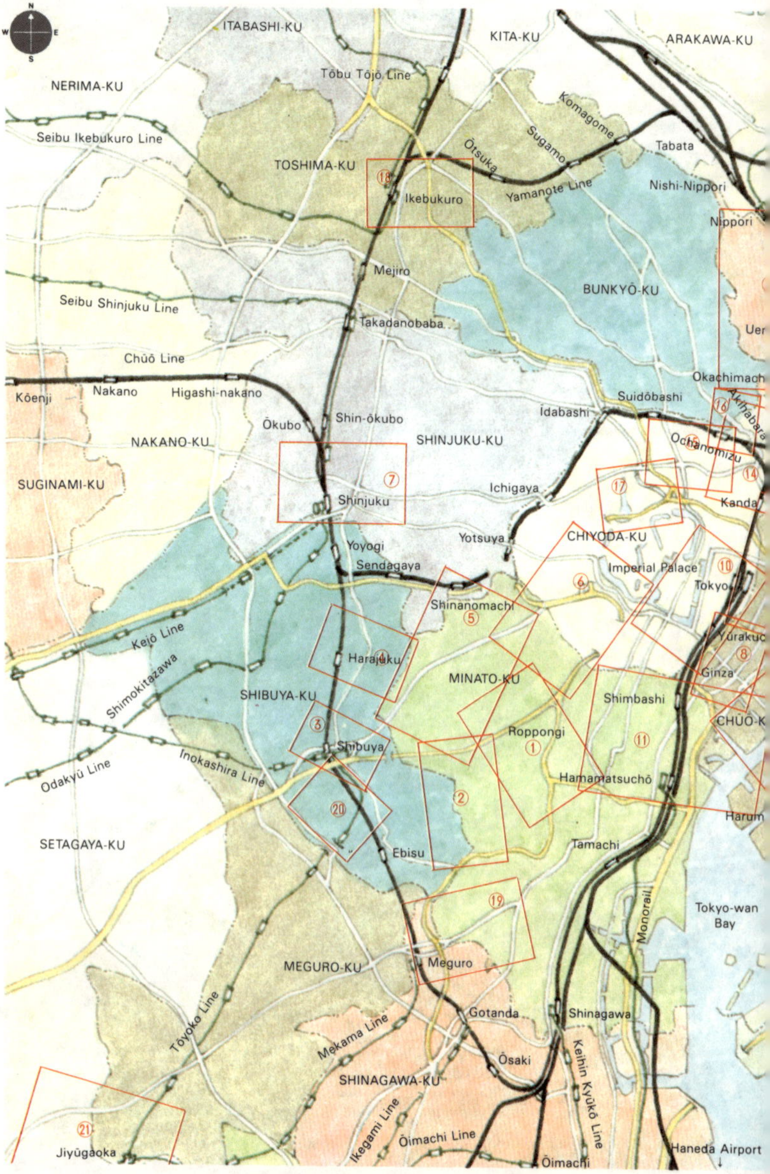

TRANSIT SYSTEM MAP

The twenty-five maps in this section cover the important districts of the city. Following are small maps of locations not found on the major maps. The maps have not been drawn in uniform scale, and directional axis varies, but the outlines of each district have been clearly marked on the greater Tokyo map and should give a fair perspective.

Map entries are marked by numbers or symbols. Next to each map is a list of the entries with the corresponding map entry number and the page number where the entry is mentioned in the text. When two or more shops are located in the same building, one number is used for all. The list of map entries is divided by categories, e.g., accommodations, restaurants, sightseeing. Abbreviations have sometimes been used to describe the type of shop, etc. The abbreviations are listed below. Landmarks, well known streets and crossings have been marked on the map. If you get lost, or are taking a taxi, ask for one of these.

Map Code
• **Shopping**

A (Antiques), AC (Arts & Crafts), AO (Art & Office Supplies), B (Books), E (Electronics), F (Fashion), FD (Food & Drink), I (Interiors), R (Records), Disc. (Discount), Misc. (Miscellaneous).

• **Nightlife**

Where not obvious, we have marked the listings as: Bar, Disco, Cabaret, G. Bar (Gay Bar), Hostess (Hostess Bar), Love H (Love Hotel), Rock (Rock & Modern Live Music), Jazz (Live), C & W (Country & Western, Live).

• **Sightseeing**

Names on the list are the standard Japanese names, but on the maps we have used the English where it will be easier to understand at a glance. Buildings found in our contemporary architecture section are marked as "Arch.".

• **Key**

×   police box
卄   shrine
卍   temple
⊠   police station
〒   post office

304 MAP

[M-1] ROPPONGI

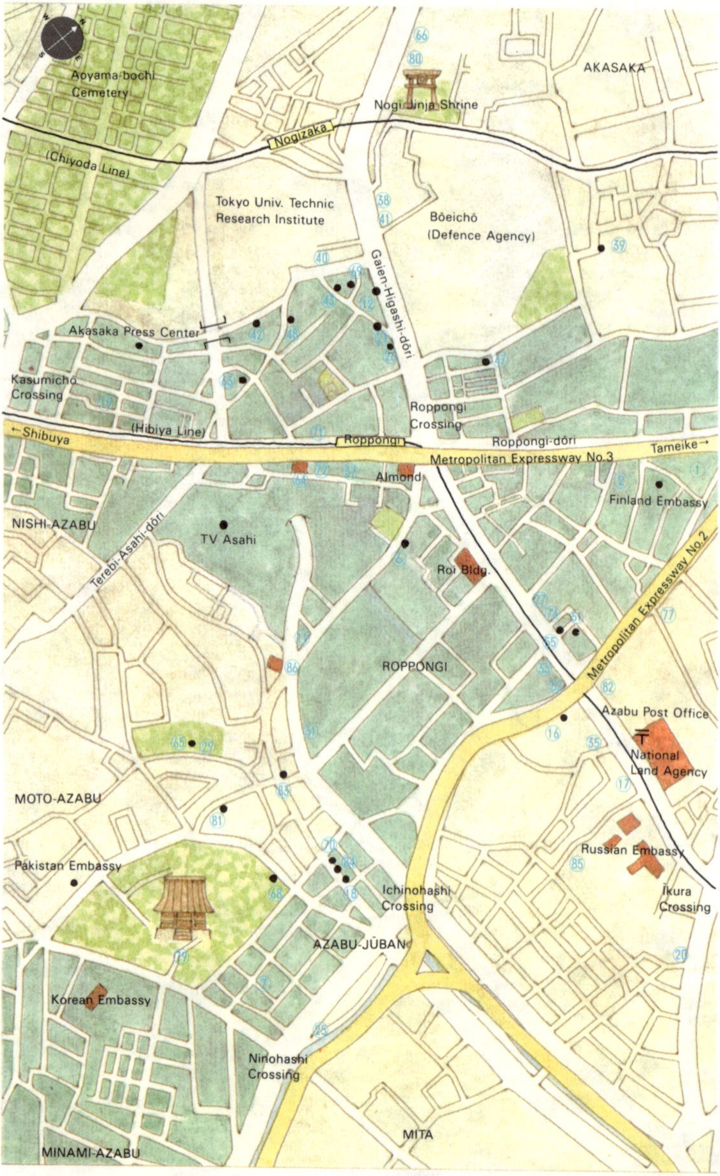

ACCOMMODATION
1. Roppongi Prince Hotel (48)

JAPANESE RESTAURANTS
2. Takamura (Kaiseki 68)
3. Hanatemari (Kaiseki 68)*
4. Minokichi (Kaiseki, Tempura 68)*
5. Fukuzushi (Sushi 71)*
6. Sushi Sei (71)
7. Matsukan (Sushi 71)
8. Yotaro (Tempura 73)*
9. Torigin (Yakitori 74)*
10. Nambantei (Yakitori 74)*
11. Ganchan (Yakitori 74)
12. Inakaya (Robatayaki 76)
13. Gonin Byakushō (Robatayaki 76)*
14. Chisen (Kushiage 77)*
15. Seryna (Beef 79)*
16. Hasejin (Beef 79)
17. Mamiana Soba (Soba 81)
18. Nagasaka Sarashina (Soba 81)
19. Inaniwa (Udon 82)
20. Nodaiwa (Unagi 82)
21. Daihachi (Rāmen 86)
22. Kappa (Home Cooking 87)*
23. Roppongi Shokudō (Home Cooking 87)*
24. Daikan Kamado (88)*

OTHER RESTAURANTS
25. Kusa no Ya (Korean 90)
26. Jojoen (Korean 90)
27. Rōgairō (Chinese 90)
28. Tong Fu (Chinese 90)*
29. Kaen (Chinese 91)
30. Aux Six Arbres (French 91)*
31. Les Choux (French 91)
32. Bofinger (French 92)*
33. A Tantôt (French 92)
34. Brasserie Bernard (French 92)*
35. Chianti (Italian 92)
5. Spago (American 93)*
36. Victoria Station (American 93)*
37. Moti (Indian 91)

COFFEE SHOPS
38. Cappuccio (94)
39. Konditorei Österreich (94)

NIGHTLIFE
40. Mint Bar (173)
41. Tabac (Bar 173)
42. Pidgeon (Bar 174)
43. Ex (Bar 174)
44. Maggie's Revenge (Bar 174)*
45. Henry Africa's (Bar 174)*
46. Charleston (Bar 174)*
47. Mr. Stamp's (Bar 175)
48. Lorne's Place (Bar 175)
49. Berni Inn (Bar 175)*
57. Vietti (Disco 176)*
50. Neo Japanesque (Disco 176)*
53. Cleo Palazzi (Disco 176)*
49. Lexington Queen (Disco 176)
1. Rajah Court (Disco 176)*
40. Ink Stick (Live, Modern 177)
52. Hot Co-Rocket (Live, Brazilian 177)
51. Cavern Club (Rock 177)
54. Kento's (Rock 177)*
55. Roppongi Pit Inn (Jazz 178)
56. Ballantine 2 (Jazz 178)*
36. Satin Doll (Jazz 178)
58. After Six (Jazz 178)*
59. Chaps (C & W 178)*
60. Midorino Yakata (Karaoke 179)*
61. Saint Julian (Karaoke 179)*
62. Casablanca (Hostess 179)*
63. Hotel Roppongi (Love H. 182)

SHOPPING
64. Wave (R, B 104)
35. Axis (I 104)
65. Boutique Yūya (F, A 108, 134)
66. Pashu (F 110)
67. Jun Murata (F 110)*
4. Madame Hanai (F 109)*
68. Blue and White (AC 116)
69. Kurofune (A 133)
70. Mamegen (FD 137)
71. Meidi-ya (FD 139)
35/72. Lapis (AO 144)
73. Oriental (Cosmetics 144)*
35. Nuno (Fabric 144)
35. Playthings (Toys 146)
74. Daichū (F, I 146)
35. Kissō (AC 124)
75. Winners (R 142)*

THEATERS
76. Haiyūza Gekijō (161)*
64. Cine Vivant Roppongi (168)

GALLERIES
77. Unac Salon (197)
35. Tokyo Designer's Space (196)
35. Ao Gallery (196)
78. News (196)*

SIGHTSEEING
79. Zempukuji (Temple 206)
80. Nogi Tei (214)
81. Austrian Embassy (Arch. 215)

HEALTH & BEAUTY
82. International Clinic (230)
83. Azabu Jūban Onsen (Bath 232)
84. Nagai Yakkyoku (231)
85. Clark Hatch (Sports 233)
86. Sweden Health Center (Gym 233)
87. Andre Bernard (Hair 236)*

OTHER RESTAURANTS (cont.)
88. Ile de France (French 92)*

*See Roppongi inset map on page 307.

[M-2] NISHI-AZABU—HIRŌ

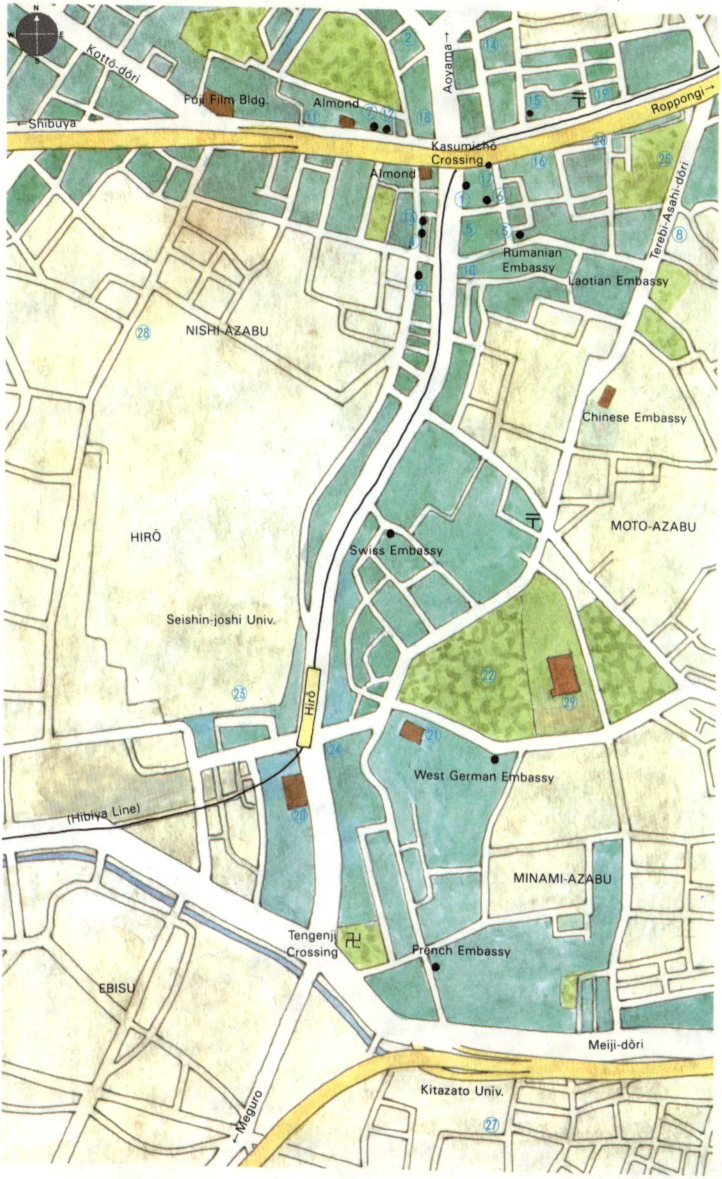

RESTAURANTS
1. Jū Jū (Korean 90)
2. Hokkaien (Chinese 90)
3. Queen Alice (French 91)
4. Bistrot de la Cite (French 92)
5. Chianti (Italian 92)
6. Al Porto (Italian 93)
7. La Boheme (Italian 93)
8. Fox Bagels (American 93)

COFFEE SHOPS
9. Ruelle de Derrière (94)
10. La Palette (94)
11. Patisserie de la Table (94)

NIGHTLIFE
12. Red Shoes (Bar 173)
13. Dick's Bar (173)
14. Val's Bar (173)
5. Chiantissimo (Bar 173)
15. Shirin (Bar 174)

SHOPPING
16. Hiromi Yoshida (F 108)
17. Arrston Volaju (F 110)
18. Saga Tōen (AC 124)
19. Washi Kōbō (AC 119, 120)
20. Meidiya (FD 139)
21. National Azabu Supermarket (FD 139)
21. National Bookstore (143)

SIGHTSEEING
22. Arisugawa Kōen (Park 210)
23. Sacred Heart International School (Arch. 215)
24. Mitsubishi Bank (Arch. 215)

HEALTH & BEAUTY
25. Ishikawa Clinic (230)
26. Kanda Clinic (230)
27. Tōyō Igaku Kenkyūjo (229)
28. Nisseki Iryō Center (230)
21. National Azabu Supermarket Pharmacy (231)

OTHERS
29. Metropolitan Central Library (293)

*Roppongi Inset Map (see page 305)

[M-3] SHIBUYA

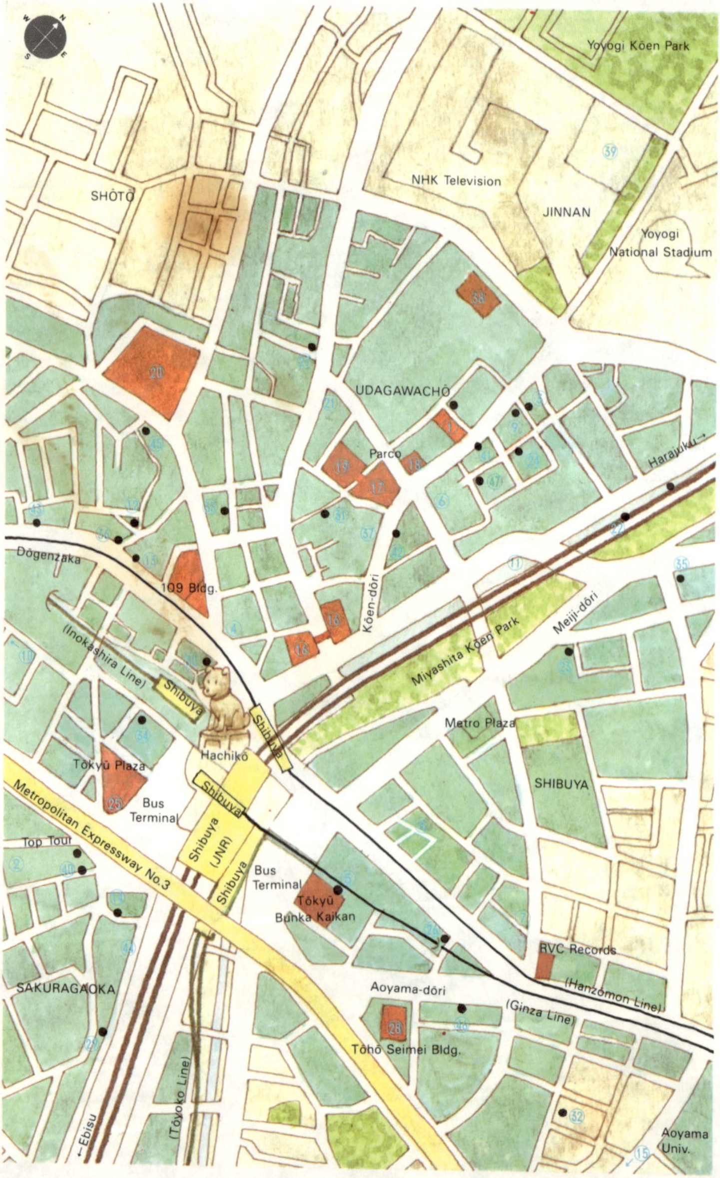

MAP 309

ACCOMMODATION
1. Shibuya Tōbu Hotel (49)
2. Hillport Hotel (49)

JAPANESE RESTAURANTS
3. Sushi Bar Sai (Sushi 71)
4. Tsunahachi (Tempura 72)
5. Nambantei (Yakitori 74)
6. I-Ro-Ha-Ni-Ho-He-To (Robata-yaki 76)
7. Chōtoku (Udon 82)
8. Hagoromo (Rāmen 86)
9. Charlie House (Rāmen 86)
10. Jizake (88)
11. Temmi (Health 89)

OTHER RESTAURANTS
12. Reikyō (Taiwanese 91)
13. Roma Sabatini (Italian 92)

COFFEE SHOPS
14. Cafe Bistro McLord (95)
15. Lawn (95)

SHOPPING
16. Seibu Dept. (102)
17. Parco Part 1 (F 103)
18. Parco Part 2 (F 103)
19. Parco Part 3 (F, I 103)
20. Tōkyū Dept. (102)
21. Tōkyū Hands (I 104)
22. Bunkaya Zakkaten (F 111)
23. Pink Dragon (F, I 111)
24. Tokyo-dō (F 111)
25. Tsukamoto (AC 116)
26. Jōnan Denki (E 114)
27. Tower Records (R 142)
28. Sumiya (R 142)
29. Meruridō (R 142)
17. Wacoal Fabrics House (Fabric 144)
30. Tellus (Shoes 146)
31. Daichū (Misc. 146)

NIGHTLIFE
32. Kay's Bar (173)
33. Mon (Bar 174)
34. The Live Inn (Rock 177)
35. Crocodile (Rock 177)
36. Aspen Glow (C & W 178)
47. EX (Bar 173)

CONCERT HALLS & THEATERS
37. Jean Jean (161)
17. Seibu Gekijō (161)
38. Shibuya Kōkaidō (161)
19. Space Part 3 (161)
39. NHK Hall (161)
40. Euro Space (Cinema 168)

MUSEUMS & GALLERIES
41. Tabacco and Salt Museum (191)
42. Gallery View (196)

HEALTH & BEAUTY
43. Dr. Uchiike (Accup. 230)
44. Shiawase Kenkō Club (230)
45. Matsuo Shika (Dental 231)
46. Pāru Onsen (Bath 232)

OTHERS
16. Akagiya Playguide (162)

[M-4] HARAJUKU

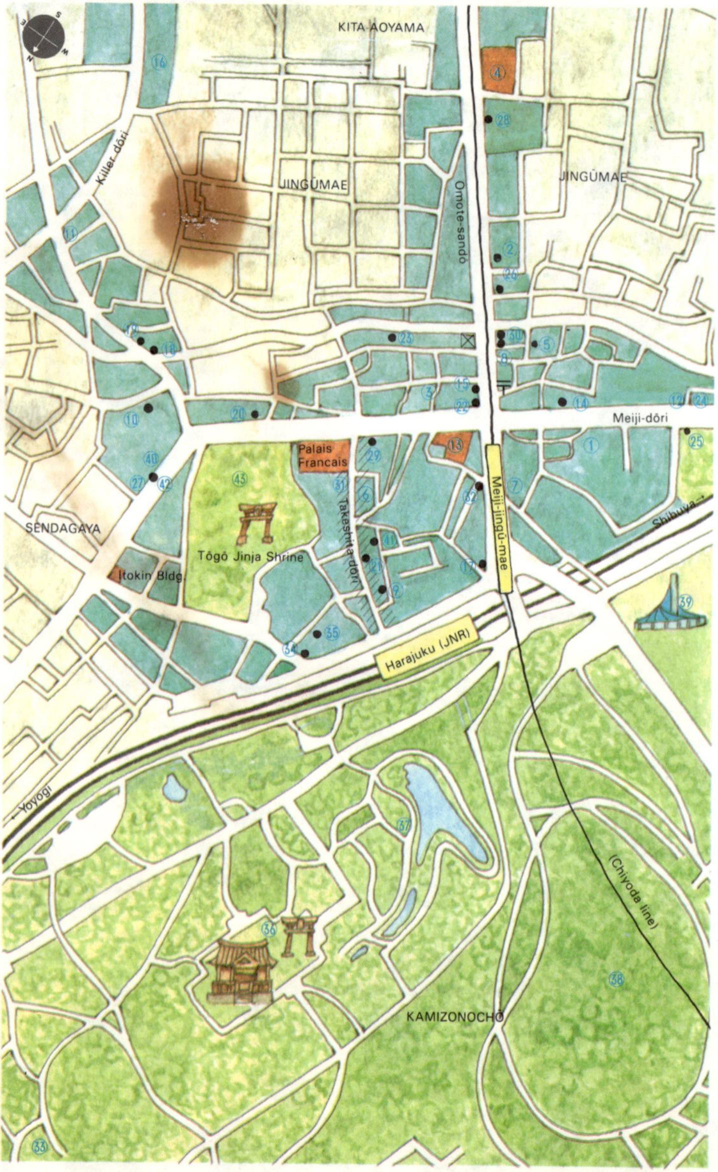

MAP 311

ACCOMMODATION
① Hotel Harajuku Trimm (49)

JAPANESE RESTAURANTS
② Genrokuzushi (Sushi 71)
③ Toriden (Yakitori 74)

OTHER RESTAURANTS
④ L'Orangerie de Paris (French 92)
⑤ La Boheme (Italian 93)
⑥ La Verde (Italian 93)

COFFEE SHOPS
⑦ Studio V (94)
⑧ Cafe de Rope (94)
⑨ Luseine-kan (94)

NIGHTLIFE
⑩ Radio Bar (173)
⑪ Night Bar (173)
⑫ Monkberry's (Bar, Disco 173)
⑤ Oh God (Bar 174)
㊷ Club D (Disco 176)

SHOPPING
⑬ La Foret (F 103)
④ Hanae Mori (F 108)
⑭ Obscure Desire of Bourgeoisie (F 108)
⑮ Milk (F 108)
⑯ Madame Nicole (F 109)
⑰ Jurgen Lehl (F 108)
⑱ Kansai Yamamoto (F 109)
⑲ Persons (F 110)
⑳ Beams (F 110)
㉑ Last Scene (F 111)
㉒ Harajuku Plaza (F 111)
㉓ Garage Paradise (F 111)
㉔ Surplus (F 111)
㉕ Dep't Store (F 111, 135)
㉒ Back Tick (F 111)
㉖ Oriental Bazaar (AC, A 116, 125, 133, 134)
④ Konjaku Nishimura (A 134)
㉗ Dynamic Audio (E 114)
㉘ Shū Uemura Beauty Boutique (Cosmetics 144)
㉖ Mori Silver (Pearls 145)
㉙ Diana (Shoes 146)
㉚ Kiddyland (Toys 146)
㉛ Takeshita-dōri (F 100, 111)

MUSEUMS & GALLERIES
㉜ Ōta Memorial Museum of Art (188)
㉝ Meiji Shrine Treasure House (190)
㉞ At Gallery (196)
㉟ Scan Video Gallery (197)

SIGHTSEEING
㊱ Meiji Jingū (Shrine 207)
㊲ Meiji Jingū Gyoen (Park 211)
㊳ Yoyogi Kōen (Park 210)
㊴ National Gymnasium (Arch. 215)
㊵ Turkish Embassy (Arch. 215)

HEALTH & BEAUTY
⑥ Isukura Yakkyoku (Pharmacy 231)
① Harajuku Trim (Health Club 234)
㊴ National Gymnasium (Swimming Pool 234)
⑬ Mod's Hair (236)
㊶ Studio Arkis Esty Harajuku Step In (Skin Care 236)

OTHERS
⑬ The Playguide La Foret (162)
㊸ Tōgō Jinja Shrine (Flea Market 134)

312 MAP

[M-5] AOYAMA

ACCOMMODATION
1. The President Hotel Aoyama (49)
2. Asia Center of Japan (49)
3. Tokyo Aoyama Kaikan (49)
4. Nihon Seinenkan (49)

JAPANESE RESTAURANTS
5. Sushi Sei (71)
6. Anri (Home Cooking 87)

OTHER RESTAURANTS
7. Daini's Table (Chinese 90)
8. Lotus Café (Chinese 91)
9. Le Chinois (Chinese 91)
10. Bindi (Indian 91)
11. La Patata (Italian 92)
12. Sabatini Aoyama (Italian 92)
13. Posh Boy (American 93)

COFFEE SHOP
14. Yoku Moku (94)

NIGHTLIFE
15. Le Club (Bar 173)
16. Oyster Bar (Bar 173)
17. Tokio (Disco 176)

SHOPPING
5. Bell Commons (F 103)
18. From First (F 103)
19. Hanae Mori (F 108)
20. Nicole (F 109)
21. Plantation (F 108)
21. Issey Miyake Men (F 110)
22. The Shirts (F 110)
23. Comme des Garçon Homme (F 110)
20. Monsieur Nicole (F 110)
24. Pashu (F 110)
25. Takeo Kikuchi (F 110)
26. Junko Koshino (F 108)
27. Crafts Center (AC 116)
28. Gallery Konohana (AC 118)
29. Isetatsu (AC 118)
30. Matsushita Associates, Inc. (A 125)
31. Morita Antiques (A 133)
32. Kammomn Antiques (A 133)
33. Kikuya Honten (FD 136)
34. Kinokuniya International (FD 139)
35. Natural House (FD 139)
36. Flex Japan (E 114)
37. Pied Piper House (R 142)
38. On Sundays (B 143)
39. Innovator Shop (I 145)
40. Design Studio Okamoto (I 145)
41. Midget (I 145)
42. Calzeria Hosono (Shoes 146)
43. Meda (Shoes 146)
44. Shū Uemura (Cosmetics 144)
45. Mujirushi Ryōhin (Misc. 146)

CONCERT HALLS & THEATERS
46. Tessenkai Nōgaku Kenshūjo (159)
47. Sōgetsu Hall (161)
4. Nihon Seinenkan Hall (161)
19. The Space (161)

MUSEUMS & GALLERIES
48. Nezu Art Museum (186)
49. Aoyama Green Gallery (196)
50. Green Collections (197)
51. Gallery Watari (197)
52. Video Earth Tokyo (197)

TRADITIONAL ARTS
47. Sōgetsu Kaikan (Ikebana 199)
53. Ohara Kaikan (Ikebana 199)

SIGHTSEEING
54. Meiji Jingū Gaien (Park 210)
55. Aoyama Bochi (Cemetery 214)
56. Geihinkan (Akasaka Detached Palace 214)
47. Sōgetsu Kaikan (Arch. 215)
18. From First Bldg. (Arch. 216)
19. Hanae Mori Bldg. (Arch. 215)
14. Yoku Moku (Arch. 216)

HEALTH & BEAUTY
57. Tani Clinic (230)
58. Tokyo Chiropractic Center (230)
35. International Vision Center (231)
59. Boy (Hair 236)
60. Peek a Boo (Hair 236)

OTHERS
61. Meiji Jingū Kyūjō (Baseball 167)
62. Far East Laboratory (Film 292)

[M-6] AKASAKA—NAGATACHŌ

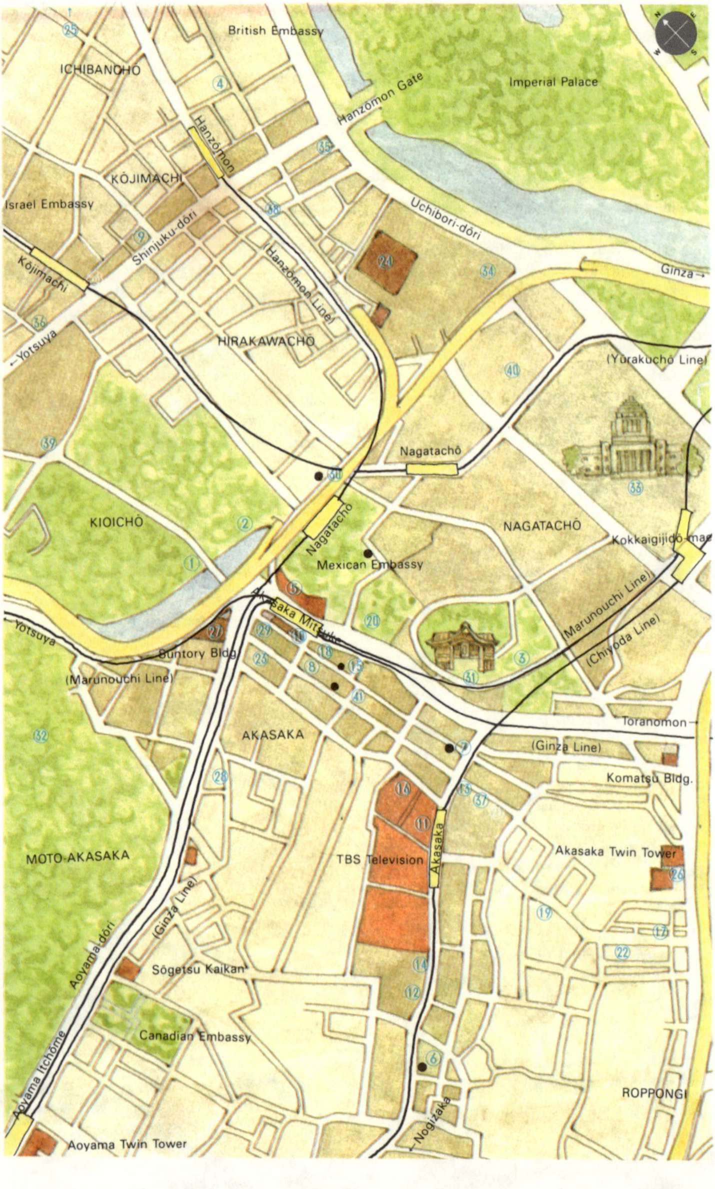

MAP 315

ACCOMMODATIONS
1. Hotel New Ōtani (47)
2. Akasaka Prince Hotel (47)
3. Capitol Tōkyū Hotel (47)
4. Diamond Hotel (48)
5. Akasaka Tōkyū Hotel (48)
6. Hotel Yōkō Akasaka (48)

JAPANESE RESTAURANTS
7. Inakaya (Robatayaki 76)
8. Kushinobō (Kushiage 77)
9. Tambaya (Unagi 82)
10. Botejū (Okonomiyaki 85)
11. Susukino (Rāmen 86)
12. Tsutsui (Yōshoku 87)
13. Hayashi (88)

OTHER RESTAURANTS
14. Anzai (Vietnamese 91)
15. Taj (Indian 91)
16. La Granata (Italian 92)
17. Mexico Lindo (Mexican 93)

NIGHTLIFE
1. Trader Vic's (Bar 174)
18. Mugen (Disco 176)
19. Cordon Blue (Cabaret 179)
20. New Latin Quarter (Cabaret 179)

SHOPPING
1. Hotel New Ōtani Arcade (105)
10. Belle Vie Akasaka (F 103)
22. Ayahata (A 134)
23. Big Shoes (146)

CONCERT HALLS & THEATERS
24. Kokuritsu Gekijō (161)
25. Albion-za (161)
26. Akasaka La Foret (161)

MUSEUMS & GALLERIES
27. Suntory Art Gallery (187)
28. Akasaka Green Gallery (196)
29. Inui Gallery (196)

ADDITIONAL ARTS
1. Seisei-an (Tea 199)
30. Sho International (Calligraphy 199)

SIGHTSEEING
31. Hie Jinja (Shrine 207)
32. Geihinkan (Akasaka Detached Palace 214)
33. National Diet Bldg. (213)
34. Supreme Court (Arch. 216)
35. Wacoal Bldg. (Arch. 215)

HEALTH & BEAUTY
36. Kōjimachi Rebirth (Sauna 233)
37. Otomiyu (Bath 232)
38. Bain Douche (Bath 232)
39. Mainichi Sports Plaza Tokyo (234)

OTHERS
40. National Diet Library (293)
41. Glass Art Akasaka (215)

[M-7] SHINJUKU

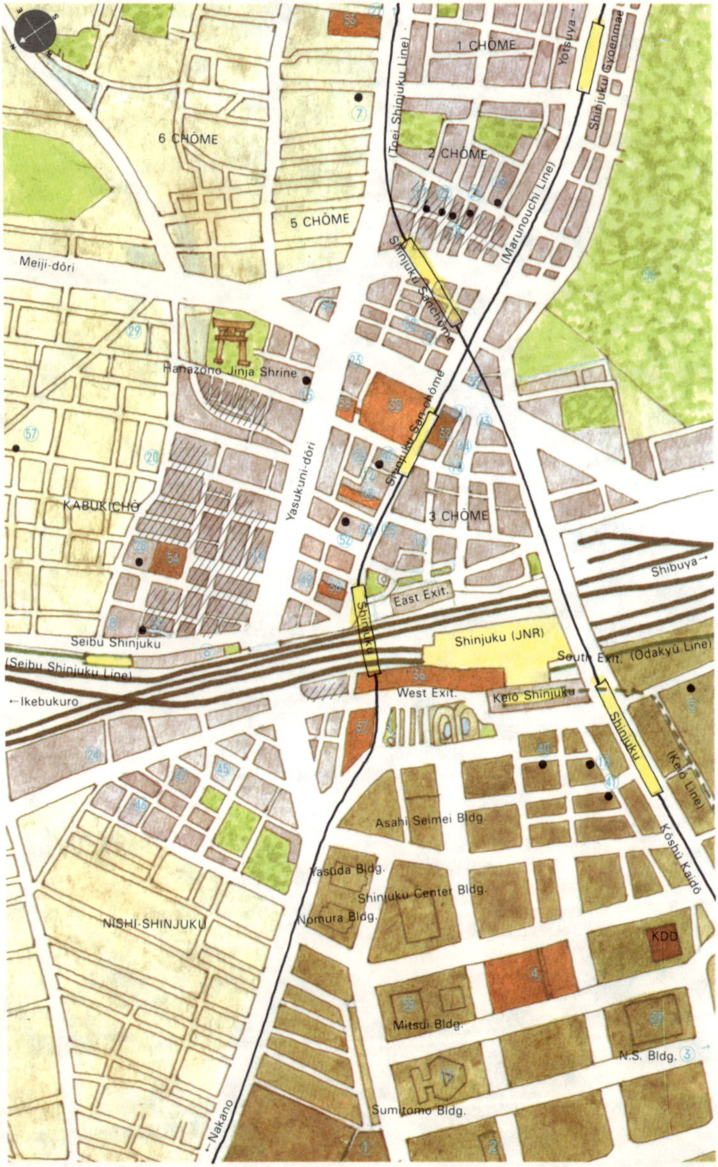

MAP

ACCOMMODATION
1. Hilton International (49)
2. Hotel Century Hyatt (50)
3. Washington Hotel (50)
4. Keiō Plaza Hotel (49)
5. Hotel Sun-oute Tokyo (50)
6. Shinjuku Prince Hotel (50)
7. Inabasō (Ryokan 53)
8. Green Plaza Shinjuku (Capsule H. 55)

JAPANESE RESTAURANTS
9. Sakaezushi Honten (Sushi 71)
10. Tsunahachi (Tempura 72)
11. Serina (Beef 79)
12. Healthmagic (Health 89)
13. Mana (Health 89)

OTHER RESTAURANTS
14. Tōkaien (Korean 90)
15. Tokyo Daihanten (Chinese 90)

COFFEE SHOP
16. Studio V (95)

NIGHTLIFE
17. 69 (174)
18. Regent Bar (G. Bar 175)
19. Peter Pan (G. Bar 175)
20. Kokuchō no Mizuumi "Black Swan Lake" (G. Bar 175)
21. Sambiki no Kobuta "3 Little Pigs" (G. Bar 175)
22. Sazae (G. Bar 175)
23. Tsubaki House (Disco 176)
2. Samba Club (Disco 177)
24. Loft (Rock 177)
25. Suzy's Bar (Rock 177)
26. Shinjuku Pit Inn (Jazz 178)
27. J (Jazz 178)
28. Wishbone (C & W 178)
29. Hotel Perrier (Love H. 182)

SHOPPING
30. Isetan Dept. (102)
31. Marui Fashion-kan (102)
32. Marui Techno-kan (E 102)
33. Marui Sports-kan (102)
34. Marui Interior-kan (102)
35. Marui Young-kan (F 102)
36. Odakyū Dept. (102)
37. Odakyū Halc (I 145)
38. Studio Alta (F 103)
39. O.A. Center (E 113)
40. Yodobashi Camera (C 114)
41. Camera no Doi (C 114)
42. Camera no Sakuraya (C 114)
43. Miyama Shōkai (C 114)
44. Disk Union (R 142)
45. Woodstock (R 142)
46. Winners (R 142)
47. UK Edison (R 142)
48. Kinokuniya (B 142)
49. Sampei Store (Disc. 144)

CONCERT HALLS & THEATERS
50. Suehirotei (159)
51. Cinema Square Tōkyū (168)
52. Shinjuku Royal (168)
53. Tokyo Kōseinenkin Kaikan (161)
48. Kinokuniya Hall (161)
54. Shinjuku Koma Gekijō (161)
54. Theater Apple (161)

GALLERY
55. Pentax Forum (197)

SIGHTSEEING
56. Shinjuku Gyoen (Garden 211)
57. Ichibankan (Arch. 216)

HEALTH & BEAUTY
58. Kōrakuen Sauna (233)
58. Ladies Sauna (233)
11. Do Sports Plaza (233)
8. Green Plaza Shinjuku (Sauna 233)

OTHERS
30. Isetan Playguide (162)

318 MAP

[M-8] GINZA

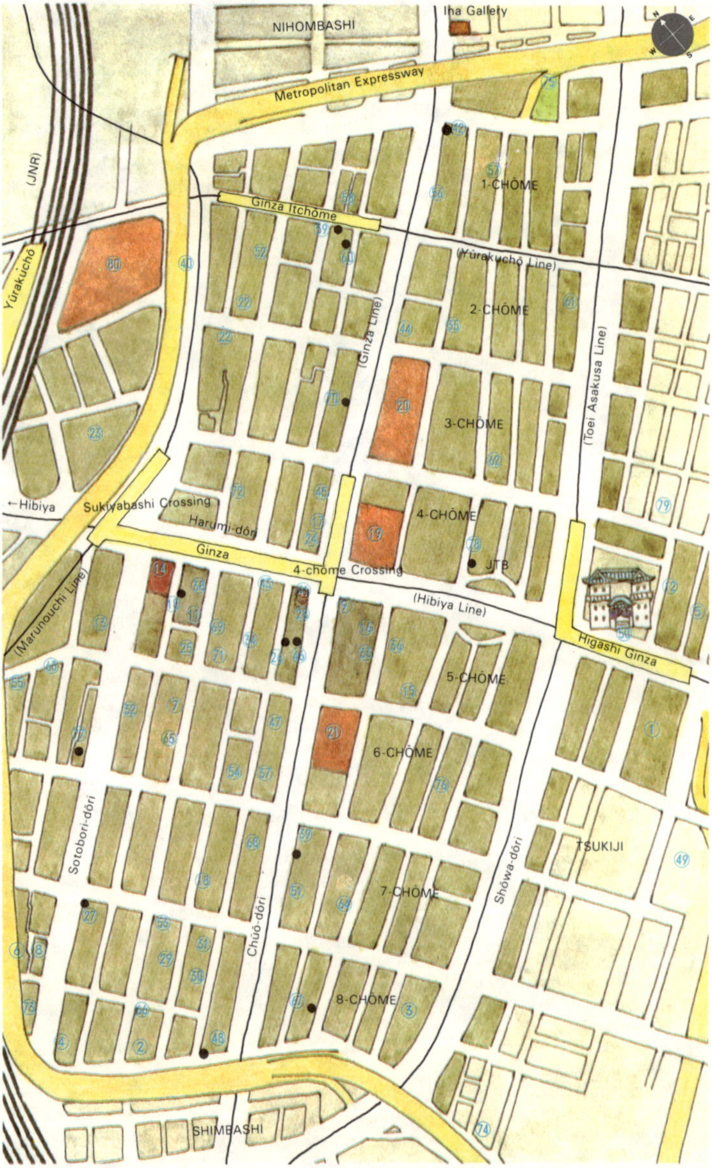

ACCOMMODATION
1. Ginza Tōkyū Hotel (46)
2. Mitsui Urban Hotel Ginza (46)
3. Ginza Dai-ichi Hotel (46)
4. Ginza Nikkō Hotel (46)
5. Hotel Atamisō (46)

JAPANESE RESTAURANTS
2. Munakata (Kaiseki 68)
6. Sushi Sei (Sushi 71)
7. Ten-ichi (Tempura 73)
8. Hīragi (Kushi-age 77)
9. Shabusen (Beef 79)
10. Ōmatsuya (Soba 81)
11. Yasuko (Oden 84)
12. Wakatsuki (Okonomiyaki 85)
13. Naokyū (Rāmen 86)

OTHER RESTAURANTS
14. Sabatini di Firenze (Italian 92)
14. Maxim de Paris (French 92)
15. Balalaika (Russian 93)

COFFEE SHOPS
16. Budō no ki (94)
17. Kimuraya (94)
18. Satō Ningyō (94)

SHOPPING
19. Mitsukoshi Dept. (101)
20. Matsuya Dept. (102)
21. Matsuzakaya Dept. (102)
22. Printemps Dept. (103)
23. Seibu Dept. (102)
24. Wakō (103)
25. Ginza To (F 103)
26. Yuki Torī (F 109)
8. Kyōto Center (AC 116)
27. Takumi (AC 116)
28. Kyūkyodō (AC 119, 121)
29. Myōgaya (AC 129)
30. Hiratsuka (AC 122)
31. Wan'ya Shoten (AC 130)
32. Shimakame (AC 128)
33. Ryūzendō (AC 121)
34. Tachikichi (AC 125)
35. Masudaya (AC 128)
36. Tsumugiya Kichihei (AC 128)
37. Kunoya (AC 129)
38. Yoitaya (AC 129)
14. Sony Showroom (E 112)
9. Technics Ginza (E 112)
39. Tōshiba Ginza Seven (E 112)
40. Hitachi Lo-D Plaza (E 112)
41. Mitsubishi Denki Showroom (E 112)
42. Maicon Base Ginza (E 114)
43. Jena (B 143)
44. Itōya (AO 144)
45. Mikimoto (Pearls 145)
46. Washington (Shoes 146)
47. Diana (Shoes 146)
48. Toy Park (146)

CONCERT HALLS & THEATERS
49. Shimbashi Embujō (159)
32. Ginza Nō Theater (159)
50. Kabukiza (159)
51. Gas Hall (161)
48. Hakuhinkan Gekijō (161)
52. Ginza Namikiza (168)

TICKET OUTLET
28. Kyūkyodō Ticket Service (162)

NIGHTLIFE
14. Pub Cardinal (Bar 174)
53. Health Angels (Bar 174)
54. Pilsen (Beer Hall 175)

MUSEUMS & GALLERIES
55. Riccar Art Museum (188)
56. Ai Gallery (195)
57. Gallery K (195)
58. G Art Gallery (195)
59. Lunami Gallery (195)
60. Gallery White Art (195)
61. Gallery Kobayashi (195)
62. Gallery Yamaguchi (195)
63. Gekkōsō Gallery (195)
64. Gallery Muramatsu (195)
65. Gallery Ueda (195)
66. Tokyo Gallery (195)
67. Gallery Te (195)
67. Gallery Q (195)
68. Kuroda Tōen (Ceramics 196)
69. Yōseidō Gallery (197)
70. Nikon Salon (Photos 197)
71. Gallery Mukai (197)
72. Nishimura Gallery (197)

SIGHTSEEING
73. Shizuoka Press Bldg. (Arch. 215)
74. Nakagin Capsule Bldg. (Arch. 215)

HEALTH & BEAUTY
75. Ginzayu (Bath 232)
22. Mod's Hair (236)
76. Tokyo Onsen Diamond Spa (233)
77. Tokyo Optical Center (231)

OTHERS
78. Ming-Yu International Library (293)
79. World Magazine Library (293)
80. Japan National Tourist Organization (240)

[M-9] NIHOMBASHI—KYŌBASHI

ACCOMMODATION
1. Hotel Kokusai Kankō (47)
2. Yaesu Fujiya Hotel (47)
3. Tokyo City Hotel (47)

JAPANESE RESTAURANTS
4. Munakata (Kaiseki 68)
5. Uogashi (Sushi 71)
6. Isehiro (Yakitori 74)
7. Mimiu (Udon 81)

SHOPPING
8. Mitsukoshi Dept. (101)
9. Takashimaya Dept. (101)
10. Daimaru Dept. (102)
11. Ishizuka (AC 116)
12. Haibara (AC 118)
13. Kamiyama Sudareten (AC 120)
14. Kuroeya (AC 123)
15. Tsurukawa Gakki-honten (AC 126)
16. Heiandō (AC 123)
17. Kiya (AC 122)
18. Saruya (AC 123)
19. Mayuyama & Co., Ltd. (A 133)
20. Yamamotoyama (FD 139)
21. Maruzen (B 143)

MARTIAL ARTS
22. Metropolitan Police Board PR Center (166)

THEATER
23. Film Center (168)

MUSEUMS & GALLERIES
24. Kite Museum (190)
25. Yamatane Museum of Art (188)
26. Bridgestone Museum of Art (188)
27. Tamura Gallery (194)
28. G Parelugon II (194)
29. Maki Gallery (195)
30. Komai Gallery (195)
31. Tokiwa Gallery (195)
32. Ina Gallery (195)
33. Nantenshi Gallery (195)
34. Kaneko Art Gallery (195)
35. Kaneko Art G1 (195)
36. Zeito Photo (197)
37. Kanransha (197)
38. Akira Ikeda Gallery (197)

SIGHTSEEING
39. Nihombashi Bridge (214)
40. Bank of Japan (Arch. 214)

OTHERS
41. Japan Travel Bureau (258)

[M-10] YŪRAKUCHŌ—HIBIYA—MARUNOUCHI

MAP 323

ACCOMMODATION
1. Imperial Hotel (46)
2. Palace Hotel (47)
3. Tokyo Marunouchi Hotel (47)
4. Tokyo Station Hotel (47)

JAPANESE RESTAURANT
5. Ajiwai (Yakitori 75)

SHOPPING
6. Sakai Kōkodō Gallery (A, AC 125)
1. Imperial Hotel Arcade (105)
7. International Arcade (AC, E 105)
7. Hayashi Kimono (A, AC 134)
8. NEC Showroom (E 113)

CONCERT HALLS & THEATERS
9. Tokyo Takarazuka Gekijō (161)
10. Nissei Gekijō (161)
11. Yomiuri Hall (162)
12. Hibiya Kōkaidō (161)
13. Ino Hall (161)
14. Teikoku Gekijō (161)

MUSEUMS & GALLERIES
15. Idemitsu Art Gallery (187)
1. Yaya Gallery (196)

TRADITIONAL ART
1. Tōkō-an (Tea 199)

SIGHTSEEING
16. Kōkyo Higashi Gyoen (Garden 211)
17. Hibiya Kōen (Park 210)
18. Kōkyo (Imperial Palace 213)
19. Nijūbashi Bridge (213)
20. Tokyo Metropolitan Goven't Offices (Arch. 215)
21. Industrial Bank of Japan (Arch. 216)
16. Imperial Music Hall (Arch. 216)

HEALTH & BEAUTY
22. American Pharmacy (231)
2. Pink Pearl (Steam Bath 233)
1. Sanwa Massage (233)

OTHERS
23. Metropolitan Hibiya Library (293)
24. Tourist Information Center (257)

[M-11] SHIBA—TORANOMON—SHIMBASHI

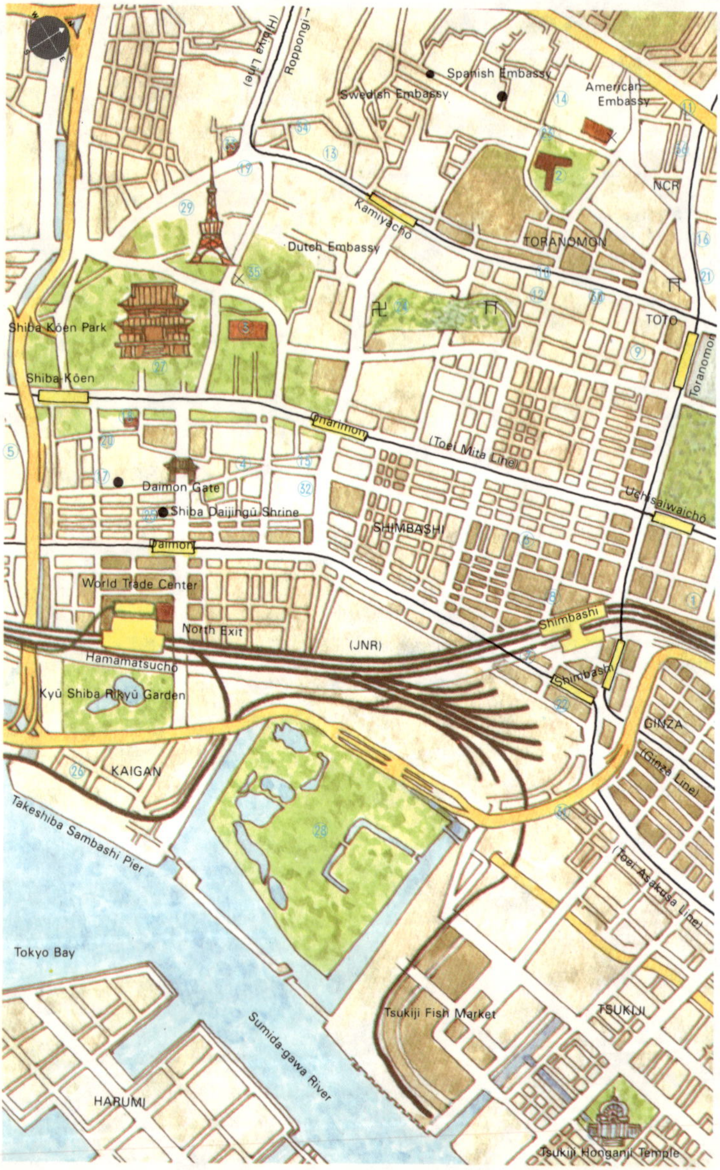

ACCOMMODATION
1. Shimbashi Daiichi Hotel (46)
2. Hotel Ōkura (48)
3. Tokyo Prince Hotel (48)
4. Shiba Park Hotel (48)
5. Tokyo Grand Hotel (48)

JAPANESE RESTAURANTS
6. Kazuya (Tonkatsu 78)
7. Shimbashi Kenkō Shizenshoku Center (Health 89)
8. Tōjimbō (Health 89)

NIGHTLIFE
9. Chitose-tei (Karaoke 179)

SHOPPING
2. Hotel Ōkura Arcade (105)
10. Japan Sword (AC 122)
11. Inachū Japan (AC 123)
12. Ishida Biwa-ten (AC 126)
13. Art Plaza Magatani (A 133)
14. The Gallery (A 133)
15. Heisandō (A 133)
16. Victor Video Center (E 112)
17. Techno Culture Center Media Bum (E 113)

CONCERT HALLS & THEATERS
18. ABC Hall (161)
19. Ikura La Foret 800/500 (161)
20. Yūbin Chokin Hall (162)
21. Toranomon Hall (161)
22. Yakult Hall (162)

MUSEUMS & GALLERIES
23. Ōkura Museum (187)
24. NHK Museum of Broadcasting (191)
25. Toleman Collection (197)
16. Video Information Center (198)
26. Gatōdō Gallery Takebashi (196)

TRADITIONAL ARTS
2. Chōshō-an (Tea 199)

SIGHTSEEING
27. Zōjōji Temple (206)
28. Hama Rikyū Teien (Garden 211)
29. Tokyo Tower (213)
30. Toranomon NN Bldg. (Arch. 215)
31. Nakagin Capsule Tower Bldg. (Arch. 215)
32. Japan Headquarters of the Red Cross (Arch. 215)
33. Noa Bldg. (Arch. 216)
34. Reiyūkai Shakaden (Arch. 216)

HEALTH & BEAUTY
35. Tokyo Medical & Surgical Clinic (230)
35. Besford Dental Office (231)
36. Matsuo Shika Iin (Dental 231)
35. The Medical Dispensary (231)
2. Hotel Ōkura Steam Bath (233)

[M-12] ASAKUSA

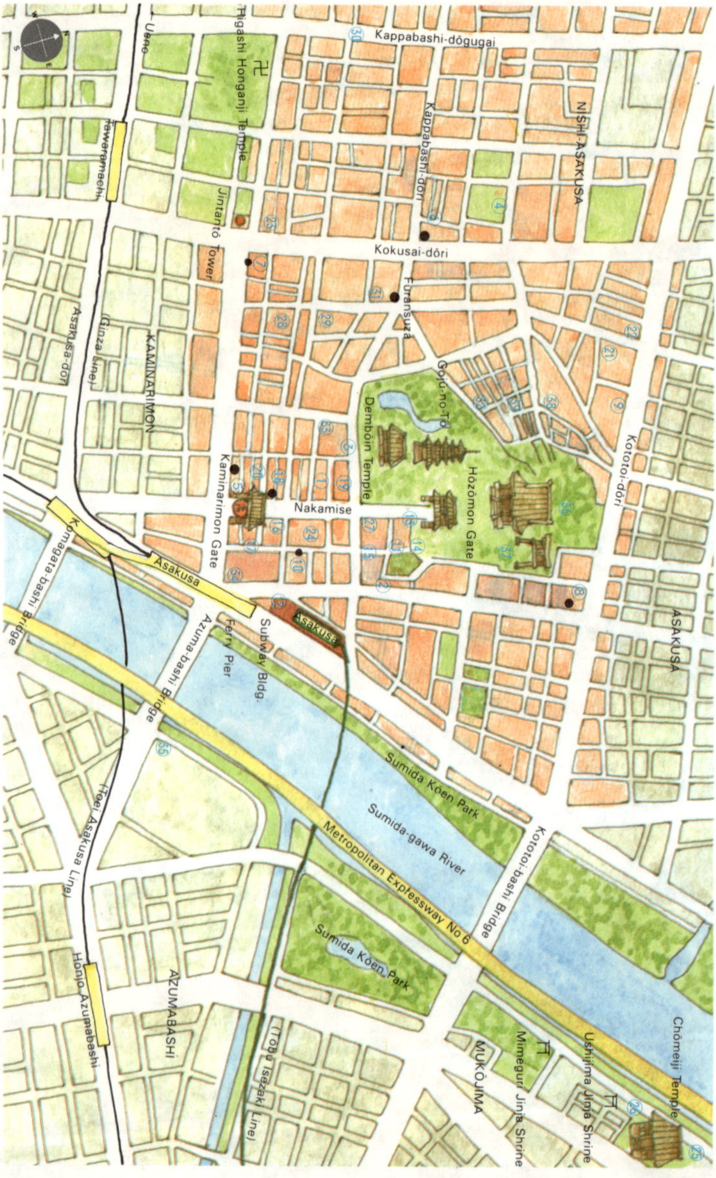

ACCOMMODATION
1. Mikawaya Bekkan (Ryokan 53)

JAPANESE RESTAURANTS
2. Miyako (Sushi 71)
3. Daikokuya (Tempura 73)
4. Kawakin (Tonkatsu 78)
5. Chin-ya (Beef 79)
6. Asakusa Imahan (Beef 79)
7. Yakko (Unagi 83)
8. Maruta-gōshi (Oden 84)
9. Tambo (Okonomiyaki 85)
10. Tatsumiya (88)
11. Kuremutsu (88)

SHOPPING
12. Matsuya Dept. (102)
13. Sukeroku (AC 117)
14. Hyakusuke (AC 131)
15. Fujiya Tenuguiten (AC 132)
16. Hōsendō Kyūami (AC 130, 132)
17. Kurodaya (AC 119)
18. Bunsendō (AC 130)
19. Yonoya (AC 131)
20. Hasetoku (AC 129)
21. Hanatō (AC 120)
22. Kiriya Gofukuten (AC 132)
23. Miyamoto Unosuke Shōten (AC 127)
24. Idaya (AC 121)
25. Kototoi Dango (FD 136)
26. Chōmeiji Sakuramochi (FD 136)
27. Kimuraya Hompo (FD 137)
28. Iriyama Sembei (FD 137)
29. Hinode Sembei (FD 137)
30. Kappabashi Wholesale Market (106)

THEATERS
31. Asakusa Engei Hall (159)
32. Asakusa Mokubatei (159)
33. Asakusa Kōkaido (161)

NIGHTLIFE
34. Kamiya Bar (174)
35. Azumabashi Beer House (175)

SIGHTSEEING
36. Sensōji Temple (206)
37. Asakusa Jinja Shrine (208)
38. Hanayashiki Yūenchi (Pleasure Ground 213)

HEALTH & BEAUTY
39. Asakusa Kannon Onsen (Bath 232)

328 MAP

[M-13] UENO

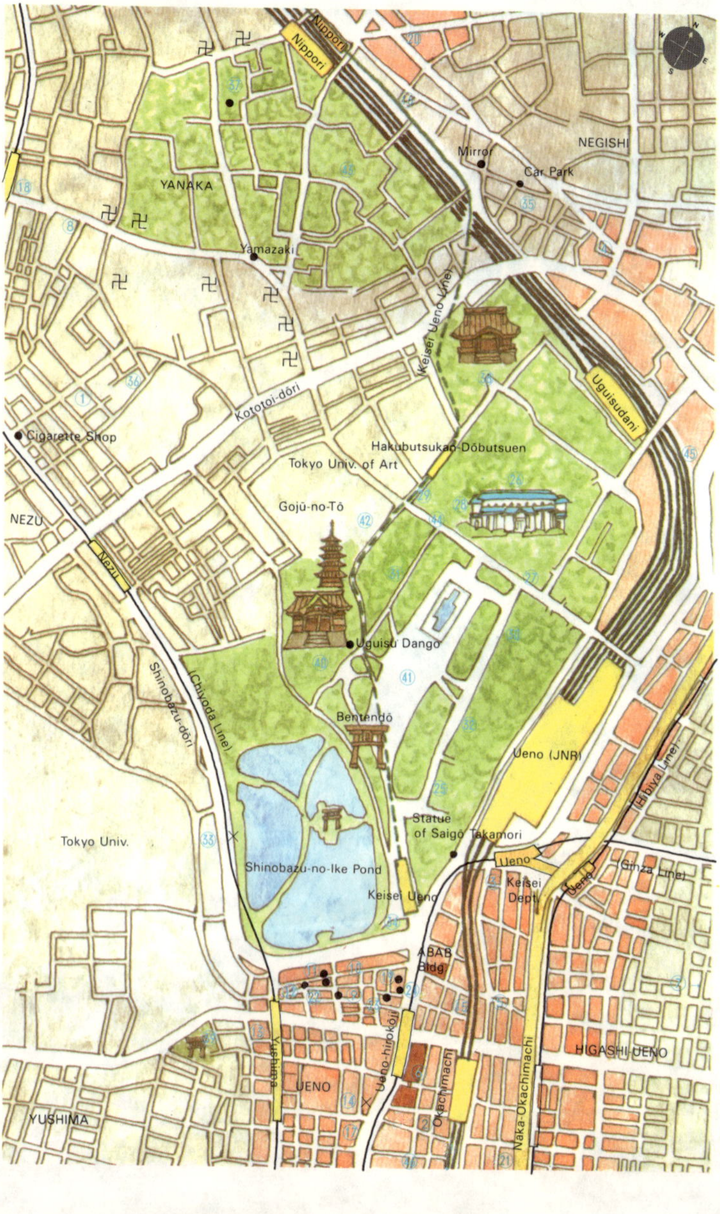

ACCOMMODATION
① Sawanoya (Ryokan 53)
JAPANESE RESTAURANTS
② Honke Ponta (Tonkatsu 78)
③ Santomo (Fugu 83)
④ Sasanoyuki (Tōfu 84)
OTHER RESTAURANT
⑤ Yansandō (Korean 90)
SHOPPING
⑥ Matsuzakaya Dept. (102)
⑦ Hashimoto (AC 117)
⑧ Isetatsu (AC 118)
⑨ Hasegawa Hakimonoten (AC 121, 129)
⑩ Kyōya (AC 122)
⑪ Dōmyō (AC 129)
⑫ Kikuya Shamisenten (AC 126)
⑬ Ishizuka Shōten (AC 120)
⑭ Sairakudō (A 125)
⑮ Nakata Shōten (A 135)
⑯ Habutae Dango (FD 136)
⑰ Usagiya (FD 137)
⑱ Kikumi Sembei (FD 137)
⑲ Shuetsu (FD 139)
⑮ Ameyoko Arcade (105)
⑳ Nippori Wholesale Market (106)
㉑ Maruboshi Denki (E 114)
㉒ Kiya (AO 144)
CONCERT HALLS & THEATERS
㉓ Hommokutei (159)
㉔ Suzumoto Engeijō (159)
㉕ Tokyo Bunka Kaikan (161)
MUSEUMS
㉖ Tokyo National Museum (186)
㉗ Tōyōkan (186)
㉘ Hyōkeikan (186)
㉙ Hōryūji Treasure House (186)
㉚ National Science Museum (191)
㉛ Tokyo Metropolitan Art Museum (188)
㉜ National Museum of Western Art (188)
㉝ Yokoyama Taikan Memorial Gallery (191)
㉞ Shitamachi Museum (189)
㉟ Museum of Calligraphy (189)
㊱ Daimyō Clock Museum (190)
㊲ Asakura Sculpture Gallery (188)
SIGHTSEEING
㊳ Kan'eiji Temple (206)
㊴ Yushima Tenjin Shrine (208)
㊵ Tōshōgū Shrine (209)
㊶ Ueno Kōen (Park 210)
㊷ Ueno Dōbutsuen (Zoo 212)
㊸ Yanaka Bochi (Cemetery 215)
㊹ Kyū Ikeda Yashiki Ōtemon (214)
HEALTH & BEAUTY
㊺ Dr. Yukio Kurosu (230)
㊻ Tsubame-yu (Bath 232)

[M-14] AKIHABARA

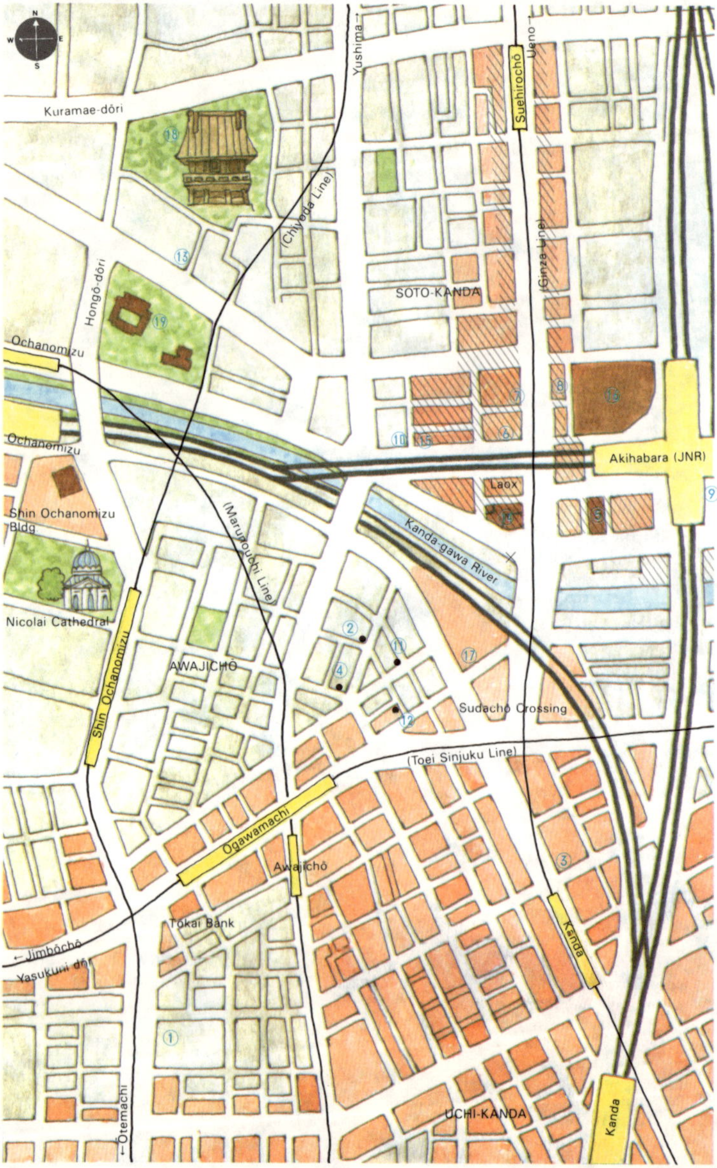

ACCOMMODATION
① Tokyo YMCA (54)
JAPANESE RESTAURANTS
② Yabu-soba (Soba 81)
③ Kikukawa (Unagi 83)
④ Shōeitei (Yōshoku 88)
SHOPPING
⑤ Radio Kaikan (E 113)
⑥ Tokyo Radio Dept. (E 113)
⑤ Kimura Musen (E 113)
⑦ Satō Musen (E 113)
⑤ Shōjin Shōkai (E 113)
⑧ Hirose Musen Audio Center (F 113)
⑤ F. Shōkai (E 113)
⑨ Rocket Honten (E 113)
⑤ Fujionkyō "Maikon" Center Ram (E 113)
⑥ Honda Tsūshō (E 114)
⑥ Wakamatsu Tsūshō (E 114)
⑩ Livina Yamagiwa (I 120)
⑪ Takemura (FD 136)
⑫ Midoriya (FD 137)
⑬ Amanoya (FD 138)
⑭ Ishimaru Denki No. 3 (R 142)
⑮ Ishimaru Denki Honten (R 142)
⑯ Kanda Fruit & Vegetable Market (107)
MUSEUM
⑰ Transportation Museum (191)
SIGHTSEEING
⑱ Kanda Myōjin Shrine (207)
⑲ Yushima Seido (213)

332 MAP

[M-15] OCHANOMIZU—JIMBŌCHŌ

ACCOMMODATION
① Hilltop Hotel (51)
② Tokyo YWCA Hostel (54)
③ YWCA Asia Youth Center (54)

RESTAURANTS
④ Sarafan (Russian 93)
⑤ Balalaika (Russian 93)

COFFEE SHOP
⑥ Rihaku (95)

SHOPPING
⑦ Gyokusendō (AC 119)
⑧ Yōmeidō Budōguten (AC 133)
⑨ Wan'ya Shoten (AC 130)
⑩ Tokyo Old Folk Craft & Antique Center (A 133)
⑪ Sanseidō (B 143)
⑫ Kitazawa Shoten (B 143)
⑬ Sancha Shobō (B 143)
⑭ Ōya Shobō (B 143)
⑮ Tuttle Bookshop (B 143)
⑯ Matsumura Shoten (B 143)
⑰ Kanda Kosho Center (B, A 143)
⑱ Hara Shobō (B 143)
⑲ Tokyo Taibunsha (B 143)
⑳ Toyoda Shobō (B 143)
㉑ Haga Shoten (B 143)
㉒ Lemon (AO 144)
㉓ Kimuraya (Disc. 144)

THEATERS
㉔ Athénée Français (168)
㉕ Iwanami Hall (168)

TRADITIONAL ARTS
㉖ Ikenobō (Ikebana 199)
㉗ Ikebana International (199)

MUSEUMS
㉘ Meiji University Archeological Collection (189)
㉘ Meiji University Criminal Museum (190)

SIGHTSEEING
㉙ Nicolai Cathedral (213)
㉔ Athénée Français (Arch. 216)

[M-16] YUSHIMA

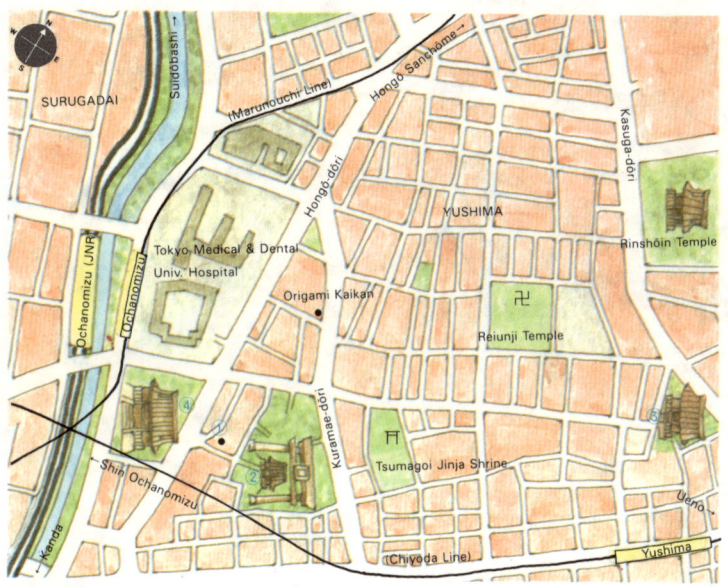

SHOPPING
① Amanoya (FD 138)
SIGHTSEEING
② Kanda Myōjin Shrine (207)
③ Yushima Tenjin Shrine (208)
④ Yushima Seidō (213)

[M-17] KUDAN

ACCOMMODATION
1. Hotel Grand Palace (51)
2. Kudan Kaikan Hotel (51)
3. Fairmont Hotel (51)
4. Hotel Kayū Kaikan (48)

NIGHTLIFE
2. Kudan Beer Garden (176)

CONCERT HALLS & THEATERS
2. Kudan Kaikan Hall (161)
5. Nihon Budōkan (161)

MUSEUMS
6. Treasure House of the Yasukuni Shrine (190)
7. Science Museum (191)
8. Tokyo National Museum of Modern Art (187)
9. Crafts Gallery of the Museum of Modern Art (187)

SIGHTSEEING
10. Yasukuni Jinja Shrine (207)
11. Kitanomaru Park (210)

[M-18] IKEBUKURO

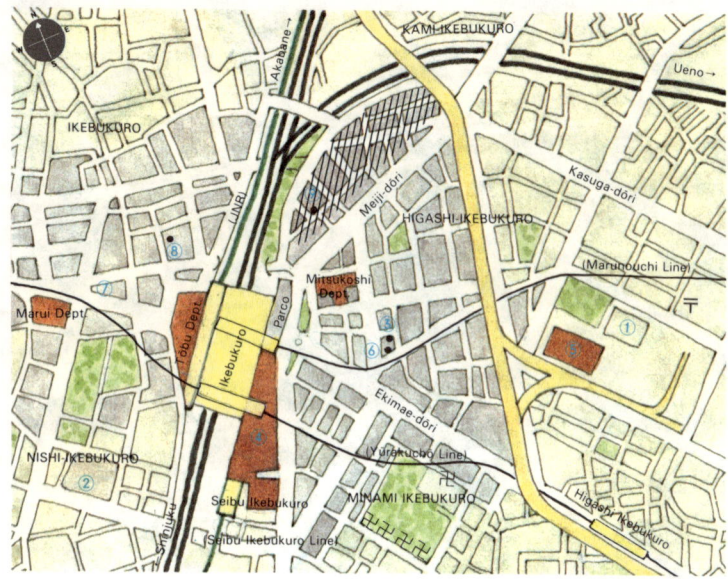

ACCOMMODATION
① Sunshine City Prince Hotel (50)
② Hotel Metropolitan (Hotel 50)
③ Hotel White City (55)

SHOPPING
④ Seibu Dept. (102)
⑤ Sunshine City (104)
⑥ Bic Camera (C 114)
⑦ Camera no Kimura (C 114)
④ Habitat (I 145)

CONCERT HALLS & THEATERS
⑧ Ikebukuro Engeijō (159)
⑨ Bungeiza (168)
④ Studio 200 (161)
⑤ Sunshine Gekijō (161)

MUSEUMS & GALLERIES
⑤ The Ancient Orient Museum (190)
④ Seibu Art Museum (188)

[M-19] MEGURO

ACCOMMODATION
① Miyako Hotel Tokyo (51)
② Gajoen Kankō Hotel (51)
③ Meguro Gajoen (Ryokan 53)

JAPANESE RESTAURANT
④ Tonki (Tonkatsu 78)

NIGHTLIFE
⑤ Meguro Emperor (Love H. 182)

SHOPPING
⑥ Gallery Meguro (A 133)
⑦ Pioneer Showroom (E 113)

MUSEUMS
⑧ Hatakeyama Museum (187)
⑨ Tokyo Metropolitan Teien Museum of Art (188)
⑩ National Park for Nature Study (191)

[M-20] DAIKAN-YAMA

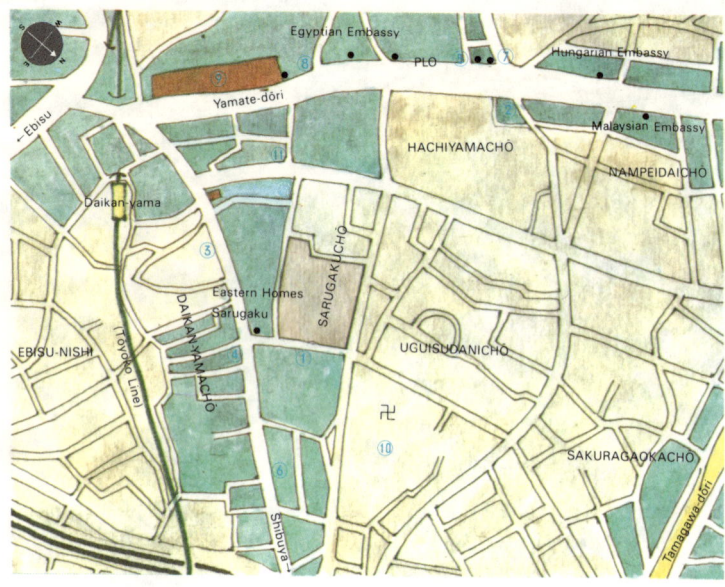

JAPANESE RESTAURANT
① Daikon-ya (Kaiseki 68)
OTHER RESTAURANTS
② Madame Toki's (French 92)
③ La Boheme (Italian 93)
NIGHTLIFE
④ Bar de Savey (173)
SHOPPING
⑤ Junko Shimada (F 108)
① Ficce Uomo (F 110)
⑥ Sabby Genteel (F, I 111, 145)
⑦ Tokio Kumagai (F, Shoes 110, 146)
SIGHTSEEING
⑧ Royal Danish Embassy (Arch. 215)
⑨ Hillside Terrace (Arch. 215)
⑩ Jōsenji Temple (Arch. 215)
HEALTH & BEAUTY
⑪ Bijin (Hair 236)

[M-21] JIYŪGAOKA

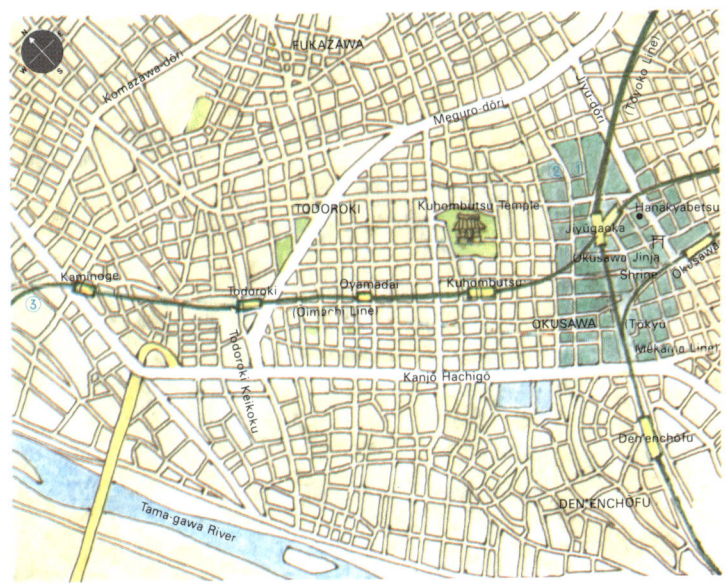

JAPANESE RESTAURANTS
1. Okajū (Robata-yaki 76)
2. Motomachi (Okonomi-yaki 85)

MUSEUM
3. Gotō Art Museum (186)

[M-22] TSUKIJI—HARUMI

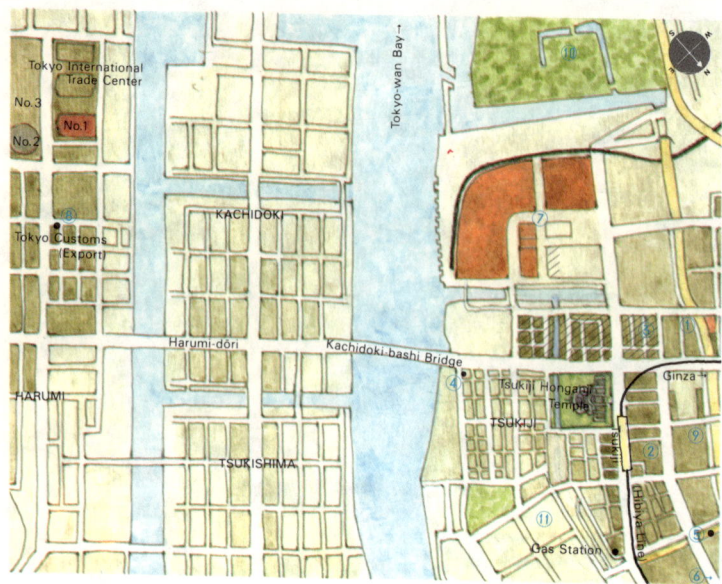

ACCOMMODATION
① Ginza Marunouchi Hotel (46)
JAPANESE RESTAURANTS
② Tamura (Kaiseki 68)
③ Tsukiji Edogin (Sushi 71)
④ Tentake (Fugu 83)
SHOPPING
⑤ Kashiwaya (AC 120)
⑥ Ōnoya Sōhonten (AC 130)
⑦ Tsukiji Fish Market (106)
MUSEUM
⑧ Furniture Museum (191)
SIGHTSEEING
⑨ Dentsū Bldg. (Arch. 215)
⑩ Hama Rikyū Teien (Garden 211)
HEALTH & BEAUTY
⑪ St. Luke's International Hospital (230)

[M-23] NINGYŌCHŌ

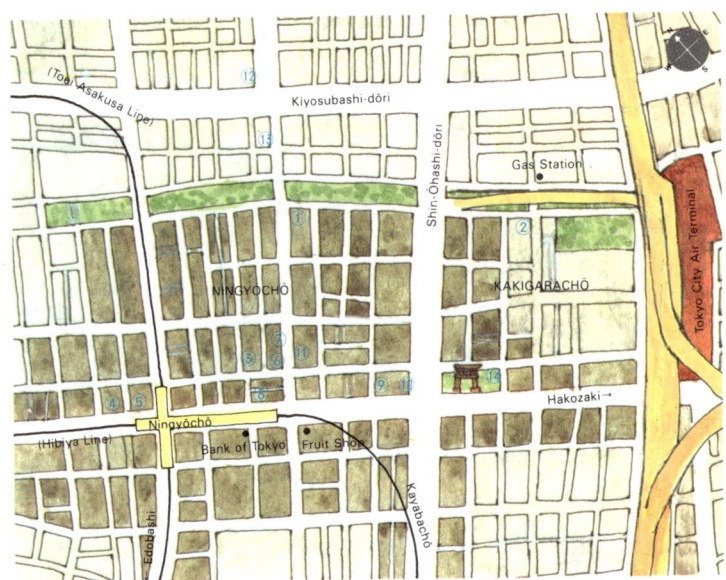

ACCOMMODATION
① Hotel Kitchō (52)
② City Pension Zem (52)
JAPANESE RESTAURANT
③ Hōmitei (Yōshoku 88)
SHOPPING
④ Ubukeya (AC 122)
⑤ Iseryū Shōten (AC 125)
⑥ Iwai Shōten (AC 119)
⑦ Bachi-ei Gakkiten (AC 126)
⑧ Kyōsendō (AC 130)
⑨ Kotobukidō Kyōgashi-tsukasa (FD 136)
⑩ Shigemori Eishindō (FD 137)
⑪ Yanagiya (FD 137)
THEATER
⑫ Meijiza (161)
MUSEUM
⑬ Kurita Museum (190)
SIGHTSEEING
⑭ Suitengū Shrine (208)

[M-24] ASAKUSABASHI

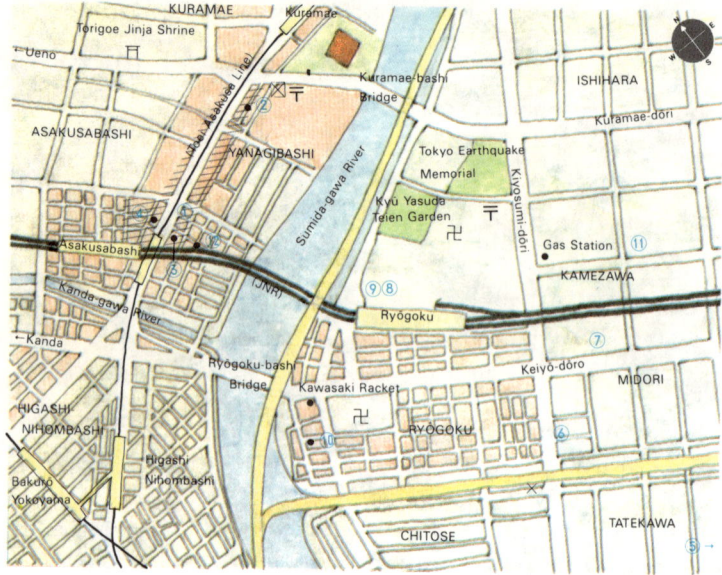

SHOPPING
① Wholesale Market (106)
② Musashiya Shōten (AC 117)
③ Kyūgetsu (AC 118)
④ Kōundō (AC 119)
⑤ Itō Oke-ten (AC 123)
⑥ Kikuya (AC 129)
⑦ Tokyo Hyakka Funabashiya (Disc. 144)

SPORTS: SUMŌ
⑨ New Kokugikan Sumō Stadium (164)
⑩ Kasugano-beya (164)
⑪ Kokonoe-beya (164)
⑫ Takasago-beya (164)

MUSEUM
⑧ Sumō Museum (191)

[M-25] FUKAGAWA—TSUKUDAJIMA

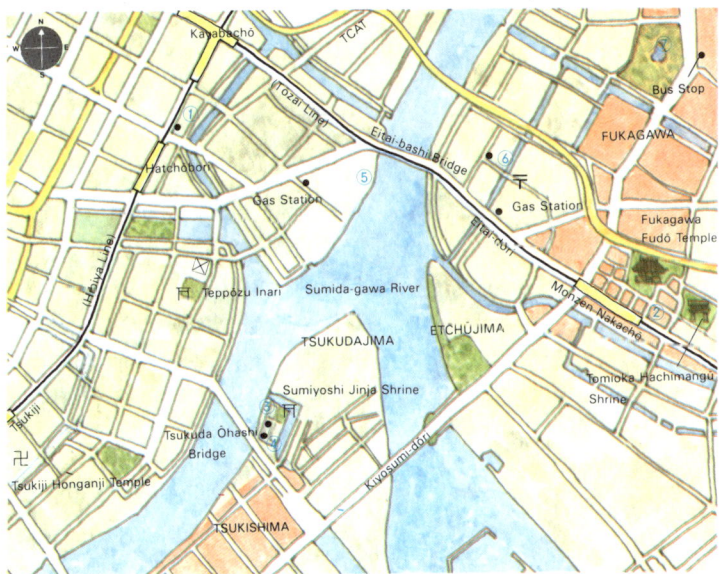

ACCOMMODATION
① Holiday Inn (52)
SHOPPING
② Miyagetsudō (FD 136)
③ Ten'yasu (FD 139)
④ Tanakaya (FD 139)
GALLERIES
⑤ Gallery Ueda Warehouse (197)
⑥ Sagachō Exhibit Space (196)
SIGHTSEEING
⑦ Kiyosumi Teien (Garden 211)

MAP LIST

Tokyo Transportation 300
Areas 302
[M-1] Roppongi 304
[M-2] Nishi-Azabu—Hirō 306
[M-3] Shibuya 308
[M-4] Harajuku 310
[M-5] Aoyama 312
[M-6] Akasaka—Nagatachō 314
[M-7] Shinjuku 316
[M-8] Ginza 318
[M-9] Nihombashi—Kyōbashi 320
[M-10] Yūrakuchō—Hibiya—Marunouchi 322
[M-11] Shiba—Toranomon—Shimbashi 324
[M-12] Asakusa 326
[M-13] Ueno 328
[M-14] Akihabara 330
[M-15] Ochanomizu—Jimbōchō 332
[M-16] Yushima 334
[M-17] Kudan 335
[M-18] Ikebukuro 336
[M-19] Meguro 337
[M-20] Daikan-yama 338
[M-21] Jiyūgaoka 339
[M-22] Tsukiji—Harumi 340
[M-23] Ningyōchō 341
[M-24] Asakusabashi 342
[M-25] Fukagawa—Tsukudajima 343
[M-26] Nakano 345
[M-27] Ōkubo 345
[M-28] Yoyogi 345
[M-29] Sendagaya 345
[M-30] Kōrakuen 346
[M-31] Yotsuya 346
[M-32] Hakusan 346
[M-33] Shibuya 346
[M-34] Shimokitazawa 347
[M-35] Komabatōdaimae 347
[M-36] Tokyo 347
[M-37] Shinagawa 347
[M-38] Shinagawa 347
[M-39] Kita-Shinagawa 348
[M-40] Ōimachi 348
[M-41] Komagome 348
[M-42] Tamanoi 349
[M-43] Iriya 349
[M-44] Kameido 349
[M-45] Horikiri Shōbuen 349
[M-46] Daishimae 350
[M-47] Honjo-Azumabashi 350
[M-48] Ōji 350

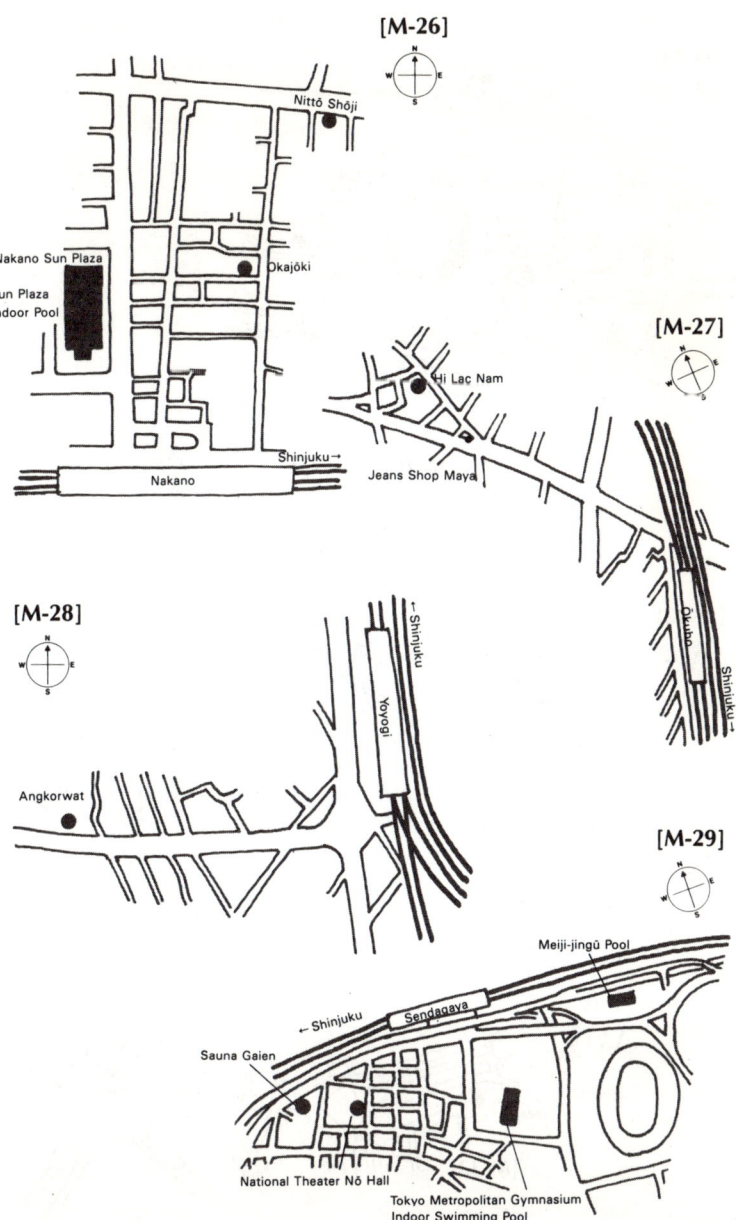

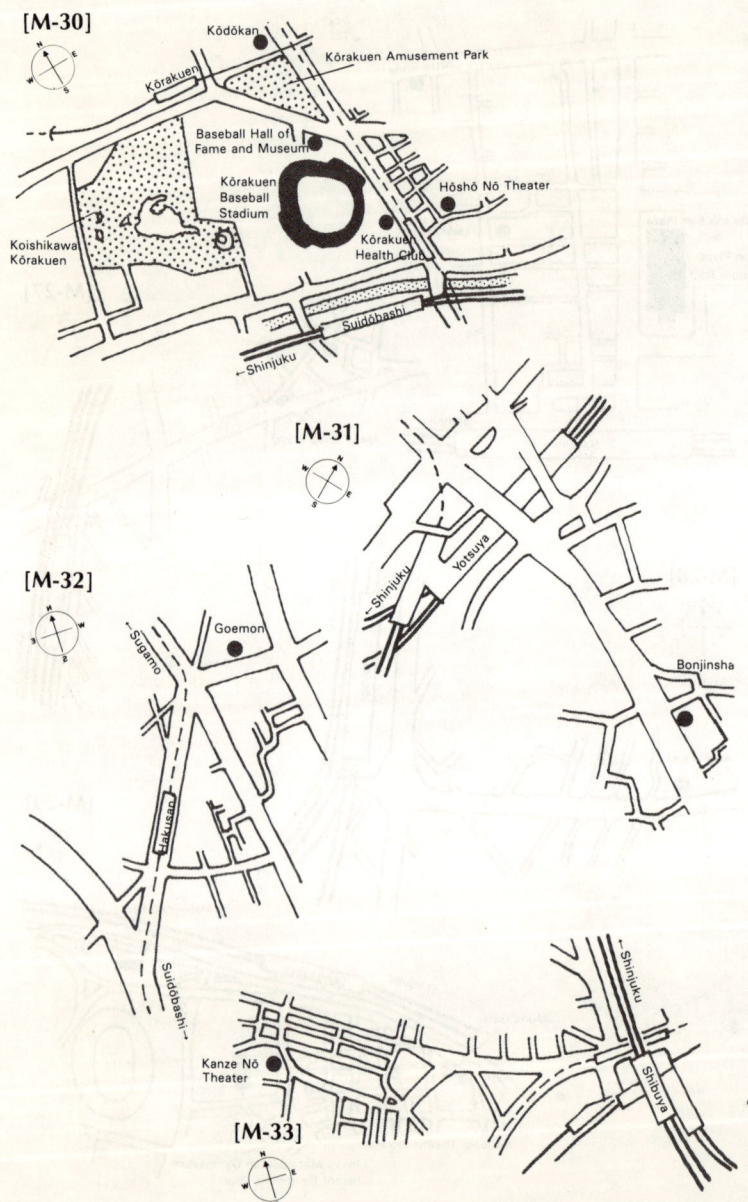

MAP 347

[M-34]

Shinjuku →
Shimokitazawa
Honda Gekijō

[M-35]

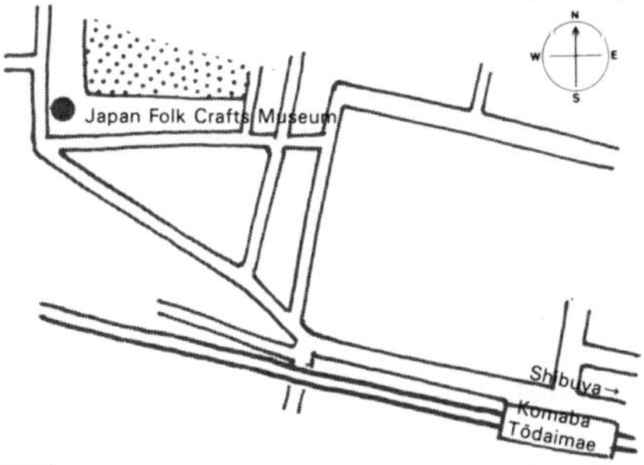

Japan Folk Crafts Museum

Shibuya →
Komaba Tōdaimae

[M-36]

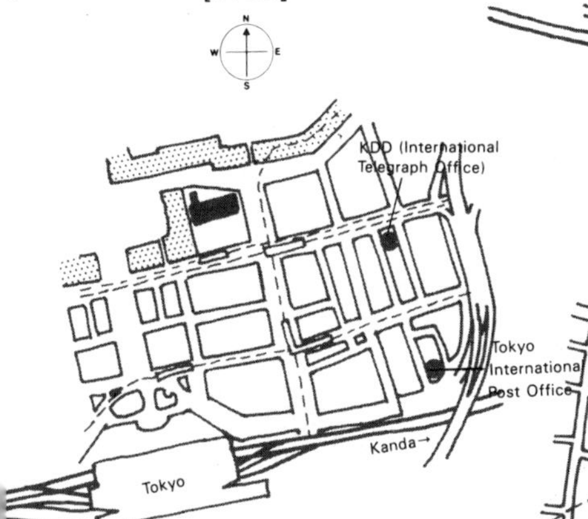

KDD (International Telegraph Office)
Tokyo International Post Office
Kanda →
Tokyo

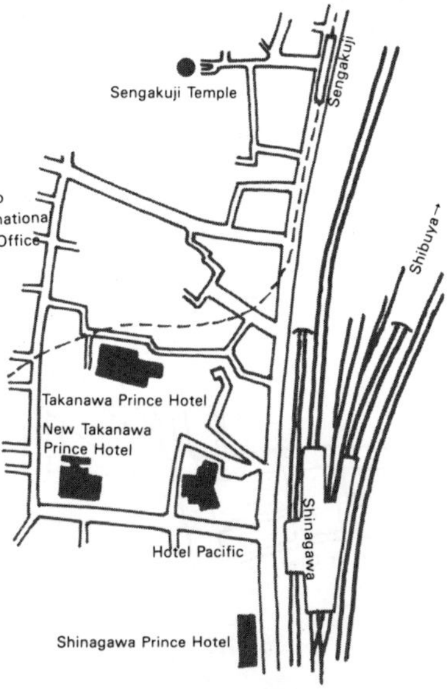

Sengakuji Temple
Sengakuji
Shibuya →

Takanawa Prince Hotel
New Takanawa Prince Hotel

[M-37]

Hotel Pacific
Shinagawa
Shinagawa Prince Hotel

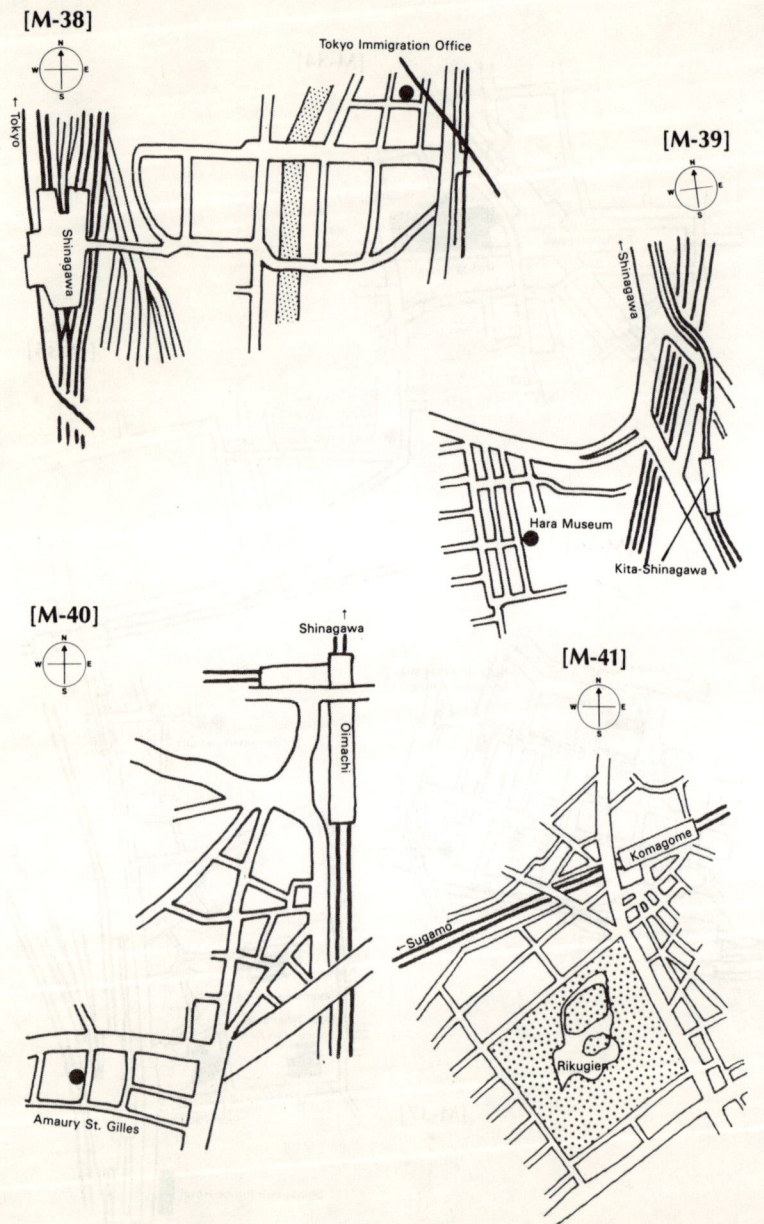

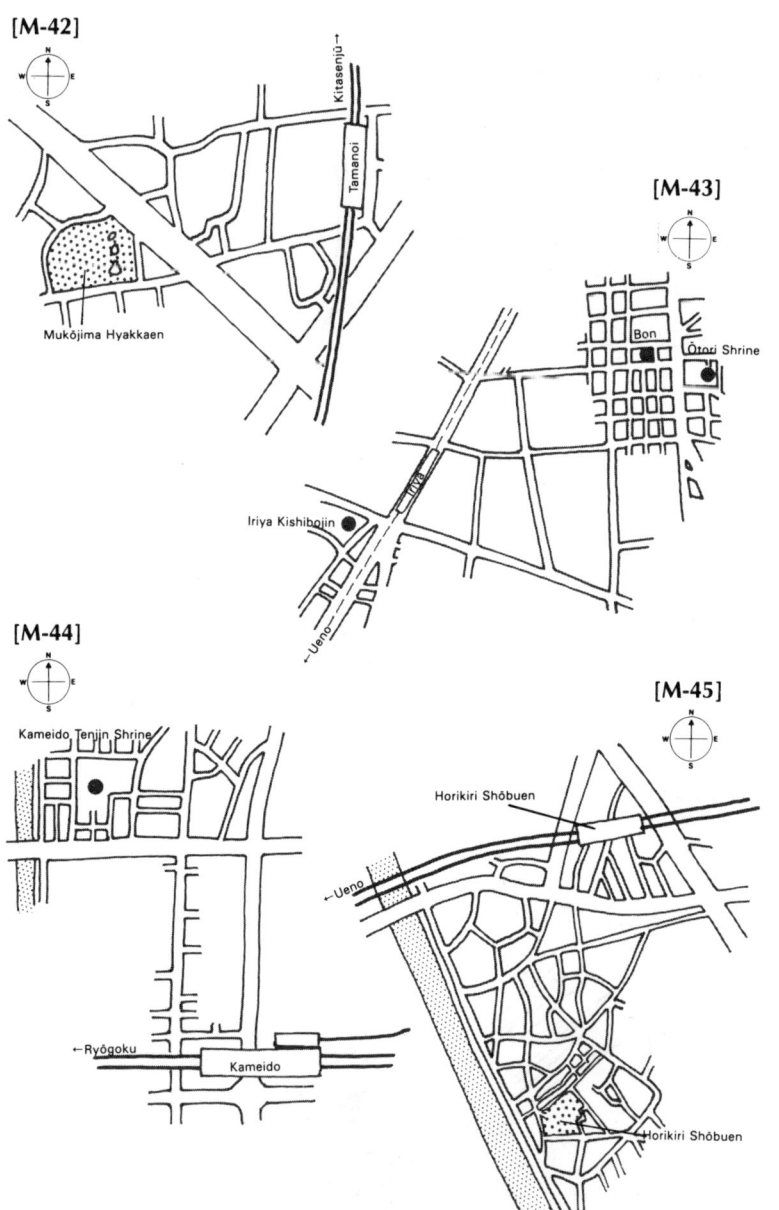

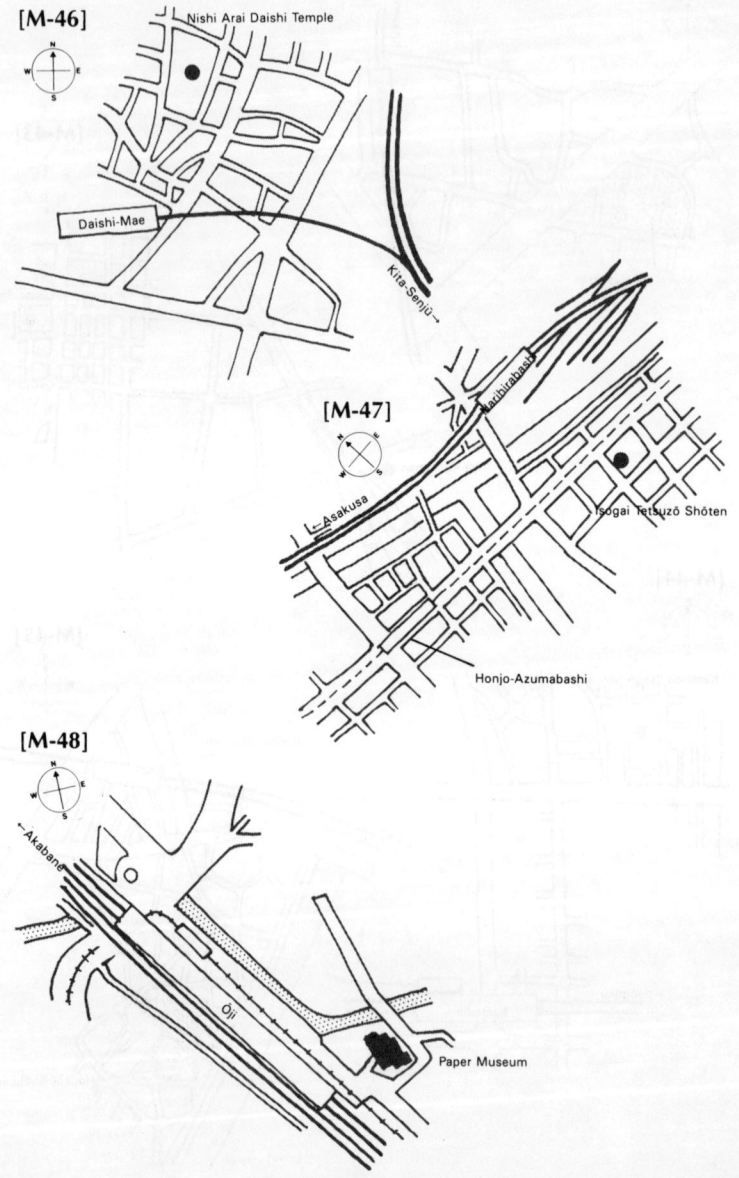

PICTURE CREDITS

18 page
●

Creative Director	Hideo MUKAI
Art Director	Koji MIZUNO
Designer	Nobuhiko SUGAYA
Copywriter	Hide NAKANO
Photographer	Hidesato IWANAMI
Stylist	Masako MABUCHI
	Yoshiko EGI
Hair Designer	Yoshio SUGIYAMA
Advertiser	MATSUYA

44 page
●

Art Director	Toshio SUZUKI
Designer	Toshio SUZUKI
Copywriter	Takashi ANDO
Photographer	Masaki NISHIMURA
Advertiser	SUNTORY

58 page
●

Art Director	Hideo MUKAI
Designer	Hideo MUKAI
Copywriter	Hideo MUKAI
Photographer	Tadao YOSHIDA
Advertiser	KIBUN

98 page
●

Creative Director	Takashi NAKAHATA
Art Director	Kaoru KASAI
Copywriter	Takashi NAKAHATA
Photographer	Masaaki KOBAYASHI
Advertiser	SONY

150 page
●

Creative Director	Kyo NIINUMA
Art Director	Kazutaka YAMASHITA
Designer	Takuji MIYAZAKI
Copywriter	Kyo NIINUMA
Illustrator	Haruo TAKINO
Advertiser	KABUKIZA THEATER

170 page
●

Art Director	Makoto NAKAMURA
Designer	Makoto NAKAMURA
Copywriter	Kesao UCHIDA
Photographer	Noriaki YOKOSUKA
Advertiser	SHISEIDO

184 page
●

Art Director	Ikko TANAKA
Designer	Tokiyoshi TSUBOUCHI
Copywriter	Kazuko KOIKE
Advertiser	SEIBU BIJUTSUKAN

202 page
●

Art Director	Shinichi HARA
Designer	Hidetake AWANO
Copywriter	Nobuko HIRASHIMA
Photographer	Takayoshi TERASHIMA
Advertiser	ALFA RECORD

228 page
●

Art Director	Yoshio HASEGAWA
Designer	Yoshio HASEGAWA
Copywriter	Takeo NAGASAWA
Photographer	Masaya SUGA
Advertiser	PARCO

238 page
●

Art Director	Nobuo SUGIMOTO
Designer	Naoko HENMI
Copywriter	Tokie INADA
Illustrator	Atsushi YOSHIDA
Advertiser	TEITO KOSOKUDO
	KOTSU EIDAN

We would like to thank all of the above people for their help and cooperation.

ACKNOWLEDGEMENTS

The TOKYO CITY GUIDE and its authors owe their thanks to a vast number of people who gave advice, recommendations, support, and enthusiasm to this project. A special thanks is owed to the following people: Mori Akira, Hara Saburō, Ichimura Suzuko, Inagaki Jirō, Hashimoto Yoshio, Ōhashi Atsushi, Shimada Masae, Watari Kōichi, Robin Thompson, Nick Bornoff, Baby and Marcy, Richard Greer, Mihara Yoshiyuki, Hasumi Yūko, Matsui Takeyoshi, Utsunomiya Sōtarō, Leonard Koren, the staff at TIC, and our editors Matsui Yōichi and Nose Chieko.

INDEX

A Tantôt 92
ABC Kaikan Hall 161
Accommodation 45
ACT Mini Theater 168
Acupuncture 229
Addresses 256
After Six 178
Ai Gallery 195
Aikidō 165
Aikidō Federation, International 165
Ajiwai 75
Akagiya Playguide 162
Akamon 213
Akasaka **28**, 47, 63, 172
Akasaka Detached Palace 214
Akasaka Green Gallery 196
Akasaka La Foret 161
Akasaka Prince Hotel 47
Akasaka Tōkyū Hotel 48
Akihabara **36**, 99, 113
Akiko Sakaizumi 108
Akira Ikeda Gallery 197
Al Porto 93
Albion-za 161
Alien Registration Card **243**, 251
Amanoya 138
Amateur Archery Federation of Japan 166
Amaury St. Gilles 196
Amazake 138
American Pharmacy 231
Ameyoko **105**, 222
Andre Bernard 236
Angkor Wat 91
Anri 87
Antiques 133
Antique Stores 133
Ao Gallery 196
Aoyama **25**, 49, 94, 100, 172
Aoyama Bochi 214
Aoyama Green Gallery 196
Aozai 91
Arai Yakushi 134
Arcade 62, **105**
Architecture 215
Arisugawa Kōen 210
Arrival 243
Arrston Volaju 110
Art Plaza Magatani 133
Art Vivant 143
Arts 185
Asakura Sculpture Gallery 188
Asakusa **38**, 100, 217
Asakusa Engei Hall 159
Asakusa Imahan 79
Asakusa Jinja **208**, 218
Asakusa Kannon Onsen 232
Asakusa Kōkaidō 161
Asakusa Mokubatei 159
Asakusabashi **41**, 106
Asia Center of Japan 49
Aspen Glow 178
At Gallery 196
Atene Gallery 195
Athénée Français 168, 216
Aux Six Arbres 91
Axis 104
Axis Building 145
Ayahata 134
Azabu Jūban Onsen 232
Azumabashi Beer House 175

Baby-sitting 291
Bachiei Gakkiten 126
Back Tick 111
Bain Douche 232
Balalaika 93

Ballantine 2 178
Bank 248
Bank of Japan 214
Bar de Savey 173
Bargain Sale 104
Bars 172
Baseball 166
Baseball Hall of Fame and Museum 191
Beams 110
Beauty Care 236
Beer Gardens 175
Beer Halls 175
Bell Commons 103
Belle Vie Akasaka 103
Berni Inn 175
Besford Dental Office 231
Bic Camera 114
Big Shoes 146
Bigi 108
Bijin 236
Bindi 91
Bingoya 132
Bistrot de La Cité 92
Biwa 126, 141
Blue and White 116
Bodaiju 89
Body and Soul 178
Bofinger 92
Bon 69
Bonjinsha 143
Book 142
Botanical Gardens 211
Botejū 85
Boutique Yūya **108**, 134
Boy 236
Brasserie Bernard 92
Brasserie Ma Pomme 92
Bridgestone Museum of Art 188
Brushes 119
Buddhism 204
Budō no Ki 94
Budōkan 214
Bungakuza 160
Bungeiza 168
Bunkaya Zakkaten 111
Bunraku 153
Bunseidō **130**, 218
Buriki no Jihatsudan 160
Buses 255
Business Assistance 290
Business Hostels 46
Business Hours 248

Cabaret 179
Cables 252
Café Bistro Mcslord 95
Café de Rope 94
Calendar 274
Calligraphy **199**, 295
Calligraphy Museum, Japan 189
Calzeria Hosono 146
Camera no Doi 114
Camera no Kimuraya 114
Camera no Sakuraya 114
Cameras 114
Capitol Tōkyū Hotel 47
Cappuccio 94
Capsule Hotels 46
Carp Banners **117**, 277
Casablanca 179
Cavern Club 177
Cemeteries 214
Ceramics **124**, 190, 196
Cha-Dōgu→Tea Ceremony Utensils
Chaps 178
Charlston 174

Charlie House 86
Cheap Accommodations 53
Cheap Fashion 110
Chianti 92
Chiantissimo 173
Chikuyūsha 127
Chin'ya 79
Chiropractic 230
Chisen 77
Chitose-tei 179
Chōchin →Paper Lanterns
Chōmeiji 217
Chōmeiji Sakura-mochi **136**, 217
Chōshō-an 199
Chōtoku 82
Chronological Table 282
Cine Vivant Roppongi 168
Cinema Square Tōkyū 168
City Pension Zem 52
Clark Hatch 141
Classical Japanese Music 141
Cleo Palazzi 176
Climate 239
Clinics 230
Clothing Size Conversion Chart 298
Club D 176
Coffee Shops 94
Combs and Hair Ornaments 130
Comme des Garçons 108
Concert Halls and Theaters 161
Confucianism 204
Contemporary Architecture 215
Contemporary Arts Gallery 192
Contemporary Prints 196
Contemporary Theater 159
Cordon Bleu 179
Cosmetics **131**, **144**
Costume Museum 190
Country and Western 178
Courier Service 291
Crackers 137
Crafts 196
Crafts Center 116
Crafts Gallery of The Museum of Modern Art 187
Credit Cards 248
Crocodile 177
Cultural Organizations 291
Currency 246
Customs 245

Daichū 147
Daiē 111
Daikan Kamado 88
Daikan-yama 24
Daikokuya 73
Daikon'ya 68
Daihachi 86
Daimaru **102**, 104
Daimyō Clock Museum 190
Daini's Table 90
Daisan Butai 160
Dango 136
Dembōin Garden 218
Design Studio Okamoto 145
Dental Care 231
Department Stores 62, **100**
Dep't Store **111**, 135
Designer Boutiques 107
Designers 107
Dēto Kissa 181
Diamond Hotel 48
Diana 146
Dick's Bar 173
Directory Assistance 291
Disc Union 142

Discos 176
Discount Shops 144
Disk Port 142
Disneyland, Tokyo 212
Do Sports Plaza 233
Dolls 117
Domestic Help 291
Domon 110
Dōmyō 129
Dr. Yukio Kurosu 230
Drums 127
Dynamic Audio 114

Earth Club 198
Eating Out 59
Economic Organizations 291
Edo Gangu →Toys
Eel 82
Eisei Bunko Foundation 187
Electricity 249
Electronics and Cameras 112
Electronics and Computers 113
Embassies 291
Emergency 292
Enka 140
Entertainment 151
Etiquette 63, 254
Euro-Space 168
EX, bar 173, German Bar 174
Expatriates' Hang-outs 174

F. Shōkai 113
Fabrics 144
Fairmont Hotel 51
Fans 130
Fashion 107
Fashion Buildings 103
Fashion Massage 181
Fast Food 62
Festival Clothing 131
Festivals 274
Ficce Uomo 110
Film Center 168
Film Processing 292
Fish Market, Tsukiji 106
Flex Japan 114
Flower Viewing Seasons 274
Folk Art 189
Folk Crafts 116
Folk Crafts Museum, Japan 189
Food, Asian 62, **89**
Food, Health 88
Food, Japanese 64
Food, Western 62, **91**
Food and Drink **135**, **249**
Foreigner's House Matsuoka 54
Fox Bagels 93
From 1st 103
Fude →Brushes
Fugu-ryōri 83
Fujionkyō "Maikon" Center Ram 113
Fujiya Tenuguiten 132
Fukagawa 41
Fukagawa Fudō 222
Fukuzushi 71
Furansuza 218
Furniture 122
Furniture Museum 191
Furniture Rental 292
Futagoyama-beya 164

G Art Gallery 195
G Parelugon 2 194
Gagaku 141, **151**
Gaien 232

Gajoen Kankō Hotel 51
Galleries 194
Gallery Konohana 118
Gallery Kyōbashi 195
Gallery Meguro 133
Gallery Mukai 197
Gallery Muramatsu 195
Gallery Q 195
Gallery Te 195
Gallery Ueda Ware House 197
Gallery Watari 197
Gallery White Art 195
Gallery Yamaguchi 195
Gallery Yō 195
Ganchan 74
Garage Paradise 111
Gardens **209**, 210
Gas Hall 161
Gatōdō Gallery Takebashi 196
Gay Bars 175
Geihinkan 214
Geijutsu-sai **158**, 281
Geisha 157
Gekidan Sanjūmaru 160
Gekidan Shiki 160
Gekkōsō Gallery 195
Genrokuzushi 71
Geta 129
Ginza **29**, 46, 63, 94, 100, 171, 195
Ginza Dai-ichi Hotel 46
Ginza Marunouchi Hotel 46
Ginza Namiki-za 168
Ginza Nikkō Hotel 46
Ginza Nō Theater 159
Ginza To 103
Ginza Tōkyū Hotel 46
Ginza-yu 232
Goemon 84
Gonin Byakushō 76
Gotō Art Museum 186
Green Collections 196
Grass Men's 110
Green Plaza Shinjuku 55
Grocery Stores 139
Guide 258
Guided Tours 216
Gyokusendō 119

Habitat 145
Habutae Dango 136
Haga Shoten 143
Hagoromo 86
Haibara 118
Hair Care 236
Haiyūza 160
Haiyūza Cinema Ten 168
Haiyūza Gekijō 161
Hakone Open-Air Museum 192
Hakuhinkan Gekijō 161
Hakusan 231
Half Moon 108
Hamamatsuchō 33
Hamarikyū Teien 211
Hanakyabetsu 225
Hanae Mori 108
Hanatemari 68
Hanatō **120**, 219
Hanayashiki Yūenchi 213
Hanazono Jinja 134
Haneda Airport 247
Harajuku **24**, 49, 100, 172, 196
Harajuku Plaza 111
Harajuku Trimm 234
Hara Museum **188**, 197
Hara Shobō 143
Hari→Acupuncture

Hasami→Scissors
Hasegawa Hakimonoten **121**, 129
Hasejin 79
Hasetoku 129
Hashimoto 117
Hatakeyama Museum 187
Hayashi 88
Hayashi Kimono 106, **134**
Health and Beauty 229
Health Angels 174
Health Club 233
Health Food 88
Healthmagic 89
Heiandō 123
Heisandō 133
Henry Africa's 174
Hi Lac Nam 91
Hibiya **31**, 46, 100
Hie Jinja 207
Hīragi 77
Hinode Sembei 137
Hiratsuka 122
Hirō 23
Hirose Musen Audio Center 113
Hibiya Kōen 210
Hibiya Kōkaidō 161
Hillport Hotel 49
Hilltop Hotel 51
Hilton International 49
Hiragana 263
Hired Car 247
Hiroko Koshino 108
Hiromi Yoshida 108
Historical Sites and Buildings 213
Hitachi Lo-D Plaza 112
Hitomi Ōkawa 108
Hōchō→Knives
Hokkaien 90
Holiday 240, 275
Holiday Inn 52
Hōmitei 88
Hommokutei 159
Honda Gekijō 161
Honda Tsūshō 114
Hongō 36
Honke Ponta 78
Horikiri Shōbuen 212
Hōryūji Treasure House 186
Hōseian 222
Hōsendō **130**, 132
Hōshō Nō Theater 159
Hospitals 230
Hostels 54
Hostess Bars 179
Hot Co-rocket 177
Hotel Atamisō 46
Hotel Century Hyatt 50
Hotel Grand Palace 51
Hotel Harajuku Trimm 49
Hotel Ibis 48
Hotel Kayū Kaikan 48
Hotel Kitchō 52
Hotel Kokusai Kankō 47
Hotel Metropolitan 50
Hotel New Ōtani **47**, 105
Hotel Ōkura **48**, 105
Hotel Ōkura Steam Bath 233
Hotel Pacific 51
Hotel Perrier 182
Hotel Roppongi 182
Hotels **45**, 181
Hotel White City 55
Hotel Yōkō Akasaka 48
Hotetoru 181
Housing 293
How To Use This Book 8

Hōzō Mon 218
Hyakusuke 131

Idaya 121
Idemitsu Art Gallery 187
Ikebana **199**, 295
Ikebana International 199
Ikebukuro **27**, 50, 100, 114, 172
Ikebukuro Sunroute Hotel 50
Ikebukuro Engeijō 159
Ikenobō 199
Ikura La Foret 161
Imperial Hotel 46
Imperial Hotel Arcade 105
Imperial Palace 213
Imperial Palace East Garden 211
Ina Gallery 195
Inabasō 53
Inachū Japan 123
Inakaya 76
Inaniwa 82
Incense 121
Ink Stick 177
Inner Garden 211
Innovator Shop 145
Ino Hall 161
Inui 196
Instruction 294
Interior 145
Interior Lamps 120
International Arcade 105
International Clinic 230
International Cuisine 62
International Post Office 251
International Vision Center 231
Iriyama Sembei 137
Irohanihoheto 76
Isehiro 74
Iseryū Shōten 125
Isetan 102
Isetan Playguide 162
Isetatsu 118
Ishida Biwaten 126
Ishii Shika 231
Ishikawa Clinic 230
Ishimaru Denki Honten 142
Ishimaru Denki No. 3 Shop 142
Ishizuka 116
Ishizuka Shōten 120
Isogai Tetsuzō Shōten 132
Isozaki Arata 216
Issey Miyake 108, 110
Isukura Yakkyoku 231
Itō Oketen 123
Itōya 144
Iwai Shōten 119
Iwanami Hall 168
Iwataya 135

J 178
Japan National Tourist Organization 240, 258
Japan Rail Pass 240
Japan Red Cross Hospital 230
Japan Sword 122
Japan Travel Bureau 216, 258
Japan Youth Hostels Association 54
Japanese Open Air Museum of Traditional Houses 192
Jazz 140, **178**
Jean Jean 161
Jena 143
JETRO 291
Jimbōchō **35**, 95
Jimbōchō Book District 143
Jindaiji 207
Jindaiji Shokubutsuen 211

Jiyūgaoka 224
Jizake 88
Jogging Courses 235
Jojoen 90
Jōkyō Gekijō 160
Jōnan Denki 114
Jonidan 163
Jonokuchi 163
Jūdō 165
Jūdō Federation, All Japan 166
Jūjū 90
Jun "Murata" 110
Jūnionkai 159
Junko Koshino 108
Junko Shimada 108
Jurgen Lehl 108
Jūryō 163

Kabuki 154
Kabukichō 180
Kabukiza 159
Kaen 91
Kaiseki-ryōri 61, 67
Kameido Tenjin 209
Kaminarimon 217
Kamiya Bar 174
Kamiyama Sudareten 120
Kammon Antiques 133
Kanda **35**, 100, 194, 225
Kanda Clinic 230
Kanda Fruit and Vegetable Market 107
Kanda Kosho Center 143
Kanda Myōjin 207
Kan'eiji 206
Kaneko Art Gallery 195
Kaneko Art G1 195
Kanji 262
Kanransha 197
Kansai Yamamoto 109
Kanze Nō Theater 159
Kappa 87
Kappabashi 99, **106**, 217
Kappabashi Wholesale Market 219
Karaoke 178
Karate 166
Kasa →Umbrellas
Kashiwaya 120
Kasugano-beya 164
Kasumichō 94, **171**
Kasumigaseki 31
Kasutera 137
Katakana 263
Katana →Swords
Katei-ryōri 61, 86
Kayabachō Pearl Hotel 52
Kay's Bar 173
Kawakin 78
Kazuya 78
Keiō Plaza Hotel 49
Keisei Skyliner 247
Kendō 166
Kendō Federation, Japan 166
Kento's 177
Keshōhin →Cosmetics
Kiba 41
Kiddyland 147
Kikukawa 83
Kikumi Sembei 137
Kikuya 129
Kikuya Honten 136
Kikuya Shamisenten 126
Kimono 104, **127**
Kimono Accessories 129
Kimono, Antique 134
Kimura Musen 113
Kimuraya (Coffee Shop) 94

Kimuraya (Discount Shop) 144
Kimuraya Hompo 137, 219
Kinokuniya 142
Kinokuniya Hall 161
Kinokuniya International 139
Kiriya Gofukuten 132
Kissō 124
Kita Rokuheita Kinen Theater 159
Kitanomaru Kōen 210
Kitazawa Shoten 143
Kite Association, Japan 190
Kite Museum 190
Kiya (Knives) 122
Kiya (Art Supplies) 144
Kiyomizu Kannon 219
Kiyosumi Garden 223
Kiyosumi Teien 211
Knives 122
Kō→Incense
Kobutsu no Daimaru 144
Kōdōkan **166**, 214
Koinobori→Carp Banners
Koishikawa Kōrakuen 210
Koishikawa Shokubutsuen 211
Kōjimachi Rebirth **230**, 233
Kokkai Gijidō 213
Kokonoe-beya 164
Kokuchō no Mizuumi 175
Kokugakuin University Archeological Collection 190
Kokugikan **164**, 214
Kokuritsu Gekijō 161
Kōkyo 213
Kōkyo Higashi Gyoen 211
Komai Gallery 195
Konditorei Österreich 94
Konjaku Nishimura 134
Kōrakuen **36**, 212
Kōrakuen Health Club 234
Kōrakuen Kyūjō 167
Kōrakuen Sauna 233
Korean 89
Kotani House 54
Koto **126**, 141
Kotobukidō 136
Kototoi Dango **136**, 217
Kōundō 119
Kudan 51
Kudan Beer Garden 176
Kudan Kaikan Hall 161
Kudan Kaikan Hotel 51
Kunoya 129
Kuramae **41**, 106
Kuremutsu 88, 218
Kurita Musen 190
Kuroda Tōen 196
Kurodaya 119, 218
Kuroeya 123
Kurofune 133
Kurokawa Kishō 215
Kusanoya 90
Kushi and Kanzashi→Combs and Hair Ornaments
Kushi-age 76
Kushinobō 77
Kyōbashi **34**, 195
Kyōgen 153
Kyōsendō 130
Kyōto Center 116
Kyōya 122
Kyū Ikeda Yashiki Ōtemon 214
Kyūdō 166
Kyūgetsu 118
Kyūkyodō 119, **121**
Kyūkyodō Ticket Service 162

La Boheme 93
La Foret 103
La Foret Museum 161
La Granata 92
La Palette 94
La Patata 92
La Verde 93
Lacquer Ware 123
Lacquered Bamboo Trunks 119
Ladies Sauna 233
Language **260**, 294
Lapis 144
Last Scene 111
Lawn 95
Le Chinois 91
Lemon 144
Les Choux 91
Lexington Queen 176
Libraries 293
Limousine Bus 246
Live Music 177
Livina Yamagiwa 120
Loft 177
L'orangerie de Paris 92
Lorne's Place 175
Lost and Found 257, 293
Lotus Café 91
Love Hotels 181
Luggage 145
Lunami Gallery 195
Luseine-kan 94

Madame Hanai 109
Madame Nicole 109
Madame Toki's 92
Magazines 297
Maggie's Revenge 174
Mainichi Sports Plaza Tokyo 234
Maikon Base Ginza 114
Mail 251
Major Hotels 45
Maki Fumihiko 215
Maki Gallery 195
Makushita 163
Mamegen 137
Mamiana Soba 81
Mana 89
Manjū 136
Mantoru 181
Martial Arts **165**, 295
Martial Arts Clothing and Equipment 133
Maruboshi Denki 114
Marui 102
Marunouchi **32**, 47
Maruta-Gōshi 84
Maruyu Shōkai 114
Maruzen 143
Masks 132
Massage 233
Masudaya 128
Matsubaya 158
Matsukan 71
Matsumura Shoten 143
Matsuo Shika In 231
Matsuri 274
Matsushita Associates, Inc. 125
Matsuya 102
Matsuzakaya 102
Mayuyama & Co., Ltd. 133
Maxim de Paris 92
Meda 146
Medicine, Asian 229
Medicine, Western 230
Meguro 51
Meguro Emperor 182
Meguro Gajoen 53

INDEX

Meidiya 139
Meiji Jingū 190, **207**
Meiji Jingū Gaien 210
Meiji Jingū Gaien Cycling Road 235
Meiji Jingū Gyoen 211
Meiji Jingū Kyūjō 167
Meiji Jingū Pool 234
Meiji Shrine Treasure House 190
Meiji University Archeological Collection 189
Meiji University Criminal Museum 190
Meiji-za 161
Men → Masks
Men's Designers and Boutiques 110
Men's Tinolas 110
Meruridō 142
Metric 249
Metropolitan Police Board, P.R. Center 166
Mexico Lindo 93
Michiko Koshino 109
Midget 145
Midori no Yakata 179
Midoriya 137
Mikawaya Bekkan 53
Mikimoto 145
Mimiu 81
Minato-ku Sports Center Pool 234
Mingei 116
Minokichi **68**, 73
Minshuku 54
Minshuku Association, Japan 54
Minshuku Center, Japan 54
Mint Bar 173
Mitsui Urban Hotel Ginza 46
Mitsubishi Denki Showroom 112
Mitsukoshi 101
Miyagetsudō 136
Miyako 71
Miyako Hotel Tokyo 51
Miyama Shōkai 114
Miyamoto Unosuke Shōten **127**, 219
MOA Museum of Art 192
Mochi 136
Modern Japanese and Western Art 187
Modern Music 177
Mod's Hair 236
Mon 174
Money 248
Monkberry's 173
Monorail 247
Monsieur Nicole 110
Mori Parts Shops 114
Mori Silver 145
Morita Antiques 133
Moti 91
Motomachi 85
Movies 167
Mr. Stamp's 175
Mugen 176
Mujirushi Ryōhin 147
Mukōjima Hyakkaen 212
Munakata 68
Murano Tōga 215
Musashiya Shōten 117
Museum of Calligraphy 189
Museums 185
Myōgaya 129

Nagai Yakkyoku 231
Nagai Yakkyoku Hifu Kōso Biganshitsu 236
Nagasaka Sarashina 81
Nagatachō 28
Nakamise-dōri 217
Nakano Sun Plaza 161
Nakata Shōten 135
Namagashi 135
Nambantei 74

Nantenshi Gallery 195
Naokyū 86
Narita **243**, 246
Narita Airport 52
Narita View Hotel 52
National Azabu Supermarket 139
National Azabu Supermarket Pharmacy 231
National Bookstore 143
National Diet Building 213
National Gymnasium Swimming Pool 234
National Museum of Western Art 188
National Park for Nature Study 191
National Science Museum 191
National Theater 159
National Theater Nō Hall 159
Natural House 139
NEC Showroom 113
Neo Japanesque 176
New Latin Quarter 179
New Religion 204
New Takanawa Prince Hotel 50
News 196
Nezu 219
Nezu Art Museum 186
Nezu Jinja 209
NHK Hall 161
NHK Museum of Broadcasting 191
Nicole 109
Night Bar 173
Nightlife 171
Nihombashi **34**, 100, 194, 225
Nihombashi Bridge 214
Nihon Seinenkan 49
Nihon Seinenkan Hall 161
Nihon Budōkan 161, 214
Nihon Ginkō 214
Nijūbashi 213
Nikolaidō 213
Nikon Salon 197
Ningyō → Doll
Ningyōchō **37**, 225
Nippori 106
Nishi-Arai-Daishi 206
Nishi-Azabu 23
Nishimura Gallery 197
Nissei Gekijō 161
Nisseki Iryō Center 230
Nittō Shōji 115
Nō **152**, 159, 279
Nodaiwa 82
Nogi Jinja 134
Nogi Tei 214
Noise 160
Nomiya **61**, 73, 171
Nōpan Kissa 181
Nozoki Gekijō 181
Nuno 144

OA Center 113
Obi 128
Ocha → Tea
Ochanomizu **36**, 51
Odakyū 102
Odakyū Halc 145
Oden 83
Oh God 174
Ohara 199
Okajōki 76
Okajū 76
Oke → Wooden buckets
Okonomiyaki 84
Ōkura Museum 187
Okusawa Jinja 225
Ōmatsuya 81
On Sundays 143
One Off 145

Onoterusaki Jinja 159
Ōnoya Sōhonten 130
Optical Care 231
Opus One 142
Oriental 144
Oriental Bazaar **116**, 125, 133, 134
Oshinko (Tsukemono)⟶Pickles
Ōta Memorial Museum of Art 188
Otomi-yu 232
Outer Garden 210
Oyster Bar 173

Packing 241
Palace Cycling Course 235
Palace Hotel 47
Paper **118**, 190
Paper Lanterns 120
Paper Museum 190
Parco **103**, 104
Parco Part 3 145
Parks **209**, 210
Pāru Onsen 232
Pashu 110
Patisserie de La Table 94
Pearls 145
Peek a Boo 236
Pentax Forum 197
Persons 110
Peter Pan 175
Pharmacies 231
Photography 197
Pickles 139
Pidgeon 174
Pied Piper House 142
Pilsen 175
Pink Dragon 111
Pink House 109
Pink Kyabarē 181
Pink Pearl 233
Pioneer Showroom 113
Playthings 147
Pleasure Grounds 212
Pool of Kumin Sōgō Undōjō 235
Poruno Rando 181
Posh Boy 93
Post Office 248, 251
Printemps 103
Printers 293
Professional and Community Service Organizations 293
Pub Cardinal 174
Public Baths 231

Queen Alice 91

Radio Bar 173
Rajah Court 176
Rajio Kaikan 113
Rakugo **157**, 159
Rāmen 85
Record Shops 141
Records 140
Reference and Recommended Reading 295
Red Shoes 173
Regent Bar 175
Reikyō 91
Removal 294
Rental Cars 247
Repairs 293
Restaurants, American 93
Restaurants, Cambodian 91
Restaurants, Chinese 90
Restaurants, French 91
Restaurants, Indian 91
Restaurants, Italian 92
Restaurants, Japanese 67

Restaurants, Mexican 93
Restaurants, Noodle 61
Restaurants, Russian 93
Restaurants, Taiwanese 91
Restaurants, Vietnamese 91
Riccar Art Museum 188
Rihaku 95
Rikugien 210
Robata-yaki 75
Rock 177
Rocket Honten 113
Rōgairō 90
Rōma Sabatini 92
Roppongi **22**, 48, 63, 94, 100, 171, 196
Roppongi Pit Inn 178
Roppongi Shokudō 87
Ruelle de Derriere 94
Ryōgoku 41
Ryokan 52
Ryōtei 61
Ryūzendō 121

Sabatini Aoyama/Pizzoria Romana Sabatini 92
Sabatini di Firenze 92
Sabby Genteel **111**, 145
Saga Tōen 124
Sagachō Exhibit Space 196
Saigō Takamori 219
Saint Julian 179
Sairakudō 125
Sakaezushi Honten 71
Sakai Kōkodō Gallery 125
Sake 138
Sakura-kai 199
Samba Club 177
Sambyakunin-Gekijō 168
Sambiki no Kobuta 175
Sampei Store 144
Sancha Shobō 143
Sandamme 163
Sankōin 69
Sanseidō 143
Sansuisō 53
Santomo 83
Sanwa Massage 233
Sarafan 93
Saruya 123
Sasanoyuki 84
Sashimono⟶Furniture
Satin Doll 178
Satō Musen 113
Satō Ningyō 94
Sauna 232
Sawanoya 53
Sazae 175
Scan Video Gallery 197
Science Museum 191
Scissors 122
Secondhand Clothes 135
Seibo Byōin 230
Seibu 101, **102**
Seibu Art Museum 188
Seibu Gekijō 161
Seibu Kyūjō 167
Seikadō Bunko Tenjikan 187
Seiroka Byōin 230
Sei-Sei an 199
Seitai 230
Seiyū 111
Sembei⟶Crackers
Sengakuji 207
Sensōji 206, 218
Sensu⟶Fans
Sentō 231
Serina 79
Shabusen 79

Shabu-Shabu 78
Shakuhachi **126**, 141
Shamisen **126**, 141
Shiawase Kenkō Club 230
Shiba **33**, 48
Shiba Park Hotel 48
Shibamata Taishakuten 206
Shibamataya 136
Shibuya **23**, 49, 95, 100, 172, 196
Shibuya Kōkaidō 161
Shibuya Sunroute Hotel 49
Shibuya Tōbu Hotel 49
Shigemori Eishindō 137
Shikki —→ Lacquer Ware
Shimakame 128
Shimbashi **33**, 46, 171
Shimbashi Daiichi Hotel 46
Shimbashi Embujō 159
Shimbashi Kenkō Shizenshoku Center 89
Shimpa 156
Shinagawa **37**, 50
Shinagawa Prince Hotel 51
Shinjuku **26**, 49, 95, 100, 114, 172
Shinjuku Gyoen 211
Shinjuku Koma Gekijō 161
Shinjuku Pit Inn 178
Shinjuku Prince Hotel 50
Shinjuku Royal 168
Shinobazu Pound 221
Shintō **204**, 274
Shipping 294
Shirin 174
Shitamachi Museum 189
Shitamachi Tour 217
Shizen Kyōikuen **191**, 212
Sho International 199
Shōchū 138
Shōeitei 88
Shoes 146, **241**
Shōgitai Kinenhi 219
Shōjin Shōkai 113
Shōjin-ryōri 68
Shopping 99
Showrooms 112
Shrines 203, **207**
Shū Uemura Beauty Boutique 144
Shuetsu 139
Sightseeing 203
69 174
Skin Care 236
Soba 80
Socks 129
Sōgetsu 199
Sōgetsu Hall 161
Sony Showroom 112
Space Part 3 161
Spago 93
Sports 162
Sports Facilities 233
St. Luke's International Hospital 230
St. Mary's International Catholic Hospital 230
Steam Baths 233
Street Food 62
Studio Arkis Esty Harajuku Step In 236
Studio ALTA 103
Studio 200 161
Studio V 109
Studio V Coffee Shop 94
Subways 253
Sudare —→ Bamboo Blinds
Suehirotei 159
Suitengū 208
Sukeroku 117
Sukiyaki 78
Sumida 217
Sumida Park 217

Sumida River 217
Sumiya 142
Sumiyoshi Jinja 223
Sumō 162
Sumō Museum 191
Sun Plaza Indoor Pool 235
Sunshine City **104**, 134
Sunshine City Prince Hotel 50
Sunshine Gekijō 161
Suntory Art Gallery 187
Supplies 241
Surplus 111
Sushi 69
Sushi Bar Sai 71
Sushi Sei 71
Susukino 86
Susy's Bar 177
Sutorippu Gekijō 181
Suzumoto Engeijō 159
Sweden Health Center 233
Swimming Pools 234
Sword Museum 190
Swords 121

Tabac 173
Tabi —→ Socks
Tachikichi & Co., Ltd. 125
Tailor 294
Taj 91
Takamura 68
Takanawa Prince Hotel 50
Takaosan Yakuōin 69
Takarazuka Kagekidan 160
Takasago-beya 164
Takashimaya **101**, 133
Takemura 136
Takeo Kikuchi 110
Takeshita-dōri 111
Tako —→ Kites
Takumi 116
Tama Dōbutsu Kōen 212
Tamagawa Seishōnen Cycling Course 235
Tambaya 82
Tambo 85
Tamura 68
Tamura Gallery 194
Tanakaya 139
Tange Kenzō 215
Tani Clinic 230
Taniguchi Yoshirō 215
Tatsumiya 88, 218
Taxes 248
Tax-Free Stores 105
Taxis 254
Tea 138
Tea Ceremony 199
Tea Ceremony Utensils 121
Technics Ginza 112
Techno Culture Center Media Bum 113
Teikoku Gekijō 161
Telegrams 251
Telephones 252
Tellus 146
Temmi 89
Temple **203**, 206
Tempura 72
Tenugui —→ Towels
Teppōzu Inari 223
Ten'ichi 73
Tenjō Sajiki 160
Tenkei Gekijō 160
Tentake 83
Ten-Yasu 139
Tessenkai Nōgaku Kenshūjo 159
The Ancient Orient Museum 190
The Gallery 133

The Live Inn 177
The Medical Dispensary 231
The Playguide La Foret 162
The President Hotel Aoyama 49
The Space 161
The Strand Bookstore 143
Theater Apple 161
TIC 257
Ticket Outlets 162
Tickets, Theaters, and Information 158
Tipping-Service 248
Tobacco and Salt Museum 191
Todoroki Keikoku (ravine) 224
Tōfu-ryōri 84
Tōgō Shrine 134
Tōhō Fujin Women's Clinic 230
Toilets 250
Tōjiki→Ceramics
Tōjimbō 89
Tōkaien 90
Tokio 176
Tokio Kumagai 110
Tokiwa Gallery 195
Tokō-an 199
Tokyo Aoyama Kaikan 49
Tokyo Bunka Kaikan 159, **161**
Tokyo Chiropractic Center 230
Tokyo City Air Terminal 52
Tokyo City Hotel 47
Tokyo Dai Hanten 91
Tokyo Designers Space 196
Tokyo Gallery 195
Tokyo Grand Hotel 48
Tokyo Hyakka Funabashiya 144
Tokyo Immigration Office 243
Tokyo International House 54
Tokyo Kōseinenkin Kaikan 161
Tokyo Kōseinenkin Kaikan Sports Center 234
Tokyo Marunouchi Hotel 47
Tokyo Medical and Surgical Clinic 230
Tokyo Metropolitan Art Museum 188
Tokyo Metropolitan Gymnasium Indoor
  Swimming Pool 234
Tokyo Metropolitan Teien Museum of Art 188
Tokyo National Museum 186
Tokyo National Museum of Modern Art 187
Tokyo Old Folk Craft and Antique Center 133
Tokyo Onsen Diamond Spa 233
Tokyo Optical Center 231
Tokyo Prince Hotel 48
Tokyo Rajio Depāto 113
Tokyo Station Hotel 47
Tokyo Swimming Center 235
Tokyo Taibunsha 143
Tokyo Takarazuka Gekijō 161
Tokyo Tower 213
Tokyo-dō 111
Tōkyū 102
Tōkyū Hands 104, 145
Tolman Collection 197
Tomioka Hachimangū 222
Tong Fū 90
Tonkatsu 77
Tonki 78
Toothpicks 123
Toranomon 48
Toranomon Hall 161
Toriden 74
Torigin 74
Toruko-buro 181
Tōshiba Ginza Seven 112
Tōshōgū **209**, 220
Tourist Information Center "TIC" 257
Tourist Services 257, 294
Tōyō Igaku Kenkyūjo 229
Toyoda Shobō 143

Tōyōkan 186
Toy Park 147
Toys 146
Tower Records 142
Towels 132
Trader Vic's 174
Traditional Arts 198
Traditional Arts and Crafts 115
Traditional Clothing and Accessories 127
Traditional Dance Accessories 132
Traditional Instruments 126
Traditional Sweets 135
Traditional Theater 151
Trains 253
Transportation Museum 191
Travel Agents 294
Travellers Checks 248
Treasure House of The Yasukuni Shrine 190
Tsubaki House 176
Tsubame-yu 232
Tsukamoto 116
Tsukiji **35**, 106
Tsukiji Edogin 71
Tsukiji Fish Market 71, **106**
Tsukudajima 41, **223**
Tsukudani 139
Tsumugiya Kichihei 128
Tsunahachi 72
Tsurukawa Gakki Honten 126
Tsutsui 87
Tsuzura→Lacquered Bamboo Trunks
Turkish Bath 181
Tuttle Book Shop 143
Tuxedo and Formal Rental 294

Ubukeya 122
Udon 81
Ueno **39**, 63, 100, 219
Ueno Kōen 210
Ueno Zoo 212
Uguisu Dango 220
Ukiyoe→Woodblock Prints
Umbrellas 120
Umewaka Nō Theater 159
Unac Salon 196
Unagi 82
Uogashi 71
UK Edison 142
US Book Overseas Service 143
Usagiya 137

Vals Bar 173
Vegetarian 68, 84, **88**, 250
Victor Video Center 112
Victoria Station 93
Video 197
Video Earth Tokyo 197
Video Information Center 198
Vietti 176
Visas 242

Wacoal Fabrics House 144
Wakamatsu Tsūshō 114
Wakatsuki 85
Wakō 103
Walking Courses 216
Wan'ya Shoten **130**, 132, 159
Waseda Shō Gekijō 160
Waseda University Tsubouchi Memorial Museum 190
Washi→Paper
Washikōbō **119**, 120
Washington 146
Washington Hotel 50
Wave **104**, 142
Western 178

INDEX

When to Travel 239
Wholesale Markets 106
Winners 142
Wishbone 178
Woodblock Prints **125**, 188, 189
Wooden Buckets 123
Woodstock 142
Workmen's Clothing 132
World Union of Karatedō Organization 166

X-rated 180

Y's 109
Y's for Men 110
Yabu-Soba 81
Yaesu Fujiya Hotel 47
Yakitori 73
Yakko 83
Yakult Hall 162
Yamamoto-Yama 139
Yamatane Museum of Art 188
Yanagiya 137
Yanaka 219
Yanaka Bochi 215
Yansandō 90
Yarai Nō Theater 159
Yashima 53
Yasukō 84
Yasukuni Jinja 190, **207**
Yaya Gallery 196
Year Conversion Chart 298
YMCA, Tokyo 54

YMCA Asia Youth Center 54
Yodobashi Camera 114
Yoitaya 129
Yōji → Toothpicks
Yokoyama Taikan Memorial Gallery 191
Yokozuna 163
Yoku Moku 94
Yōmeido Budōguten 133
Yomiuri Hall 162
Yonoya 131
Yōseidō Gallery 197
Yōshoku **61**, **87**
Yotaro 73
Youth Hostels 54
Yoyogi Kōen 210
Yūbinchokin Hall 162
Yuki Torī 109
Yume no Yūminsha 160
Yūrakuchō **31**, 63, 75, 172
Yushima **36**, 225
Yushima Seidō 213
Yushima Tenjin 208
YWCA Hostel, Japan 54
YWCA Hostel, Tokyo 54
YWCA Sadohara Hostel, Tokyo 54

Zeito Photo 197
Zempukuji 206
Zen 198, 204
Zōjōji 206
Zoo 212
Zōri 129

INTRODUCTION

HOW TO USE THIS BOOK

CONTENTS

TOKYO

ACCOMMODATION

EATING OUT

SHOPPING

ENTERTAINMENT

NIGHT LIFE

ARTS

SIGHTSEEING

HEALTH AND BEAUTY

THE BASICS

LANGUAGE

APPENDIX

MAP

INDEX